# Data Storage

Edited by

Prof. Florin Balasa

**Data Storage**

Edited by Prof. Florin Balasa

**Republished by InTech**

Janeza Trdine 9, 51000 Rijeka, Croatia



**Technical Editor** Maja Jakobovic

**Cover Designer** Dino Smrekar

Additional hard copies can be obtained from orders@intechopen.com

Data Storage,
Edited by Prof. Florin Balasa
p. cm.
ISBN 978-953-307-063-6

For EU product safety concerns:
IN TECH d.o.o., Prolaz Marije Krucifikse Kozulić 3, 51000 Rijeka, Croatia,
info@intechopen.com or visit our website at intechopen.com.

# Meet the editor

Florin Balasa received the Ph.D. degree in computer science from the Polytechnical University of Bucharest, Bucharest, Romania, in 1994, and the Ph.D. degree in electrical engineering from the Katholieke Universitiet Leuven, Leuven, Belgium, in 1995. From 1990 to 1995, he was with the Interuniversity Microelectronics Center (IMEC), Leuven, Belgium. From 1995 to 2000, he was a Senior Deisgn Automation Engineer at the Advanced Technology Division of Conexant Systems (formerly Rockwell Semiconductor Systems), Newport Beach, CA. He is currently an Associate Professor of Computer Science at the Southern Utah University. Dr. Balsa was a recipient of the US National Science Foundation CAREER Award.

# Preface

Many different forms of storage, based on various natural phenomena, has been invented. So far, no practical universal storage medium exists, and all forms of storage have some drawbacks. Therefore, a computer system usually contains several kinds of storage, each with an individual purpose.

Traditionally, the most important part of a digital computer is the central processing unit (CPU or, simply, a processor), because it actually operates on data, performs calculations, and controls all the other components. Without a memory, a computer would merely be able to perform fixed operations and immediately output the result. It would have to be reconfigured to change its behavior. This is acceptable for devices such as desk calculators or simple digital signal processors. Von Neumann machines differ in that they have a memory in which they store their operating instructions and data. Such computers are more versatile in that they do not need to have their hardware reconfigured for each new program, but can simply be reprogrammed with new in-memory instructions. Most modern computers are von Neumann machines.

In practice, almost all computers use a variety of memory types, organized in a storage hierarchy around the CPU, as a trade-off between performance and cost. Generally, the lower a storage is in the hierarchy, the lesser its bandwidth (the amount of transferred data per time unit) and the greater its latency (the time to access a particular storage location) is from the CPU. This traditional division of storage to primary, secondary, tertiary and off-line storage is also guided by cost per bit.

Primary storage (or main memory, or internal memory), often referred to simply as memory, is the only one directly accessible to the CPU. The CPU continuously reads instructions stored there and executes them as required. Any data actively operated on is also stored there in uniform manner.

As the random-access memory (RAM) types used for primary storage are volatile (i.e., they lose the information when not powered), a computer containing only such storage would not have a source to read instructions from, in order to start the computer. Hence, non-volatile primary storage containing a small startup program is used to bootstrap the computer, that is, to read a larger program from non-volatile secondary storage to RAM and start to execute it.

Secondary storage (or external memory) differs from primary storage in that it is not directly accessible by the CPU. The computer usually uses its input/output channels to access secondary storage and transfers the desired data using intermediate area in the primary storage. The secondary storage does not lose the data when the device is powered down – it is non-volatile. Per unit, it is typically also two orders of magnitude less expensive than primary storage. In modern computers, hard disk drives are usually used as secondary storage. The time taken to access a given byte of information stored on a hard disk is typically a few milliseconds. By contrast, the time taken to access a given byte of information stored in a RAM is measured in nanoseconds. This illustrates the very significant access-time difference which distinguishes solid-state memory from rotating magnetic storage devices: hard disks are typically about a million times slower than memory. Rotating optical storage devices, such as CD and DVD drives, have even longer access times. Some other examples of secondary storage technologies are: flash memory (e.g. USB flash drives), floppy disks, magnetic tape, paper tape, punched cards, stand-alone RAM disks, and Zip drives.

Tertiary storage or tertiary memory provides a third level of storage. Typically it involves a robotic mechanism which will mount (insert) and dismount removable mass storage media into a storage device according to the system's demands; this data is often copied to secondary storage before use. It is primarily used for archival of rarely accessed information since it is much slower than secondary storage (e.g. tens of seconds). This is primarily useful for extraordinarily large data stores, accessed without human operators. Typical examples include tape libraries and optical jukeboxes.

Off-line storage is a computer data storage on a medium or a device that is not under the control of a processing unit. In modern personal computers, most secondary and tertiary storage media are also used for off-line storage. Optical discs and flash memory devices are most popular, while in enterprise uses, magnetic tape is predominant. This book presents several advances in different research areas related to data storage, from the design of a hierarchical memory subsystem in embedded signal processing systems for data-intensive applications, to data representation in flash memories, to the data recording and retrieval in conventional optical data storage systems and the more recent holographic systems, to applications in medicine requiring massive image databases.

In optical storage systems, sensitive stored patterns can cause failure in data retrieval and decrease the system reliability. Modulation codes play the role of shaping the characteristics of stored data patterns. In conventional optical data storage systems, information is recorded in a one-dimensional spiral stream. The major concern of modulation codes for these systems is to separate the binary 1's by a number of binary 0's.

The holographic data storage systems are regarded as the next-generation optical data storage due to an extremely high capacity and ultra-fast transfer rate. In holographic systems, information is stored as pixels on two-dimensional pages. Different from the conventional optical data storage, the additional dimension inevitably brings new considerations to the design of modulation codes. The primary concern is that interferences between pixels are omni-directional. Moreover, interferences between pixels are imbalanced: since pixels carry different intensities to represent different bits of information, pixels with higher intensities tend to corrupt the signal fidelity of pixels with lower intensities more than the other way around.

Chapter 1 analyzes different modulation codes for optical data storage. It first addresses types of constraints of modulation codes. Afterwards, the one-dimensional modulation codes, adopted in the current optical storage systems (like EFM for CD's, EFMPlus for DVD's, 17PP for Blu-ray discs), are presented. Next, the chapter focuses on two-dimensional modulation codes for holographic data storage systems – the block codes and the strip codes. It further discusses the advantages and disadvantages of variable-length modulation codes in contrast to fixed-length modulation codes.

Chapter 2 continues the discussion on holographic data storage systems, giving an overview on the processing of retrieved signals. Even with modulation codes, two channel defects - inter-pixel interferences and misalignments - are major causes for degradation of the retrieved image and, thus, degradation in detection performance. Misalignments severely distort the retrieved image and several solutions for compensating misalignment - itera- 2 tive cancellation by decision feedback, oversampling with re-sampling, interpolation with rate conversion - are presented in the chapter. Equalization and detection are the signal processing operations for the final data detection in the holographic data storage reading procedure, restoring the stored information from the interferenceinflicted signal. In contrast to the classical de-convolution method based on linear minimum mean squared error (LMMSE) equalization, that suffers from a model mismatch due to the inherent nonlinearity of the channel, the chapter presents two nonlinear detection algorithms that achieve a better performance than the classical LMMSE at the cost of a higher complexity.

Chapter 3 describes recent advances towards three-dimensional (3D) optical data storage systems. One of the methods for 3D optical data storage is based on volume holography. The physical mechanism is photochromism, which is a reversible transformation of a single chemical species between two states having different absorption spectra and refractive indices. This allows for holographic multiplexing recording and reading. Another technique for 3D optical data storage is the bit-by-bit memory at the nanoscale, which is based on the confinement of multiphoton absorption to a very small volume because of its nonlinear dependence of excitation intensity.

Both organic and anorganic materials are convenient for 3D data storage. These materials must satisfy several norms for storing and reading: resistance to aging due to temperature and recurrent reading, high-speed response for high-rate data transfer, no optically scattering for multilayer storage. The chapter presents experiments with two particular media: a photosensitive (zinc phosphate) glass containing silver and a spin state transition material. Flash memories have become the dominating member in the family of non-volatile memories. Compared to magnetic and optical recording, flash memories are more suitable for mobile, embedded, and mass-storage applications. The reasons include their high speed, physical robustness, and easy integration with other circuits. In a flash memory, cells (floating-gate transistors) are organized into blocks. While it is relatively easy to inject charge into a cell (operation called writing or programming), to remove charge from a cell (operation called erasing), the whole block containing it must be erased to the ground level and then reprogrammed. This block erasure operation not only significantly reduces the speed, but also reduces the lifetime of the flash memory.

Chapter 4 analyzes coding schemes for rewriting data in flash memories. The interest to this problem comes from the fact that if data are stored in the conventional way, even to change one bit in the data may necessitate to lower some cell's charge level, which would lead to the costly block erasure operation. This study discusses the Write Asymmetric Memory (WAM) model for flash memories, where the cells' charge levels are changing monotonically before each erasure operation. The chapter also presents a data representation scheme called Rank Modulation whose aim is to eliminate both the problem of overshooting (injecting a higher charge level than desired) while programming cells, and also to tolerate better asymmetric shifts of the cells' charge levels.

Chapter 5 deals with data compression which is becoming an essential component of high-speed data communication and storage. Lossless data compression is the process of encoding ("compressing") a body of data into a smaller body of data, which can, at a later time, be uniquely decoded ("decompressed") back to the original data. In contrast, lossy data compression yields by decompression only some approximation of the original data. Several lossless data compression techniques have been proposed in the past - starting with Huffman code. This chapter focuses on a more recent lossless compression approach - the Lempel-Ziv (LZ) algorithm - whose princi- ple is to find the longest match between a recently received string stored in the input buffer and an incoming string; once the match is located, the incoming string is represented with a position tag and a length variable, linking it to the old existing one, thus achieving a more concise representation than the input data. The chapter presents an area- and speed-efficient systolic array implementation of the LZ compression algorithm. The systolic array can operate at a higher clock rate than other architectures (due to the nearest-neighbor communication) and can be easily implemented and tested due to regularity and homogeneity.

Although the CPU performance has considerably improved, the speed of file system management of huge information is considered as the main factor that affects computer system performance. The I/O bandwidth is limited by magnetic disks whose rotation speed and seek time has improved very slowly (although the capacity and cost per megabyte has increased much faster). Chapter 6 discusses problems related to the reliability of a redundant array of independent disks (RAID) system, which is a generally used solution since 1988 referring to the parallel access of data separated on several disks. A RAID system can be configured in various ways to get a fair compromise between data access speed, system reliability, and size of storage. The general trade-off is to increase data access speed by writing the data into more places, hence increasing the amount of storage. On the other hand, more disks cause a lower reliability: this, together with the data redundancy, cause a need for additional algorithms to enhance the reliability of valuable data. The chapter presents recent solutions for the use of Reed- Solomon code in a RAID system in order to correct single random error and double erasures. The proposed RAID system is expandable in terms of correction capabilities and presents an integrated concept: the modules at the disk level mainly deal with burst or random errors in disks, while the control level does the corrections for multiple failures of the system.

A grid is a collection of computers and storage resources, addressing collaboration, data sharing, and other patterns of interaction that involve distributed resources. Since the grid typically consists nowadays of hundreds or even thousands of storage and computing nodes, key challenges faced by high-performance storage systems are manageability, scalable administration, and monitoring of system state. Chapter 7 presents a scalable distributed system consisting of an administration module that manages virtual storage resources according to their workloads, based on the information collected by a monitoring module. Since the major concern in a conventional data storage distributed system is the data access performance, the focus was on static performance parameters not related to the nodes load. In contrast, the current system is designed based on the principle that the whole system's performance is affected not only by the behavior of each individual application, but also by the execution of different applications combined together. The new system takes into account the utilization percentage of system resources, like CPU load, disk load, network load. It offers a flexible and simple model that collects information on the nodes' state and uses its monitoring knowledge together with a prediction model to efficiently place data during runtime execution in order to improve the overall data access performance.

Many multidimensional signal processing systems, particularly in the areas of multimedia and telecommunications, are synthesized to execute data-intensive applications, the data transfer and storage having a significant impact on both the system performance and the major cost parameters - power and area. In particular, the memory subsystem is, typically, a major contributor to the overall energy budget of the entire system. The dynamic energy consumption is caused by memory accesses, whereas the static energy consumption is due to leakage currents. Savings of dynamic energy can be potentially obtained by accessing frequently used data from smaller on-chip memories rather than from the large off-chip main memory, the problem being how to optimally assign the data to the memory layers. As on-chip storage, the scratch-pad memories (SPM's) - compiler-controlled static RAM's, more energy-efficient than the hardware-managed caches - are widely used in embedded systems, where caches incur a significant penalty in aspects like area cost, energy consumption, and hit latency. Chapter 8 presents a power-aware memory allocation methodology. Starting from the high-level behavioral specification of a given application, where the code is organized in sequences of loop nests and the main data structures are multidimensional arrays, this framework performs the assignment of the multidimensional signals to the memory layers - the on-chip scratch-pad memory and the off-chip main memory - the goal being the reduction of the dynamic energy consumption in the memory subsystem. Based on the assignment results, the framework subsequently performs the mapping of signals into the memory layers such that the overall amount of data storage be reduced. This software system yields a complete allocation solution: the exact storage amount on each memory layer, the mapping functions that determine the exact locations for any array element (scalar signal) in the specification, metrics of quality for the allocation solution, and also an estimation of the dynamic energy consumption in the memory subsystem using the CACTI power model.

Network-on-a-Chip (NoC) is a new approach to design the communication subsystem of System-on-a-Chip (SoC) - paradigm referring to the integration of all components of a computer or other electronic system into a single integrated circuit, implementing digital, analog, mixed-signal, and sometimes radio-frequency functions, on a single chip substrate. In a NoC system, modules such as processor cores, memories, and specialized intellectual property (IP) blocks exchange data using a network that brings notable improvements over the conventional bus system. An NoC is constructed from multiple point-to-point data links interconnected by temporary storage elements called switches or routers, such that messages can be relayed from any source module to any destination module over several links, by making routing decisions at the switches. The wires in the links of NoC are shared by many signals, different from the traditional integrated circuits that have been designed with dedicated point-to-point connections - with one wire dedicated to each signal. In this way, a high level of parallelism is achieved, because all links in NoC can operate simultaneously on different data packets. As the complexity of integrated circuits keeps growing, NoC provides enhanced throughput and scalability in comparison with previous communication architectures (dedicated signal wires, shared buses, segmented buses with bridges), reducing also the dynamic power dissipation (as signal propagation in wires across the chip require multiple clock cycles).

Chapter 9 discusses different trade-offs in the design of efficient NoC, including both elements of the network - interconnects and storage elements. This chapter introduces a high-throughput architecture, which is applied to different NoC topologies: butterfly fat-free (BFT), a mesh interconnect topology called CLICH´E , Octagon, and SPIN. A power dissipation analysis for all these high-throughput architectures is presented, followed by a discussion on the throughput improvement and an overhead analysis.

Data acquisition and data storage are requirements for many applications in the area of sensor networks. Chapter 10 discusses different protocols for interfacing smart sensors and mobile devices with non-volatile memories.

A "smart sensor" is a transducer that provides functions to generate a correct representation of a sensed or controlled quantity. Networks of smart sensors have an inbuilt ability to sense and process information, and also to send selected information to external receivers (including other sensors). The nodes of such networks - the smart sensors - require memory capabilities in order to store data, either temporarily or permanently. The non-volatile memories (whose content need not be periodically refreshed) used in the architecture of smart sensors include all forms of read-only memories (ROM's) - such as programmable read-only memories (PROM's), erasable programmable read-only memories (EPROM's), electrically erasable programmable read-only memories (EEPROM's) - and flash memories. Sometimes, random access memories powered by batteries are used as well.

The communication between the sensor processing unit and the non-volatile memory units is done using different communications protocols. For instance, the 1-wire interface protocol - developed by Dallas Semiconductor - permits digital communications through twisted-pair cables and 1-wire components over a 1-wire network; the 2-wire interface protocol - developed by Philips - performs communication functions between intelligent control devices, general-purpose (including memories) and application-specific circuits along a bi-directional 2-wire bus (called the Inter-Integrated Circuit or the I2C-bus).

The chapter also presents memory interface protocols for mobile devices, like the CompactFlash (CF) memory protocol - introduced by SanDisk Corporation - used in flash memory card applications where small form factor, low-power dissipation, and ease-of-design are crucial considerations; or the Secure Digital (SD) memory protocol - the result of a collaboration between Toshiba, SanDisk, and MEI (Panasonic) - specifically designed to meet the security, capacity, performance, and environment requirements inherent to the newly-emerging audio and video consumer electronic devices, as well as smart sensing networks (that include smart mobile devices, such as smart phones and PDA's).

The next chapters present complex applications from different fields where data storage plays a significant part in the system implementation.

Chapter 11 presents a complex application of an array of sensors, called the electronic nose. This system is used for gas analysis when exposed to a gas mixture and water vapour in a wide range of temperatures. The large amount of data collected by the electronic nose is able to provide high-level information, to make characterizations of different gases. The electronic nose utilizes an efficient and affordable sensor array that shows autonomous and intelligent capabilities. An application of this system is the separation of butane and propane - (normally) gaseous hydrocarbons derived from natural gas or refinery gas streams. A neural network with feed forward back propagation training algorithm is used to detect each gas with different sensors. Fuzzy logic is also used because it enhances discrimination techniques among sensed gases. A fuzzy controller is used to detect the concentration of each gas in the mixture based on three parameters: temperature, output voltage of the microcontroller, and the variable resistance related to each sensor.

With the steady progress of the technology of digital imaging and the rapid increase of the data storage capacity, the capability to manipulate massive image databases over the Internet is used nowadays both in clinical medicine - to assist diagnosis - and in medical research and teaching. The traditional image has been replaced by Computer Radiography or Digital Radiography derived imagery, Computed Tomography, Magnetic Resonance Imaging (MRI), and Digital Subtraction Angiography. This advance reduces the space and cost associated with X-ray films, speeds up hospital management procedures, improving also the quality of the medical imagery-based diagnosis. Chapter 12 presents a complex system where a grid-distributed visual medical knowledge and medical image database was integrated with radiology reports and clinical information on patients in order to support the diagnostic decision making, therapeutic strategies, and to reduce the human, legal, and financing consequences of medical errors. This system started being used on the treatment of dementia - a brain generative disease or a group of symptoms caused by various diseases and conditions - to establish a prototype system integrating content-based image retrieval (CBIR) and clinical information from electronic medical records (EMR).

Chapter 13 describes a data storage application from the food industry. The food legislation in the European Union imposes strict regulations on food traceability in all the stages of production, transformation, and distribution. The back or suppliers traceability refers to the capability of having knowledge of the products that enter a food enterprise and their origin and suppliers. The internal or process traceability refers to the information about what is made, how and when it is made, and the identification of the product. The forward or client traceability refers to the capability of knowing the products delivered, when and to whom they have been supplied. The chapter describes a traceability system called the radio-frequency identification (RFID). This is a contactless method for data transfer, carried out through electromagnetic waves. RFID tags (transponders), consisting of a microchip and an antenna, represent the physical support for storing the information required to perform a complete traceability of the products, as well as facilitate the collection of data required by the technical experts of regulatory boards in charge of quality certification. The RFID read/write device creates a weak electromagnetic field. When a RFID tag passes through this field, the microchip of the transponder wakes up and can send/receive data without any contact to the reader. The communication gets interrupted when the tag leaves the field, but the data on the tag remains stored.

Prof. Florin Balasa
*Dept. Computer Science and Information Systems*
*Southern Utah University*

# Contents


Preface VII

1. Modulation Codes for Optical Data Storage 001
Tzi-Dar Chiueh and Chi-Yun Chen

2. Signal Processing in Holographic Data Storage 018
Tzi-Dar Chiueh and Chi-Yun Chen

3. Optical data storage in photosensitive glasses and spin state transition compounds 034
Matthieu Bellec, Lionel Canioni, Arnaud Royon, Bruno Bousquet, Jérôme Degert and Eric Freysz

4. Data Representation for Flash Memories 053
Anxiao (Andrew) Jiang and Jehoshua Bruck

5. Design and Implementation of FPGA- based Systolic Array for LZ Data Compression 075
Mohamed A. Abd El Ghany, Magdy A. El-Moursy and Aly E. Salama

6. Design of Simple and High Speed Scheme to Protect Mass Storages 093
Ming-Haw Jing, Yan-Haw Chen, Zih-Heng Chen, Jian-Hong Chen and Yaotsu Chang

7. Administration and Monitoring Service for Storage Virtualization in Grid Environments 107
Salam Traboulsi

8. Power-Aware Memory Allocation for Embedded Data-Intensive Signal Processing Applications 117
Florin Balasa, Ilie I. Luican, Hongwei Zhu and Doru V. Nasui

9. High Throughput Architecture for High Performance NoC 133
Mohamed A. Abd El Ghany, Magdy A. El-Moursy and Mohammed

10. Non-volatile memory interface protocols for smart sensor networks and mobile devices 157
Octavian Postolache, Pedro Silva Girão and José Miguel Dias Pereira

11. Electronic Nose System and Artificial Intelligent Techniques for Gases Identification 176
Iman Morsi

12. Medical Image Intelligent Access Integrated with Electronic Medical Records System for Brain Degenerative Disease 202
Mei-Ju Sua, Po-Hsun Chengb, Sao-Jie Chena, Chung-Yi Yangd, Ping-Kung Yipf, Daniel Racoceanugh and Heng-Shuen Chence

13. Use of RFID tags for data storage on quality control in cheese industries 214
Raquel Pérez-Aloe, José M. Valverde, Antonio Lara, Fernando Castaño, Juan M. Carrillo, José González and Isidro Roa

1

# Modulation Codes for Optical Data Storage

Tzi-Dar Chiueh and Chi-Yun Chen
*National Taiwan University*
*Taipei, Taiwan*

## 1. Introduction

In optical storage systems, sensitive stored patterns can cause failure in data retrieval and decrease the system reliability. Modulation codes play the role of shaping the characteristics of stored data patterns in optical storage systems. Among various optical storage systems, holographic data storage is regarded as a promising candidate for next-generation optical data storage due to its extremely high capacity and ultra-fast data transfer rate. In this chapter we will cover modulation codes for optical data storage, especially on those designed for holographic data storage.

In conventional optical data storage systems, information is recorded in a one-dimensional spiral stream. The major concern of modulation codes for these optical data storage systems is to separate binary ones by a number of binary zeroes, i.e., run-length-limited codes. Examples are the eight-to-fourteen modulation (EFM) for CD (Immink et al., 1985), EFMPlus for DVD (Immink, 1997), and 17 parity preserve-prohibit repeated minimum run-length transition (17PP) for Blu-ray disc (Blu-ray Disc Association, 2006). Setting constraint on minimum and maximum runs of binary zeros results in several advantages, including increased data density, improved time recovery and gain control and depressed interference between bits.

In holographic data storage systems, information is stored as pixels on two-dimensional (2-D) pages. Different from conventional optical data storage, the additional dimension inevitably brings new consideration to the design of modulation codes. The primary concern is that interferences between pixels are omni-directional. Besides, since pixels carry different intensities to represent different information bits, pixels with higher intensities intrinsically corrupt the signal fidelity of those with lower intensities more than the other way around, i.e., interferences among pixels are imbalanced. In addition to preventing vulnerable patterns suffering from possible interferences, some modulation codes also focus on decoder complexity, and yet others focus on achieving high code rate. It is desirable to consider all aspects but trade-off is matter-of-course. Different priorities in design consideration result in various modulation codes.

In this chapter, we will first introduce several modulation code constraints. Next, one-dimensional modulation codes adopted in prevalent optical data storage systems are discussed. Then we turn to the modulation codes designed for holographic data storage. These modulation codes are classified according to the coding methods, i.e., *block codes* vs. *strip codes*. For block codes, code blocks are independently produced and then tiled to form a whole page. This guarantees a one-to-one relationship between the information bits and the associated code blocks. On the contrary, strip codes produce code blocks by considering the current group of information bits as well as other code blocks. This type of coding complicates the encoding procedure but can ensure that the constraints be satisfied across block boundary. We will further discuss variable-length modulation codes, which is a contrast to fixed-length modulation codes. Variable-length modulation codes have more freedom in the design of code blocks. With a given code rate, variable-length modulation codes can provide better modulated pages when compared to fixed-length modulation codes. However, variable-length modulation codes can suffer from the *error propagation* problem where a decoding error of one code block can lead to several ensuing decoding errors.

## 2. Constraints

Generally speaking, constraints of modulation codes are designed according to the channel characteristics of the storage system. There are also other considerations such as decoder complexity and code rate. In conventional optical data storage systems, information carried in a binary data stream is recorded by creating marks on the disk with variable lengths and spaces between them. On the other hand, information is stored in 2-D data pages consisting of ON pixels and OFF pixels in holographic data storage system. The holographic modulation codes encode one-dimensional information streams into 2-D code blocks. The modulated pages created by tiling code blocks comply with certain constraints, aiming at reducing the risk of corrupting signal fidelity during writing and retrieving processes. Due to the additional dimension, other considerations are required when designing constraints for holographic modulation codes. In the following some commonly adopted constraints are introduced.

### 2.1 Run-Length Limited Constraint

The run-length limited constraint is widely adopted in optical storage systems. Examples are the eight-to-fourteen modulation (EFM) in CD, EFMPlus in DVD, and the 17 parity preserve-prohibit repeated minimum run-length transition (17PP) in Blu-ray disc. Due to the different reflectivity states, peak detection is the most common receiver scheme. To reliably detect peaks, separation on the order of 1.5-2 mark diameters is required between marks (McLaughlin, 1998). The run-length limited constraint thus sets limits to the frequency of ones in the data stream to avoid the case where large run-length of zeros causes difficulty of timing recovery and streams with small run-length of zeros have significant high-frequency components that can be severely attenuated during readout.

From one-dimensional track-oriented to 2-D page-based technology, the run-length between "1"s (or ON pixels) has to be extended to 2-D. Two run-length limited constraints for 2-D patterns have been proposed. One constraint sets upper and lower bounds to run-length of zeros in both horizontal and vertical directions (Kamabe, 2007). The other one sets upper and lower bounds to 2-D spatial distance between any two ON pixels (Malki et al., 2008; Roth et al., 2001). See Fig. 1 for illustration of this 2-D run-length limited constraint.

### 2.2 Conservative Constraint

The conservative constraint (Vardy et al., 1996) requires at least a prescribed number of transitions, i.e., 1→0 or 0→1, in each row and column in order to avoid long periodic stretches of contiguous light or dark pixels. This is because a large area of ON pixels results in a situation similar to over-exposure in photography. The diffracted light will illuminate the dark region and lead to false detection. An example of such detrimental pattern is shown in Fig. 2.

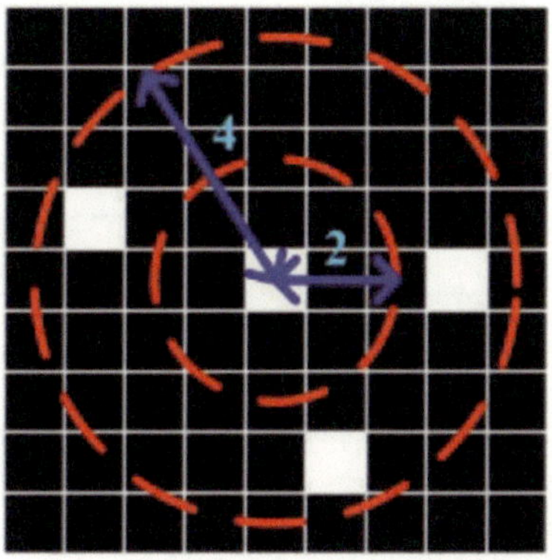


Fig. 1. Illustration of the 2-D run-length limited constraint based on 2-D spatial distance with lower and upper bounds of two and four, respectively.

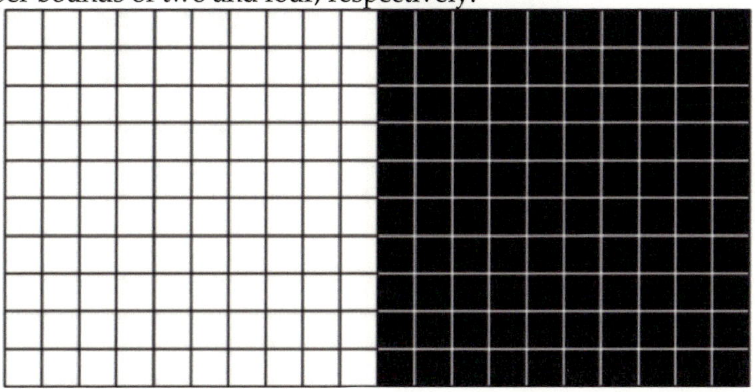

Fig. 2. A pattern forbidden by the conservative constraint (Blaum et al., 1996).

### 2.3 Low-Pass Constraint

The low-pass constraint (Ashley & Marcus, 1998; Vadde & Vijaya Kumar, 2000) excludes code blocks with high spatial frequency components, which are sensitive to inter-pixel interference induced by holographic data storage channels. For example, an ON pixel tends to be incorrectly detected as "0" when it is surrounded by OFF pixels and similarly an OFF pixel tends to be incorrectly detected as "1" when surrounded by ON pixels. Therefore, such patterns are forbidden under the low-pass constraint.

In fact, the low-pass constraints can be quite strict so that the legal code patterns have good protection against high-frequency cutoff. This is, however, achieved at the cost of lower code rate because few code blocks satisfy this constraint. Table 1 lists five low-pass constraints and examples that violate these constraints.

| Constraints | Examples of forbidden patterns |
|---|---|
| At least one ON/OFF pixel exists among eight nearest neighboring pixels of an ON/OFF pixel. | 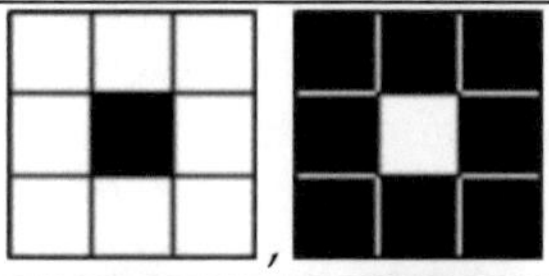 |
| At least one ON/OFF pixel exists among four nearest neighboring pixels of an ON/OFF pixel. | 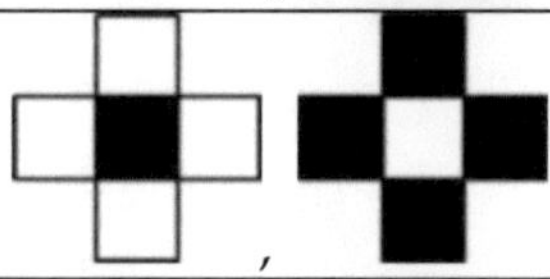 |
| At least two ON/OFF pixels exist among four nearest neighboring pixels of an ON/OFF pixel. | 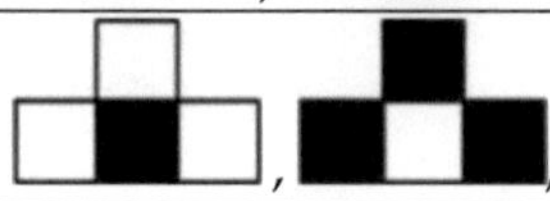 etc. |
| No ON/OFF pixels are isolated either horizontally or vertically. | 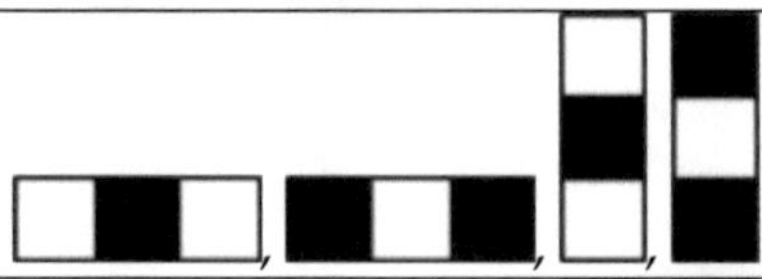 |
| No ON/OFF pixels are isolated either horizontally, vertically or diagonally. | 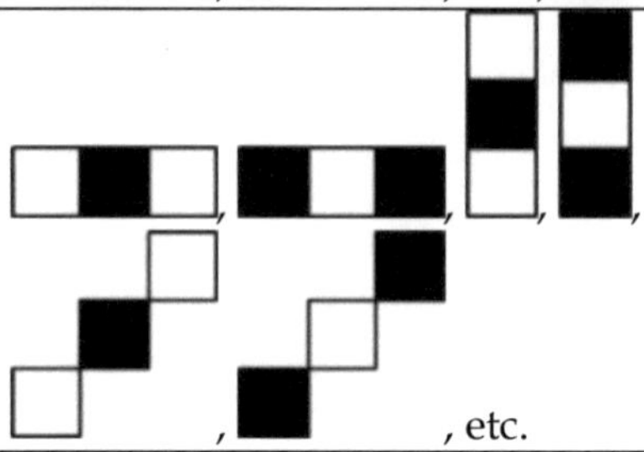 etc. |

Table 1. Low-pass constraints and examples of forbidden patterns.

### 2.4 Constant-Weight Constraint

The weight of a page is defined as the ratio of the number of ON pixels over the number of all pixels. With a constant-weight page, low-complexity correlation detection can be efficiently implemented (Coufal et al., 2000; Burr & Marcus, 1999; Burr et al., 1997). Two kinds of weight distribution garner interests of researchers. One is balanced weight, which makes the numbers of ON pixels and OFF pixels the same. The other is sparse weight, which makes the number of ON pixels less than that of OFF pixels. Balanced-weight modulation codes have higher code rates than sparse-weight modulation codes with the same code block size. However, due to imbalanced interference between ON pixels and OFF pixels, OFF pixels are favored as they cause lower level of interference. Therefore, sparse codes enable more data pages that can be superimposed at the same location on the recording medium by reducing optical exposure and increasing diffraction efficiency (the ratio of the power of the diffracted beam to the incident power of that beam) per pixel (Daiber et al., 2003). In addition, the probability of undesirable patterns can be reduced by decreasing ON pixel density. To be more exact, up to 15% improvement of total memory capacity can be achieved by sparse codes with the page weight decreased to 25% (King & Neifeld, 2000).

### 2.5 Summary

We have introduced four types of constraints for modulation codes commonly adopted in optical data storage: run-length limited, conservative, low-pass and constant-weight constraints. The run-length limited constraint focuses on the density of ON pixels. The conservative constraint considers the frequency of transitions between ON and OFF pixels. The low-pass constraint helps avoid those patterns vulnerable to inter-pixel interference effects in the holographic data storage systems. As for the constant-weight constraint, it enables a simple decoding scheme by sorting pixel intensities. Sparse modulation codes further decrease the probability of vulnerable patterns and increase the number of recordable pages.

## 3. One-Dimensional Modulation Codes

The modulation codes adopted by current optical data storage systems, i.e., CD, DVD, and Blu-ray disc, are developed according to the run-length limited constraint. As we mentioned previously, short runs result in small read-out signal power which tends to cause errors while long runs cause failure in time recovery. Therefore, a run-length limited code in the non-return-to-zero (NRZ) notation requires the number of "0"s between two "1"s to be at least $d$ and at most $k$. The real bits recorded on the disc are then transformed from NRZ to non-return-to-zero inverted (NRZI) format consisting of sequence of runs which changes polarity when a "1" appears in the NRZ bit stream, as shown in Fig. 3.

Under the EFM rule adopted by CD, 8-bit information sequences are transformed into 14-bit codewords using a table. The 14-bit codewords satisfy the (2, 10)-run-length limited constraint in the NRZ notation, that is, two "1"s are always separated by at least two "0"s and at most ten "0"s. To make sure bits across two adjacent codewords also comply with the run-length limited constraint, three emerging bits precede every 14-bit codeword. Although two merging bits are sufficient to meet this requirement, one additional bit is used in order to do DC-control, that is, make the *running digital sum*, which is the sum of bit value (±1) from the start of the disc up to the specified position, close to zero as much as possible. Therefore, total 17 bits are needed to store eight information bit in the EFM code.

The EFMPlus code used in DVD translates sequences of eight information bit into 16-bit codewords satisfying the (2, 10)-run-length limited constraint. Unlike EFM, which is simply realized by a look-up table, EFMPlus code exploits a finite state machine with four states. No merging bits are required to promise no violation across codewords. In addition, to circumvent error propagation, the encoder is further designed to avoid state-dependent decoding.

Blu-ray disc boosts data capacity by further shrinking physical bit size recorded on the disc, leading to severer interference than CD and DVD. In Blu-ray disc, the 17PP modulation code follows the (1, 7)-run-length limited constraint and exploits a new DC-control mechanism. The DC-control is realized by inserting DC-bits at certain DC-control points in the information stream. The polarity of the corresponding NRZI bit stream is flipped if a DC-bit is set as "1" while the polarity remains if a DC-bit is set as "0". Therefore, the best DC-free bit stream that makes the running digital sum closest to zero can be obtained by properly setting the DC-bits. The DC-control mechanism is illustrated in Fig. 4.

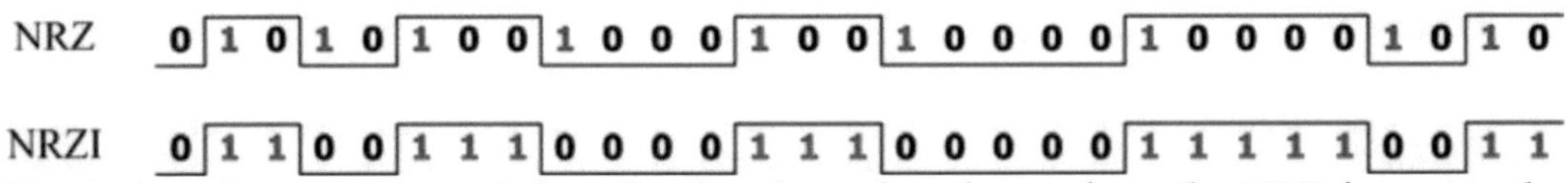


Fig. 3. Actual patterns recorded on the disc through a change from the NRZ format to the NRZI format.

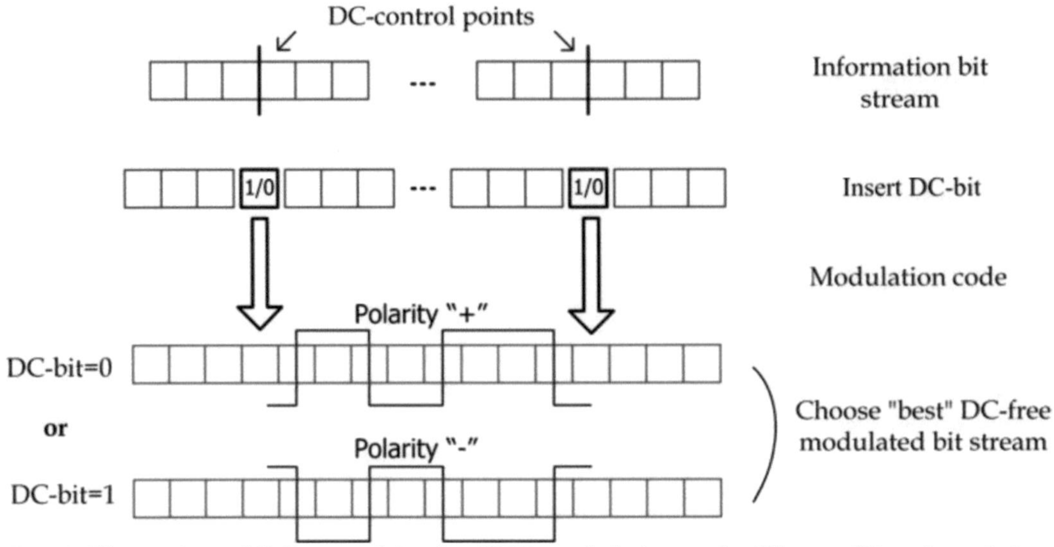


Fig. 4. Illustration of DC control in the 17PP modulation code (Blu-ray Disc Association, 2006).

## 4. Block Codes for Holographic Data Storage

A block code used in holographic data storage maps a sequence of information bits into a 2-D code block in a one-to-one manner. The encoded blocks are tiled to create a whole page. The ratio of the number of information bits to the number of block pixels is called *code rate*. For example, a simple block code, named *differential code*, uses two pixels to represent one bit and achieves a code rate of 1/2. Its code blocks are illustrated in Fig. 5. Basically, higher code rate is preferred since less redundant pixels are included and more information is carried in the final modulated page. For this purpose, enlarging block size or changing the average intensity is applied (Kume et al., 2001). Fig. 6 illustrates a 5:9 block code with a code rate of 5/9 and a 6:9 block code with a code rate of 2/3. With two of nine pixels in a code block turned ON, there exist $C_2^9 = 36$ possible code blocks. Therefore, these coded blocks are sufficient to represent five information bits, giving a 5:9 block code. Similarly, with three of nine pixels in a code block turned ON, there are $C_3^9 = 84$ possible coded blocks, thus achieving a 6:9 block code.

However, a larger block size may deteriorate decoding performance due to biased intensity throughout the block. Higher intensity also degrades the quality of reconstructed images according to the sparse code principle. On the other hand, increasing the number of possible code blocks (and thus code rate) often leads to more complex decoding. Hence, modulation

code design is a trade-off among higher code rate, simpler decoder and satisfactory BER performance.
Block codes indeed provide a simple mapping in encoding and decoding. However, the risk of violating constraints becomes significant when tiling multiple blocks together since illegal patterns may occur across the boundary of neighboring blocks. To circumvent this problem, additional constraints may be required. Unfortunately, more constraints can eliminate some patterns that would have been legitimate. To maintain the code rate, a larger block size is called for.

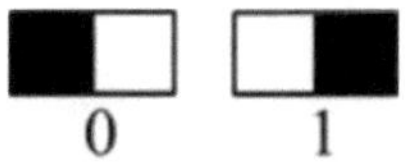


Fig. 5. Differential code.

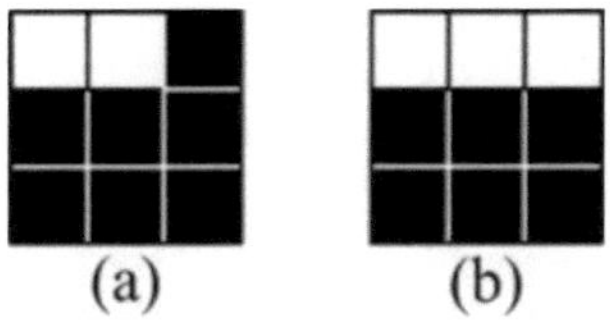


Fig. 6. (a) A code block in the 5:9 block code and (b) a code block in the 6:9 block code.

### 4.1 6:8 Balanced Block Code

The 6:8 balanced block code (Burr et al., 1997) is one of the most common block modulation codes used in the holographic data storage systems. A group of six information bits is encoded into a 2×4 block with exactly four ON pixels and four OFF pixels, satisfying the balanced constraint. Since $C_4^8 = 70$ is larger than $2^6$=64, we choose 64 patterns from 70 code blocks and assign Gray code to these blocks . Correlation detection (Burr et al., 1997) is also proposed to decode such block code. In this method the correlations between the retrieved block and all code blocks are computed and the code block with the maximum correlation to the received block is declared the stored pattern.

### 4.2 6:8 Variable-Weight Block Code

The constant-weight constraint can have negative impacts on the achievable code rate of a modulation code. For instance, if we apply a sparse constant-weight constraint to a 2×4 block code and require two ON pixels and six OFF pixels in every code block, then there are only 28 legal code blocks, giving four information bits and a low code rate of 1/2.
The 6:8 variable-weight modulation code (Chen & Chiueh, 2007) is a sparse block modulation code with variable weight and relatively high code rate. Similar to the 6:8 balanced block code, the variable-weight code encodes a group of six data bits into a 2×4 block. There are $C_1^8 = 8$ codewords with one ON pixel and $C_3^8 = 56$ codewords with three ON pixels, enough to represent 6-bit information. This design decreases the weight of a modulated page from 50% to 34.38%. Therefore, the variable-weight code provides better BER performance with the same coding scheme as the 6:8 balanced code performance due to lower interference level from fewer ON pixels.

### 4.3 Codeword Complementing Block Modulation Code

The codeword complementing block modulation code (Hwang et al., 2003) adopts an indirect encoding scheme so as to satisfy the pseudo-balanced constraint and thus achieve uniform spectrum of the modulated pages. The coding procedure consists of two steps: *constant weight encoding* and *selective complementary encoding*. The constant weight encoder maps input information bits into one-dimensional constant-weight codewords. Each one-dimensional $N$-bit codeword forms a row in an $(N+1)\times N$ code matrix. Then, some rows are flipped according to the elements in the last row of the current code matrix. If a pixel in the last row is "1", the selective complementary encoder flips the corresponding row. In this way, the final $N\times N$ modulated block has constant weight and relatively uniform spectrum in the Fourier plane. An example of the codeword complementing block modulation code encoding process with $N$=11 is illustrated in Fig. 7.

The decoding procedure is simple. By calculating the average intensity of each row of a retrieved block, rows that have been complemented by the selective complementary encoder are easily identified and the polarities of the pixels are reversed. Moreover, the last row in the code matrix can be decided. Decoding the constant weight encoded blocks is achieved by first sorting the intensity of the received pixels in each codeword and marking proper number of pixels with higher intensity as "ON" and the other pixels of the codeword as "OFF." Then information bits are obtained by inverse mapping of constant weight encoding.

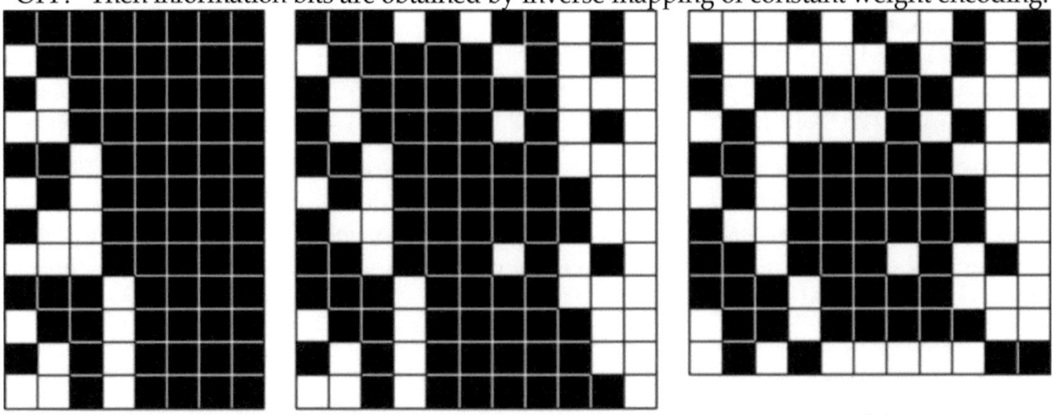

(a) (b) (c)

Fig. 7. Illustration of codeword complementing block modulation code encoding process ($N$=11). (a) Input information block, (b) constant weight encoded block and (c) selective complementary encoded block (Hwang et al., 2003).

### 4.4 Conservative Codes

Conservative codes are designed to satisfy the conservative constraint discussed previously. The coding scheme consists of a set of modulation blocks which is used as masks for the pixel-wise exclusive-OR operation with input information blocks. The encoded output blocks will be conservative of strength $t$, meaning that there exist no less than $t$ transitions in each row and column. A method based on an error correcting code having minimum Hamming distance $d$ and $d\geq 2t-3$ is proposed in (Vardy et al., 1996).

First define a mapping $\varphi$: $F_n \rightarrow E_n$ as follows:

$$\varphi(\mathbf{x}) = \mathbf{x} \oplus \sigma(\mathbf{x}) \tag{1}$$

where $F_n$ is the set of all binary column vectors and $E_n$ is the subset of $F_n$ consisting of all even-weight vectors; σ(**x**) is the 1-bit cyclic downward shift of a column vector **x**. Given two sets of codewords, $C_1$ and $C_2$, produced by two (*t*-2)-error correcting codes of length *m* and *n*, respectively, two sets of column vectors {$\mathbf{a}_1$, $\mathbf{a}_2$,..., $\mathbf{a}_n$} and {$\mathbf{b}_1$, $\mathbf{b}_2$, ..., $\mathbf{b}_m$} are obtained by inverse-mapping of φ-1(C1) and φ-1(C2). A theorem in (Vardy et al., 1996) states that for any vector x in Fn, if $\mathbf{x} \oplus \mathbf{a}_i$ has less than t transitions, $\mathbf{x} \oplus \mathbf{a}_j$ will have has at least t transitions for all j≠i.

Next one constructs matrices $A_1$,$A_2$,$A_n$ and $B_1$,$B_2$,$B_m$ all with the size of *m*×*n*, from the aforementioned sets of column vectors, {$\mathbf{a}_0$, $\mathbf{a}_1$,..., $\mathbf{a}_n$} and {$\mathbf{b}_0$, $\mathbf{b}_1$, ..., $\mathbf{b}_m$}. $\mathbf{A}_i$ is formed by tiling $\mathbf{a}_i$ *n* times horizontally while $B_j$ is formed by tiling transposed bj m times vertically.

$$\mathbf{A}_i = [\mathbf{a}_i \mid \mathbf{a}_i \mid \cdots \mid \mathbf{a}_i], \quad i = 1, ..., n \tag{2}$$

$$\mathbf{B}_j = \begin{bmatrix} \mathbf{b}_j^T \\ \hline \mathbf{b}_j^T \\ \hline \vdots \\ \hline \mathbf{b}_j^T \end{bmatrix}, \quad j = 1, ..., m \tag{3}$$

Finally, a modulation block is obtained by component-wise exclusive-OR of an $\mathbf{A}_i$ and a $\mathbf{B}_j$. On the total, there are (*m*+1)×(*n*+1) such modulation blocks. With such modulation block construction, it can be shown that pixel-wise exclusive-OR operation of an input information block with a modulation block yields an modulated block that satisfies the conservative constraint with strength *t*. To indicate which modulation block is applied, several bits are inserted as an extra row or column to each recorded page.

### 4.5 Block Code with 2-D Run-Length-Limited Constraint

In 2-D run-length limited block codes, only the minimum distance ($d_{min}$) between ON pixels is enforced. Codebook design involves an exhaustive search of all possible binary blocks and prunes any blocks containing two ON pixels with a square distance smaller than $d_{min}$. A mapping between segments of information bits and these code blocks is then developed.

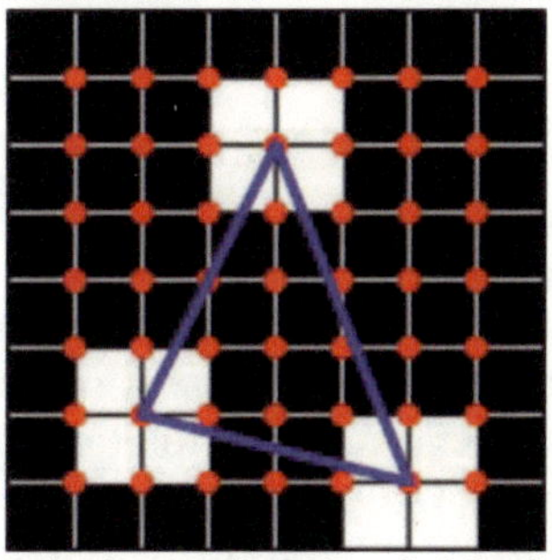

Fig. 8. An example of 8×8 block with three all-ON sub-blocks (Malki et al., 2008).

In (Malki et al., 2008), a fixed number of all-ON sub-blocks are present in each code block. This scheme lets the proposed code comply with the constant-weight constraint automatically. An example of three 2×2 all-ON sub-blocks is shown in Fig. 8. For an 8×8 block without any constraints, there are (8-1)×(8-1)=49 possible positions for each sub-block, denoted by filled circles. The value of $d_{min}$ determines the available number of legal code blocks.

## 5. Strip Codes for Holographic Data Storage

In contrast to block codes, which create modulated pages by tiling code blocks independently, strip codes exploit a finite state machine to encode information streams taking adjacent blocks into consideration. The name of "strip" comes from dividing a whole page into several non-overlapping strips and encoding/decoding within each strip independently. To decode such modulation codes, a *sliding block decoder* (Coufal et al., 2000) is required. Such a decoder has a decoding window containing preceding (memory), current and subsequent (anticipation) blocks.

Strip codes provide an advantage of ensuring that the modulated patterns across borders of blocks can still comply with the prescribed constraints if the coding scheme is well designed. However, additional constraints for patterns across borders of strips are still required. These additional constraints are called *strip constraints* (Ashley & Marcus, 1998; Coufal et al., 2000). Another advantage of strip codes is their better error-rate performance due to the fact that adjacent modulated blocks are used to help decode the current block.

In terms of the decoding procedure, strip codes need decoders with higher complexity when compared with block codes. Another concern for strip codes is that using a finite state machine as the encoder may fail to achieve the 2-D capacity C (Ashley & Marcus, 1998) defined as

$$C = \lim_{h,w \to \infty} \frac{\log_2(N(h,w))}{hw}, \tag{4}$$

where $N(h,w)$ is the number of legal code blocks on an $h \times w$ block.

Strip codes solve problems of violating constraints across block borders by considering adjacent modulated blocks during encoding/decoding operation of the current block. As such, better conformance to the constraints and BER performance are attained at the cost of higher encoding/decoding complexity.

### 5.1 8:12 Balanced Strip Code

The 8:12 strip modulation code proposed in (Burr et al.,1997) is a typical balanced strip code. A page is first divided into non-overlapping strips with height of two pixels. Balanced code blocks with size of 2×6 are prepared in advance with minimum Hamming distance of four. During encoding, a finite state machine with four states is used to map 8-bit information into a 2×6 block based on the current state and input information bits, achieving a code rate of 2/3. The process goes on until a complete modulated page is obtained. As for decoding, the Viterbi decoder can be adopted for better performance. The 8:12 modulation code is block-decodable and can be decoded using the correlation detection. However, the error rate performance will not be as good as those using Viterbi decoders.

### 5.2 9:12 Pseudo-Balanced Strip Code

The 9:12 pseudo-balanced code (Hwang et al., 2002) is a strip code which maps 9-bit information into a 12-bit codeword with a code rate of ¾. It is similar to the 8:12 balanced

modulation code, but with higher code rate by relaxing the balanced constraint to allow certain degree of codeword imbalance. The 9:12 pseudo-balanced code maps information bits to codewords according to a trellis with eight diverging and eight merging states. Each branch represents a set of 64 pseudo-balanced 12-bit codewords with minimum Hamming distance of four. These codewords are divided into 16 groups. The most-significant three information bits of the current data word and the most-significant three bits of the previous data word indicate the states in the previous stage and the current stage, respectively. The codeword set is determined uniquely by these two states. The least-significant six bits of the current information word are used to select a codeword within the set.
The decoding is similar to Viterbi decoder for trellis codes (Proakis, 2001). First, the best codeword with respect to the acquired codeword for each codeword set is found. The index of that best codeword and the associate distance are recorded. Then the Viterbi algorithm finds the best state sequence using those aforementioned distances as branch metrics. In (Hwang et al., 2002), it is shown that the 9:12 pseudo-balanced code, though with a higher code rate, provides similar performance as the 8:12 balanced strip code.

### 5.3 2-D Low-Pass Codes

Previously, several low-pass constraints which prohibit some particular patterns with high spatial frequency components are introduced. Strip codes are better suited for compliance with these constraints since they can control patterns across block borders more easily.

| Current state | Input information bits | | | | | | | | | | | | | | | |
|---|---|---|---|---|---|---|---|---|---|---|---|---|---|---|---|---|
| | 000 | | 001 | | 010 | | 011 | | 100 | | 101 | | 110 | | 111 | |
| 1 | 00<br>00 | 1 | 10<br>10 | 1 | 01<br>01 | 2 | 11<br>11 | 2 | 11<br>01 | 2 | 01<br>11 | 2 | 00<br>11 | 3 | 11<br>00 | 4 |
| 2 | 00<br>00 | 1 | 10<br>10 | 1 | 01<br>01 | 2 | 11<br>11 | 2 | 00<br>10 | 1 | 10<br>00 | 1 | 00<br>11 | 3 | 11<br>00 | 4 |
| 3 | 00<br>00 | 1 | 10<br>10 | 1 | 01<br>01 | 2 | 11<br>11 | 2 | 00<br>10 | 1 | 01<br>11 | 2 | 00<br>11 | 3 | 11<br>00 | 4 |
| 4 | 00<br>00 | 1 | 10<br>10 | 1 | 01<br>01 | 2 | 11<br>11 | 2 | 11<br>01 | 2 | 10<br>00 | 1 | 00<br>11 | 3 | 11<br>00 | 4 |

Table 2. Encoder for the third constraint in Table 1 (Ashley & Marcus, 1998).

| Code block | 00<br>00 | 10<br>10 | 01<br>01 | 11<br>11 | 00<br>10 | 11<br>01 | 10<br>00 | 01<br>11 | 00<br>11 | 11<br>00 |
|---|---|---|---|---|---|---|---|---|---|---|
| Information bits | 000 | 001 | 010 | 011 | 100 | 100 | 101 | 101 | 110 | 111 |

Table 3. Decoder for the third constraint in Table 1 (Ashley & Marcus, 1998).

Besides, the high-frequency patterns may not only appear within strips but also across strips. *Strip constraint* is therefore very important when we require a low-pass property over the whole modulated page. Below is an example of the strip constraint applying to a strip code that satisfies the low-pass constraint. Given a forbidden pattern in Table 1 with height $L$, a strip constraint banning the top/bottom $m$ top/bottom rows of this forbidden pattern to appear in the top/bottom of the current strip, where $m$ is between $L/2$ and $L$. With this extra strip constraint, it is guaranteed that the low-pass constraint will be satisfied across strip boundary. Table 2 and Table 3 are an example of encoder/decoder designed for the third constraint in Table 1. Using a finite state machine with four states, the encoder transforms three information bits into a 2×2 code block based on the current state. The code block and the next state are designated in the Table 2. The three information bits are easily decoded from the single retrieved block. The mapping manner is shown in Table 3.

## 6. Variable-Length Modulation Codes for Holographic Data Storage

In Sections 4 and 5, we have introduced block codes and strip codes for holographic data storage, respectively. The code rates of the modulation codes we discussed are generally fixed. This kind of modulation codes is called *fixed-length* since they map a fixed number of information bits into a fixed-size code block. To allow for more flexibility in modulation codes, *variable-length* modulation codes were proposed. With such modulation codes, a variable number of information bits are mapped into a variable-size code block. Despite its advantage of more freedom in choosing legal code blocks that comply with certain constraints, variable-length modulation codes need a more elaborate decoding scheme to correctly extract code blocks without causing error propagation.

A variable-length modulation code designed to obey the low-pass constraint is proposed in (Pansatiankul & Sawchuk, 2003). It eliminates patterns which contain high spatial frequency not only within blocks but also across block borders. With this strict constraint and a given code rate, variable-length modulation codes produce better modulated pages than fixed-length modulation codes. Instead of preventing forbidden patterns such as those listed in Table 1, (Pansatiankul & Sawchuk, 2003) sets maximum numbers of ON pixels surrounding an OFF pixel. The notation of this variable-length modulation code is ($[m_1, m_2, \ldots]$, $[n_1, n_2, \ldots]$; $[k_1, k_2, \ldots]$; $\alpha$, $\beta$), where $m_i$ and $n_i$ are the size of 2-D blocks, $k_i$ is the length of one-dimensional input information bits, $\alpha$ is a maximum number of ON pixels in the four connected neighbor positions surrounding an OFF pixel and $\beta$ *is* another maximum number of ON pixels in the rest four of eight nearest neighbor positions surrounding an OFF pixel. Parts of the modulated page produced by (4,[1,2,3];[2,4,6];2,3) and (1,[4,6,8]; [2,3,4];3,0) variable-length modulation codes are given in Fig. 9. Rectangles indicate 3×3 blocks with highest allowable number of ON-pixels around an OFF-pixel according to the respective ($\alpha$, $\beta$) constraints.

The encoding process is the same as those in conventional block codes, giving a one-to-one manner between information bits and code blocks. In contrast to the straightforward encoding scheme, the decoding has the challenge of correctly determining the size of the current code block to do inverse-mapping. A decoding scheme for the (4,[1,2,3];[2,4,6];2,3) variable-length modulation code is provided in (Pansatiankul & Sawchuk, 2003). We first grab a 4×1 retrieved block and compare it to all 4×1 code blocks corresponding to 2-bit information. Note that in (4,[1,2,3];[2,4,6];2,3) variable-length modulation code, all 4×2 and 4×3 coded patterns are designed to have an all-OFF last column. If we cannot find a 4×1 code block that is close to the retrieved block and the next column contains only OFF pixels, we enlarge the retrieved block size from 4×1 to 4×2 and compare it to all 4×2 code blocks corresponding to 4-bit information. If still we cannot find any good 4×2 code block, then an error is declared. Similarly, we can check the second column to the right of the current 4×2 retrieved block for all OFF pixels and enlarge the retrieved block to 4×3 if the check turns out positive. Then compare the extended retrieved block to all 4×3 code blocks corresponding to 6-bit information. Similarly, an error is declared when no code block matches the retrieved block.

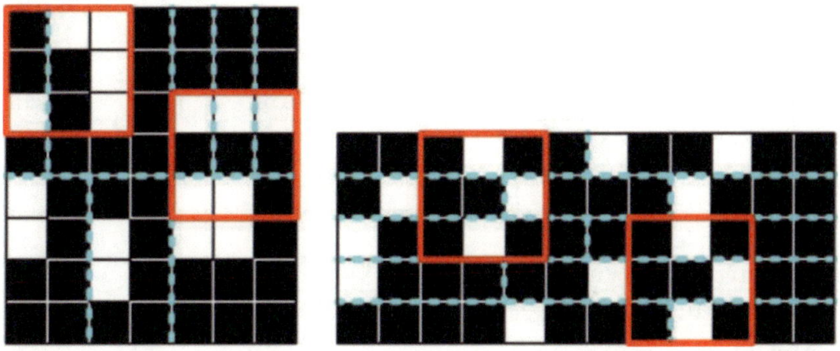

Fig. 9. Sample modulated page produced by two variable-length modulation codes (Pansatiankul & Sawchuk, 2003).

## 7. Conclusion

In this chapter, modulation codes for optical data storage have been discussed. At first, four types of constraints are introduced, including run-length limited, conservative, low-pass and constant-weight constraints. Since high spatial frequency components tend to be attenuated during recording/reading procedures and long runs of OFF pixels increase difficulty in tracking, the former three types of constraints are proposed to avoid these adverse situations as much as possible. On the other hand, the constant-weight constraint gives modulated pages that are easier to decode. In addition, experiments indicate that better performance can be obtained for modulation codes that have sparse weight.

Based on the constraints, several modulation codes are discussed. The one-dimensional modulation codes adopted in current optical storage systems, i.e., EFM for CD, EFMPlus for DVD and 17PP for Blu-ray disc, are first introduced. All of these modulation codes are developed for the run-length limited constraint.

Next, we focus on 2-D modulation codes for holographic data storage systems. They are classified into block codes and strip codes. Information bits and code blocks have a one-to-one relationship in block codes whose encoder/decoder can be simply realized by look-up tables. However, block codes cannot guarantee that patterns across block borders comply with the required constraints. This shortcoming can be circumvented by strip codes, which produce code blocks based on not only the input information bits but also neighboring modulated blocks. A finite state machine and a Viterbi decoder are typical schemes for the encoding and decoding of the strip codes, respectively.

Variable-length modulation codes, in contrast to fixed-length modulation codes, do not fix the number of input information bits or the code block size. The relaxed design increases the number of legal patterns and provides better performance than the fixed-length modulation codes with the same code rate. However, error propagation problems necessitate a more elaborated decoder scheme.

Finally, comparisons among different types of modulation codes introduced in this chapter are listed in Table 4 and Table 5.

| | Block code | Strip codes |
|---|---|---|
| One-to-one manner between information bits and code blocks | Yes | No |
| Constraint satisfaction across block borders | Difficult | Simple |
| Encoding/decoding complexity | Low | High |

Table 4. Comparison between block codes and strip codes.

| | Fixed-length | Variable-length |
|---|---|---|
| Freedom of choosing legal pattern | Low | High |
| Error propagation problem during decoding | No | Yes |
| BER performance with the same code rate | Poor | Good |
| Code rate with the same BER performance | Low | High |

Table 5. Comparison between fixed-length and variable-length modulation codes

## 8. References

Ashley, J. J. & Marcus, B. H. (1998). Two-dimensional low-pass filtering codes. *IEEE Trans. on Comm.*, Vol. 46, No. 6, pp. 724-727, ISSN 0090-6778

Blaum, M.; Siegel, P. H., Sincerbox, G. T., & Vardy, A. (1996). Method and apparatus for modulation of multi-dimensional data in holographic storage. *US patent* (Apr. 1996) 5,510,912

Blu-ray Disc Association (2006). *White paper Blu-ray disc format: 1. A physical format specifications for BD-RE*, 2nd edition

Burr, G. W.; Ashley, J., Coufal, H., Grygier, R. K., Hoffnagle, J. A., Jefferson, C. M., & Marcus,B. (1997). Modulation coding for pixel-matched holographic data storage. *Optics Letters*, Vol. 22, No. 9, pp. 639-641, ISSN 0146-9592

Burr, G. W. & Marcus, B. (1999). Coding tradeoffs for high density holographic data storage. *Proceedings of the SPIE*, Vol. 3802, pp. 18–29, ISSN 0277-786X

Coufal, H. J.; Psaltis, D. & Sincerbox, G. T. (Eds.). (2000). *Holographic data storage*, Springer-Verlag, ISBN 3-540-66691-5, New York

Chen, C.-Y. & Chiueh, T.-D. A low-complexity high-performance modulation code for holographic data storage, *Proceedings of IEEE International Conference on Electronics, Circuits and Systems*, pp. 788-791, ISBN 978-1-4244-1377-5, Dec. 2007, Morocco

Daiber, A. J.; McLeod, R. R. & Snyder, R. (2003). Sparse modulation codes for holographic data storage. *US patent* (Apr. 2003) 6,549,664 B1

Hwang, E.; Kim, K., Kim, J., Park, J. & Jung, H. (2002). A new efficient error correctible modulation code for holographic data storage. *Jpn. J. Appl. Phys.*, Vol. 41, No. 3B, pp. 1763-1766, ISSN 0021-4922

Hwang, E.; Roh, J., Kim, J., Cho, J., Park, J. & Jung, H. (2003).A new two-dimensional pseudo-random modulation code for holographic data storage. *Jpn. J. Appl. Phys.*, Vol. 42, No. 2B, pp. 1010-1013, ISSN 0021-4922

Immink, K. A.; Nijboer, J. G., Ogawa, H. & Odaka, K. (1985). Method of coding binary data. *U.S. Patent* (Feb. 1985) 4,501,000

Immink, K. A. (1997). Method of converting a series of m-bit information words to a modulated signal, method of producing a record carrier, coding device, decoding device, recording device, reading device, signal, as well as record carrier. *U.S. Patent* (Dec. 1997) 5,696,505

Kamabe, H. (2007). Representation of 2 dimensional RLL constraint, *Proceedings of IEEE International Symposium on Information Theory (ISIT),* pp. 1171-1175, ISBN 978-1-4244-1397-3, Jun. 2007, Nice

King, B. M. & Neifeld, M. A. (2000). Sparse modulation coding for increased capacity in volume holographic storage. *Applied Optics,* Vol. 39, No. 35, pp. 6681-6688, ISSN 0003-6935

Kume, T.; Yagi, S., Imai, T. & Yamamoto, M. (2001). Digital holographic memory using two-dimensional modulation code. *Jpn. J. Appl. Phys.,* Vol. 40, No. 3B, pp. 1732-1736, ISSN 0021-4922

Malki, O.; Knittel, J., Przygodda, F., Trautner, H. & Richter, H. (2008). Two-dimensional modulation for holographic data storage systems. *Jpn. J. Appl. Phys.*, Vol. 47, No. 7, pp. 5993-5996, ISSN 0021-4922

McLaughlin, S. W. (1998). Shedding light on the future of SP for optical recording. *IEEE Signal Processing Magazine,* Vol. 15, No. 4, pp. 83-94, ISSN 1053-5888

Pansatiankul, D. E. & Sawchuk, A. A. (2003). Variable-length two-dimensional modulation coding for imaging page-oriented optical data storage systems. *Applied Optics,* Vol. 42, No. 26, pp. 5319-5333, ISSN 0003-6935

Proakis, J. G. (2001) *Digital Communications,* McGraw-Hill Science/Engineering/Math; 4th edition, ISBN 0-07-232111-3, International

Roth, R. M.; Siegel, P. H. & Wolf, J. K. (2001). Efficient coding schemes for the hard-square model. *IEEE Trans. on Info. Theory,* Vol. 47, No. 3, pp. 1166-1176, ISSN 0018-9448

Vadde, V. & Vijaya Kumar, B.V.K. (2000). Performance comparison of equalization and low-pass coding for holographic storage, *Conference Digest Optical Data Storage,* pp. 113-115, ISBN 0-7803-5950-X, May 2000

Vardy, A.; Blaum, M., Siegel, P. H., & Sincerbox, G. T. (1996). Conservative arrays: multidimensional modulation codes for holographic recording. *IEEE Trans. on Info. Theory,* Vol. 42, No. 1, pp. 227-230, ISSN 0018-9448

# Signal Processing in Holographic Data Storage

Tzi-Dar Chiueh and Chi-Yun Chen
*National Taiwan University*
*Taipei, Taiwan*

## 1. Introduction

Holographic data storage (HDS) is regarded as a potential candidate for next-generation optical data storage. It has features of extremely high capacity and ultra-fast data transfer rate. Holographic data storage abandons the conventional method which records information in one-dimensional bit streams along a spiral, but exploits two-dimensional (2-D) data format instead. Page access provides holographic data storage with much higher throughput by parallel processing on data streams. In addition, data are saved throughout the volume of the storage medium by applying a specific physical principle and this leads data capacity on the terabyte level.

Boosted data density, however, increases interferences between stored data pixels. Moreover, the physical limits of mechanical/electrical/optical components also result in misalignments in the retrieved images. Typical channel impairments in holographic data storage systems include misalignment, inter-pixel interferences and noises, which will be discussed in the following. One channel model that includes significant defects, such as misalignment, crosstalk among pixels, finite pixel fill factors, limited contrast ratio and noise, will also be introduced.

The overall signal processing for holographic data storage systems consists of three major parts: modulation codes, misalignment compensation, equalization and detection. A block diagram of such a system is illustrated in Fig. 1. Note that in addition to the three parts, error-correcting codes (ECC) help to keep the error rate of the retrieved information under an acceptable level. This topic is beyond the scope of the chapter and interested readers are referred to textbooks on error-correcting codes.

To help maintain signal fidelity of data pixels, modulation codes are designed to comply with some constraints. These constraints are designed based on the consideration of avoiding vulnerable patterns, facilitation of timing recovery, and simple decoder implementation. Modulation codes satisfying one or more constraints must also maintain a high enough code rate by using as few redundant pixels as possible. The details are discussed in the chapter on "Modulation Codes for Optical Data Storage."

Even with modulation codes, several defects, such as inter-pixel interferences and misalignments, can still cause degradation to the retrieved image and detection performance. Misalignments severely distort the retrieved image and thus are better handled before regular equalization and detection. Iterative cancellation by decision feedback, oversampling with resampling, as well as interpolation with rate conversion are possible solutions for compensating misalignment.

Equalization and detection are the signal processing operations for final data decision in the holographic data storage reading procedure. Over the years, many approaches have been proposed for this purpose. For one, linear minimum mean squared error (LMMSE) equalization is a classical de-convolution method. Based on linear minimum mean squared error (LMMSE) equalization, nonlinear minimum mean squared error equalization can handle situations where there exists model mismatch. On the other hand, maximum likelihood page detection method can attain the best error performance theoretically. However, it suffers from huge computation complexity. Consequently, there have been several detection algorithms which are modifications of the maximum likelihood page detection method, such as parallel decision feedback equalization (PDFE) and two-dimensional maximum a posteriori (2D-MAP) detection.

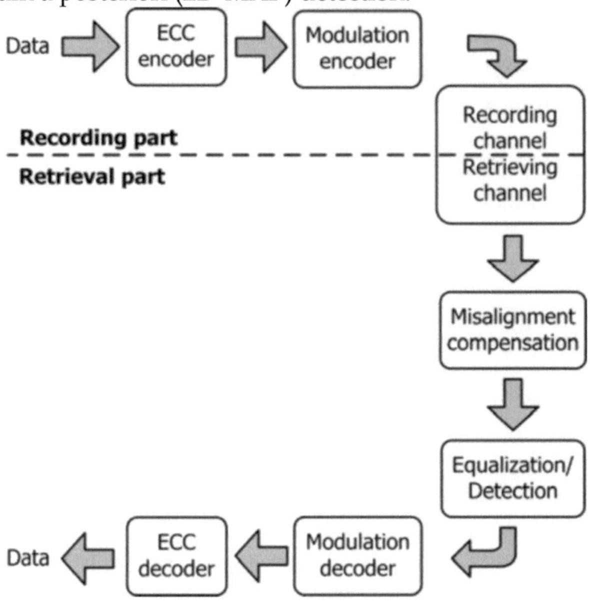


Fig. 1. Block diagram of signal processing in holographic data storage systems.

## 2. Recording and Retrieving Process

Holographic data storage systems store information carried by the interfered patterns within the recording media. The interfered pattern is created by one *object beam* and one *reference beam*. A *spatial light modulator* is adopted in holographic data storage systems to produce object beams, which is similar to a three-dimensional (3-D) object from which light is scattered and thus recorded in conventional holography. The spatial light modulator displays information in a 2-D format and modulates the intensity, phase or both intensity and phase of light beams. The 2-D data pages can consist of binary pixels (ON and OFF) or gray-scale pixels (Burr et al., 1998; Das et al., 2009). Spatial light modulators can be implemented by liquid crystal displays, digital micro-mirror devices, etc.

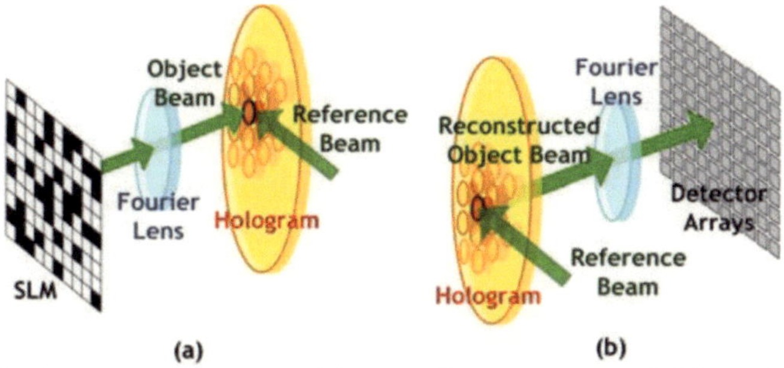


Fig. 2. Holographic data storage system: (a) recording process and (b) retrieving process (Chen et al., 2008).

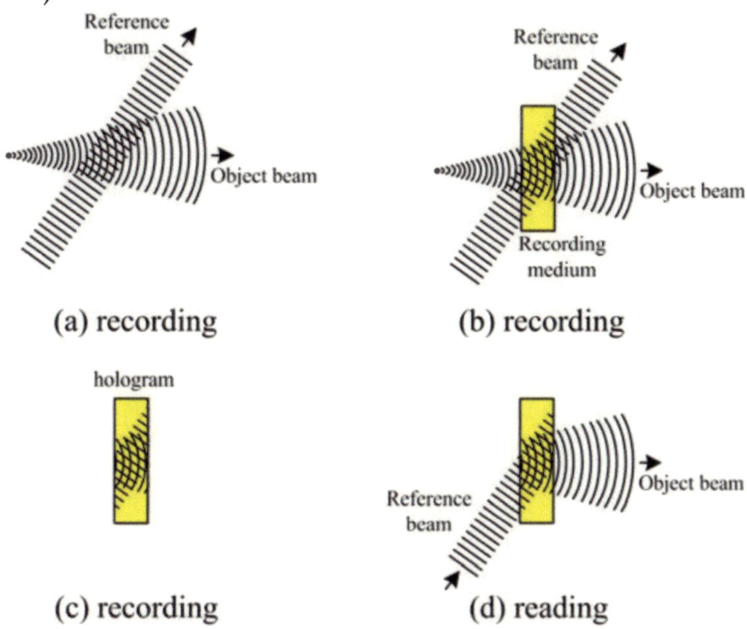


Fig. 3. Illustration of recording and reading process (InPhase).

With the spatial light modulator well controlled by the computer, information-carrying object beams can be created by passing a laser light through or being reflected by the spatial light modulator. Next, the object beam is interfered with a reference beam, producing an interferes pattern, namely, a *hologram*, which then leads to a chemical and/or physical change in the storage medium. By altering one or more characteristics of the reference beam, e.g., angle, wavelength, phase or more of them, multiple data pages can be superimposed at the same location. The process is called *multiplexing*. There are many multiplexing methods; interested readers can refer to (Coufal et al., 2000) for more details.
Reference beams of data pages at a certain location in the recording medium are like addresses of items in a table. In other words, data pages can be distinguished by the reference beam which interfered with the corresponding object beam. Therefore, by illuminating the recording medium with the reference beam from a proper incident angle, with a proper wavelength and phase, a certain object beam can be retrieved and then captured by the detector array at the receiving end. The stored information is processed by

transforming captured optical signals to electrical signals. The detector array is usually a charge coupled device (CCD) or a complementary metal oxide semiconductor (CMOS) image sensor. Minimum crosstalk from other pages when retrieving individual pages is attributed to a physical property called *Bragg effect*. Fig. 2 shows an example of the holographic data storage systems and Fig. 3 illustrates more details in the recording and reading processes.

## 3. Channel Defects

Ideally, a pixel of the spatial light modulator is directly imaged onto a detector pixel in a pixel-matched holographic data storage system. Such perfect correspondence is practically difficult to maintain due to non-ideal effects in holographic data storage channel that distort light signal and deteriorate signal fidelity. These non-ideal effects are called *channel defects*. Like most communication systems, optical storage systems have channel defects. Boosted storage density makes holographic data storage signals especially sensitive to interferences, noise or any tiny errors in storage media and optical/mechanical fabrication. From the spatial light modulator to the detector, from optical to mechanical, quite a few factors have significant influence on retrieved signals.

Laser light intensity determines the signal-to-noise ratio (SNR) but the intensity may not be uniform across the whole page. Usually, corners of data pages are darkerdue to the Gaussian wave front of the light source. This phenomenon and variations of light intensity over a page both are categorized as non-uniformity effect of light intensity. Non-uniformity of the retrieved signal level may cause burst errors at certain parts of data pages. Another factor is the contrast ratio, which is defined as the intensity ratio between an ON pixel and an OFF pixel. Ideally the contrast ratio is infinite. However, the OFF pixels actually have non-zero intensity in the spatial light modulator plane. A finite contrast ratio between the ON and OFF pixels makes the detection of pixel polarity more cumbersome. Another non-ideal effect is related to fill factors of spatial light modulator pixels and detector pixels. A fill factor is defined as the ratio of active area to the total pixel area, which is less than unity in real implementation.

Crosstalk is actually the most commonly discussed channel defect. We discuss two kinds of crosstalk here, including inter-pixel interference and inter-page interference. Inter-pixel interference is the crosstalk among pixels on the same data page. It results from any or combination of the following: band-limiting optical apertures, diffraction, defocus and other optical aberrations. Inter-page interference is caused by energy leakage from other data pages. This can be caused by inaccuracy of the reference beam when a certain data page is being retrieved. As more pages are stored in the medium, inter-page interference becomes a higher priority in holographic data storage retrieval. How good the interference can be handled determines to a large extent the number of date pages that can be superimposed.

Mechanical inaccuracies bring about another type of channel defects. Errors in the optical subsystem, mechanical vibration and media deformation can lead to severe misalignment, namely *magnification, translation* and *rotation*, between the recorded images and the retrieved images. Even without any inter-pixel interference or other optical distortions, misalignments still destroy the retrieval results entirely, especially in pixel-matched systems. Fig. 4 shows an example of misalignments $(\gamma_x, \gamma_y, \sigma_x, \sigma_y, \theta)$, where $\gamma_x, \gamma_y$ are the magnification factors in the X- and Y- directions, respectively; $\sigma_x, \sigma_y$ are the translation in the range of ±0.5 pixel along the X- and Y- directions, respectively; and the rotation angle, $\theta$, is positive in the counter-clockwise direction.

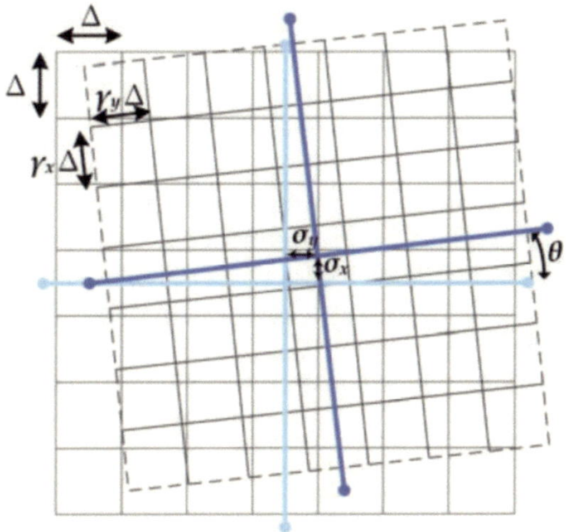


Fig. 4. Misalignment effects: magnification, translation and rotation of a detector page with respect to a spatial light modulator page.

Optical and electrical noises are inevitable in holographic data storage systems. They include crosstalk noise, scattering noise, shot noise and thermal noise. Optical noise occurs during the read-out process when the storage medium is illuminated by coherent reference beams, resulting from optical scatter, laser speckle, etc. Electrical noise, such as shot noise and thermal noise, occurs when optical signals are captured by detector arrays and converted into electrical signals.

## 4. Channel Model

A holographic data storage channel model proposed in (Chen et al., 2008), shown in Fig. 5, includes several key defects mentioned in Section 3. Multiple holographic data storage channel impairments including misalignment, inter-pixel interference, fill factors of spatial light modulator and CCD pixels, finite contrast ratio, oversampling ratio and noises are modeled. The input binary data sequence, $A(i, j)$, takes on values in the set $\{1, 1/\varepsilon\}$, where $\varepsilon$ is a finite value called the amplitude contrast ratio. The spatial light modulator has a pixel shape function $p(x, y)$ given by

$$p(x,y)=\Pi\left(\frac{x}{ff_{SLM}\Delta}\right)\cdot\Pi\left(\frac{y}{ff_{SLM}\Delta}\right), \tag{1}$$

where $ff_{SLM}$ represents the spatial light modulator's linear fill factor, the symbol $\Delta$ represents the pixel pitch and $\Pi(\cdot)$ is the unit rectangular function. Another factor that contributes to inter-pixel interference is the *point spread function*, a low-pass spatial behavior with impulse response $h_A(x, y)$ resulted from the limited aperture of the optics subsystem. This point spread function is expressed as

$$h_A(x,y)=h_A(x)h_A(y), \tag{2}$$

where

$$h_A(x) = (D/\lambda f_L)\mathrm{sinc}(xD/\lambda f_L). \tag{3}$$

Note that $D$ is the width of the square aperture, $\lambda$ is the wavelength of the incident light, and $f_L$ represents the focal length. The corresponding frequency-domain transfer function $H_A(f_x, f_y)$ in this case is the ideal 2-D rectangular low-pass filter with a cut-off frequency equal to $D/2\lambda f_L$.

A CCD/CMOS image sensor is inherently a square-law integration device that detects the intensity of the incident light. The image sensor transforms the incoming signals from the continuous spatial domain to the discrete spatial domain. Quantization in space causes several errors due to offsets in sampling frequency, location, and orientation. Magnification, translation and rotation are modeled as ($\gamma_x$, $\gamma_y$, $\sigma_x$, $\sigma_y$, $\theta$), as explained previously. In addition, the oversampling ratio $M$, the pixel ratio between spatial light modulator and CCD/CMOS sensor, is another factor to be considered.

Taking all the aforementioned effects into account, we have the final image sensor output at the $(k, l)^{th}$ pixel position given by

$$C_m(k,l) = \int_{\Lambda_X}\int_{\Lambda_Y} \left| \left[ \sum_a \sum_b A(i+a, j+b)h(x - a\Delta, y - b\Delta) \right] + n_o(x', y') \right|^2 dy'dx' + n_e(k,l) \tag{4}$$

where

$$\begin{aligned} \Lambda_X &= \left[ \left( \frac{k - ff_{CCD}/2}{M\gamma_x} + \sigma_x \right)\Delta, \ \left( \frac{k + ff_{CCD}/2}{M\gamma_x} + \sigma_x \right)\Delta \right] \\ \Lambda_Y &= \left[ \left( \frac{l - ff_{CCD}/2}{M\gamma_y} + \sigma_y \right)\Delta, \ \left( \frac{l + ff_{CCD}/2}{M\gamma_y} + \sigma_y \right)\Delta \right] \end{aligned} \tag{5}$$

and

$$\begin{aligned} x' &= x\cos\theta + y\sin\theta \\ y' &= -x\sin\theta + y\cos\theta \end{aligned}. \tag{6}$$

The subscript $m$ in $C_m(k, l)$ indicates misalignment; $h(x, y)$ in Eq. (4) is also known as a *pixel spread function* and $h(x, y) = p(x, y) \otimes h_A(x, y)$; $ff_{CCD}$ represents the CCD image sensor linear fill factor; $n_o(x', y')$ and $n_e(k, l)$ represent the optical noise and the electrical noise associated with the $(k, l)^{th}$ pixel, respectively. Translation and magnification effects are represented by varying the range of integration square as in Eq. (5), while the rotational effect is represented by transformation from the x-y coordinates to the x'-y' coordinates as in Eq. (6).

The probability density function of optical noise $n_o(x', y')$ can be described as a circular Gaussian distribution and its intensity distribution has Rician statistics. On the other hand, the electrical noise $n_e(k, l)$ is normally modeled as an additive white Gaussian noise with zero mean (Gu et al., 1996).

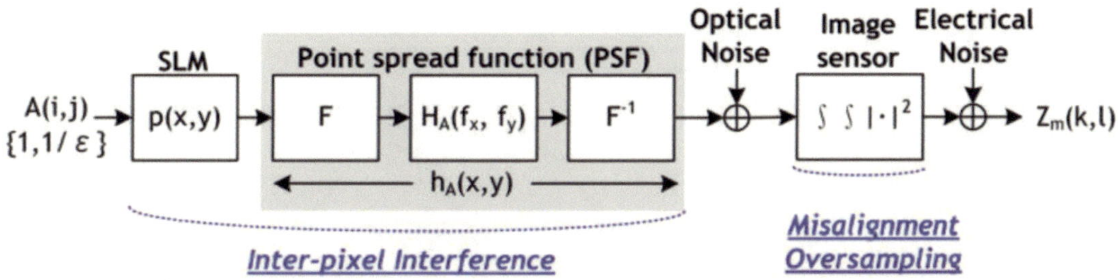

Fig. 5. Block diagram of a complete holographic data storage channel model.

## 5. Misalignment Compensation

Misalignments in retrieved images need be detected and compensated. To avoid information loss in the case that the detector array receives only part of a data page, a larger detector array or redundant (guard) pixels surrounding the information-carrying spatial light modulator pages can be employed. Moreover, a misalignment estimation procedure based on training pixels is needed before actual compensation. In fact, the estimation needs to be performed locally due to non-uniformity of channel effects. Toward this end, a page is divided into blocks of a proper size and training pixels are deployed in every block for local misalignment estimation. One possible estimation method is correlation based. In this method, the correlations of the received pixels and the known training pixels with different values of magnification, translation and rotation are first computed. The parameter setting with the maximum correlation is regarded as the estimation outcome. With the misalignments estimated, the retrieved images need be compensated before the modulation decoder decides the stored information. In the following several compensation schemes will be introduced.

### 5.1 Decision Feedback

Two decision feedback algorithms capable of dealing with translation and rotational misalignment compensation are proposed in (Menetrier & Burr, 2003) and (Srinivasa & McLaughlin, 2005), respectively. The iterative detection method exploits decision feedback to eliminate misalignment effects simultaneously. Hereafter, we explain the algorithm by using a one-dimensional translation effect in the pixel-matched system with a simplified channel model. A received pixel $C_m(k, l)$ can be represented as a function of two adjacent spatial light modulator pixels, $A(k\text{-}1, l)$ and $A(k, l)$, as shown in Fig. 6 and Eq. (7).

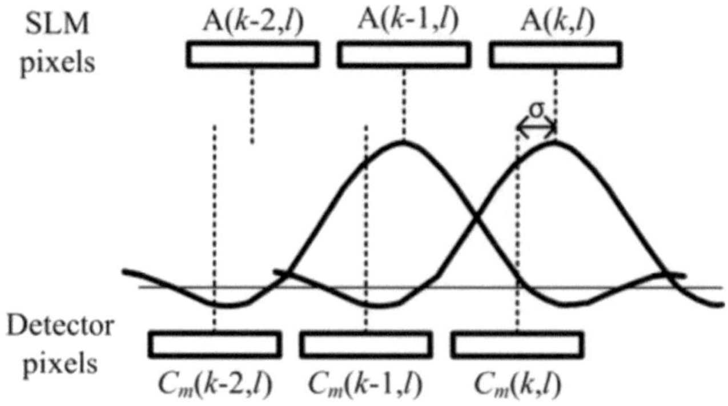


Fig. 6. Illustration of one-dimensional translation effect with parameter $\sigma$ (Menetrier & Burr, 2003).

$$C_m(k,l) = \int_{-ff_{CCD}/2}^{ff_{CCD}/2} \int_{-ff_{CCD}/2}^{ff_{CCD}/2} \left[\sqrt{A(k,l)}h(x-\sigma,y) + \sqrt{A(k-1,l)}h(x-\sigma+1,y)\right]^2 dxdy \tag{7}$$

Rewriting Eq. (7), we have

$$C_m(k,l) = A(k,l)H_{00}(\sigma) + 2\sqrt{A(k,l)A(k-1,l)}H_{01}(\sigma) + A(k-1,l)H_{11}(\sigma). \tag{8}$$

It is clear that if $C_m(k, l)$ and $A(k\text{-}1, l)$ are known, $A(k, l)$ can be calculated according to Eq. (8). The decision feedback detection scheme is based on this observation. If $\sigma$ is positive in the horizontal direction, then the scheme starts from the pixel at the top-left corner $C_m(0, 0)$, $A(0, 0)$ (the corner pixel) is first detected assuming that $A(-1, 0)$ is zero. With $A(0, 0)$ decided, decision feedback detection moves to detect the next pixel $A(1, 0)$ and repeats the same process until all pixels are detected. When the translation is only in the horizontal dimension, all rows can be processes simultaneously.

Extending the above case to 2-D, the retrieved pixel is a function of four spatial light modulator pixels

$$\begin{aligned} C_{m,s} &= A_s H_{ss} + A_h H_{hh} + A_v H_{vv} + A_d H_{dd} \\ &+ 2\sqrt{A_s A_h} H_{sh} + 2\sqrt{A_s A_v} H_{sv} + 2\sqrt{A_s A_d} H_{sd} , \\ &+ 2\sqrt{A_h A_v} H_{hv} + 2\sqrt{A_h A_d} H_{hd} + 2\sqrt{A_v A_d} H_{vd} \end{aligned} \tag{9}$$

where subscript $s$ is for self, $h$ for horizontal, $v$ for vertical and $d$ for diagonal. With the same principle used in the one-dimensional decision feedback detection, one must detect three pixels, horizontal, vertical and diagonal, before detecting the intended pixel. If both $\sigma_x$ and $\sigma_y$ are positive, again we start from the top-left pixel calculating $A(0, 0)$ assuming that pixel $A(0, -1)$, $A(-1, -1)$, and $A(-1, 0)$ are all zeros. The process is repeated row by row until all pixels are detected.

A similar detection scheme for images with rotational misalignment is proposed in (Srinivasa & McLaughlin, 2005). The process is somewhat more complicated because a pixel's relationship with associated SLM pixels depends on its location. For example, if the detector array has rotational misalignment of an angle in the clockwise direction as shown in Fig. 7, a pixel at the left top portion is a function of $A(k, l)$, $A(k, l\text{-}1)$, $A(k\text{+}1, l\text{-}1)$ and $A(k\text{+}1, l)$, while pixel at the right-bottom corner is a function of $A(k, l)$, $A(k\text{-}1, l)$, $A(k\text{-}1, l\text{+}1)$ and $A(k, l\text{+}1)$. Therefore, iterative decision feedback detection has to be performed differently depending on the location of the current pixel.

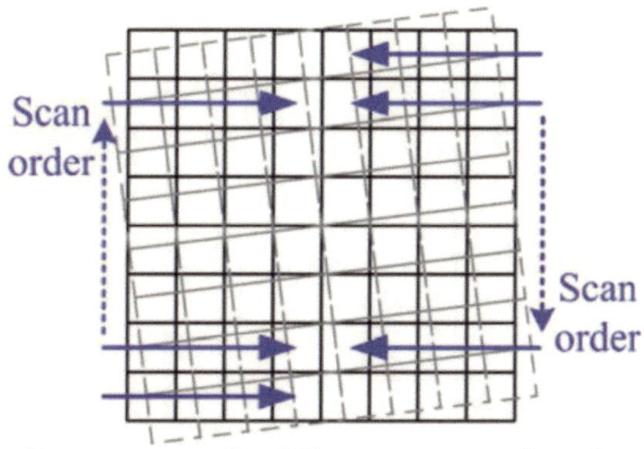


Fig. 7. Rotational misalignment entails different scan orders for the decision feedback cancellation detection in different portions of a page (Srinivasa & McLaughlin, 2005).

### 5.2 Oversampling and Resampling

Oversampling is a good way to handle the magnification effect and avoid the situation that a detector pixel is larger than a spatial light modulator pixel, leading to information loss. Besides, even if there is no magnification effect, a sub-Nyquist oversampling is necessary when the translation misalignment is around 0.5 pixel (Ayres et al., 2006b). With oversampling, the misalignment compensation task is no more than resampling.

The resampling process is actually a combination of misalignment compensation and equalization which will be discussed later. The resampling coefficients can be deduced by using the minimum mean-square-error (MMSE) criterion. With different sets of misalignment parameters, different sets of coefficients can be designed. For example, 20×20 sets of coefficients are required to handle 2-D translation misalignment with 5% precision. The number of coefficients needed to handle all possible misalignment situations can lead to a large memory size. Besides, oversampling uses more detector pixels to represent spatial light modulator pixels, thus decreasing stored information and recording density.

### 5.3 Interpolation and Rate Conversion

To compensate misalignments and convert the retrieved pixel rate to that of the stored data pixels, a 2-D filter capable of interpolation and rate conversion is proposed in (Chen et al., 2008). Interpolation can tackle translation and rotational misalignments. Rate conversion then converts the pixel rate to obtain pixel-matched pages free of misalignments.

Pixels in the captured images can be realigned by either 2-D interpolators or 2-D all-pass fractional delay filters (Pharris, 2005). A simple example is the bilinear filter shown in Fig. 8.

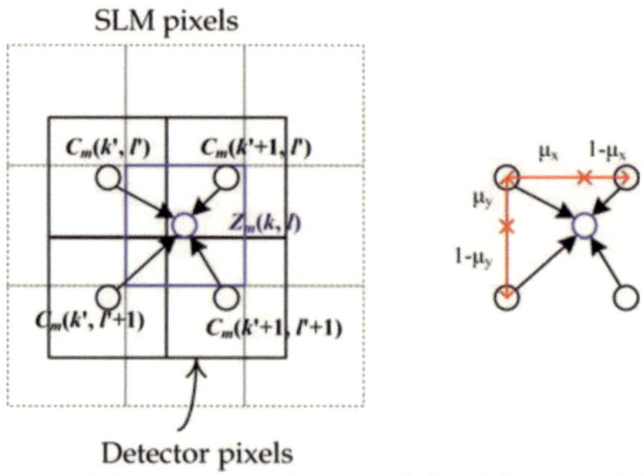


Fig. 8. Realignment by using a bilinear interpolator with local fractional displacement $\mu_x$ and $\mu_y$.

The reconstructed pixel corresponding to a spatial light modulator pixel is given by

$$\begin{aligned} Z_m(k,l) = & (1-\mu_x)\cdot(1-\mu_y)\cdot C_m(k',l') + \mu_x\cdot(1-\mu_y)\cdot C_m(k'+1,l') \\ & + (1-\mu_x)\cdot\mu_y\cdot C_m(k',l'+1) + \mu_x\cdot\mu_y\cdot C_m(k'+1,l'+1) \end{aligned}, \tag{10}$$

where $Z_m$ and $C_m$ are the realigned and misaligned images, respectively.
In general, the 2-D interpolator can be formulated as

$$Z_m(k,l) = \sum_{(p,q)\in S} f(\mu_x - p) f(\mu_y - q) C_m(k'+p, l'+q), \tag{11}$$

where $f(\cdot)$ is the one-dimensional impulse response of the corresponding interpolator; $S$ is the input range of the 2-D interpolators; $\mu_x$ and $\mu_y$ indicate the local fractional displacement from the nearest pixel ($k'$, $l'$) at $C_m$ in horizontal and vertical directions, respectively. The relationship between the local fractional displacement $\mu_x$ and $\mu_y$ and the corresponding pixel position $k'$ and $l'$ on the misaligned image $C_m$ can be expressed as

$$\begin{aligned} \tilde{k} &= (k\cos\theta - l\sin\theta + \sigma_x)\cdot M\cdot\gamma_x, \\ \tilde{l} &= (k\sin\theta + l\cos\theta + \sigma_y)\cdot M\cdot\gamma_y \end{aligned} \tag{12}$$

where $M$ is the oversampling ratio and

$$\begin{aligned} k' &= \lfloor \tilde{k} \rfloor, \quad \mu_x = \tilde{k} - k' \\ l' &= \lfloor \tilde{l} \rfloor, \quad \mu_y = \tilde{l} - l' \end{aligned}. \tag{13}$$

To further enhance the realigned image quality, higher-order filters can be adopted. In (Chen et al., 2008), a 6×6-tap raised-cosine interpolator provides a better choice with acceptable complexity and satisfactory performance than other filters.
The rate-conversion filter can properly restore oversampled images that have suffered magnification effect to pixel-matched images for ensuing pixel detection. Without loss of generality, the rate-conversion filter can be formulated as

$$Z(i,j) = \sum_{p=P_{\min}}^{P_{\max}} \sum_{q=Q_{\min}}^{Q_{\max}} v_x(p) v_y(q) Z_m(k+p, l+q), \tag{14}$$

where $Z_m$ indicates the realigned pixels and the weights $v_x(p)$ and $v_y(p)$ depend on the magnification factors $\gamma_x$ and $\gamma_y$ as well as the oversampling ratio $M$.

The realignment interpolator and the rate-conversion filter can be combined to reduce complexity. First, both 2-D filters are separated into two respective one-dimensional operations. Second, the realignment interpolators and the rate-conversion filters are integrated to construct a misalignment-compensation block that consists of one-dimensional compensation in the horizontal direction and one-dimensional compensation in the vertical direction. With such rearrangement, 84% reduction in additions and 74% reduction in multiplications are achieved (Chen et al., 2008).

## 6. Equalization and Detection

In general, equalization and detection is the final step of signal readout in holographic data storage. At this stage, most of the distortion caused by misalignments should have been removed. The remaining channel effects are mainly inter-pixel interference and noises. Equalization tries to eliminate impairments on the page by making its pixel intensity distribution as close to that of the spatial light modulator page as possible. A certain number of known pixels are needed to train the equalizer coefficients. For instance, assume that pixels on the distorted page are formulated as

$$\mathbf{Y} = \mathbf{HX}+\mathbf{N}, \tag{15}$$

where **Y** indicates the pixels on the distorted page; **H** is the pixel spread function of the channel; **X** indicates the pixels on the SLM page and **N** indicates the noises. Equalization is done by computing $\mathbf{H}^{-1}\mathbf{Y}$, where $\mathbf{H}^{-1}$ denotes the equalizer coefficients. There are several well-known techniques for estimating these coefficients. However, as the holographic data storage channel is nonlinear, the simplistic linear equalizer may have model mismatch, making it ineffective.

Detection generates final decision for each pixel. The simplest detection is a slicer which determines a binary pixel as "1" if the intensity is higher than a certain threshold and "0" otherwise. The slicer must be preceded by equalization to achieve acceptable BER performance. There exist other detection algorithms that operate without equalization. However, they need additional channel state information for effective operation.

### 6.1 MMSE Equalization

LMMSE equalization is a popular equalization method in communication systems. In holographic data storage systems, LMMSE equalization has to be extended to two-dimensional (Singla & O'Sullivan, 2004; Chugg et al., 1999; Keskinoz & Vijaya Kumar, 1999; Choi & Baek, 2003; Ayres et al., 2006a). Assume that the 2-D equalizer has (2*K*-1)×(2*K*-1) taps and its output is given by

$$\hat{A}(i,j)=\sum_{m=-K}^{K}\sum_{n=-K}^{K}w(m,n)Z(i-m,j-n), \tag{16}$$

where $w(m, n)$ is the $(m, n)^{th}$ tap of the equalizer, and $Z(i, j)$ is the $(i, j)^{th}$ pixel of retrieved data page. The LMMSE equalizer calculates $w(m, n)$ that minimizes the average squared error between equalized output and actual stored pixel, i.e.,

$$\min\left\{E\left[\left|\hat{A}(i,j)-A(i,j)\right|^2\right]\right\}, \tag{17}$$

based on the MMSE criterion. According to the orthogonal principle (Haykin, 2002), we can make use of auto-correlation of the received pixels and the cross-correlation between the received and the desired pixels to solve for the optimal coefficients through the following equations

$$R_{AZ}(p,q)=\sum_{m=-K}^{K}\sum_{n=-K}^{K}w(m,n)R_{ZZ}(p-m,q-n)=w(p,q)\otimes R_{ZZ}(p,q), \tag{18}$$

where $\otimes$ denotes convolution and

$$\begin{aligned}R_{AZ}(p,q)&=E[A(i,j)Z(i-p,j-q)]\\ R_{ZZ}(p,q)&=E[Z(i,j)Z(i-p,j-q)]\end{aligned}. \tag{19}$$

(Keskinoz & Vijaya Kumar, 1999) provided a simple way to calculate equalizer coefficients by applying Fourier transformation to Eq. (18). The equalizer coefficients can then be obtained by

$$w(p,q)=IFFT\{FFT[R_{AZ}(p,q)]/FFT[R_{ZZ}(p,q)]\}. \tag{20}$$

Unfortunately, linear equalizers can suffer from model mismatch and render them ineffective since the holographic data storage channel is inherently nonlinear. To this end, nonlinear equalization was also proposed (Nabavi & Vijaya Kumar, 2006; He & Mathew, 2006).

### 6.2 Parallel Decision Feedback Equalization

Decision feedback equalization was proposed in (King & Neifeld, 1998) and (Keskinoz & Vijaya Kumar, 2004). The algorithm iteratively detects pixels while considering the interferences from neighboring pixels based on decisions that have been made in the previous iterations. The process is executed on each pixel independently. The detection results will converge after several iterations. Hereafter in this chapter, we called this method *parallel decision feedback equalization (PDFE).*

PDFE is actually a simplified version of the optimal maximum likelihood page detection algorithm which has a search space as large as an entire page and is thus impractical in actual implementation. PDFE breaks the whole page into small blocks whose size equals the extent of the channel pixel spread function and uses iterations to achieve near maximum likelihood performance.

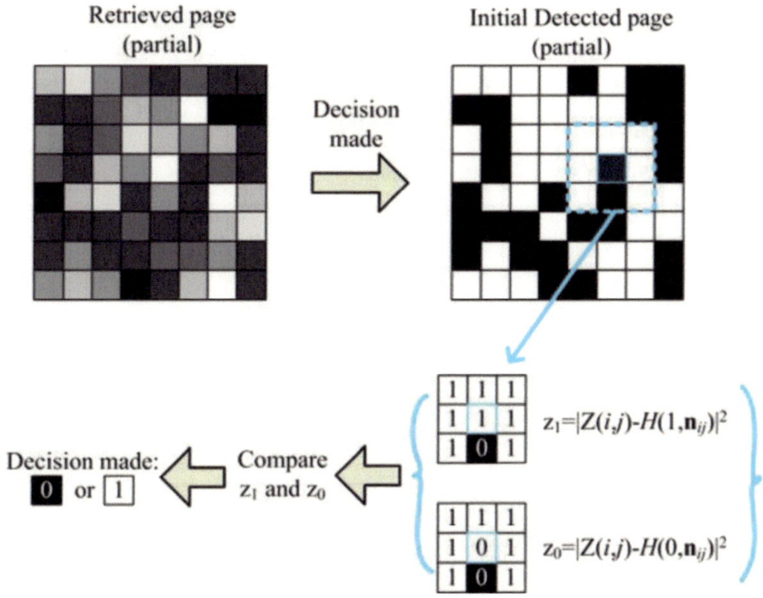


Fig. 9. Illustration of PDFE.

Assume that we consider inter-pixel interference within a range of 3×3 pixels and there exist no misalignment effects and the retrieved images have been made pixel-matched. Parallel decision feedback equalization starts with computing hard decision for each pixel. Then two hypotheses are tested to find the best decision for the current pixel. The process is shown in Fig. 9. With eight surrounding pixels given by decisions from the previous iteration, the central (current) pixel is decided as "1" or "0" according to

$$\begin{aligned} \hat{A}(i,j)=1 \quad if \quad \left|Z(i,j)-H(1,\mathbf{n}_{ij})\right|^2 < \left|Z(i,j)-H(0,\mathbf{n}_{ij})\right|^2, \\ \hat{A}(i,j)=0 \quad if \quad \left|Z(i,j)-H(1,\mathbf{n}_{ij})\right|^2 > \left|Z(i,j)-H(0,\mathbf{n}_{ij})\right|^2 \end{aligned} \tag{21}$$

where $H(A(i,j), \mathbf{n}_{ij})$ is the inter-pixel-interference-inflicted channel output with $A(i,j)$=0 or 1 and a neighborhood pattern expressed as a binary vector, $\mathbf{n}_{ij}$, consisting of the eight binary pixels.

The performance of parallel decision feedback equalization depends on the correctness of channel estimation and good initial condition. With inaccurate channel information or too many errors in the initial condition, PDFE will have poor overall performance as initial errors can propagate throughout the entire page.

### 6.3 2D-MAP

*Two-dimensional maximum a posteriori* (2D-MAP) detection, proposed in (Chen et al., 1998) as the 2-D[4] (Two-Dimensional Distributed Data Detection) algorithm, is actually the well-known max-log-MAP algorithm. It is also a simplified sub-optimal maximum likelihood page detection algorithm. Different from PDFE, the extrinsic information of each pixel is now taken into consideration during searching for optimal decisions. Therefore, more than two cases are tested in 2D-MAP. In this algorithm, a log-likelihood ratio (LLR) for each pixel is used as extrinsic information and is maintained throughout the iterative process. An LLR with higher absolute value indicates a greater probability of the pixel being "1" or "0." As the iteration goes on, the LLR value at each pixel will be re-calculated based on the knowledge of the previous LLR values of its eight neighbors. In all likelihood, this process makes each and every LLR move away from the origin and all pixel decisions become more and more certain.

The procedure of the 2D-MAP detection comprises *likelihood computation* and *update*. In a binary holographic data storage system, the likelihood computation formulas are given by

$$\begin{aligned} LL1_U^{(k)}(i,j) &= \min_{N_{ij}}\left\{\frac{1}{2N_0}\left|Z(i,j)-H(1,\mathbf{n}_{ij})\right|^2+\mathbf{d}_{ij}^{(k-1)}\bullet\mathbf{n}_{ij}\right\}. \\ LL0_U^{(k)}(i,j) &= \min_{N_{ij}}\left\{\frac{1}{2N_0}\left|Z(i,j)-H(0,\mathbf{n}_{ij})\right|^2+\mathbf{d}_{ij}^{(k-1)}\bullet\mathbf{n}_{ij}\right\} \end{aligned} \tag{22}$$

Again $H(A(i,j), \mathbf{n}_{ij})$ is the inter-pixel interference-inflicted channel output with $A(i,j) = 0$ or 1 and a neighborhood pattern expressed as a binary vector, $\mathbf{n}_{ij}$, consisting of the eight binary pixels; $N_{ij}$ is the set of all possible neighborhood patterns. In addition, $\mathbf{d}^{(k-1)}$ is a vector consisting of the corresponding LLR values of neighboring pixels in the $(k-1)^{th}$ iteration and the symbol ' ' represents inner product of two vectors. In the above, all misalignment effects and oversampling have been properly handled and the only remaining channel effect is inter-pixel interference and noises. LLRs are updated at the end of each iteration. To avoid sudden changes in the LLR values, a forgetting factor $\beta$ is applied and the updated LLR takes the form of

$$L^{(k)}(i,j) = (1-\beta)L^{(k-1)}(i,j) + \beta\left\{LL1_U^{(k)}(i,j) - LL0_U^{(k)}(i,j)\right\}, \tag{23}$$

The value of $\beta$ can affect the speed and accuracy of convergence. A larger $\beta$ leads to faster convergence but may lead to poor detection performance.

With the help of soft information, 2D-MAP indeed has better performance but with much higher complexity than PDFE. In (Chen et al., 2008) several complexity reduction schemes, including iteration, candidate, neighborhood and addition reduction, are proposed and thus up to 95% complexity is saved without compromising the detection performance.

## 7. Conclusion

This chapter gives an overview to the processing of retrieved signals in holographic data storage systems. The information to be stored is arranged in a 2-D format as binary or gray-level pixels and recorded by interference patterns called hologram. The fact that multiple holograms can be superimposed at the same location of the recording medium leads to volume storage that provides very high storage capacity.

Two important channel defects, misalignments and inter-pixel interferences, are major causes for degradation in detection performance and their model is formulated mathematically. Several misalignments compensation algorithms are introduced. One algorithm adopts decision feedback to handle misalignments and interference simultaneously. Pixels are detected one by one after cancelling interference from neighboring pixels. The scan orders should be carefully designed when misalignments may involve pixels coming from other directions. Another algorithm makes use of oversampling, and then resample at location. Another algorithm combines interpolation and rate conversion to compensate various misalignments effects.

Equalization and detection are crucial steps in restoring stored information from the interference-inflicted signal. Albeit its popularity and low complexity, LMMSE equalization algorithm suffers from the problem of model mismatch as the holographic data storage channel is inherently nonlinear. In light of this fact, two nonlinear detection algorithms, both simplified versions of the optimal maximum likelihood page detection, are introduced. They achieve better performance than the LMMSE method at the cost of higher complexity.

## 8. References


Ayres, M.; Hoskins, A., & Curtis, K. (2006a). Processing data pixels in a holographic data storage system. WIPO patent (Sep. 2006) WO/2006/093945 A2

Ayres, M.; Hoskins, A., & Curtis, K. (2006b). Image oversampling for page-oriented optical data storage. *Applied Optics*, Vol. 45, No. 11, pp. 2459–2464, ISSN 0003-6935

Burr, G. W.; Coufal, H., Hoffnagle, J. A., Jefferson, C. M., & Neifeld, M. A. (1998). Gray-scale data pages for digital holographic data storage. *Optics Letters*, Vol. 23, No. 15, pp. 1218–1220, ISSN 0146-9592

Chen, X.; Chugg, K. M. & Neifeld, M. A. (1998). Near-optimal parallel distributed data detection for page-oriented optical memories. *IEEE J. Sel. Top. Quantum Electron.*, Vol. 4, No. 5, pp. 866–879, ISSN 1077-260X

Chen, C.-Y.; Fu, C.-C. & Chiueh, T.-D. (2008). Low-complexity pixel detection for images with misalignments and inter-pixel interference in holographic data storage. *Applied Optics*, vol. 47, no. 36, pp. 6784–6795, ISSN 0003-6935

Choi, A.-S. & Baek, W.-S. (2003). Minimum mean-square error and blind equalization for digital holographic data storage with intersymbol interference. *Jpn. J. Appl. Phys.*, Vol. 42, No. 10, pp. 6424–6427, ISSN 0021-4922

Chugg, K. M.; Chen, X., Neifeld, M. A. (1999). Two-dimensional equalization in coherent and incoherent page-oriented optical memory. *J. Opt. Soc. Am. A*, Vol. 16, No. 3, pp. 549–562, ISSN 1084-7529

Coufal, H. J.; Psaltis, D. & Sincerbox, G. T. (Eds.). (2000). *Holographic data storage,* Springer-Verlag, ISBN 3-540-66691-5, New York

Das, B.; Joseph, J., Singh, K. (2009). Phase modulated gray-scale data pages for digital holographic data storage. *Optics Communications*, Vol. 282, No. 11, pp. 2147–2154, ISSN 0030-4018

Gu, C.; Dai, F., & Hong, J. (1996). Statistics of both optical and electrical noise in digital volume holographic data storage. *Electronic Letters*, Vol. 32, No. 15, pp.1400–1402, ISSN 0013-5194

Haykin, S. (2002). *Adaptive filter theory*, Prentice Hall, 4th edition, ISBN 0130901261

He, A. & Mathew, G. (2006). Nonlinear equalization for holographic data storage systems. *Applied Optics*, Vol. 45, No. 12, pp. 2731–2741, ISSN 0003-6935

InPhase website: http://www.inphase-technologies.com

Keskinoz, M. & Vijaya Kumar, B. V. K. (1999). Application of linear minimum mean-squared-error equalization for volume holographic data storage. *Applied Optics*, Vol. 38, No. 20, pp. 4387–4393, ISSN 0003-6935

Keskinoz M. & Vijaya Kumar, B. V. K. (2004). Discrete magnitude-squared channel modeling, equalization, and detection for volume holographic storage channels. *Applied Optics*, Vol. 43, No. 6, pp. 1368–1378, ISSN 0003-6935

King, B. M. & Neifeld, M. A. (1998). Parallel detection algorithm for page-oriented optical memories. *Applied Optics*, Vol. 37, No. 26, pp. 6275–6298, ISSN 0003-6935

Menetrier, L. & Burr, G. W. (2003). Density implications of shift compensation postprocessing in holographic storage systems. *Applied Optics*, Vol. 42, No. 5, pp. 845–860, ISSN 0003-6935

Nabavi, S. & Vijaya Kumar, B. V. K. (2006). Application of linear and nonlinear equalization methods for holographic data storage. *Jpn. J. Appl. Phys.*, Vol. 45, No. 2B, pp. 1079–1083, ISSN 0021-4922

Pharris, K. J. (2005). Methods and systems for holographic data recovery. *U.S. Patent* (Jan. 2005) 20050018263 A1

Singla, N. & O'Sullivan, J. A. (2004). Minimum mean squared error equalization using priors for two-dimensional intersymbol interference. *Proceedings of IEEE International Symposium on Information Theory (ISIT)*, pp. 130, ISBN 0-7803-8280-3, Jun. 2004, Chicago

Srinivasa, S. G. & McLaughlin, S. W. (2005). Signal recovery due to rotational pixel misalignments. *Proceedings of IEEE International Conference on Acoustics, Speech, and Signal Processing (ICASSP)*, Vol. 4, iv/121- iv/124, ISBN 0-7803-8874-7, Mar. 2005, Philadelphia

# 3

# Optical data storage in photosensitive glasses and spin state transition compounds

Matthieu Bellec, Lionel Canioni, Arnaud Royon, Bruno Bousquet, Jérôme Degert and Eric Freysz
*Centre de Physique Moléculaire Optique et Hertzienne (CPMOH), University of Bordeaux France*
Thierry Cardinal and Jean-François Létard
*Institut de Chimie de la Matière Condensée de Bordeaux (ICMCB), University of Bordeaux France*

## 1. Introduction

Up to now, the common media for optical data storage are the discs (blue ray technology for example). However, by definition, this technology is limited to two dimensions. The necessity for increasing data storage capacity requires the use of three-dimensional (3D) optically based systems. One of the methods for 3D optical data storage is based on volume holography. The physical mechanism is photochromism, which is defined as a reversible transformation of a single chemical species between two states that have different absorption spectra and refractive indices. This allows for holographic multiplexing recording and reading, such as wavelength (Rakuljic et al., 1992), angular (Mok, 1993), shift (Psaltis et al., 1995) and phase encoding. Another promising 3D optical data storage system is the bit-by-bit memory at the nanoscale (Li et al., 2007). It is based on the confinement of multi-photon absorption to a very small volume because of its nonlinear dependence on excitation intensity. This characteristic provides an income for activating chemical or physical processes with high spatial resolution in three dimensions. As a result there is less cross talk between neighbouring data layers. Another advantage of multi-photon excitation is the use of infrared (IR) illumination, which results in the reduction of scattering and permits the recording of layers at a deep depth in a thick material. Two-photon 3D bit recording in photopolymerizable (Strickler & Webb, 1991), photobleaching (Pan et al., 1997; Day & Gu, 1998) and void creation in transparent materials (Jiu et al., 2005; Squier & Muller, 1999) has been demonstrated with a femtosecond laser. Recording densities could reach terabits per cubic centimeter. Nevertheless, these processes suffer from several drawbacks. The index modulation associated with high bit density limits the real data storage volume due to light scattering. The fluorescence can limit the data transfer rate and the lifetime of the device.

Thanks to various available compositions, ease of implementation, stability and transparency, both organic and inorganic materials are convenient for 3D data storage. To be good candidates for 3D optical data storage, these materials must satisfy several norms

for the storing and the reading: Resistance to ageing due to temperature and recurrent reading. Moreover, high-speed response for high rate data transfer, no optically scattering for multilayer storage, erasure and eventually record with a grayscale to increase the data density could be incontrovertible advantages.
Here, we present two particular media: A photosensitive glass (zinc phosphate glass containing silver) in which the contrast mechanism is neither a change in refractive index nor a change in absorption, but a change in the third-order susceptibility ($\chi^{(3)}$) induced by femtosecond laser irradiation (Canioni et al., 2008); and a spin state transition material.

## 2. Photosensitive glass

### 2.1. Data storage medium: Photosensitive zinc phosphate glass containing silver

Glasses with composition $40P_2O_5$-$4Ag_2O$-55ZnO-$1Ga_2O_3$ (mol%) were prepared for 3D data storage using a standard melt quench technique. $(NH_4)_2HPO_4$, ZnO, $AgNO_3$ and $Ga_2O_3$ in powder form were used as raw materials and placed with the appropriate amount in a platinum crucible. A heating rate of about 1°C.min$^{-1}$ has been conducted up to 1000 °C. The melt was then kept at this last temperature (1000 °C) from 24 to 48 hours. Following this step, the liquid was poured into a brass mold after a short increase of the temperature at 1100°C in order to access the appropriate viscosity. The glass samples obtained were annealed at 320 °C (55 °C below the glass transition temperature) for 3 hours, cut (0.5 to 1 mm-thick) and optically polished. The glass possesses an absorption cut-off wavelength at 280 nm (due to the silver ions associated absorption band around 260 nm) and emits fluorescence mainly around 380 nm when excited at 260 nm. This intrinsic fluorescence is due to $Ag^+$ isolated in the glass (Belharouak et al., 1999).
The processed glass is highly photosensitive and was originally developed as a gamma irradiation dosimeter (Schneckenburger et al., 1981; Dmitryuk et al., 1996). Following exposure to gamma rays, the glass presents a broad UV absorption band, and when excited by UV radiation, emits homogeneous fluorescence which intensity is proportional to the irradiation dosage. This fluorescence is attributed to the presence of silver nanoclusters.

### 2.2. Silver nanoclusters formation following IR femtosecond irradiation

When an IR femtosecond laser is focused inside the photosensitive glass, a nonlinear multiphoton interaction occurs (in this case 4-photon-absorption) at the vicinity of the focal volume. Photoelectrons are ejected from the valence to the conduction band of the glass (Jones & Reiss, 1977; Stuart et al., 1996; Keldysh, 1965). In a similar manner to the mechanism utilized in a dosimeter (Schneckenburger et al., 1981; Dmitryuk et al., 1996), the released electrons are trapped within a few picoseconds by silver $Ag^+$ ions to form silver $Ag^0$ atoms. Then, due to the high laser repetition rate, the accumulation of the deposited laser energy increases the local temperature leading to the $Ag^0$ diffusion. Mobile $Ag^0$ atoms are trapped by the $Ag^+$ ions to form silver clusters $Ag_m^{x+}$ with the number of atoms $m<10$ and the ionization degree x. Since this is produced by a highly nonlinear interaction, the silver nanoclusters can be distributed in 3D inside the glass in an area that is smaller than the laser beam diameter (Sun et al., 2001). More details on the silver nanoclusters distribution in this glass can be found in (Bellec et al., 2009). The photo-induced silver nanoclusters have characteristic properties well adapted for the 3D optical data storage.

## 2.3. Silver nanoclusters spectral and optical properties

The photosensitive glass is irradiated using a femtosecond laser source emitting 440 fs, 9 MHz repetition rate pulses at 1030 nm. The laser mode is $TEM_{00}$, and the output polarization is TM. The maximum output average power is close to 6 W, which results in a maximum energy per pulse of 600 nJ. Acousto-optic filtering permits the tuning of the pulse energy and the repetition rate for perfect control of the accumulated effect. The femtosecond laser is focused using a reflective 36× objective with a 0.52 numerical aperture (NA) (working distance 15 mm) to a depth of 200 mm in the glass. The beam waist is estimated to be 1 mm. Spectroscopic properties (*i.e.* absorption and emission spectra) of the silver nanoclusters are shown in Fig 1. A transmission confocal setup, with a 36× - 0.52 NA reflective objective, is used for spectroscopy. A UV diode emitting at 405 nm with an appropriate emission filter, and a white light source are used to obtain emission and absorption spectra. All spectra are measured using a spectrometer equipped with a CCD camera. Figure 1(a) shows the absorbance difference between the irradiated region (experimental conditions: Irradiance $I$ = 6 $TW.cm^{-2}$; Number of pulses N = $10^6$) and the non-irradiated region. An absorption band appears at 345 nm. The emission spectrum of the fluorescent species when excited in the UV is presented in Fig. 1(b). A wide band centered at 580 nm is observed. These spectral properties can be attributed to the photoinduced silver nanoclusters (Dmitryuk et al., 1996; Dai et al., 2007).

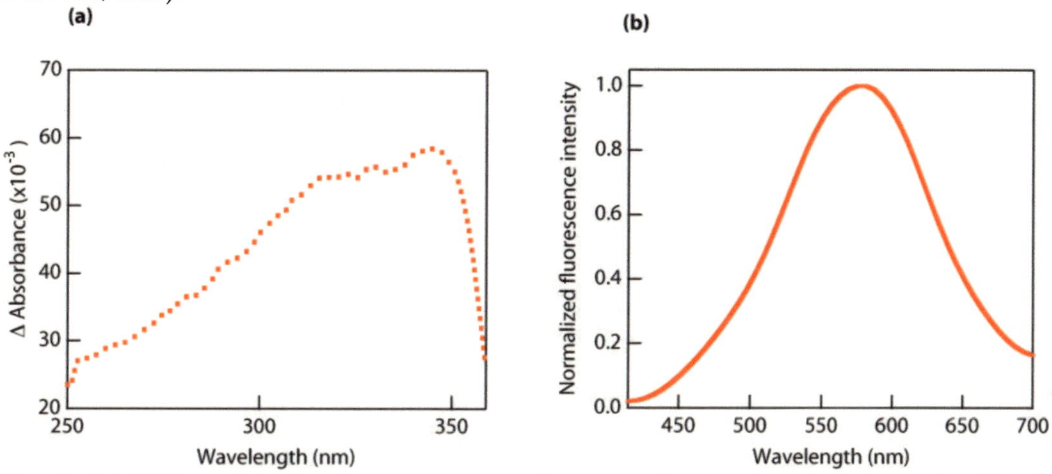


Fig. 1. (a) Differential absorbance spectrum between the irradiated and non-irradiated regions; (b) Emission spectrum (excitation wavelength, 405 nm) of the irradiated region. Experimental laser irradiation conditions: $I$ = 6 $TW.cm^{-2}$, $N$ = $10^6$. Differential absorbance and emission spectra are assigned to laser induced Ag clusters.

The optical properties of the silver nanoclusters are studied for different irradiation conditions by white light, epifluorescence and third-harmonic generation (THG) microscopy. Thus, the glass is exposed to different irradiance levels (x axis) between 4 $TW.cm^{-2}$ and 10 $TW.cm^{-2}$ and a different number of pulses (y axis) from $10^2$ to $10^6$, as shown on the experimental map sketch in Fig. 2(a). The sample is manipulated through patterning of bits with a bit spacing of 20 mm using a precision *xyz* stage. Epiwhite light and epifluorescence microscopy are performed with commercial microscopes. A transmission confocal setup, with a 36× - 0.52 NA reflective objective, is used for THG data collection. The

THG signal is filtered from the fundamental one by an emission bandpass filter @ (350 ± 50) nm and is collected with a photomultiplier tube. In our case, THG is excited with the same laser at low energy 10 nJ/pulse, but practically, a cheaper laser, such as a femtosecond fiber laser, could be used. Indeed, with a minimum energy of 0.1 nJ and an irradiance of $10^{10}$ W.cm$^{-2}$ (corresponding to an average power of 10 mW with a 100 MHz repetition rate), more than one third-harmonic photon by incoming pulse can be detected (Brocas et al., 2004).

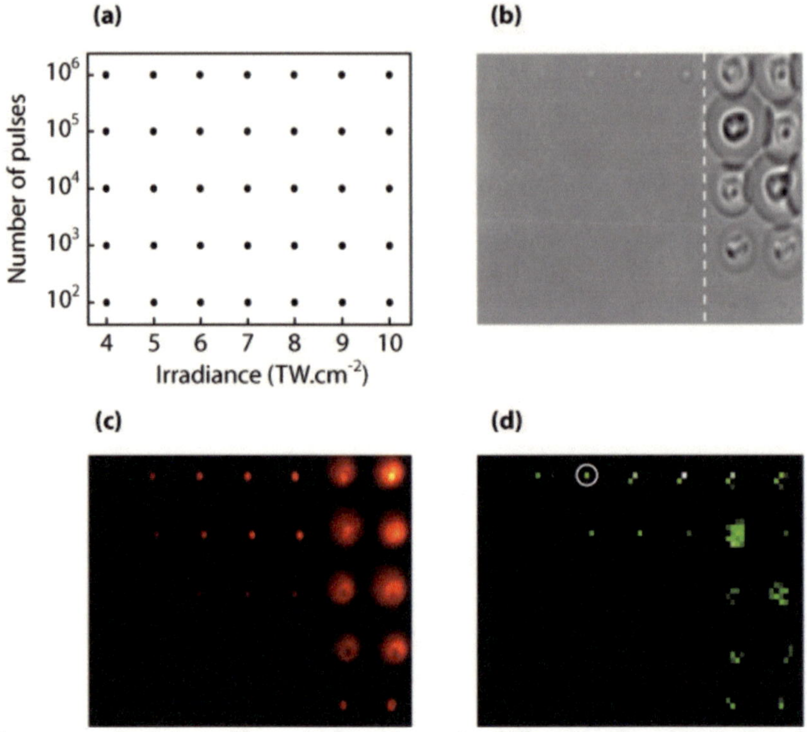


Fig. 2. Microscopy imaging of laser-induced species following the experimental map sketch. (a) x axis, laser irradiance; y axis, number of laser pulses, 6×5 bits pattern; spacing, 20 mm. (b) Epiwhite light microscopy image reveals linear refractive index modifications; vertical dashed line, damage threshold. (c) Epifluorescence microscopy image (excitation wavelength, 365 nm; emission filter, (610 ± 40) nm). (d) THG image (excitation wavelength, 1030 nm; emission filter, (350 ± 50) nm); encircled area, data storage irradiation conditions ($I$ = 6×TW.cm$^{-2}$, $N = 10^6$).

Transmission, fluorescence, and THG readout images of bits recorded with different irradiance levels and laser shots are presented in figures 2(b)–2(d). Figure 2(b) shows changes in refractive index. The damage threshold is achieved at an irradiance of 9 TW cm$^{-2}$, which is delimited by a vertical dashed line. At irradiances below this line, no apparent modifications are observed except for the high accumulated area in the upper part of Fig. 2(b). Nevertheless, in Fig. 2(c), we observe that fluorescence is obtained in regions where the refractive index is not modified. The same behavior is observed on the THG image in Fig. 2(d).

The THG image confirms that the induced Ag clusters absorb at 343 nm, corresponding to the resonant third-harmonic of the laser wavelength. Indeed, a coherent third-harmonic signal could be generated by each center due to the resonant absorption. The irradiated region is in the weak absorption regime and allows an enhancement of the third harmonic signal (Shen, 1984; Barille et al., 2002). Moreover, the image contrast is proportional to $|\chi_R^{(3)} - \chi_{NR}^{(3)}|^2$, where $\chi_R^{(3)}$ and $\chi_{NR}^{(3)}$ are the third-order susceptibilities of the irradiated (resonant) and non-irradiated (nonresonant) regions (Barille et al., 2002). The signal is due to the electronic contribution to $\chi^{(3)}$, since only the electronic polarization is able to quickly respond to a high frequency all-optical field excitation. Therefore, at the vicinity of the nonlinear interface between the Ag clusters and the glass matrix, a coherent third-harmonic signal can be generated under femtosecond laser excitation at 1030 nm.

Thus, as illustrated in Fig 3, the data can be stored inside the glass by femtosecond laser irradiation below the refractive index modification threshold. Thanks to thermal cumulative effects, stable Ag nanoclusters are created, giving rise to the formation of a nonlinear resonant interface (Fig. 3(a)). THG readout becomes possible using the same laser with less energy (Fig. 3(b)).

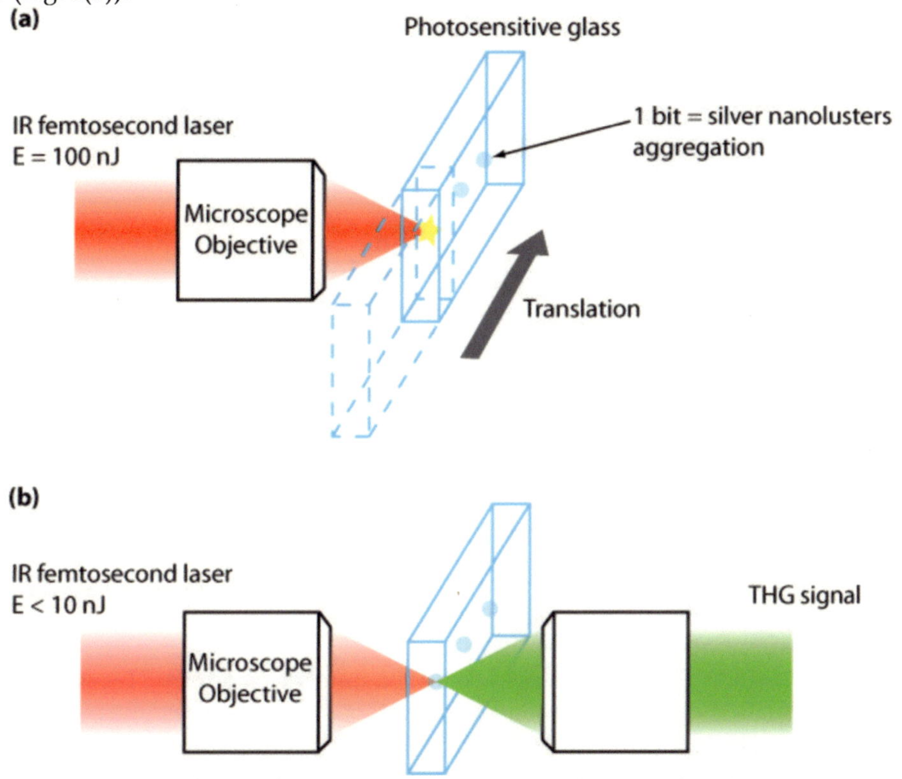


Fig. 3. Writing and reading processes. (a) Data are stored inside the photosensitive glass by focusing an IR femtosecond laser. 1 bit corresponds to a silver nanoclusters aggregation which presents no refractive index modifications. (b) Using the same laser with less energy, the third-harmonic signal can be collected.

### 2.4. Reading process by third-harmonic generation

To demonstrate the 3D optical data storage performance according to the principle explained before, a 3D bit pattern embedded in the photosensitive glass is written and read by a THG imaging setup. To achieve a high bit density in the volume, the change in refractive index must be kept as low as possible to minimize the effect of scattering of the reading beam while the change in $\chi^{(3)}$ must be as high as possible. We choose to work below the damage threshold to minimize the refractive index modification and optimize creation of aggregates by the accumulated effect (the corresponding area is encircled in Fig. 2(d)). The sample is irradiated with a laser irradiance of 6 TW.cm$^{-2}$ and with $10^6$ pulses. Three layers of data are embedded 200 mm inside the sample. Each layer contains a pattern of 12×12 bits with a bit spacing of 3 mm. The letters U, B, and the numeral 1 (for University Bordeaux 1) are recorded in the first, second, and third layers, respectively, with a layer spacing of 10 mm in the *z* direction. As shown previously, the same laser is used for the reading procedure but with a lower irradiance. By scanning the sample in *xyz* through the focus, the three layers (U, B, and 1) are reconstructed and presented in Fig. 3.

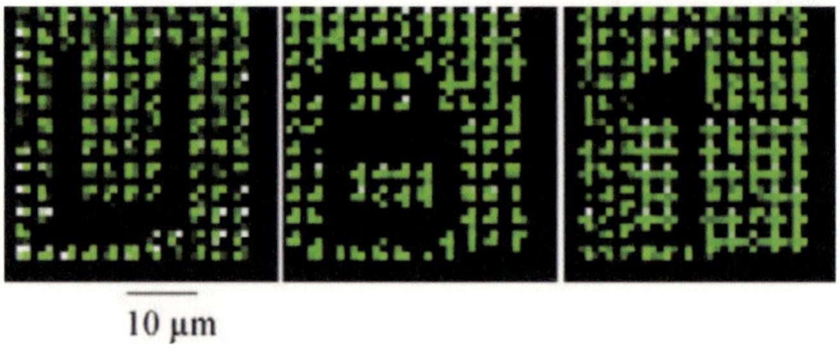


Fig. 4. THG readout of the three layers containing the bit patterns U, B, and 1, recorded in the bulk of the glass (bit spacing, 3 mm; layer spacing, 10 mm). Laser writing parameters: $I$ = 6 TW.cm$^{-2}$, $N = 10^6$. The three THG images present high signal-to-noise ratio and no cross talk.

As expected by the THG mechanism, an image with high contrast and no cross talk is observed in Fig. 3. The main advantages of this technique compared to usual 3D data storage are no photobleaching, no change in linear refractive index, and therefore no scattering. Moreover, the THG signal is coherent and gives rise to a rather intense, directional, and less divergent beam with a high signal-to-noise ratio. Due to the fast THG response, the reading speed is limited only by the pulse duration.

### 2.5. Grayscale encoding

Fig. 2(d) shows that the THG signal depends on the number of pulses. This can be used to encode the information onto a grayscale. Using an acousto-optic modulator, the number of pulses is well controlled. As presented in the Fig. 4, the THG response for an irradiance $I$ = 6 TW.cm$^{-2}$ is linear with the number of pulses between $1\times10^4$ and $5\times10^4$ pulses. Considering the readout error, the encoding becomes possible with a 16 levels grayscale (4 bits).

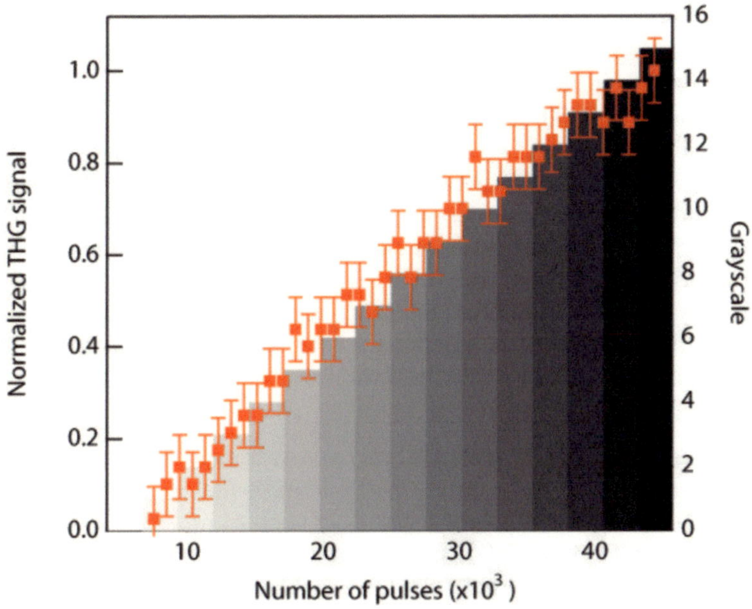


Fig. 5. THG signal versus number of the laser pulses with $I$ = 6 TW.cm$^{-2}$. The information can be grayscale encoded.

### 2.6. 3D optical data storage stability

The photo-written glasses were submitted to different thermal treatments below the transition temperature of the glass $T_g$ = 375 °C at 100 °C, 200 °C, 300 °C, 350 °C during 3 h and above $T_g$ at 400 °C during 20 min. The THG signal is not modified for temperatures below $T_g$ but disappears for temperatures higher than $T_g$. The recording is erased only after thermal treatment at 400 °C during 20 min corresponding to a total reorganization of the glass. Then, bits could be rewritten inside the glass after polishing. Thus we can state that recording is very stable in standard conditions (up to 85 °C). In our reading conditions, 10 nJ/pulse, the THG signal is not modified, even after several hours of unstopped exposure (corresponding to $10^{10}$ readings). Indeed, the Ag clusters are created only if enough photoelectrons are produced (threshold process). This is the reason why no modification appears during the reading process.

### 2.7. 3D optical data storage capacity

In our experimental conditions (bit spacing, 3 mm; layer spacing, 10 mm), 1 Gbit.cm$^{-3}$ could be stored inside the glass. Better performances can be achieved with a high NA objective (NA = 1.4) even if the objective working distance limits the number of layers. According to Chen & Xie (Chen and Xie, 2002), the THG can reach radial and axial resolutions of 250 and 400 nm, respectively. Thus a storage capacity in the range of Tbits.cm$^{-3}$ is possible in the glass. Considering the grayscale encoding, this value can be increased.

## 3. Spin state transition materials

Spin-crossover systems are a paradigmatic example of bistable optical materials. In such materials, the optical properties can be changed from one state to another through external stimuli such as temperature (T), pressure (P) or light (hν). As the system switches between the two states, its optical properties drastically change in the visible and near IR spectral ranges. These properties were demonstrated in many molecular samples at low temperature. It is only very recently that we have shown that pulsed light irradiations make possible to switch the optical properties of such bistable systems at room temperature. The mechanism responsible for the switching in these particles has also been elucidated. It indicates that less than a thousand photons are required to photo-switch a single nanoparticle of 60 nm in diameter. The offered prospects by such materials in optical and material sciences are therefore very rich and promising.

### 3.1. Data recording within the hysteresis loop at low temperature

In the last thirty years, the interest in molecular materials that makes possible the storing of a digital information has considerably increased. In such a context, the molecular bistability associated to the spin-crossover (SCO) phenomenon has triggered important research activities. Indeed, the change of the spin state in a SCO material can be induced reversibly in a solid state by adjusting or applying different constraints such as temperature, pressure, light intensity or pulsed magnetic field (Gutlich et al., 1994; Bousseksou et al., 2000). The SCO phenomenon induces for instance an important and reversible change of the optical absorbance or of the magnetic susceptibility of the studied medium. The first photomagnetic effect in an iron(II) SCO material was reported by Decurtins et al. in 1984. At low temperature ($T \leq 50$ K), these authors demonstrated the possibility to convert a compound with a low spin (LS, S=0) state into a compound with a metastable high spin (HS, S=2) using green light laser beam irradiation. This phenomenon, called Light-Induced Excited Spin-State Trapping (LIESST), was extended later by Hauser, who showed that red light switches the system back to the LS state (reverse-LIESST) (Hauser, 1996). This effect triggered a lot of interest, but most of the published studies have failed to demonstrate the LIESST effect at high temperature. In fact, above 50 K, the photo-induced HS state usually decays within a few minutes. To overcome this limitation, an interesting approach would be to work within the thermal hysteresis loop of a SCO material. Indeed, within the hysteresis loop, both HS and LS states are thermodynamically stable. The first spin change reported in a thermal hysteresis was, in fact, induced using intense magnetic pulses (Bousseksou et al., 2000). However, for practical applications, the use of such external perturbation is not realistic. The first influence of light on a thermal hysteresis loop was described by Renz et al. in 2000. This effect, named Light Perturbed Thermal Hysteresis (LiPTH) was observed under continuous laser irradiation. Depending on the laser wavelength, the hysteresis loop was shifted towards lower temperature or higher temperature. However, the phenomenon relaxes as soon as the laser light is switched-off and considerably limits its application for data storage. Recently, light-induced valence tautomeric conversion was reported in some cobalt-iron Prussian Blue analogs at room temperature (Shimamoto et al., 2002; Liu et al., 2003). It was shown that a single laser pulse converts the electronic state from $Fe^{II}$(S=0)-CN-$Co^{II}$(S=0) to $Fe^{III}$(S=1/2)-CN-$Co^{II}$(S=3/2). The reverse phenomenon has also been observed (Liu et al., 2003). This phenomenon was explained using the so-called domino effect (Koshino & Ogawa, 1998): When the concentration of the local excited HS state is higher than a critical value, all the system commutes from an LS to an HS state. According to these experiments, one may wonder if a single laser pulse may also induce the same phenomena in a cooperative iron(II) SCO material. To demonstrate it, we have selected the [Fe(PM-BiA)$_2$(NCS)$_2$] (PM-BiA = N-2'-pyridylmethylene-4-aminobiphenyl) complex which exhibits a well defined abrupt hysteresis around 170 K (Létard et al., 1998; Létard et al., 2003). We have shown that, under certain conditions, the use of a single pulse laser in the center of the thermal hysteresis loop leads to a LS $\rightarrow$ HS photo-conversion (Freysz et al., 2004). Compared to the experiments reported on valence tautomeric compounds, our results indicated that the final state reached after a laser excitation is neither a pure HS nor a pure LS state, but it is instead a "mixture" of HS/LS domains. Since the system is firstly photo-excited into the HS state and then slowly relaxes to mixture of HS/LS state, our results cannot be accounted by the so-called domino effect.

The set-up we used to perform these experiments is sketched on Figure 6a. The sample, a powder composed of micro crystallites (a few microns in radius) is sandwiched in between two optical windows and is placed into a cryostat. The specular light reflected by the sample was collected and sent to a 150 mm spectrometer to select the wavelength centered at 600 nm. The resolution of the spectrometer was set to be ~ 2 nm. At the exit of the spectrometer, the light was collected by a photomultiplier connected to a 1 Mega Ohm load. The voltage drop across this load was recorded versus the temperature of the sample in the cryostat. As shown in Figure 6b, this reflection set-up makes possible to record the temperature hysteresis loop of the studied sample. To first record the LS to HS state transitions, the sample is shined with a white light continuum and the light reflected by the sample and transmitted at 600 nm through the spectrometer is recorded by the photo-multiplier. The typical evolution of the reflectivity versus the temperature increase or decrease is presented in Figure 6b. These data are in very good agreement with the measurements performed with a SQUID.

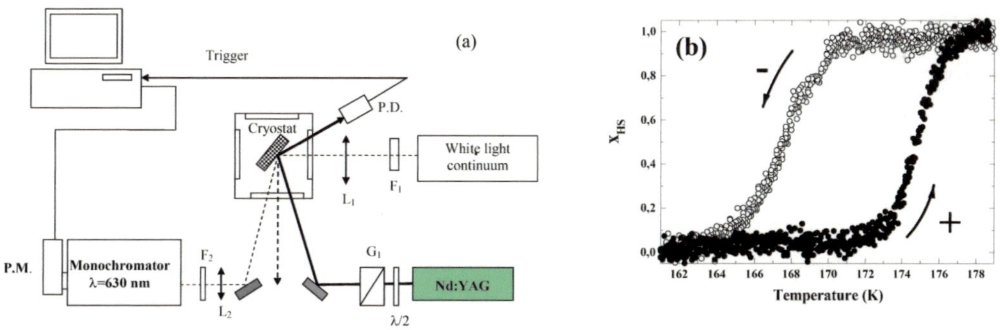


Fig. 6. (a) Sketch of the experimental set-up used to induce and measure the laser induced spin state transition. (b) Evolution of the reflected light versus the temperature. The temperature is either decreased from 180 K to 160 K or increased from 160 K To 180 K. $X_{HS}$ is the molar fraction of molecules in the HS state.

Using this set-up, we have studied the effect of pulsed light on the sample. In this later case, a single laser pulse (Q-switched nanosecond frequency doubled $Nd^{3+}$:YAG laser, $\lambda_0$=0.532 µm, pulse width 8 ns; energy between 0.5 and 10 mJ) was focused on a spot of about 3 mm in diameter and only a small fraction of the light reflected by the sample at 600 nm within the laser spot area was imaged and recorded by the spectrometer. As shown in Figure 7a, when the sample is cooled at 140 K, a temperature below the hysteresis loop, we clearly record a temporal evolution of the reflectivity of the sample. According to our calibration, our data clearly show that all the sample probed by the reflected light is brought into the HS state. Moreover, within 0.5 second, it relaxes back to the LS state. By studying the evolution of the HS fraction within the laser spot versus the energy of the laser pulse, we note that the number of HS particles steadily increases versus the energy of the laser pulse up to an energy of ~ 1 mJ. Above 1 mJ, which corresponds to a fluence of 14 mJ.cm$^{-2}$ per pulse, all the probed molecules are photo-converted in HS state and the signal saturates. This situation remains until 9 mJ, when a surface photo-degradation of the sample occurs. In conclusion, below the thermal hysteresis and between 78 and 140 K, the photo-induced HS state is not stable. We noted its lifetime decreases from hours (at 60 K) to minutes (at 78 K) and to second (at 140 K) (Degert et al., 2005).

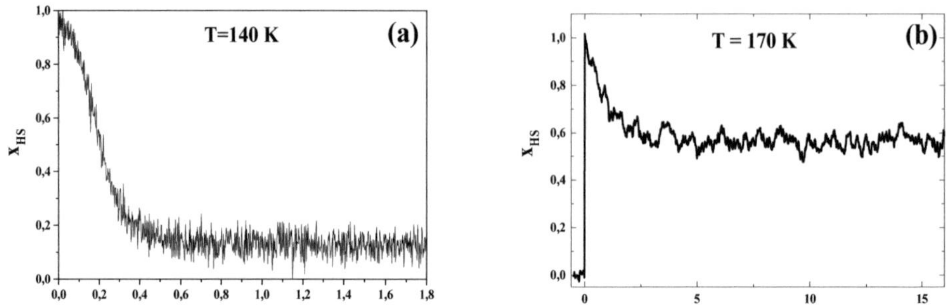


Fig. 7. HS → LS relaxation curves (a) At 140 K below the hysteresis loop. (b) At 170 K within the hysteresis loop. The sample was firstly cooled down to a pure LS state and then carefully warmed

Let us now consider the influence of a 1 mJ laser pulse when the sample is set at a temperature within the thermal hysteresis loop. The sample was firstly set into the LS configuration by slowly cooling it and then carefully warming it at $T_1$= 166 K, *i.e.* the region at the beginning of the thermal hysteresis loop. The sample was then excited with a single laser pulse. As reported on Figure 7a, immediately after the single laser pulse, all the probed particles reach the HS state, but they relax back to the LS state. This clearly indicates firstly, that the photo-induced excited HS state is not stable, even within the hysteresis loop and secondly, that the LS → HS transition cannot be induced by the photo-excitation of HS molecules. This observation also considerably limits the contribution of a domino effect associated with the excitation of the molecular HS state under our experimental conditions. We then warmed the sample at 170K, *i.e.* the region in the centre of the thermal hysteresis loop, and again excited it with a single laser pulse. Similarly to what reported on Figure 7b, immediately after the single laser pulse, all the probed particles reach the HS state. But this time, they neither relax toward the pure HS state nor the initial LS state. The final situation after relaxation can be regarded as a "mixture" of HS/LS particles. At first, this result is interesting in regard to the opened problem of the thermal effect accompanying the optical excitation of the sample. Indeed, if an artificial and important temperature increase ($\Delta T > 10$ K) associated with the absorption of the particles brought the sample in the HS state, it

should, at first glance, remain within this state. This is clearly not the reported experimental result. Moreover, we have also shown that additional laser pulses do not affect the measured HS/LS ratio (Freysz et al., 2004). We have also demonstrated the stability of the photo-induced mixture state within the hysteresis loop. When one steadily increases the temperature of the sample, it remains within this "mixture" state until it reaches the upper and lower temperature branch of the hysteresis loop, respectively labelled $T_{1/2\downarrow}$ and $T_{1/2\uparrow}$. For temperatures higher than $T_{1/2\uparrow}$, all the particles of the sample are converted in the HS state. This latter result demonstrates, if necessary, that the sample is not damaged by the laser pulse. This point was confirmed by the repetition of the experiment many times on the same sample, which did not show any degradation.
Although these experiments were interesting in demonstrating optical data recording in spin state compounds within the hysteresis loop, their practical use was quite limited.

### 3.2. Data recording within the hysteresis loop and at room temperature

One year after our work, it has been shown that different compounds can be photo-switched at room temperature using a single Nd:YAG Q-switched laser pulse (Bonhommeau et al., 2005). However, the details of the mechanisms giving rise to the switching of the spin state compound within the thermal hysteresis was difficult to evidence (Fouché et al., 2009). In order to investigate these mechanisms, we have carried out an optical study of the SCO complex $[Fe(NH_2trz)_3](NO_3)_2\ 3H_2O$ coordination polymer ($NH_2trz$ = 4-amino-1,2,4-triazole) known to display a well-defined thermal hysteresis loop at room temperature.

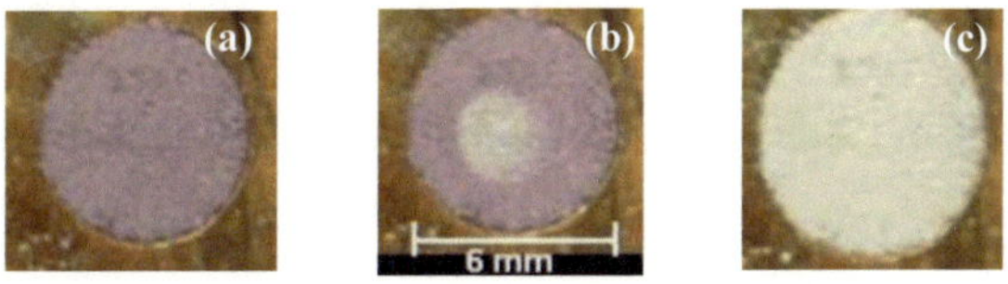


Fig. 8. $[Fe(NH_2trz)_3](NO_3)_2\ 3H_2O$ sample in the LS state (a), the HS state (c) and after photo-excitation by a single laser pulse within the hysteresis loop of the compound (b).

As shown in Fig. 8, the colour of the powder, which is pink when the sample is in the LS state (Fig 8a), becomes almost completely white when the sample is in the HS state (Fig. 8c). Indeed, in the LS state, this material displays a broad absorption band at around 520 nm, which is characteristic of the d-d transition of $Fe^{2+}$ ($^1A_{1g} \rightarrow {}^1T_{1g}$), while in the HS state a d-d-transition is recorded at lower energy in the near-infrared region (830 nm). Figure 8b shows the state of the sample impacted by a sequence of pulses yielded by a frequency tripled Nd:YAG laser that delivers pulses at 355nm which duration is ~ 6ns and fluence on the sample is $E_p$ ~ 52 mJ.cm$^{-2}$. The same experiment has also been performed using pulses with the same fluence but centred at 532 nm. In both cases, we noticed that the central part of the sample impacted by the laser pulse becomes white. The sample remains as it is as long as its temperature is kept within the thermal hysteresis loop. For instance, the whole sample recovers its original pink colour when its temperature is below 10 °C. This clearly indicates that within the hysteresis loop, the micro-crystallites of the compound impacted by the laser pulses are brought in the HS state.

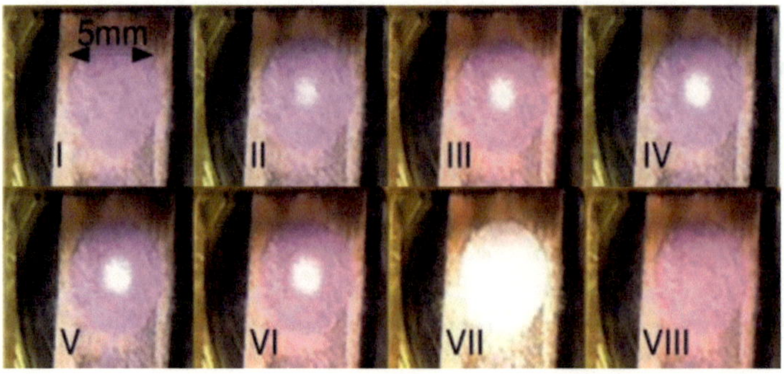


Fig. 9. (I) and (VII) colour of the sample in the LS state. Evolution of the sample set in the thermal hysteresis loop and impacted by (II) one pulse, (III) two pulses, (IV) three pulses, (V) four pulses, (VI) five pulses. (VIII) Colour of the sample impacted by five laser pulse and cooled back in the LS state.

We have also recorded the evolution of the sample versus the laser excitation. Firstly, we noticed that below a certain laser fluence, the sample remains unchanged. Above this threshold fluence, the final state of the compounds depends on both the laser fluence and the number of laser pulses used to excite the sample. As shown in Fig. 9, the central part of the sample shined by the laser beam that is initially in the LS state (I) becomes whiter and whiter as the number of excitation pulses increases ( Fig. 9 II to 9 VI). The pictures in Fig. 9VII and 9VIII underline that, for temperature above or below the hysteresis loop, the sample recovers its HS or LS state. This indicates that the sample is not altered by the laser excitation. This experiment also indicates that grayscale encoding is also possible in these materials.

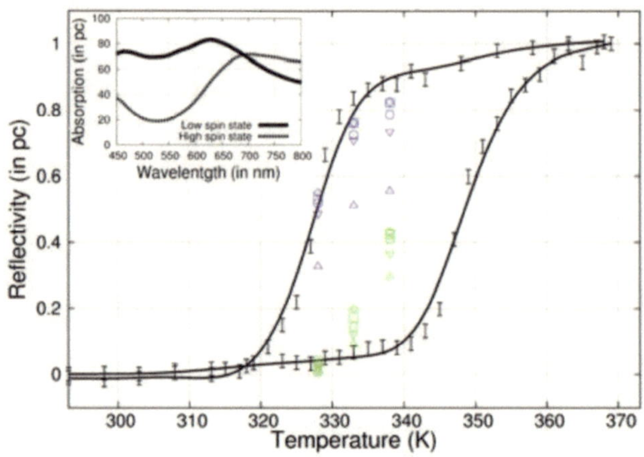


Fig. 10. In solid line: Thermal hysteresis loop deduced from the optical reflectivity and irradiation studies performed at 328 K, 333 K and 338 K by one (△), two (▽), three (O), four (□) and five (◇) pulses at 355 nm (in blue) and 532 nm (in green) with a fluence of 52 $mJ.cm^{-2}$. The inset is the absorption of the powder in the HS and LS states.

To be more quantitative about the final state reached by the sample after each laser pulse, we have replaced the monochromator by a spectrometer and we have recorded the spectrum of the light reflected by the sample after each laser pulse. This enables to fix the state of the sample within the hysteresis loop (Fig. 10). These last data clearly indicate that one can easily perform data recording in this compound. However, they also stress that data recording is easier when the absorption coefficient of the sample is higher. This also clearly underlines that the laser induced heating of the sample is of central importance. To clearly evidence the mechanism responsible for data recording in these materials, we have performed a nanosecond time resolved reflectivity measurement that is described below.

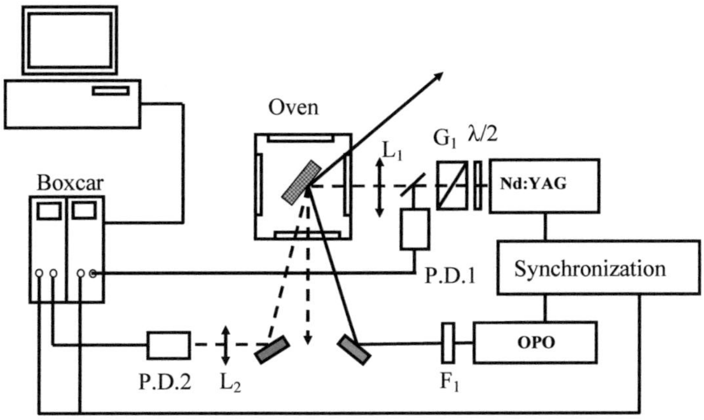


Fig. 11. Nanosecond time resolved pump-probe set-up.

### 3.2. Kinetic of the data recording

#### 3.2.1. Pump-probe time resolved nanosecond set-up

The optical set-up depicted in Fig. 11 has been designed to record the kinetic of the LS to HS state transition with a nanosecond time resolution. The sample placed in an oven is excited by a "pump" pulse provided by a nanosecond Optical Parametric Oscillator (OPO Panther EX from Continuum), this latter being pumped by a Q-switched-nanosecond-frequency-tripled Nd:YAG laser emitting at $\lambda_0$ = 355 nm (Surelite II from Continuum). The signal and the idler pulses (pulse duration $\tau_{pump}$ ~ 6 ns), produced by a parametric frequency conversion in a type II BBO crystal, are spatially separated by dichroïc mirrors. The OPO is tuneable from 400 to 680 nm and from 720 to 2500 nm. At $\lambda_0$ = 400 nm, the maximum pulse excitation energy is ~ 20 mJ. In practice, we adjusted the fluence on the sample by focusing more or less tightly the laser beam. To measure the sample reflectivity change ($\Delta$R) induced by the pump pulse, a "probe" pulse generated by a frequency doubled and Q-switched Nd:YAG laser ($\tau_{probe}$ ~ 6 ns) was used. The probe pulse light diffused by the sample at an angle of 30° was collected by a fast photodiode which output signal is sent in a first boxcar gated integrator. To compensate for pulse to pulse energy fluctuations, the probe pulse reflected by an uncoated optical window placed in front of the sample is used as a reference pulse. It is collected by a second fast photodiode which output signal is connected to a second boxcar gated integrator. The relative sample reflectivity is determined by dividing the signal delivered by the two photodiodes. To control the delay between the pump and probe pulses, the two Nd:YAG lasers are synchronized using a home build-electronic device. This device, that also delivers the signal that triggers the boxcar gates, makes it possible to temporally delay, from few nanoseconds up to few seconds, the light pulses delivered by these two systems. To limit the impact of OPO fluctuations, we measure the energy of each OPO pulse and only kept the data corresponding to an OPO pulse energy within ± 5% of the mean OPO energy value. The signal to noise ratio of our data is further improved by averaging the data over ten laser shots. Finally, to measure the actual reflectivity change of the sample, we record for each pump-probe time delay the relative reflectivity of the sample with and without the pump pulse. In the actual set-up, the sample, a powder composed of micro crystallites a few microns in radius, is sandwiched in between two optical windows and placed into a thermally regulated oven. This set-up has been mainly used when the temperature of the sample is set slightly below the hysteresis loop. In such a case the sample recovers its initial LS state after each pump pulse. Therefore, under these experimental conditions, one records both the formation and the relaxation of the HS fraction induced by the pump pulse.

### 3.2.2. Experimental results

The reflectivity change ($\Delta R \sim 8\%$) induced by a pump pulse fluence of $E_p \sim 18$ mJ.cm$^{-2}$ is presented in Fig. 12 for a sample at 283 K.

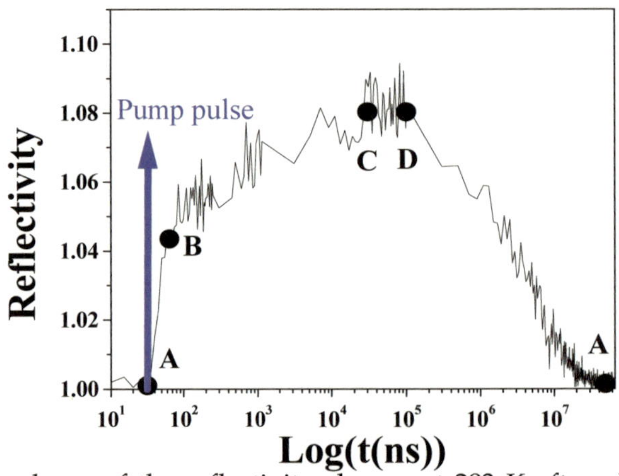


Fig. 13. Time dependence of the reflectivity change at 283 K after photo-excitation with a pump pulse of fluence $E_p \sim 9$ mJ.cm$^{-2}$.

To grasp all the complexity of the dynamic, we have chosen to present our data on a temporal logarithmic scale. Using this scale, one clearly evidences that the growing and the relaxation of the reflectivity is governed by different characteristic times. Figure 12 also indicates that, to register the complete evolution of the system after the pulse excitation, the reflectivity has to be recorded over at least five decades of time. This stresses the advantage of our experimental set-up in which one can adjust continuously the sampling steps along the experiment.

### 3.2.3. Temporal evolution of the sample within the phase diagram

We have demonstrated that the dynamic of the reflectivity change presented in Fig. 12 can be assigned to respectively:

- The heating of a thin layer (~ 400 nm) of the sample for $0 < t \leq 200$ ns.
- The diffusion of the heat toward the bulk sample and the growing of the HS fraction within the thin layer for 200 ns $\leq t \leq$ 100 μs.
- The relaxation of the HS fraction within the thin layer for 100 μs $\leq t \leq$ 100 ms.

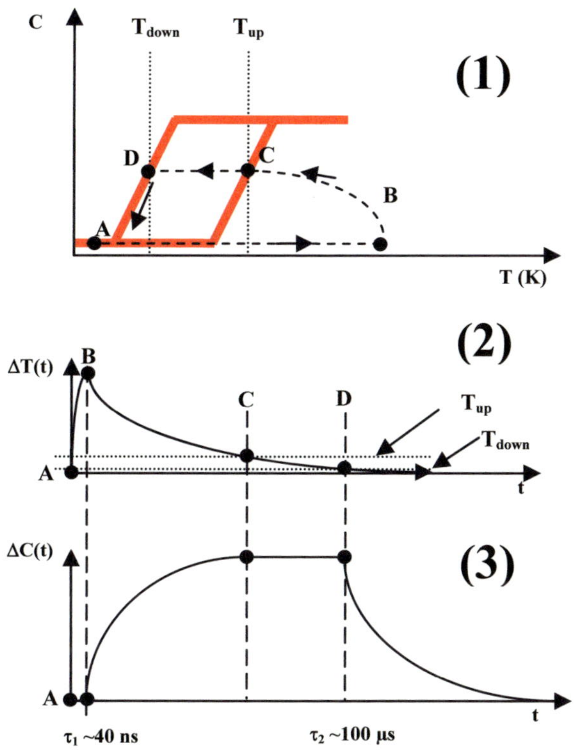


Fig. 14. Mechanisms that account for the laser pulse induced SCO at the vicinity of the thermal hysteresis loop.

As depicted in Fig. 14, this experiment makes also possible to follow the temporal evolution of the sample within the HS concentration, temperature (*i.e.* (C,T)) phase diagram of the compound outside the hysteresis loop (Fouché et al., to be published). Upon laser excitation, absorption of the pump energy takes place in a very thin layer $L_p$ (~ 400 nm). As a result, the temperature of this layer increases drastically and is maximum about 40 ns after the laser excitation and sets the sample layer at the point B of the (C,T) diagram. The heat subsequently diffuses toward the bulk sample. Hence, the temperature of the layer steadily decreases so that the sample layer is moving within the phase diagram. The evolution of the HS fraction is less abrupt. During the heating of the layer, it remains almost constant and then it starts to increase. The growth lasts as long as the temperature of the layer has not reached the ascending branch of the hysteresis loop (point C of the phase diagram). Then, as long as the temperature of the layer remains within the thermal hysteresis loop (*i.e.* between the point C and D of the phase diagram), the HS fraction remains constant. It decreases as soon as the temperature of the layer reaches the descending branch of the hysteresis loop (point D of the phase diagram).

### 3.2.4. Mechanisms responsible for data recording within the hysteresis loop

The results recorded when the temperature of the sample was set below the hysteresis loop and presented in the previous section makes possible to understand the evolution of the sample when its temperature is set within the hysteresis loop as depicted in Fig.9. Figure 15 shows the evolution of the sample after each laser pulse.

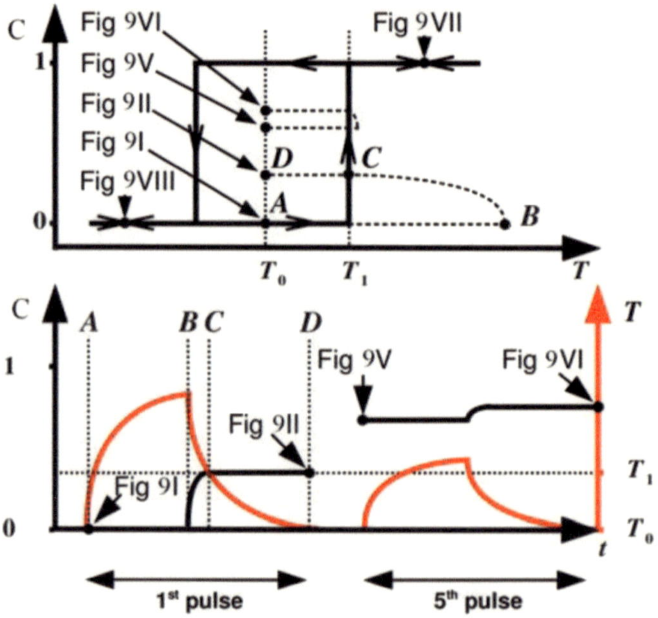


Fig. 15. Path in the phase diagram followed by the sample after each laser shot and evolution of the temperature (grey line) and the HS fraction (black line) of the sample after each laser shot.

At first, just after the laser excitation, the absorption of the pulse by a thin layer of the sample induces a local heating. Within a hundred of nanoseconds, the absorbed energy heats the system; its temperature rises up very quickly at a temperature where the LS state is unstable. The higher the absorption coefficient is, the higher the temperature increase is. Thus the sample is thermally quenched (A → B), whereas only a very small HS fraction appears. Then, the sample cools and an increase of the HS fraction takes place (B → C). As shown in Fig. 14, this process lasts about 100 μs. Once the ascending branch of the hysteresis loop is reached, the HS fraction no longer evolves and the created HS fraction coexists with the LS fraction. Finally, the powder reaches the temperature of the oven (C → D). The whole process takes about 1 ms. The sample has then reached a state where its absorption coefficient decreases. Indeed, as shown in inset of the Fig. 10, the absorption of the sample in the HS state is reduced at both 532 nm and 355 nm. Thus, for the subsequent laser pulses, the laser induced heating is less and less important, the growth lasts less and less time and the increase of the HS fraction is less and less important. After a few pulses, the sample has reached a state located within the thermal hysteresis loop (Fig. 14). In the last case, one can further improve the LS to HS conversion efficiency by increasing the laser pulse energy. Based on this scenario, the highest efficiency recorded at 355 nm is directly accounted by the highest absorption of the sample in the blue spectral range (inset of Fig. 10), leading to a greater heating of the sample.

### 3.3. Future and prospects

Our on going study deals with bistable nanoparticles with controlled sizes, shapes and optical properties. Such particles offer many prospect for data recording. Our computations indicate that less than a thousand of photons are required to photo-switch a single nanoparticle of 60 nm in diameter. On the other hand, we are also performing experiments that make possible to understand and to master the physical mechanisms responsible for the photo-switching of these nanoparticles inserted in different controlled polymeric environments. We are also currently testing their practical uses for holographic data recording.

## 4. References


Barille, R.; Canioni, L.; Sarger, L. & Rivoire, G. (2002). Nonlinearity measurements of thin films by third-harmonic-generation microscopy, *Phys. Rev. E*, 66, 067602

Belharouak, I.; Parent, C.; Tanguy, B.; Le Flem, G. & Couzy, M. (1999). Silver aggregates in photoluminescent phosphate glasses of the '$Ag_2O$-ZnO-$P_2O_5$' system, *J. Non-Cryst. Solids.*, 244, 238-249

Bellec, M; Royon, A.; Bousquet, B.; Bourhis, K.; Treguer, M.; Cardinal, T.; Richardson, M. & Canioni, L. (2009), Beat the diffraction limit in 3D direct laser writing in photosensitive glass, *Opt. Exp.*, 17, 10304-10318

Bousseksou, A; Negre, N.; Goiran, M.; Salmon, L.; Tuchagues, J.P.; Boillot, M.L.; Boukheddaden, K. & Varret, J. F. (2000), Dynamic triggering of a spin-transition by a pulsed magnetic field, *Eur. Phys. J.* B, 13, 451

S. Bonhommeau, G. Molnar, A. Galet, A. Zwick, J.A. Real, J.J. McGarvey & A. Bousseksou (2005), One-Shot-Laser-Pulse-Induced Reversible Spin Transition in the Spin Crossover Complex {Fe(C4H4N2)[Pt(CN)4]} at Room Temperature, *Angew. Chem. Int. Ed.*, 44 4069

Brocas, A.; Canioni, L. & Sarger, L. (2004). Efficient selection of focusing optics in non linear microscopy design through THG analysis, *Opt. Exp.*, 12, 2317-2322

Canioni, L.; Bellec, M; Royon, A.; Bousquet, B. & Cardinal, T. (2008). Three-dimensional optical data storage using third-harmonic generation in silver zinc phosphate glass. *Opt. Lett.*, 33, 360-362

Chen, J. & Xie, S. (2002). Green's function formulation of third-harmonic generation microscopy, *J. Opt. Soc. Am. B*, 19, 1604

Dai, Y.; Hu, X.; Wang, C.; Chen, D.; Jiang, X.; Zhu, C.; Yu, B. & Qiu, J. (2007). Fluorescent Ag nanoclusters in glass induced by an infrared femtosecond laser, *Chem. Phys. Lett.*, 439, 81

Day, D. & Gu, M. (1998). Effects of Refractive-Index Mismatch on Three-Dimensional Optical Data-Storage Density in a Two-Photon Bleaching Polymer, *Appl. Opt.*, 37, 6299-6304

Decurtins, S.; Gütlich, P.; Köhler, C.P.; Spiering, H. & Hauser, A. (1984), Light-induced excited spin state trapping in a transition-metal complex: The hexa-1-propyltetrazole-iron (II) tetrafluoroborate spin-crossover system, *Chem. Phys. Lett.*, 105, 1-4.

Degert, J.; Lascoux, N.; Montant, S.; Létard, S.; Freysz, E.; Chastanet, G. & Létard, J.-F. (2005), Complete temperature study of the relaxation from the high-spin state to low-spin state in a strongly cooperative spin crossover compound, *Chem. Phys. Lett.* 415, 206-210

Dmitryuk, A. V.; Paramzina, S. E.; Perminov, A. S.; Solov'eva, N. D. & Timofeev, N. T. (1996). The influence of glass composition on the properties of silver-doped radiophotoluminescent phosphate glasses, *J. Non-Cryst. Solids*, 202, 173-177

Fouché, O.; Degert, J.; Jonusauskas, G.; Baldé, C.; Desplanche, C.; Létard, J.-F. & Freysz, E. (2009), Laser induced spin state transition: Spectral and temporal evolution, *Chem. Phys. Lett.*, 469, 274-278

Freysz E, Montant S, Letard S & Létard J.F. (2004), Single laser pulse induces spin state transition within the hysteresis loop of an Iron compound, *Chem. Phys. Lett.*, 394, 318-323

Jiu, H.; Tang, H.; Zhou, J.; Xu, J.; Zhang, Q.; Xing, H.; Huang, W. & Xia, A. (2005). Sm(DBM)3Phen-doped poly(methylmethacrylate) for three-dimensional multilayered optical memory, *Opt. Lett.*, 30, 774-776

Gütlich, P.; Hauser, A. & Spiering, H. (1994), Thermal and Optical Switching of Iron(II) Complexes, *Angew. Chem. Int. Ed. Engl.*, 33, 2024-2054

Hauser, A. (1986), Reversibility of light-induced excited spin state trapping in the Fe(ptz)6(BF4)2, and the Zn1−xFex(ptz)6(BF4)2 spin-crossover systems, *Chem. Phys. Lett.* 124, 543-548

Jones, H. D. & Reiss, H. R. (1977). Intense-field effects in solids, *Phys. Rev. B*, 16, 2466-2473

Keldysh, L. V. (1965). Ionization in the field of a strong electromagnetic wave, *Sov. Phys. JEPT*, 20, 1307-1314

Koshino, K. & Ogawa, T (1998), Domino effects in photoinduced structural change in one-dimensional systems, *J. Phys. Soc. Jap.* 67, 2174

Létard, J.-F.; Guionneau, P.; Rabardel, L.; Howard, J. A. K.; Goeta, A. E.; Chasseau, D. & Kahn, O. (1998), Structural, Magnetic, and Photomagnetic Studies of a Mononuclear Iron(II) Derivative Exhibiting an Exceptionally Abrupt Spin Transition. Light-Induced Thermal Hysteresis Phenomenon, *Inorg. Chem*, 37, 4432-4441

Létard, J.-F.; Chastanet, G.; Nguyen, O.; Marcen, S.; Marchivie, M.; Guionneau, P.; Chasseau, D.; Gütlich, P. (2003), Spin Crossover Properties of the [Fe (PM-BiA) 2 (NCS) 2] Complex-Phases I and II, *Monatshefte für Chemie* 134, 165

Li, X.; Bullen, C.; Chon, J. W. M.; Evans, R. A. & Gu, M. (2007). Two-photon-induced three-dimensional optical data storage in CdS quantum-dot doped photopolymer, *Appl. Phys. Lett.*, 90, 161116

Liu, H.W.; Matsuda, K.; Gu, Z.Z.; Takahashi, K.; Cui, A.L.; Nakajima, R.; Fujishima, A. & Sato, O. (2003), Reversible Valence Tautomerism Induced by a Single-Shot Laser Pulse in a Cobalt-Iron Prussian Blue Analog, *Phys. Rev. Lett.* 90, 167403

Mok, F. K. (1993). Angle-multiplexed storage of 5000 holograms in lithium niobate, *Opt. Lett.*, 18, 915-917

Pan, S.; Shih, A.; Liou, W.; Park, M.; Bhawalkar, J.; Swiatkiewicz, J.; Samarabandu, J.; Prasad, P. N. & Cheng, P. C. (1997). *Scanning* 19, 156

Psaltis, D.; Levene, M.; Pu, A. & Barbastathis, G. (1995). Holographic storage using shift multiplexing, *Opt. Lett.*, 20, 782-784

Rakuljic, G. A.; Leyva, V. & Yariv, A. (1992). Optical data storage by using orthogonal wavelength-multiplexed volume holograms, *Optics Letters*, 17, 1471-1473

Renz, F.; Spiering, H.; Goodwin, H.A. & Gütlich, P (2000), Light-perturbed hysteresis in an iron (II) spin-crossover compound observed by the Mössbauer effect, *Hyperfine Interactions* 126, 155

Schneckenburger, H.; Regulla, D. F. & Unsöld, E. (1981). Time-resolved investigations of radiophotoluminescence in metaphosphate glass dosimeters, *Appl. Phys. A*, 26, 23-26

Shen, Y. R. (1984). *The Principles of Nonlinear Optics*, Wiley

Squier, J. & Muller, M. (1999). Third-harmonic generation imaging of laser-induced breakdown in glass, *Appl. Opt.*, 38, 5789-5794

Strickler, J. H. & Webb, W. W. (1991). Three-dimensional optical data storage in refractive media by two-photon point excitation, *Opt. Lett.*, 16, 1780-1782

Stuart, B. C.; Feit, M. D.; Herman, S.; Rubenchik, A. M.; Shore, B. W. & Perry, M. D. (1996). Nanosecond-to-femtosecond laser-induced breakdown in dielectrics, *Phys. Rev. B*, 53, 1749-1761

Sun, H. B.; Tanaka, T.; Takada, K. & Kawata, S. (2001). Finer features for functional microdevices, *Nature*, 412, 697-698

Shimamoto, N.; Ohkoshi, S.-S.; Sato, O. & Hashimoto, K. (2002), One-Shot-Laser-Pulse-Induced Cooperative Charge Transfer Accompanied by Spin Transition in a Co-Fe Prussian Blue Analog at Room Temperature, *Chem. Lett.*, 31, 486

# 4

# Data Representation for Flash Memories

Anxiao (Andrew) Jiang
*Computer Science and Engineering Dept.*
*Texas A&M University*
*College Station, TX 77843, U.S.A.*
*ajiang@cse.tamu.edu*

Jehoshua Bruck
*Electrical Engineering Department*
*California Institute of Technology*
*Pasadena, CA 91125, U.S.A.*
*bruck@caltech.edu*

In this chapter, we introduce theories on data representation for flash memories. Flash memories are a milestone in the development of the data storage technology. The applications of flash memories have expanded widely in recent years, and flash memories have become the dominating member in the family of non-volatile memories. Compared to magnetic recording and optical recording, flash memories are more suitable for many mobile-, embedded- and mass-storage applications. The reasons include their high speed, physical robustness, and easy integration with circuits.
The representation of data plays a key role in storage systems. Like magnetic recording and optical recording, flash memories have their own distinct properties, including block erasure, iterative cell programming, etc. These distinct properties introduce very interesting coding problems that address many aspects of a successful storage system, which include efficient data modification, error correction, and more. In this chapter, we first introduce the flash memory model, then study some newly developed codes, including codes for rewriting data and the rank modulation scheme. A main theme is understanding how to store information in a medium that has asymmetric properties when it transits between different states.

## 1. Modelling Flash Memories

The basic storage unit in a flash memory is a floating-gate transistor [3]. We also call it a cell. Charge (e.g., electrons) can be injected into the cell using the hot-electron injection mechanism or the Fowler-Nordheim tunnelling mechanism, and the injected charge is trapped in the cell. (Specifically, the charge is stored in the floating-gate layer of the transistor.) The charge can also be removed from the cell using the Fowler-Nordheim tunnelling mechanism. The amount of charge in a cell determines its threshold voltage, which can be measured. The operation of injecting charge into a cell is called *writing* (or *programming*), removing charge is called *erasing*, and measuring the charge level is called *reading*. If we use two discrete charge levels to store data, the cell is called *single-level cell* (SLC) and can store one bit. If we use $q > 2$ discrete charge levels to store data, the cell is called *multi-level cell* (MLC) and can store $\log_2 q$ bits.

A prominent property of flash memories is *block erasure*. In a flash memory, cells are organized into blocks. A typical block contains about $10^5$ cells. While it is relatively easy to inject charge into a cell, to remove charge from any cell, the whole block containing it must be erased to the ground level (and then reprogrammed). This is called block erasure. The block erasure operation not only significantly reduces speed, but also reduces the lifetime of the flash memory [3]. This is because a block can only endure about $10^4 \sim 10^6$ erasures, after which the block may break down. Since the breaking down of a single block can make the whole memory stop working, it is important to balance the erasures performed to different blocks. This is called *wear leveling*. A commonly used wear-leveling technique is to balance erasures by moving data among the blocks, especially when the data are revised [10].

There are two main types of flash memories: NOR flash and NAND flash. A NOR flash memory allows random access to its cells. A NAND flash partitions every block into multiple sections called pages, and a page is the unit of a read or write operation. Compared to NOR flash, NAND flash may be much more restrictive on how its pages can be programmed, such as allowing a page to be programmed only a few times before erasure [10]. However, NAND flash enjoys the advantage of higher cell density.

The programming of cells is a noisy process. When charge is injected into a cell, the actual amount of injection is randomly distributed around the aimed value. An important thing to avoid during programming is overshooting, because to lower a cell's level, erasure is needed. A commonly used approach to avoid overshooting is to program a cell using multiple rounds of charge injection. In each round, a conservative amount of charge is injected into the cell. Then the cell level is measured before the next round begins. With this approach, the charge level can gradually approach the target value and the programming precision is improved. The corresponding cost is the slowing down in the writing speed.

After cells are programmed, the data are not necessarily error-proof, because the cell levels can be changed by various errors over time. Some important error sources include *write disturb* and *read disturb* (disturbs caused by writing or reading), as well as leakage of charge from the cells (called the *retention problem*) [3]. The changes in the cell levels often have an asymmetric distribution in the up and the down directions, and the errors in different cells can be correlated.

In summary, flash memory is a storage medium with asymmetric properties. It is easy to increase a cell's charge level (which we shall call *cell level*), but very costly to decrease it due to block erasure. The NAND flash may have more restrictions on reading and writing compared to NOR flash. The cell programming uses multiple rounds of charge injection to shift the cell level monotonically up toward the target value, to avoid overshooting and improve the precision. The cell levels can change over time due to various disturb mechanisms and the retention problem, and the errors can be asymmetric or correlated.

## 2. Codes for Rewriting Data

In this section, we discuss coding schemes for rewriting data in flash memories. The interest in this problem comes from the fact that if data are stored in the conventional way, even to change one bit in the data, we may need to lower some cell's level, which would lead to the costly block erasure operation. It is interesting to see if there exist codes that allow data to be rewritten many times without block erasure.

The flash memory model we use in this section is the *Write Asymmetric Memory (WAM)* model [16].

**Definition 1.** WRITE ASYMMETRIC MEMORY (WAM) *In a write asymmetric memory, there are $n$ cells. Every cell has $q \geq 2$ levels: levels $0, 1, \cdots, q-1$. The level of a cell can only increase, not decrease.*

The Write Asymmetric Memory models the monotonic change of flash memory cells before the erasure operation. It is a special case of the *generalized write-once memory (WOM)* model, which allows the state transitions of cells to be any acyclic directed graph [6, 8, 29].
Let us first look at an inspiring example. The code can write two bits twice in only three single-level cells. It was proposed by Rivest and Shamir in their celebrated paper that started the study of WOM codes [29].
We always assume that before data are written into the cells, the cells are at level 0.

**Example 2.** *We store two bits in three single-level cells (i.e., $n = 3$ and $q = 2$). The code is shown in Fig. 1. In the figure, the three numbers in a circle represent the three cell levels, and the two numbers beside the circle represent the two bits. The arrows represent the transition of the cells. As we can see, every cell level can only increase.*
*The code allows us to write the two bits at least twice. For example, if want to write "10", and later rewrite them as "01", we first elevate the cell levels to "0,1,0", then elevate them to "0,1,1".*

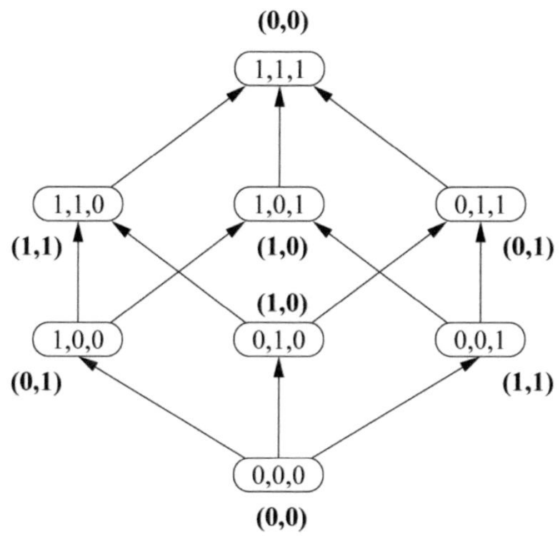


Fig. 1. Code for writing two bits twice in three single-level cells.

In the above example, a rewrite can completely change the data. In practice, often multiple data variables are stored by an application, and every rewrite changes only one of them. The joint coding of these data variables are useful for increasing the number of rewrites supported by coding. The rewriting codes in this setting have been named *Floating Codes* [16].

**Definition 3.** FLOATING CODE
*We store $k$ variables of alphabet size $\ell$ in a write asymmetric memory (WAM) with $n$ cells of $q$ levels. Every rewrite changes one of the $k$ variables.*
*Let $(c_1, \cdots, c_n) \in \{0, 1, \cdots, q-1\}^n$ denote the state of the memory (i.e., the levels of the $n$ cells). Let $(v_1, \cdots, v_k) \in \{0, 1, \cdots, \ell-1\}^k$ denote the data (i.e., the values of the $k$ variables). For any*

*two memory states* $(c_1, \cdots, c_n)$ *and* $(c'_1, \cdots, c'_n)$, *we say* $(c_1, \cdots, c_n) \geq (c'_1, \cdots, c'_n)$ *if* $c_i \geq c'_i$ *for* $i = 1, \cdots, n$.
*A floating code has a decoding function* $F_d$ *and an update function* $F_u$. *The decoding function*

$$F_d : \{0, 1, \cdots, q-1\}^n \rightarrow \{0, 1, \cdots, \ell - 1\}^k$$

*maps a memory state* $s \in \{0, 1, \cdots, q-1\}^n$ *to the stored data* $F_d(s) \in \{0, 1, \cdots, \ell - 1\}^k$. *The update function (which represents a rewrite operation),*

$$F_u : \{0, 1, \cdots, q-1\}^n \times \{1, 2, \cdots, k\} \times \{0, 1, \cdots, \ell - 1\} \rightarrow \{0, 1, \cdots, q-1\}^n,$$

*is defined as follows: if the current memory state is* $s$ *and the rewrite changes the* $i$*-th variable to value* $j \in \{0, 1, \cdots, \ell - 1\}$, *then the rewrite operation will change the memory state to* $F_u(s, i, j)$ *such that* $F_d(F_u(s, i, j))$ *is the data with the* $i$*-th variable changed to the value* $j$. *Naturally, since the memory is a write asymmetric memory, we require that* $F_u(s, i, j) \geq s$.
*Let* $t$ *denote the number of rewrites (including the first write) guaranteed by the code. A floating code that maximizes* $t$ *is called optimal.*

The code in Fig. 1 is in fact a special case of the floating code, where the number of variables is only one. More specifically, the parameters for it is $k = 1, \ell = 4, n = 3, q = 2$ and $t = 2$.
Let us look at an example of floating codes for two binary variables.

**Example 4.** *We store two binary variables in a Write Asymmetric Memory with* $n$ *cells of* $q$ *levels. Every rewrite changes the value of one variable. The Floating codes for* $n = 1$, 2 *and* 3 *are shown in Fig. 2. As before, the numbers in a circle represent the memory state, the numbers beside a circle represent the data, and the arrows represent the transition of the memory state triggered by rewriting. With every rewrite, the memory state moves up by one layer in the figure. For example, if* $n = 3, q \geq 3$ *and a sequence of rewrites change the data as*

$$(0,0) \rightarrow (1,0) \rightarrow (1,1) \rightarrow (0,1) \rightarrow (1,1) \rightarrow \cdots$$

*the memory state changes as*

$$(0,0,0) \rightarrow (1,0,0) \rightarrow (1,0,1) \rightarrow (1,0,2) \rightarrow (1,1,2) \rightarrow \cdots$$

*The three codes in the figure all have a periodic structure, where every period contains* $2n - 1$ *layers (as shown in the figure) and has the same topological structure. From one period to the next, the only difference is that the data* $(0,0)$ *is switched with* $(1,0)$, *and the data* $(1,1)$ *is switched with* $(0,1)$. *Given the finite value of* $q$, *we just need to truncate the graph up to the cell level* $q - 1$.

The floating codes in the above example are generalized in [16] for any value of $n$ and $q$ (but still with $k = \ell = 2$), and are shown to guarantee

$$t = (n-1)(q-1) + \lfloor \frac{q-1}{2} \rfloor$$

rewrites. We now prove that this is optimal. First, we show an upper bound to $t$, the number of guaranteed rewrites, for floating codes [16].

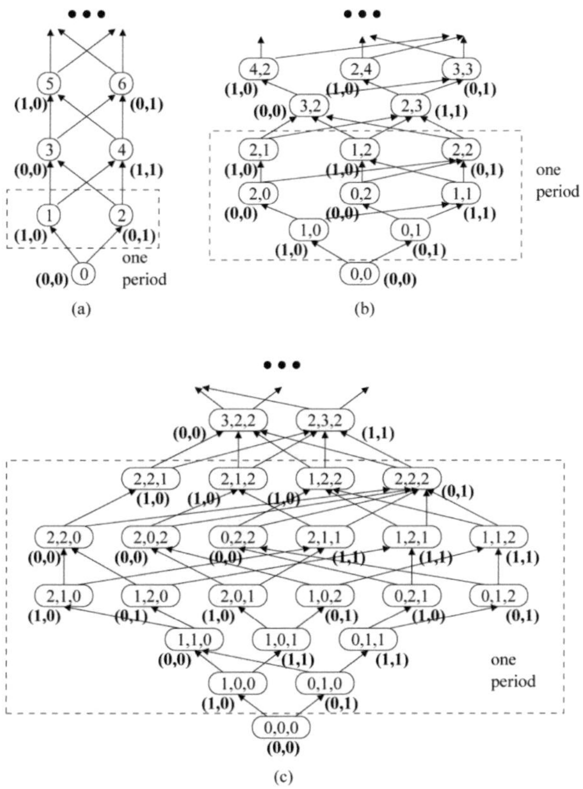


Fig. 2. Three examples of an optimal floating code for $k = 2, l = 2$ and arbitrary $n, q$. (a) $n = 1$. (b) $n = 2$. (c) $n = 3$.

**Theorem 5.** *For any floating code, if $n \geq k(l-1) - 1$, then*

$$t \leq [n - k(l-1) + 1] \cdot (q-1) + \lfloor \frac{[k(l-1)-1] \cdot (q-1)}{2} \rfloor;$$

*if $n < k(l-1) - 1$, then*

$$t \leq \lfloor \frac{n(q-1)}{2} \rfloor.$$

*Proof.* First, consider the case where $n \geq k(\ell - 1) - 1$. Let $(c_1, c_2, \cdots, c_n)$ denote the memory state. Let $W_A = \sum_{i=1}^{k(\ell-1)-1} c_i$, and let $W_B = \sum_{i=k(\ell-1)}^{n} c_i$. Let's call a rewrite operation "adversarial" if it either increases $W_A$ by at least two or increases $W_B$ by at least one. Since there are $k$ variables and each variable has the alphabet size $\ell$, a rewrite can change the variable vector in $k(\ell - 1)$ different ways. However, since $W_A$ is the summation of only $k(\ell - 1) - 1$ cell levels, there are at most $k(\ell - 1) - 1$ ways in which a rewrite can increase $W_A$ by one. So there must be an "adversarial" choice for every rewrite.
Consider a sequence of adversarial rewrites operations supported by a generic floating code. Suppose that $x$ of those rewrite operations increase $W_A$ by at least two, and suppose that $y$ of them increase $W_B$ by at least one. Since the maximum cell level is $q - 1$, we get $x \leq$

$\lfloor \frac{[k(l-1)-1]\cdot(q-1)}{2} \rfloor$ and $y \leq [n - k(l-1) + 1] \cdot (q-1)$. So the number of rewrites supported by a floating code is at most $x + y \leq [n - k(l-1) + 1] \cdot (q-1) + \lfloor \frac{[k(l-1)-1]\cdot(q-1)}{2} \rfloor$.

The case where $n < k(\ell - 1) - 1$ can be analyzed similarly. Call a rewrite operation "adversarial" if it increases $\sum_{i=1}^{n} c_i$ by at least two. It can be shown that there is always a adversarial choice for every rewrite, and any floating code can support at most $t \leq \lfloor \frac{n(q-1)}{2} \rfloor$ adversarial rewrites. □

When $k = \ell = 2$, the above theorem gives the bound $t \leq (n-1)(q-1) + \lfloor \frac{q-1}{2} \rfloor$. It matches the number of rewrites guaranteed by the floating codes of Example 4 (and their generalization in [16]). So these codes are optimal.

Let us pause a little to consider the two given examples. In Example 2, two bits can be written twice into the three single-level cells. The total number of bits written into the memory is four (considering the whole history of rewriting), which is more than the number of bits the memory can store at any given time (which is three). In Example 4, every rewrite changes one of two binary variables and therefore reflects one bit of information. Since the code guarantees $(n-1)(q-1) + \lfloor \frac{q-1}{2} \rfloor$ rewrites, the total amount of information "recorded" by the memory (again, over the history of rewriting) is $(n-1)(q-1) + \lfloor \frac{q-1}{2} \rfloor \approx nq$ bits. In comparison, the number of bits the memory can store at any give time is only $n \log_2 q$.

Why can the total amount of information written into the memory (over the multiple rewrites) exceed $n \log_2 q$, the maximum number of bits the memory can store at any give time? It is because only the current value of the data needs to be remembered. Another way to understand it is that we are not using the cells sequentially. As an example, if there are $n'$ single level cells and we increase one of their levels by one, there are $n'$ choices, which in fact reflects $\log_2 n'$ bits of information (instead of one bit).

We now extend floating codes to a more general definition of rewriting codes. First, we use a directed graph to represent how rewrites may change the stored data. This definition was proposed in [19].

**Definition 6.** GENERALIZED REWRITING
*The stored data is represented by a directed graph $\mathcal{D} = (V_{\mathcal{D}}, E_{\mathcal{D}})$. The vertices $V_{\mathcal{D}}$ represent all the values that the data can take. There is a directed edge $(u, v)$ from $u \in V_{\mathcal{D}}$ to $v \in V_{\mathcal{D}}$, $v \neq u$, iff a rewriting operation may change the stored data from value $u$ to value $v$. The graph $\mathcal{D}$ is called the* data graph *and the number of its vertices, corresponding to the input-alphabet size, is denoted by $L = |V_{\mathcal{D}}|$. Without loss of generality (w.l.o.g.), we assume the data graph to be strongly connected.*

It is simple to see that when the above notion is applied to floating codes, the alphabet size $L = \ell^k$, and the data graph $\mathcal{D}$ has constant in-degree and out-degree $k(\ell - 1)$. The out-degree of $\mathcal{D}$ reveals how much change in the data a rewrite operation can cause. It is an important parameter. In the following, we show a rewriting code for this generalized rewriting model. The code, called *Trajectory Code*, was presented in [19].

Let $(c_1, \cdots, c_n) \in \{0, 1, q-1\}^n$ denote the memory state. Let $V_{\mathcal{D}} = \{0, 1, \cdots, L-1\}$ denote the alphabet of the stored data. Let's present the trajectory code step by step, starting with its basic building blocks.

### *Linear Code and Extended Linear Code*

We first look at a *Linear Code* for the case $n = L - 1$ and $q = 2$. It was proposed by Rivest and Shamir in [29].

**Definition 7.** LINEAR CODE FOR $n = L - 1$ AND $q = 2$
*The memory state* $(c_1, \cdots, c_n)$ *represents the data*

$$\sum_{i=1}^{n} ic_i \mod (n+1).$$

*For every rewrite, change as few cells from level 0 to level 1 as possible to get the new data.*

We give an example of the Linear Code.

**Example 8.** *Let* $n = 7, q = 2$ *and* $L = 8$*. The data represented by the memory state* $(c_1, \cdots, c_7)$ *is*

$$\sum_{i=1}^{7} ic_i \mod 8.$$

*If the rewrites change the data as* $0 \to 3 \to 5 \to 2 \to 4$*, the memory state can change as* $(0,0,0,0,0,0,0) \to (0,0,1,0,0,0,0) \to (0,1,1,0,0,0,0) \to (0,1,1,0,1,0,0) \to (0,1,1,1,1,1,0)$.

The following theorem shows that the number of rewrites enabled by the Linear Code is asymptotically optimal in $n$, the number of cells. It was proved in [29].

**Theorem 9.** *The Linear Code guarantees at least* $\frac{n+1}{4} + 1$ *rewrites.*

*Proof.* We show that as long as at least $\frac{n+1}{2}$ cells are still of level 0, a rewrite will turn at most two cells from level 0 to level 1. Let $x \in \{0, 1, \cdots, n\}$ denote the current data value, and let $y \in \{0, 1, \cdots, n\}$ denote the new data value to be written, where $y \neq x$. Let $z$ denote

$$y - x \mod (n+1).$$

If the cell $c_z$ is of level 0, we can simply change it to level 1. Otherwise, let

$$S = \{i \in \{1, \cdots, n\} | c_i = 0\},$$

and let

$$T = \{z - s \mod (n+1) \mid s \in S\}.$$

Since $|S| = |T| \geq \frac{n+1}{2}$ and $|S \cup T| < n$ (zero and $z$ are in neither set), the set $S \cap T$ must be nonempty. Their overlap indicates a solution to the equation

$$z = s_1 + s_2 \mod (n+1)$$

where $s_1$ and $s_2$ are elements of $S$. □

When $n \geq L$ and $q \geq 2$, we can generalize the Linear Code in the following way [19]. First, suppose $n = L$ and $q \geq 2$. We first use level 0 and level 1 to encode (as the Linear Code does), and let the memory state represent the data $\sum_{i=1}^{n} ic_i \mod n$. (Note that rewrites here will not change $c_n$.) When the code can no longer support rewriting, we increase all cell levels (including $c_n$) from 0 to 1, and start using cell levels 1 and 2 to store data in the same way as above, except that now, the data represented by the memory state $(c_1, \cdots, c_n)$ uses the formula $\sum_{i=1}^{n} i(c_i - 1) \mod n$. This process is repeated $q - 1$ times in total. The general decoding function is therefore

$$\sum_{i=1}^{n} i(c_i - c_n) \mod n.$$

Now we extend the above code to $n \geq L$ cells. We divide the $n$ cells into $b = \lfloor n/L \rfloor$ groups of size $L$ (some cells may remain unused), and sequentially apply the above code to the first group of $L$ cells, then to the second group, and so on. We call this code the *Extended Linear Code*.

**Theorem 10.** *Let $2 \leq L \leq n$. The Extended Linear Code guarantees $n(q-1)/8 = \Theta(nq)$ rewrites.*

*Proof.* The Extended Linear Code essentially consists of $(q-1)\lfloor \frac{n}{L} \rfloor \geq \frac{(q-1)n}{2L}$ Linear Codes. □

### *Code for Large Alphabet Size L*

We now consider the case where $L$ is larger than $n$. The rewriting code we present here will reduce it to the case $n = L$ studied above [19]. We start by assuming that $n < L \leq 2^{\sqrt{n}}$.

**Construction 11.** REWRITING CODE FOR $n < L \leq 2^{\sqrt{n}}$
*Let $b$ be the smallest positive integer value that satisfies $\lfloor n/b \rfloor^b \geq L$.*
*For $i = 1, 2, \ldots, b$, let $v_i$ be a symbol from an alphabet of size $\lfloor n/b \rfloor \geq L^{1/b}$. We may represent any symbol $v \in \{0, 1, \cdots, L-1\}$ as a vector of symbols $(v_1, v_2, \ldots, v_b)$. Partition the $n$ flash cells into $b$ groups, each with $\lfloor n/b \rfloor$ cells (some cells may remain unused). Encoding the symbol $v$ into $n$ cells is equivalent to the encoding of each $v_i$ into the corresponding group of $\lfloor n/b \rfloor$ cells. As the alphabet size of each $v_i$ equals the number of cells it is to be encoded into, we can use the Extended Linear Code to store $v_i$.*

**Theorem 12.** *Let $16 \leq n \leq L \leq 2^{\sqrt{n}}$. The code in Construction 11 guarantees*

$$\frac{n(q-1)\log n}{16 \log L} = \Theta(\frac{nq \log n}{\log L})$$

*rewrites.*

*Proof.* We first show that for $b$ – the smallest positive integer value that satisfies $\lfloor n/b \rfloor^b \geq L$ – it holds that

$$b \leq \frac{2 \log L}{\log n}.$$

Note that for all $1 \leq x \leq \frac{\sqrt{n}}{2}$, we have $\lfloor n/x \rfloor^x \geq n^{x/2}$. Since $16 \leq n \leq L \leq 2^{\lfloor \sqrt{n} \rfloor}$, it is easy to verify that

$$\frac{2 \log L}{\log n} \leq \frac{\sqrt{n}}{2}.$$

Therefore,

$$\lfloor \frac{n \log n}{2 \log L} \rfloor^{\frac{2 \log L}{\log n}} \geq n^{\frac{\log L}{\log n}} = L,$$

which implies the upper bound for $b$.
Using Construction 11, the number of rewrites possible is bounded by the number of rewrites possible for each of the $b$ cell groups. By Theorem 10 and the above upper bound for $b$, this is at least

$$\lfloor \frac{n}{b} \rfloor \cdot \frac{q-1}{8} \geq (\frac{n \log n}{2 \log L} - 1)\frac{q-1}{8} = \Theta\left(\frac{nq \log n}{\log L}\right).$$

□

For the codes we have shown so far, we have not mentioned any constraint on the data graph $\mathcal{D}$. Therefore, the above results hold for the case where the data graph is a complete graph. That is, a rewrite can change the data from any value to any other value. We now show that the above codes are asymptotically optimal. For the Linear Code and the Extended Linear Code, this is easy to see, because every rewrite needs to increase some cell level, so the number of rewrites cannot exceed $n(q-1) = O(nq)$. The following theorem shows that the rewriting code in Construction 11 is asymptotically optimal, too [19].

**Theorem 13.** *When $n < L-1$ and the data graph $\mathcal{D}$ is a complete graph, a rewriting code can guarantee at most $O(\frac{nq \log n}{\log L})$ rewrites.*

*Proof.* Let us consider some memory state $s$ of the $n$ flash cells, currently storing some value $v \in \{0, 1, \cdots, L-1\}$. The next rewrite can change the data into any of the other $L-1$ values. If we allow ourselves $r$ operations of increasing a single cell level of the $n$ flash cells (perhaps, operating on the same cell more than once), we may reach $\binom{n+r-1}{r}$ distinct new states. Let $r$ be the maximum integer sastisfying $\binom{n+r-1}{r} < L-1$. So for the next rewrite, we need at least $r+1$ such operations in the worst case. Since we have a total of $n$ cells with $q$ levels each, the number of rewrite operations is upper bounded by

$$\frac{n(q-1)}{r+1} \leq \frac{n(q-1)}{\lfloor \frac{\log(L-1)}{1+\log n} \rfloor + 1} = O(\frac{nq \log n}{\log L}).$$

□

### *Trajectory Code Construction*

Let's now consider more restricted rewrite operations. In many applications, a rewrite often changes only a (small) part of the data. So let's consider the case where a rewrite can change the data to at most $\Delta$ new values. This is the same as saying that in the data graph $\mathcal{D}$, the maximum out-degree is $\Delta$. We call such graph $\mathcal{D}$ a *Bounded Out-degree Data Graph.*

The code to be shown is given the name *Trajectory Code* in [19]. Its idea is to record the path in $\mathcal{D}$ along which the data changes, up to a certain length. When $\Delta$ is small, this approach is particularly helpful, because recording which outgoing edge a rewrite takes (one of $\Delta$ choices) is more efficient than recording the new data value (one of $L > \Delta$ choices).

We first outline the construction of the Trajectory Code. Its parameters will be specified soon. Let $n_0, n_1, n_2, \ldots, n_d$ be $d+1$ positive integers such that $\sum_{i=0}^{d} n_i = n$ is the number of cells. We partition the $n$ cells into $d+1$ groups, each with $n_0, n_1, \ldots, n_d$ cells, respectively. We call them *registers* $S_0, S_1, \ldots, S_d$.

The encoding uses the following basic scheme: we start by using register $S_0$, called the *anchor*, to record the value of the initial data $v_0 \in \{0, 1, \cdots, L-1\}$. For the next $d$ rewrite operations we use a differential scheme: denote by $v_1, \ldots, v_d \in \{0, 1, \cdots, L-1\}$ the next $d$ values of the rewritten data. In the $i$-th rewrite, $1 \leq i \leq d$, we store in register $S_i$ the identity of the edge $(v_{i-1}, v_i) \in E_{\mathcal{D}}$. ($E_{\mathcal{D}}$ and $V_{\mathcal{D}}$ are the edge set and vertex set of the data graph $\mathcal{D}$, respectively.) We do not require a unique label for all edges globally, but rather require that *locally*, for each vertex in $V_{\mathcal{D}}$, its out-going edges have unique labels from $\{1, \cdots, \Delta\}$, where $\Delta$ denotes the maximal out-degree in the data graph $\mathcal{D}$.

Intuitively, the first $d$ rewrite operations are achieved by encoding the *trajectory* taken by the input data sequence starting with the anchor data. After $d$ such rewrites, we repeat the process by rewriting the next input from $\{0,1,\cdots,L-1\}$ in the anchor $S_0$, and then continuing with $d$ edge labels in $S_1,\cdots,S_d$.
Let us assume a sequence of $s$ rewrites have been stored thus far. To decode the last stored value all we need to know is $s \mod (d+1)$. This is easily achieved by using $\lceil t/q \rceil$ more cells (not specified in the previous $d+1$ registers), where $t$ is the total number of rewrite operations we would like to guarantee. For these $\lceil t/q \rceil$ cells we employ a simple encoding scheme: in every rewrite operation we arbitrarily choose one of those cells and raise its level by one. Thus, the total level in these cells equals $s$.
The decoding process takes the value of the anchor $S_0$ and then follows $(s-1) \mod (d+1)$ edges which are read consecutively from $S_1, S_2, \cdots$. Notice that this scheme is appealing in cases where the maximum out-degree of $\mathcal{D}$ is significantly lower than the alphabet size $L$.
Note that each register $S_i$, for $i=0,\ldots,d$, can be seen as a *smaller rewriting code* whose data graph is a *complete graph* of either $L$ vertices (for $S_0$) or $\Delta$ vertices (for $S_1,\ldots,S_d$). We use either the Extended Linear Code or the code of Construction 11 for rewriting in the $d+1$ registers.
The parameters of the *Trajectory Code* are shown by the following construction. We assume that $n \le L \le 2^{\sqrt{n}}$.

**Construction 14.** TRAJECTORY CODE FOR $n \le L \le 2^{\sqrt{n}}$
*If* $\Delta \le \lfloor \frac{n \log n}{2 \log L} \rfloor$, *let*

$$d = \lfloor \log L / \log n \rfloor = \Theta(\log L / \log n).$$

*If* $\lfloor \frac{n \log n}{2 \log L} \rfloor \le \Delta \le L$, *let*

$$d = \lfloor \log L / \log \Delta \rfloor = \Theta(\log L / \log \Delta).$$

*In both cases, set the size of the* $d+1$ *registers to* $n_0 = \lfloor n/2 \rfloor$ *and* $n_i = \lfloor n/(2d) \rfloor$ *for* $i = 1,\ldots d$. *If* $\Delta \le \lfloor \frac{n \log n}{2 \log L} \rfloor$, *apply the code of Construction* 11 *to register* $S_0$, *and apply the Extended Linear Code to registers* $S_1,\cdots,S_d$. *If* $\lfloor \frac{n \log n}{2 \log L} \rfloor \le \Delta \le L$, *apply the code of Construction* 11 *to the* $d+1$ *registers* $S_0,\cdots,S_d$.

The next three results show the asympotically optimality of the Trajectory Code (when $\Delta$ is small and large, respectively) [19].

**Theorem 15.** *Let* $\Delta \le \lfloor \frac{n \log n}{2 \log L} \rfloor$. *The Trajectory Code of Construction* 14 *guarantees* $\Theta(nq)$ *rewrites.*

*Proof.* By Theorems 10 and 12, the number of rewrites possible in $S_0$ is equal (up to constant factors) to that of $S_i$ ($i \ge 1$):

$$\Theta\left(\frac{n_0 q \log n_0}{\log L}\right) = \Theta\left(\frac{nq \log n}{\log L}\right) = \Theta\left(\frac{nq}{d}\right) = \Theta\left(n_i q\right)$$

Thus the total number of rewrites guaranted by the Trajectory Code is $d+1$ times the bound for each register $S_i$, which is $\Theta(nq)$. □

**Theorem 16.** *Let* $\lfloor \frac{n \log n}{2 \log L} \rfloor \le \Delta \le L$. *The Trajectory Code of Construction* 14 *guarantees* $\Theta\left(\frac{nq \log n}{\log \Delta}\right)$ *rewrites.*

*Proof.* By Theorem 12, the number of rewrites possible in $S_0$ is:

$$\Theta\left(\frac{n_0 q \log n_0}{\log L}\right) = \Theta\left(\frac{nq \log n}{\log L}\right)$$

Similarly the number of rewrites possible in $S_i$ $(i \geq 1)$ is:

$$\Theta\left(\frac{n_i q \log n_i}{\log \Delta}\right) = \Theta\left(\frac{nq \log n}{d \log \Delta}\right) = \Theta\left(\frac{nq \log n}{\log L}\right).$$

Here we use the fact that as $d \leq \log L$ it holds that $d = o(n)$ and $\log n_i = \Theta(\log n - \log d) = \Theta(\log n)$. Notice that the two expressions above are equal. Thus, as in Theorem 15, we conclude that the total number of rewrites guaranteed by the Trajectory Code is $d+1$ times the bound for each register $S_i$, which is $\Theta\left(\frac{nq \log n}{\log \Delta}\right)$. □

The rewriting performance shown in the above theorem matches the bound shown in the following theorem. We omit its proof, which interested readers can find in [19].

**Theorem 17.** *Let $\Delta > \lfloor \frac{n \log n}{2 \log L} \rfloor$. There exist data graphs $\mathcal{D}$ of maximum out-degree $\Delta$ such that any rewriting code for $\mathcal{D}$ can guarantee at most $O\left(\frac{nq \log n}{\log \Delta}\right)$ rewrites.*

We have so far focused on rewriting codes with asymptotically optimal performance. It is interesting to study rewriting codes that are strictly optimal, like the floating code in Example 4. Some codes of this kind have been studied in [16, 17]. In some practical applications, more specific forms of rewriting can be defined, and better rewriting codes can be found. An example is the *Buffer Code* defined for streaming data [2]. Besides studying the worst-case performance of rewriting codes, the expected rewriting performance is equally interesting. Some rewriting codes for expected performance are reported in [7, 19].

## 3. Rank Modulation

We focus our attention now on a new data representation scheme called *Rank Modulation* [21, 23]. It uses the relative order of the cell levels, instead the absolute values of cell levels, to represent data. Let us first understand the motivations for the scheme.

Fast and accurate programming schemes for multi-level flash memories are a topic of significant research and design efforts. As mentioned before, the flash memory technology does not support charge removal from individual cells due to block erasure. As a result, an interative cell programming method is used. To program a cell, a sequence of charge injection operations are used to shift the cell level cautiously and monotinically toward the target charge level from below, in order to avoid undesired global erasures in case of overshoots. Consequently, the attempt to program a cell requires quite a few programming cycles, and it works only up to a moderate number of levels per cell.

In addition to the need for accurate programming, the move to more levels in cells also aggravates the reliability problem. Compared to single-level cells, the higher storage capacity of multi-level cells are obtained at the cost of a smaller gap between adjacent cell levels. Many of the errors in flash memories are asymmetric, meaning that they shift the cell levels more likely in one direction (up or down) than the other. Examples include the write disturbs, the read disturbs, and the charge leakage. It will be interesting to design coding schemes that tolerate asymmetric errors better.

The *Rank Modulation* scheme is therefore proposed in [21, 23], whose aim is to eliminate both the problem of overshooting while programming cells, and to tolerate asymmetric errors better. In this scheme, an ordered set of $n$ cells stores the information in the permutation induced by the charge levels of the cells. In this way, no discrete levels are needed (i.e., no need for threshold levels) and only a basic charge-comparing operation (which is easy to implement) is required to read the permutation. If we further assume that the only programming operation allowed is raising the charge level of one of the cells above the current highest one (namely, *push-to-top*), then the overshoot problem is no longer relevant. Additionally, the technology may allow in the future the decrease of all the charge levels in a block of cells by a constant amount smaller than the lowest charge level (*block deflation*), which would maintain their relative values, and thus leave the information unchanged. This can eliminate a designated erase step, by deflating the entire block whenever the memory is not in use.
Let's look at a simple example of rank modulation. Let $[n]$ denote the set of integers $\{1,2,\cdots,n\}$.

**Example 18.** *We partition the cells into groups of three cells each. Denote the three cells in a group by cell 1, cell 2, and cell 3. We use a permutation of* $[3]$ – $[a_1, a_2, a_3]$ – *to represent the relative order of the three cell levels as follows: cell* $a_1$ *has the highest level, and cell* $a_3$ *has the lowest level. (The cell levels considered in this section are real numbers. So no two cells can practically have the same level.)*
*The three cells in a group can introduce six possible permutations:* $[1,2,3], [1,3,2], [2,1,3], [2,3,1], [3,1,2], [3,2,1]$. *So they can store up to* $\log_2 6$ *bits of information. To write a permutation, we program the cells from the lowest level to the highest level. For example, if the permutation to write is* $[2,3,1]$, *we first program cell 3 to make its level higher than that of cell 1, then program cell 2 to make its level higher than that of cell 3. This way, there is no risk of overshooting.*

In this section, we use $n$ to denote the number of cells in a group. As in the example, we use a permutation of $[n]$ – $[a_1, a_2, \cdots, a_n]$ – to denote the relative order of the cell levels such that cell $a_1$ has the highest level and cell $a_n$ has the lowest level.
Once a new data representation method is defined, tools of coding are required to make it useful. In this section, we focus on two tools: codes for rewriting, and codes for correcting errors.

### 3.1 Rewriting Codes for Rank Modulation

Assume that the only operation we allow for rewriting data is the "push-to-top" operation: injecting charge into a cell to make its level higher than all the other cell levels in the same cell group. Note that the push-to-top operation has no risk of overshooting. Then, how to design good rewriting codes for rank modulation?
Let $\ell$ denote the alphabet size of the data symbol stored in a group of $n$ cells. Let the alphabet of the data symbol be $[\ell] = \{1,2,\cdots,\ell\}$. Assume that a rewrite can change the data to any value in $[\ell]$. In general, $\ell$ might be smaller than $n!$, so we might end up having permutations that are not used. On the other hand, we can map several distinct permutations to the same symbol $i \in [\ell]$ in order to reduce the rewrite cost. We use $S_n$ to denote the set of $n!$ permutations, and let $W_n \subseteq S_n$ denote the set of states (i.e., the set of permutations) that are used to represent information symbols. As before, for a rewriting code we can define two functions, a *decoding function*, $F_d$, and an *update function*, $F_u$.

**Definition 19.** *The decoding function* $F_d : W_n \to [\ell]$ *maps every state* $s \in W_n$ *to a value* $F_d(s)$ *in* $[\ell]$. *Given an "old state"* $s \in W_n$ *and a "new information symbol"* $i \in [\ell]$, *the update function* $F_u : W_n \times [\ell] \to W_n$ *produces a state* $F_u(s,i)$ *such that* $F_d(F_u(s,i)) = i$.

The more push-to-top operations are used for rewriting, the closer the highest cell level is to the maximum level possible. Once it reaches the maximum level possible, block erasure will be needed for the next rewrite. So we define the rewriting cost by measuring the number of push-to-top operations.

**Definition 20.** *Given two states* $s_1, s_2 \in W_n$, *the* cost *of changing* $s_1$ *into* $s_2$, *denoted* $\alpha(s_1 \to s_2)$, *is defined as the minimum number of "push-to-the-top" operations needed to change* $s_1$ *into* $s_2$.

For example, $\alpha([1,2,3] \to [2,1,3]) = 1$, $\alpha([1,2,3] \to [3,2,1]) = 2$.

**Definition 21.** *The* worst-case rewriting cost *of a code is defined as* $\max_{s \in W_n, i \in [\ell]} \alpha(s \to F_u(s,i))$. *A code that minimized this cost is called* optimal.

Before we present an optimal rewriting code, let's first present a lower bound on the worst-case rewriting cost. Define the *transition graph* $G = (V, E)$ as a directed graph with $V = S_n$, that is, with $n!$ vertices representing the permutations in $S_n$. For any $u, v \in V$, there is a directed edge from $u$ to $v$ iff $\alpha(u \to v) = 1$. $G$ is a regular digraph, because every vertex has $n-1$ incoming edges and $n-1$ outgoing edges. The diameter of $G$ is $\max_{u,v \in V} \alpha(u \to v) = n-1$.
Given a vertex $u \in V$ and an integer $r \in \{0, 1, \ldots, n-1\}$, define the *ball* centered at $u$ with radius $r$ as $\mathcal{B}_r^n(u) = \{v \in V \mid \alpha(u \to v) \leq r\}$, and define the *sphere* centered at $u$ with radius $r$ as $\mathcal{S}_r^n(u) = \{v \in V \mid \alpha(u \to v) = r\}$. Clearly,

$$\mathcal{B}_r^n(u) = \bigcup_{0 \leq i \leq r} \mathcal{S}_r^n(u).$$

By a simple relabeling argument, both $|\mathcal{B}_r^n(u)|$ and $|\mathcal{S}_r^n(u)|$ are independent of $u$, and so will be denoted by $|\mathcal{B}_r^n|$ and $|\mathcal{S}_r^n|$ respectively.

**Lemma 22.** *For any* $0 \leq r \leq n-1$,

$$|\mathcal{B}_r^n| = \frac{n!}{(n-r)!}$$

$$|\mathcal{S}_r^n| = \begin{cases} 1 & r = 0 \\ \frac{n!}{(n-r)!} - \frac{n!}{(n-r+1)!} & 1 \leq r \leq n-1. \end{cases}$$

*Proof.* Fix a permutation $u \in V$. Let $P_u$ be the set of permutations having the following property: for each permutation $v \in P_u$, the elements appearing in its last $n-r$ positions appear in the same relative order in $u$. For example, if $n = 5$, $r = 2$, $u = [1,2,3,4,5]$ and $v = [5,2,1,3,4]$, the last 3 elements of $v$ – namely, $1,3,4$ – have the same relative order in $u$. It is easy to see that given $u$, when the elements occupying the first $r$ positions in $v \in P_u$ are chosen, the last $n-r$ positions become fixed. There are $n(n-1)\cdots(n-r+1)$ choices for occupying the first $r$ positions of $v \in P_u$, hence $|P_u| = \frac{n!}{(n-r)!}$. We will show that a vertex $v$ is in $\mathcal{B}_r^n(u)$ if and only if $v \in P_u$.

Suppose $v \in \mathcal{B}_r^n(u)$. It follows that $v$ can be obtained from $u$ with at most $r$ "push-to-the-top" operations. Those elements pushed to the top appear in the first $r$ positions of $v$, so the last $n-r$ positions of $v$ contain elements which have the same relative order in $u$, thus, $v \in P_u$. Now suppose $v \in P_u$. For $i \in [n]$, let $v_i$ denote the element in the $i$-th position of $v$. One can transform $u$ into $v$ by sequentially pushing $v_r, v_{r-1}, \ldots, v_1$ to the top. Hence, $v \in \mathcal{B}_r^n(u)$. We conclude that $|\mathcal{B}_r^n(u)| = |P| = \frac{n!}{(n-r)!}$. Since $\mathcal{B}_r^n(u) = \bigcup_{0 \le i \le r} \mathcal{S}_i^n(u)$, the second claim follows. □

The following lemma shows a lower bound to the worst-case rewriting cost.

**Lemma 23.** *Fix integers $n$ and $\ell$, and define $\rho(n,\ell)$ to be the smallest integer such that $|\mathcal{B}^n_{\rho(n,\ell)}| \ge \ell$. For any code $W_n$ and any state $s \in W_n$, there exists $i \in [\ell]$ such that $\alpha(s \to F_u(s,i)) \ge \rho(n,\ell)$, i.e., the worst-case rewriting cost of any code is at least $\rho(n,\ell)$.*

*Proof.* By the definition of $\rho(n,\ell)$, $|\mathcal{B}^n_{\rho(n,\ell)-1}| < \ell$. Hence, we can choose $i \in [\ell] \setminus \{F_d(s') \mid s' \in \mathcal{B}^n_{\rho(n,\ell)-1}(s)\}$. Clearly, by our choice $\alpha(s \to F_u(s,i)) \ge \rho(n,\ell)$. □

We now present a rewriting code construction. It will be shown that the code achieves the minimum worst-case rewriting cost. First, let us define the following notation.

**Definition 24.** *A* prefix sequence $\theta = [a^{(1)}, a^{(2)}, \ldots, a^{(m)}]$ *is a sequence of $m \le n$ distinct symbols from $[n]$. The* prefix set $P_n(\theta) \subseteq S_n$ *is defined as all the permutations in $S_n$ which start with the sequence $\theta$.*

We are now in a position to construct the code.

**Construction 25.** Rewriting Code for Rank Modulation
*Arbitrarily choose $\ell$ distinct prefix sequences, $\theta_1, \ldots, \theta_\ell$, each of length $\rho(n,\ell)$. Let us define $W_n = \bigcup_{i\in[\ell]} P_n(\theta_i)$ and map the states of $P_n(\theta_i)$ to $i$, i.e., for each $i \in [\ell]$ and $s \in P_n(\theta_i)$, set $F_d(s) = i$. Finally, to construct the update function $F_u$, given $s \in W_n$ and some $i \in [\ell]$, we do the following: let $[a_i^{(1)}, a_i^{(2)}, \ldots, a_i^{(\rho(n,\ell))}]$ be the first $\rho(n,\ell)$ elements which appear in all the permutations in $P_n(\theta_i)$. Apply push-to-top operations on the elements $a_i^{(\rho(n,\ell))}, \ldots, a_i^{(2)}, a_i^{(1)}$ in $s$ to get a permutation $s' \in P_n(\theta_i)$ for which, clearly, $F_d(s') = i$. Set $F_u(s,i) = s'$.*

**Theorem 26.** *The code in Construction 25 is optimal in terms of minimizing the worst-case rewriting cost.*

*Proof.* It is obvious from the description of $F_u$ that the worst-case rewriting cost of the construction is at most $\rho(n,\ell)$. By Lemma 23 this is also the best we can hope for. □

**Example 27.** *Let $n = 3$, $\ell = 3$. Since $|\mathcal{B}_1^3| = 3$, it follows that $\rho(n,\ell) = 1$. We partition the $n! = 6$ states into $\frac{n!}{(n-\rho(n,\ell))!} = 3$ sets, which induce the mapping:*

$$P_3([1]) = \{[1,2,3],[1,3,2]\} \mapsto 1,$$
$$P_3([2]) = \{[2,1,3],[2,3,1]\} \mapsto 2,$$
$$P_3([3]) = \{[3,1,2],[3,2,1]\} \mapsto 3.$$

*The cost of any rewrite operation is 1.*

If a probability distribution is known for the rewritten data, we can also define the performance of codes based on the average rewriting cost. This is studied in [21], where an variable-length prefix-free code is optimized. It is shown that the average rewriting cost of this prefix-free code is within a small constant approximation ratio of the minimum possible cost of all codes (prefix-free codes or not) under very mild conditions.

### 3.2 Error-correcting Codes for Rank Modulation

Error-correcting codes are often essential for the reliability of data. An error-correcting rank modulation code is a subset of permutations that are far from each other based on some distance measure. The distance between permutations needs to be defined appropriately according to the error model. In this section, we define distance as the number of adjacent transpositions. We emphasize, however, that this is not the only way to define distance. The results we present here were shown in [23].

Given a permutation, an *adjacent transposition* is the local exchange of two adjacent elements in the permutation: $[a_1, \ldots, a_{i-1}, a_i, a_{i+1}, a_{i+2}, \ldots, a_n]$ is changed to $[a_1, \ldots, a_{i-1}, a_{i+1}, a_i, a_{i+2}, \ldots, a_n]$.

In the rank modulation model, the minimal change to a permutation caused by charge-level drift is a single adjacent transposition. Let us measure the number of errors by the minimum number of adjacent transpositions needed to change the permutation from its original value to its erroneous value. For example, if the errors change the permutation from $[2,1,3,4]$ to $[2,3,4,1]$, the number of errors is two, because at least two adjacent transpositions are needed to change one into the other: $[2,1,3,4] \to [2,3,1,4] \to [2,3,4,1]$.

For two permutations $A$ and $B$, define their distance, $d(A,B)$, as the minimal number of adjacent transpositions needed to change $A$ into $B$. This distance measure is called the *Kendall Tau Distance* in the statistics and machine-learning community [24], and it induces a metric over $S_n$. If $d(A,B) = 1$, $A$ and $B$ are called *adjacent*. Any two permutations of $S_n$ are at distance at most $\frac{n(n-1)}{2}$ from each other. Two permutations of maximum distance are a reverse of each other.

*Basic Properties*

**Theorem 28.** *Let $A = [a_1, a_2, \ldots, a_n]$ and $B = [b_1, b_2, \ldots, b_n]$ be two permutations of length $n$. Suppose that $b_p = a_n$ for some $1 \le p \le n$. Let $A' = [a_1, a_2, \ldots, a_{n-1}]$ and $B' = [b_1, \ldots, b_{p-1}, b_{p+1}, \ldots, b_n]$. Then,*

$$d(A,B) = d(A',B') + n - p.$$

The above theorem can be proved by induction. It shows a recursive algorithm for computing the distance between two permutations. Let $A = [a_1, a_2, \ldots, a_n]$ and $B = [b_1, b_2, \ldots, b_n]$ be two permutations. For $1 \le i \le n$, let $A_i$ denote $[a_1, a_2, \ldots, a_i]$, let $B_i$ denote the subsequence of $B$ that contains only those numbers in $A_i$, and let $p_i$ denote the position of $a_i$ in $B_i$. Then, since $d(A_1, B_1) = 0$ and $d(A_i, B_i) = d(A_{i-1}, B_{i-1}) + i - p_i$, for $i = 2, 3, \ldots, n$, we get

$$d(A,B) = d(A_n, B_n) = \frac{(n-1)(n+2)}{2} - \sum_{i=2}^{n} p_i.$$

**Example 29.** *Let* $A = [1,2,3,4]$ *and* $B = [4,2,3,1]$. *Then* $A_1 = [1]$, $A_2 = [1,2]$, $A_3 = [1,2,3]$, $A_4 = [1,2,3,4]$, $B_1 = [1]$, $B_2 = [2,1]$, $B_3 = [2,3,1]$, $B_4 = [4,2,3,1]$. *We get*

$$\begin{aligned} d(A_1, B_1) &= 0, \\ d(A_2, B_2) = d(A_1, B_1) + 2 - p_2 &= 0 + 2 - 1 = 1, \\ d(A_3, B_3) = d(A_2, B_2) + 3 - p_3 &= 1 + 3 - 2 = 2, \\ d(A_4, B_4) = d(A_3, B_3) + 4 - p_4 &= 2 + 4 - 1 = 5. \end{aligned}$$

*Indeed,* $d(A, B) = \frac{(n-1)(n+2)}{2} - \sum_{i=2}^{n} p_i = \frac{(4-1)(4+2)}{2} - (1 + 2 + 1) = 5$.

We now define a coordinate system for permutations. We fix $A = [1,2,\ldots,n]$. For every permutation $B = [b_1, b_2, \ldots, b_n]$, we define its *coordinates* as $X_B = (2 - p_2, 3 - p_3, \ldots, n - p_n)$. Here $p_i$ is defined as above for $2 \leq i \leq n$. Clearly, if $X_B = (x_1, x_2, \ldots, x_{n-1})$, then $0 \leq x_i \leq i$ for $1 \leq i \leq n - 1$.

**Example 30.** *Let* $A = [1,2,3,4,5]$. *Then* $X_A = (0,0,0,0)$. *If* $B = [3,4,2,1,5]$, *then* $X_B = (1,2,2,0)$. *If* $B = [5,4,3,2,1]$, *then* $X_B = (1,2,3,4)$. *The full set of coordinates for* $n = 3$ *and* $n = 4$ *are shown in Fig. 3 (a) and (c), respectively.* □

The coordinate system is equivalent to a form of Lehmer code (or Lucas-Lehmer code, inversion table) [26]. It is easy to see that two permutations are identical if and only if they have the same coordinates, and any vector $(y_1, y_2, \ldots, y_{n-1})$, $0 \leq y_i \leq i$ for $1 \leq i \leq n - 1$, is the coordinates of some permutation in $S_n$. So there is a one-to-one mapping between the coordinates and the permutations.

Let $A \in S_n$ be a permutation. For any $0 \leq r \leq \frac{n(n-1)}{2}$, the set $\mathcal{B}_r(A) = \{B \in S_n \mid d(A, B) \leq r\}$ is a *ball* of radius $r$ centered at $A$. A simple relabeling argument suffices to show that the size of a ball does not depend on the choice of center. We use $|\mathcal{B}_r|$ to denote $|\mathcal{B}_r(A)|$ for any $A \in S_n$. We are interested in finding the value of $|\mathcal{B}_r|$. The following theorem presents a way to compute the size of a ball using polynomial multiplication.

**Theorem 31.** *For* $0 \leq r \leq \frac{n(n-1)}{2}$, *let* $e_r$ *denote the coefficient of* $x^r$ *in the polynomial* $\prod_{i=1}^{n-1} \frac{x^{i+1}-1}{x-1}$. *Then* $|\mathcal{B}_r| = \sum_{i=0}^{r} e_r$.

*Proof.* Let $A = [1,2,\ldots,n]$. Let $B = [b_1, b_2, \ldots, b_n]$ be a generic permutation. Let $X_B = (y_1, y_2, \ldots, y_{n-1})$ be the coordinates of $B$. By the definition of coordinates, we get $d(A, B) = \sum_{i=1}^{n-1} y_i$. The number of permutations at distance $r$ from $A$ equals the number of integer solutions to $\sum_{i=1}^{n-1} y_i = r$ such that $0 \leq y_i \leq i$. That is equal to the coefficient of $x^r$ in the polynomial $\prod_{i=1}^{n-1}(x^i + x^{i-1} + \cdots + 1) = \prod_{i=1}^{n-1} \frac{x^{i+1}-1}{x-1}$. Thus, there are exactly $e_r$ permutations at distance $r$ from $A$, and $|\mathcal{B}_r| = \sum_{i=0}^{r} e_i$. □

Theorem 31 induces an upper bound for the sizes of error-correcting rank-modulation codes. By the sphere-packing principle, for such a code that can correct $r$ errors, its size cannot exceed $n!/|\mathcal{B}_r|$.

### *Embedding of Permutation Adjacency Graph*

Define the adjacency graph of permutations, $G = (V, E)$, as follows. The graph $G$ has $|V| = n!$ vertices, which represent the $n!$ permutations. Two vertices $u, v \in V$ are adjacent if and only if $d(u, v) = 1$. $G$ is a regular undirected graph with degree $n - 1$ and diameter $\frac{n(n-1)}{2}$. To study the topology of $G$, we begin with the follow theorem.

**Lemma 32.** *For two permutations $A = [a_1, a_2, \ldots, a_n]$ and $B = [b_1, b_2, \ldots, b_n]$, let their coordinates be $X_A = (x_1, x_2, \ldots, x_{n-1})$ and $X_B = (y_1, y_2, \ldots, y_{n-1})$. If A and B are adjacent, then $\sum_{i=1}^{n-1} |x_i - y_i| = 1$.*

The above lemma can be proved by induction. Interested readers can see [23] for details.
Let $L_n = (V_L, E_L)$ denote a $2 \times 3 \times \cdots \times n$ linear array graph. $L_n$ has $n!$ vertices $V_L$. Each vertex is assigned integer coordinates $(x_1, x_2, \ldots, x_{n-1})$, where $0 \leq x_i \leq i$ for $1 \leq i \leq n-1$. The distance between vertices of $L_n$ is the $L_1$ distance, and two vertices are adjacent (i.e., have an edge between them) if and only if their distance is one.
We now build a bijective map $P : V \to V_L$. Here $V$ is the vertex set of the adjacency graph of permutations $G = (V, E)$. For any $u \in V$ and $v \in V_L$, $P(u) = v$ if and only if $u, v$ have the same coordinates. By Lemma 32, if two permutations are adjacent, their coordinates are adjacent in $L_n$. So we get:

**Theorem 33.** *The adjacency graph of permutations is a subgraph of the $2 \times 3 \times \cdots \times n$ linear array.*

We show some examples of the embedding in Fig. 3. It can be seen that while each permutation has $n-1$ adjacent permutations, a vertex in the array can have a varied degree from $n-1$ to $2n-3$. Some edges of the array do not exist in the adjacency graph of permutations.

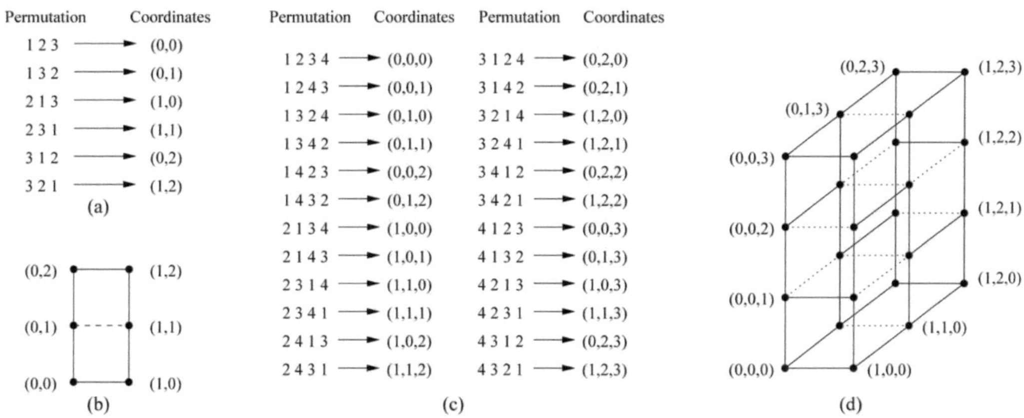

Fig. 3. Coordinates of permutations, and embedding the adjacency graph of permutations, $G$, in the $2 \times 3 \times \cdots \times n$ array, $L_n$. In the two arrays, the solid lines are the edges in both $G$ and $L_n$, and the dotted lines are the edges only in $L_n$. (a) Coordinates of permutations for $n = 3$. (b) Embedding $G$ in $L_n$ for $n = 3$. (c) Coordinates of permutations for $n = 4$. (d) Embedding $G$ in $L_n$ for $n = 4$.

The observation that the permutations' adjacency graph is a subgraph of a linear array shows an approach to design error-correcting rank-modulation codes based on Lee-metric codes. We skip the proof of the following theorem due to its simplicity.

**Theorem 34.** *Let C be a Lee-metric error-correcting code of length $n-1$, alphabet size no less than $n$, and minimum distance $d$. Let $C'$ be the subset of codewords of $C$ that are contained in the array $L_n$. Then $C'$ is an error-correcting rank-modulation code with minimum distance at least $d$.*

*Single-error-correcting Rank-Modulation Code*

We now present a family of rank-modulation codes that can correct one error. The code is based on the perfect sphere packing in the Lee-metric space [11]. The code construction is as follows.

**Construction 35.** (SINGLE-ERROR-CORRECTING RANK-MODULATION CODE)
*Let $C_1$, $C_2$ denote two rank-modulation codes constructed as follows. Let $A$ be a general permutation whose coordinates are $(x_1, x_2, \ldots, x_{n-1})$. Then $A$ is a codeword in $C_1$ if and only if the following equation is satisfied:*

$$\sum_{i=1}^{n-1} ix_i \equiv 0 \pmod{2n-1}.$$

*$A$ is a codeword in $C_2$ if and only if the following equation is satisfied:*

$$\sum_{i=1}^{n-2} ix_i + (n-1) \cdot (-x_{n-1}) \equiv 0 \pmod{2n-1}.$$

*Between $C_1$ and $C_2$, choose the code with more codewords as the final output.* □

We analyze the code size of Construction 35.

**Lemma 36.** *The rank-modulation code built in Construction 35 has a minimum cardinality of $\frac{(n-1)!}{2}$.*

*Proof.* Let $H = (V_H, E_H)$ be a $2 \times 3 \times \cdots \times (n-1) \times (2n-1)$ linear array. Every vertex in $H$ has integer coordinates $(x_1, x_2, \ldots, x_{n-1})$, where $0 \leq x_i \leq i$ for $1 \leq i \leq n-2$, and $-n+1 \leq x_{n-1} \leq n-1$.
Given any choice of $(x_1, x_2, \ldots, x_{n-2})$ of the coordinates, we would like to see if there is a solution to $x_{n-1}$ (note that $-n+1 \leq x_{n-1} \leq n-1$) that satisfies the following equation:

$$\sum_{i=1}^{n-1} ix_i \equiv 0 \pmod{2n-1}.$$

Since $\sum_{i=1}^{n-1} ix_i = (n-1)x_{n-1} + \sum_{i=1}^{n-2} ix_i$, and $n-1$ and $2n-1$ are co-prime integers, there is exactly one solution to $x_{n-1}$ that satisfies the above equation. If $x_{n-1} \geq 0$, clearly $(x_1, x_2, \ldots, x_{n-1})$ are the coordinates of a codeword in the code $C_1$. If $x_{n-1} \leq 0$, then $\sum_{i=1}^{n-2} ix_i + (n-1) \cdot [-(-x_{n-1})] \equiv 0 \pmod{2n-1}$, so $(x_1, x_2, \ldots, x_{n-2}, -x_{n-1})$ are the coordinates of a codeword in the code $C_2$.
Since $0 \leq x_i \leq i$ for $1 \leq i \leq n-2$, there are $(n-1)!$ ways to choose $x_1, x_2, \ldots, x_{n-2}$. Each choice generates a codeword that belongs either to $C_1$ or $C_2$. Therefore, at least one of $C_1$ and $C_2$ has cardinality no less than $\frac{(n-1)!}{2}$. □

**Lemma 37.** *The rank-modulation code built in Construction 35 can correct one error.*

*Proof.* It has been shown in [11] that for an infinite $k$-dimensional array, vertices whose coordinates $(x_1, x_2, \ldots, x_k)$ satisfy the condition $\sum_{i=1}^{k} ix_i \equiv 0 \pmod{2k+1}$ have a minimum $L_1$ distance of 3. Let $k = n-1$. Note that in Construction 35, the codewords of $C_1$ are a subset of the above vertices, while the codewords in $C_2$ are a subset of the mirrored image of the above vertices, where the last coordinate $x_{n-1}$ is mapped to $-x_{n-1}$. Since the permutations' adjacency graph is a subgraph of the array, the minimum distance of $C_1$ and $C_2$ is at least 3. Hence, the code built in Construction 35 can correct one error. □

**Theorem 38.** *The code built in Construction* 35 *is a single-error-correcting rank-modulation code whose cardinality is at least half of optimal.*

*Proof.* Every permutation has $n-1$ adjacent permutations, so the size of a radius-1 ball, $|\mathcal{B}_1|$, is $n$. By the sphere packing bound, a single-error-correcting rank-modulation code can have at most $\frac{n!}{n} = (n-1)!$ codewords. The code in Construction 35 has at least $(n-1)!/2$ codewords. □

## 4. Extended Information Theoretic Results

Flash memory is a type of constrained memory. There has been a history of distinguished theoretical study on constrained memories. It includes the original work by Kuznetsov and Tsybakov on coding for defective memories [25]. Further developments on defective memories include [12, 14]. The write once memory (WOM) [29], write unidirectional memory (WUM) [28, 30, 32], and write efficient memory [1, 9] are also special instances of constrained memories. Among them, WOM is the most related to the Write-Asymmetric Memory model studied in this chapter.

Write once memory (WOM) was defined by Rivest and Shamir in their original work [29]. In a WOM, a cell's state can change from 0 to 1 but not from 1 to 0. This model was later generalized with more cell states in [6, 8]. The objective of WOM codes is to maximize the number of times that the stored data can be rewritten. A number of very interesting WOM code constructions have been presented over the years, including the tabular codes, linear codes, etc. in [29], the linear codes in [6], the codes constructed using projective geometries [27], and the coset coding in [5]. Fine results on the capacity of WOM have been presented in [8, 13, 29, 33]. Furthermore, error-correcting WOM codes have been studied in [35]. In all the above works, the rewriting model assumes no constraints on the data, namely, the data graph $\mathcal{D}$ is a complete graph.

With the increasing importance of flash memories, new topics on coding for flash memories have been studied in recent years. For the efficient rewriting of data, floating codes and buffer codes were defined and studied in [16] and [2], respectively. A floating code jointly encodes multiple variables, and every rewrite changes one variable. A buffer code, on the other hand, records the most recent data of a data stream. More results on floating codes that optimize the worst-case rewriting performance were presented in [17, 34]. Floating codes that also correct errors were studied in [15]. In [19], the rewriting problem was generalized based on the data graph model, and trajectory codes for complete data graphs and bounded-degree data graphs were presented. The paper [19] also contains a summary and comparison of previous results on rewriting codes.

Optimizing rewriting codes for expected performance is also an interesting topic. In [7], floating codes of this type were designed based on Gray code constructions. In [19], randomized WOM codes of robust performance were proposed.

The rank modulation scheme was proposed and studied in [21, 23]. In addition to rewriting [21] and error correction [23], a family of Gray codes for rank modulation were also presented [21]. One application of the Gray codes is to map rank modulation to the conventional multi-level cells. A type of convolutional rank modulation codes, called *Bounded Rank Modulation*, was studied in [31].

To study the storage capacity of flash memories, it is necessary to understand how accruately flash cells can be programmed using the iterative and monotonic programming method. This was studied in [18] based on an abstract programming-error model.

The errors in flash cell levels often have an asymmetric property. In [4], error-correcting codes that correct asymmetric errors of limited magnitude were designed for flash memories.
In a storage system, to avoid the accumulation of errors, a common practice is to write the correct data back into the storage system once the errors accumulated in the data reach a certain threshold. This is called *memory scrubbing*. In flash memories, however, memory scrubbing is more difficult because to write one correct codeword back into the system, the whole block needs to be erased. A new type of error-correcting codes, called *Error-Scurbbing Codes*, were defined in [20] for multi-level cells. It is shown that even if the only allowed operation is to increase cell levels, a higher rate of ECC can be still achieved by actively scrubbing errors.
The block erasure property of flash memories affects not only rewriting and cell programming, but also data movement. In [22], it is shown that by appropriately using coding, the number of erasures needed for moving data among $n$ NAND flash blocks can be reduced by a factor of $O(\log n)$.
The rewriting codes and the rank modulation scheme are useful not only for flash memories, but also for other constrained memories. A promonent example is the phase-change memory (PCM). In a phase-change memory, a memory cell can be switched between a crystalline state and an amorphous state. Intermediate states are also possible. Since changing the cell to the crystalline state takes a substantially longer time than changing it to the amorphous state, the memory is closely related to the Write-Asymmetric Memory model. How to program PCM cells with more intermediate states fast and reliably is an active ongoing topic. The rank modulation scheme may provide an effective tool in this area.

## Acknowledgment

We would like to thank all our co-authors for their collaborative work in this area. In particular, we would like to thank Mike Langberg and Moshe Schwartz for many of the main results discussed in this chapter.

## 5. References

[1] R. Ahlswede and Z. Zhang, "On multiuser write-efficient memories," *IEEE Trans. on Inform. Theory*, vol. 40, no. 3, pp. 674–686, 1994.
[2] V. Bohossian, A. Jiang and J. Bruck, "Buffer codes for asymmetric multi-level memory," in *Proc. IEEE International Symposium on Information Theory (ISIT)*, 2007, pp. 1186-1190.
[3] P. Cappelletti, C. Golla, P. Olivo and E. Zanoni (*Ed.*), *Flash memories*, Kluwer Academic Publishers, 1st Edition, 1999.
[4] Y. Cassuto, M. Schwartz, V. Bohossian and J. Bruck, "Codes for multilevel flash memories: Correcting asymmetric limited-magnitude errors," in *Proc. IEEE International Symposium on Information Theory (ISIT)*, Nice, France, June 2007, pp. 1176-1180.
[5] G. D. Cohen, P. Godlewski, and F. Merkx, "Linear binary code for write-once memories," *IEEE Trans. on Inform. Theory*, vol. IT-32, no. 5, pp. 697–700, Sep. 1986.
[6] A. Fiat and A. Shamir, "Generalized "write-once" memories," *IEEE Trans. on Inform. Theory*, vol. IT-30, no. 3, pp. 470–480, May 1984.
[7] H. Finucane, Z. Liu and M. Mitzenmacher, "Designing floating codes for expected performance," in *Proc. 46th Annual Allerton Conference*, 2008.
[8] F. Fu and A. J. Han Vinck, "On the capacity of generalized write-once memory with state transitions described by an arbitrary directed acyclic graph," *IEEE Trans. on Inform. Theory*, vol. 45, no. 1, pp. 308–313, Jan. 1999.

[9] F. Fu and R. W. Yeung, "On the capacity and error-correcting codes of write-efficient memories," *IEEE Trans. on Inform. Theory*, vol. 46, no. 7, pp. 2299–2314, Nov. 2000.
[10] E. Gal and S. Toledo, "Algorithms and data structures for flash memories," in *ACM Computing Surveys*, vol. 37, no. 2, pp. 138-163, June 2005.
[11] S. W. Golomb and L. R. Welch, "Perfect codes in the Lee metric and the packing of polyominoes," *SIAM J. Appl. Math.*, vol. 18, no. 2, pp. 302–317, Jan. 1970.
[12] A. J. Han Vinck and A. V. Kuznetsov, "On the general defective channel with informed encoder and capacities of some constrained memories," *IEEE Trans. on Inform. Theory*, vol. 40, no. 6, pp. 1866–1871, 1994.
[13] C. D. Heegard, "On the capacity of permanent memory," *IEEE Trans. on Inform. Theory*, vol. IT-31, no. 1, pp. 34–42, Jan. 1985.
[14] C. D. Heegard and A. A. E. Gamal, "On the capacity of computer memory with defects," *IEEE Trans. on Inform. Theory*, vol. IT-29, no. 5, pp. 731–739, Sep. 1983.
[15] A. Jiang, "On the generalization of error-correcting WOM codes," in *Proc. IEEE International Symposium on Information Theory (ISIT'07)*, 2007, pp. 1391-1395.
[16] A. Jiang, V. Bohossian and J. Bruck, "Floating codes for joint information storage in write asymmetric memories," in *Proc. IEEE International Symposium on Information Theory (ISIT)*, 2007, pp. 1166-1170.
[17] A. Jiang and J. Bruck, "Joint coding for flash memory storage," in *Proc. IEEE International Symposium on Information Theory (ISIT)*, 2008, pp. 1741-1745.
[18] A. Jiang and J. Bruck, "On the capacity of flash memories," in *Proc. International Symposium on Information Theory and Its Applications (ISITA)*, 2008, pp. 94-99.
[19] A. Jiang, M. Langberg, M. Schwartz and J. Bruck, "Universal rewriting in constrained memories," in *Proc. IEEE International Symposium on Information Theory (ISIT)*, Seoul, Korea, June-July 2009. Technical report online at `http://www.paradise.caltech.edu/papers/etr096.pdf`.
[20] A. Jiang, H. Li and Y. Wang, "Error scrubbing codes for flash memories," in *Proc. Canadian Workshop on Information Theory (CWIT)*, May 2009, pp. 32-35.
[21] A. Jiang, R. Mateescu, M. Schwartz and J. Bruck, "Rank modulation for flash memories," in *Proc. IEEE International Symposium on Information Theory (ISIT)*, 2008, pp. 1731-1735.
[22] A. Jiang, R. Mateescu, E. Yaakobi, J. Bruck, P. Siegel, A. Vardy and J. Wolf, "Storage coding for wear leveling in flash memories," in *Proc. IEEE International Symposium on Information Theory (ISIT'09)*, Seoul, Korea, June-July 2009.
[23] A. Jiang, M. Schwartz and J. Bruck, "Error-correcting codes for rank modulation," in *Proc. IEEE International Symposium on Information Theory (ISIT)*, 2008, pp. 1736-1740.
[24] M. Kendall and J. D. Gibbons, *Rank correlation methods.* Oxford University Press, NY, 1990.
[25] A. V. Kuznetsov and B. S. Tsybakov, "Coding for memories with defective cells," *Problemy Peredachi Informatsii*, vol. 10, no. 2, pp. 52–60, 1974.
[26] D. H. Lehmer, "Teaching combinatorial tricks to a computer," in *Proc. Sympos. Appl. Math. Combinatorial Analysis*, vol. 10, Amer. Math. Soc., Providence, R.I., pp. 179-193, 1960.
[27] F. Merkx, "WOM codes constructed with projective geometries," *Traitment du Signal*, vol. 1, no. 2-2, pp. 227–231, 1984.
[28] W. M. C. J. van Overveld, "The four cases of write unidirectional memory codes over arbitrary alphabets," *IEEE Trans. on Inform. Theory*, vol. 37, no. 3, pp. 872–878, 1991.
[29] R. L. Rivest and A. Shamir, "How to reuse a 'write-once' memory," *Information and Control*, vol. 55, pp. 1-19, 1982.

[30] G. Simonyi, "On write-unidirectional memory codes," *IEEE Trans. on Inform. Theory*, vol. 35, no. 3, pp. 663–667, May 1989.
[31] Z. Wang, A. Jiang and J. Bruck, "On the capacity of bounded rank modulation for flash memories," in *Proc. IEEE International Symposium on Information Theory (ISIT)*, Seoul, Korea, June-July 2009.
[32] F. M. J. Willems and A. J. Vinck, "Repeated recording for an optical disk," in *Proc. 7th Symp. Inform. Theory in the Benelux*, May 1986, Delft Univ. Press, pp. 49-53.
[33] J. K. Wolf, A. D. Wyner, J. Ziv, and J. Korner, "Coding for a write-once memory," *AT&T Bell Labs. Tech. J.*, vol. 63, no. 6, pp. 1089–1112, 1984.
[34] E. Yaakobi, A. Vardy, P. H. Siegel and J. K. Wolf, "Multidimensional flash codes," in *Proc. 46th Annual Allerton Conference*, 2008.
[35] G. Zémor and G. Cohen, "Error-correcting WOM-codes," *IEEE Trans. on Inform. Theory*, vol. 37, no. 3, pp. 730–734, May 1991.

# 5

# Design and Implementation of FPGA- based Systolic Array for LZ Data Compression

Mohamed A. Abd El Ghany, Magdy A. El-Moursy* and Aly E. Salama**
*Electronics Engineering Dept., German University in Cairo, Cairo, Egypt*
*Electronics Research Institute, Cairo, Egypt, Mentor Graphics Corporation, Cairo, Egypt**
*Electronics and communication Dept., Cairo University, Cairo, Egypt***

## 1. Introduction

Data compression is becoming an essential component of high speed data communications and storage. Lossless data compression is the process of encoding ("compressing") a body of data into a smaller body of data which can, at a later time, be uniquely decoded ("decompressed") back to the original data. In lossy compression, the decompressed data contains some approximation of the original data.

Hardware implementation of data compression algorithms is receiving increasing attention due to exponential expansion in network traffic and digital data storage usage. Many lossless data compression techniques have been proposed in the past and widely used, e.g., Huffman code (Huffman, 1952) ; (Gallager, 1978);( Park & Prasanna, 1993), arithmetic code (Bodden et al., 2004);(Said, 2004);(Said, 2003); (Howard & Vetter, 1992), run-length code (Golomb, 1966), and Lempel–Ziv (LZ) algorithms (Ziv & Lempel, 1977);( Ziv & Lempel, 1978);(Welch, 1984);(Salomon, 2004). Among those, LZ algorithms are the most popular when no prior knowledge or statistical characteristics of the data being compressed are available. The principle of the LZ algorithms is to find the longest match between the recently received string which is stored in the input buffer and the incoming string. Once this match is located, the incoming string is represented with a position tag and a length variable linking the new string to the old existing one. Since the repeated data is linked to an older one, more concise representation is achieved and compression is performed. The latency of the compression process is defined by the number of clock cycles needed to produce a codeword (matching results).

To fulfill real-time requirements, several hardware realizations of LZ and its variants have been presented in the literature. Different hardware architectures, including content addressable memory (CAM) (Lin & Wu, 2000);(Jones, 1992);(Lee & Yang, 1995), Systolic array (Ranganathan & Henriques, 1993);(Jung & Burleson, 1998);(Hwang & Wu, 2001), and embedded processor (Chang et al., 1994), have been proposed in the past. The microprocessor approach is not attractive for real- time applications, since it does not fully explore hardware parallelism (Hwang & Wu, 2001). CAM has been considered one of the fastest architectures to search for a given string in a long world, which is necessary process in LZ. A CAM- based LZ data compressor can process one input symbol per clock cycle, regardless of the buffer length and string length. A CAM- based LZ can achieve optimum speed for compression.

However, CAMs require highly complex hardware and dissipate high power. The CAM approach performs string matching through full parallel search, while the systolic-array approach exploits pipelining.
As compared to CAM- based designs, systolic –array-based designs are slower, but better in hardware cost and testability (Hwang & Wu, 2001); (Hwang & Wu, 1995); (Hwang & Wu, 1997). Preliminary design for systolic – array contains thousands of processing elements (PEs) (Ranganathan & Henriques, 1993). High speed designs were then reported later, requiring only tens of PEs (Jung & Burleson, 1998);(hwang et al., 2001). A technique to enhance the efficiency of systolic- array approach which is used to implement Lempel- Ziv algorithm is described in this chapter. A parallel technique for LZ-based data compression is presented. The technique employs transforming a data–dependent algorithm to a data - independent algorithm. A control variable is introduced to indicate early completion which improves the latency. The proposed implementation is area and speed efficient. The effect of the input buffer length on the compression ratio is analyzed. An FPGA implementation for the proposed technique is carried out. The implemented design verifies that data can be compressed and decompressed on-the- fly which opens new areas of research in data compression.
The organization of this chapter is as follows: In Section 2, the LZ compression algorithm is explained. The results and comments about some software simulations are discussed. The dependency graph (DG) to investigate the data dependency of every computation step in the algorithm is shown. The most recent systolic array architecture is described and an area and speed efficient architecture is proposed in Section 3. In Section 4, the proposed systolic array structure is compared with the most recent structures (Hwang et al., 2001) in terms of area, and latency. An FPGA implementation for the proposed architecture showing the real time operations is demonstrated in Section 5. Finally, conclusions are provided in Section 6.

## 2. Lempel-ziv coding algorithm

The LZ algorithm was proposed by Ziv and Lempel in (Ranganathan & Henriques, 1993). The relationship between $n$ and $Ls$ for optimal compression performance is briefly examined. The data dependency of every computation step in the LZ compression algorithm is investigated.

### 2.1 The compression algorithm:

The LZ algorithm and its variants use a sliding window that moves a long with the cursor. The window can be divided into two parts, the part before the cursor, called the dictionary, and the part starting at the cursor, called the look-ahead buffer. The lengths of these two parts are input parameters to compression algorithm. The basic algorithm is very simple, and loops executing the following steps:

1. Find the longest match of a string starting at the cursor and completely contained in the look-ahead buffer to a string starting in the dictionary.
2. Output a triple parameter ($I_p$, $L_{max}$, $S$) containing the position $I_p$ of the occurrence in the window, the length $L_{max}$ of the match and the next symbol $S$ past the match.
3. Move the cursor $L_{max} + 1$ symbols forward.

Let us consider an example with window length of ($n$=9) and look-ahead buffer length ($Ls=3$) shown in Fig. 1.
Let the content of the window be denoted *as* $X_i$, $i = 0,1,\ldots,n-1$ and that of the look-ahead buffer be $Y_j$, $j = 0,1,\ldots Ls$-1 (i.e., $Y_j = X_{i+n-Ls}$). According to LZ algorithm, the content of look-ahead buffer is compared with the dictionary content starting from $X0$ to $X_{n-Ls-1}$ to find the longest match length. If the best match in the window is found to start from position $I_p$ and the match length is $L_{max}$. Then $L_{max}$ symbols will be represented by a codeword ($I_p$, $L_{max}$). The codeword length is $Lc$:

$$Lc = 1 + [\log_2 (n-L_s)] + [Log_2 L_s] \quad \text{bits} \qquad (1)$$

Lc is fixed. Assume $w$ bits are required to represent a symbol in the window, $l = [log2\ Ls]$ bits are required to represent Lmax, and $p = [log2\ (n-Ls)]$ bits are required to represent $Ip$. Then the compression ratio is $(l + p) / (Lmax * w)$, where $0 \le Lmax \le Ls$. Hence the compression ratio depends on the match situation.

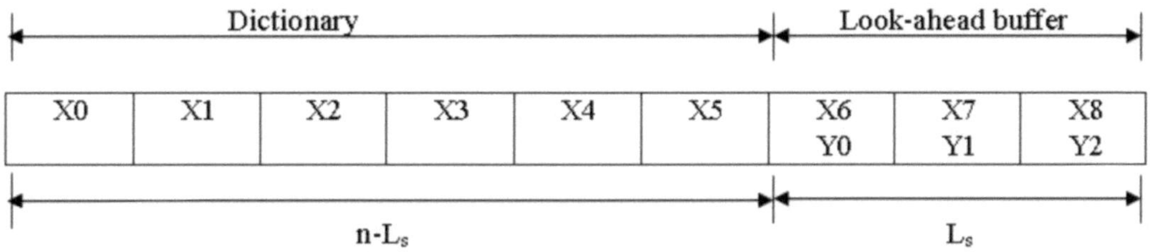


Fig. 1. window of the LZ compressor example

The codeword design and the choice of widow length are crucial in achieving maximum compression. The LZ technique involves the conversion of variable length substrings into fixed length codewords that represent the pointer and the length of the match. Hence, selection of values of $n$ and $L_s$ can greatly influence the compression efficiency of the LZ algorithm.

### 2.2 Compression Algorithm Paramters Selection

Simulation for the performance of the LZ algorithm for different buffers lengths is performed using the Calgary corpus and the Silesia Corpus (Deorowicz, 2003) [16], as shown in Fig. 2 and Fig. 3, respectively. In these experiments, the codeword is up to 2 bytes long.
From Fig. 2 and Fig. 3, the compression ratio decreases when $n$ exceeds 1024. The above improvement in the compression ratio can be obtained only when $L_s$ = 8, 16, or 32. Based on the results, the best $L_s$ for a good compression ratio is $2^4$. Increasing $L_s$ beyond that will require a much faster growing $n$ (as well as hardware cost and computation time), with saturating or even decreasing compression ratio. The reason is that repeating patterns tend to be short, and that increasing $L_s$ and $n$ also increases the codeword length ($l + p$). To achieve a good performance for different data formats, $L_s$ may range from 8 to 32, while $n$ may be from 1k to 8 k. The simulation results verify the results proposed in (Arias et al., 2004).

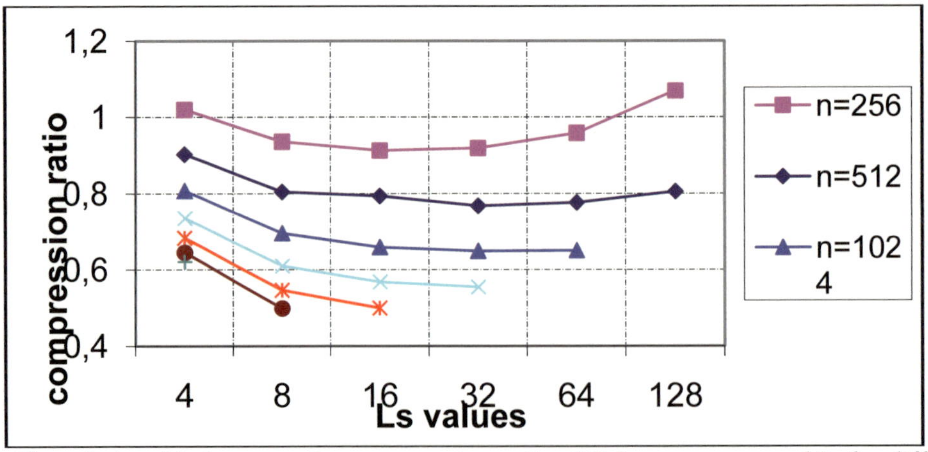


Fig. 2. The relationship between the compression ratio of Calgary corpus and *Ls* for different values of *n*

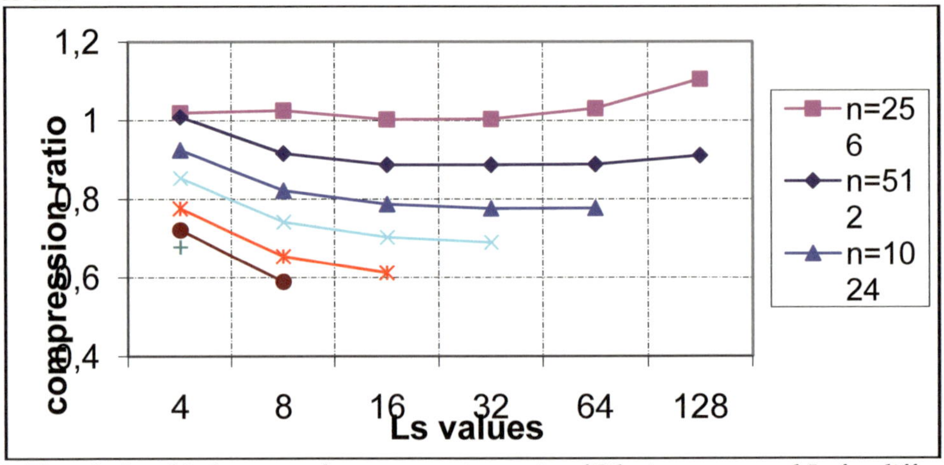


Fig. 3. The relationship between the compression ratio of Silesia corpus and *Ls* for different values of *n*.

**2.3 Dependency graph:**

A dependency graph (DG) is a graph that shows the dependence of the computations that occur in an algorithm. The DG of the LZ algorithm can be obtained as shown in Fig. 4. In the DG, L (match length) and E (match signal) are propagated from cell to cell. *X* (content of the window) and *Y* (content of the look-ahead buffer) are broadcast horizontally and diagonally to all cells, respectively. The DG shown in Fig. 4 is called a global DG, because it contains global signals. The global DG can be transformed into a localized DG, by propagating the input data *Y* and *X* from cell to cell instead of broadcasting them. Processor assignment can be done by projection of the DG onto the surface normal to the projection vector selected. After processor assignment, the events are scheduled using a schedule vector.

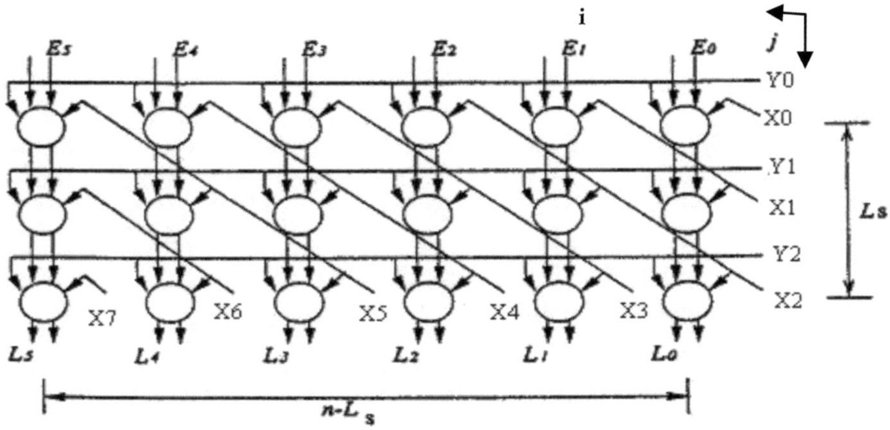


Fig. 4. The dependence graph of the LZ compression algorithm.

## 3. Systolic array architecture

The hardware architectures of LZ data compression demonstrate that systolic array compressors are better in hardware cost and testability. The main difference between systolic arrays and other architectures is that systolic arrays can operate at a higher clock rate (due to nearest-neighbor communication) and can easily be implemented and tested (due to regularity and homogeneity). In the following subsections, the most recent systolic array architectures are described. The high performance architecture is proposed.

### 3.1 Design-1

This architecture was first proposed in (Ziv & Lempel, 1977). The space-time diagram and its final array architecture are given in Fig. 5, where D represents a unit delay on the signal line between two processing elements. In Table 1, the six –sets of comparisons have to be done in sequence in order to find the maximum matching substring.

| (1) | (2) | (3) | (4) | (5) | (6) |
|---|---|---|---|---|---|
| X0- Y0 | X1- Y0 | X2- Y0 | X3- Y0 | X4- Y0 | X5- Y0 |
| X1- Y1 | X2- Y1 | X3- Y1 | X4- Y1 | X5- Y1 | X6- Y1 |
| X2- Y2 | X3- Y2 | X4- Y2 | X5- Y2 | X6- Y2 | X7- Y2 |

Table 1. The six- sets of required comparisons

Let us consider six processing elements (PE's) in parallel, each performing one vertical set of comparisons. Each processing element would require 3 time units ($L_s$ =3) to complete its set of comparisons. As shown in Fig. 5, the delay blocks in each PE delay the *Y* by two time steps and the X by one time step. A space- time diagram is used to illustrate the sequence of comparisons as performed by each PE. The data brought into PE0 are routed systolically through each processor from left to right. In the first time unit, X0 and Y0 are compared at PE0. In the second time unit, X1 and Y1 are compared, X0 flows to PE1, and Y0 is delayed by one cycle (time unit). In the third time unit, X2 andY2 are compared at PE0. At this time, Y0 gets to PE1along with X1, and PE1 performs its first comparison at the third cycle, PE0 completes all its required comparisons and stores an integer specifying the number of successful comparisons in a register called $L_i$. Another register called $L_{max}$, holds the maximum matching length obtained from the previous PE's. In the fourth time unit, PE0 compares the values of $L_{max}$ (which for PE0 is 0) and $L_i$, and the greater of the two is sent to the $L_{max}$ register of the next PE. The result of the $L_i$ - $L_{max}$ comparison is sent to the next PE after a delay of one time unit for proper synchronization. Finally, the $L_{max}$ value emerging out from the last PE (PE5 in this case) is the length of the longest matching substring. There is another register called PE's id, whose contents are passed along with the $L_{max}$ value to the next PE. Its contents indicate the id of the processor element where the $L_{max}$ value occurred which becomes the pointer to the match.

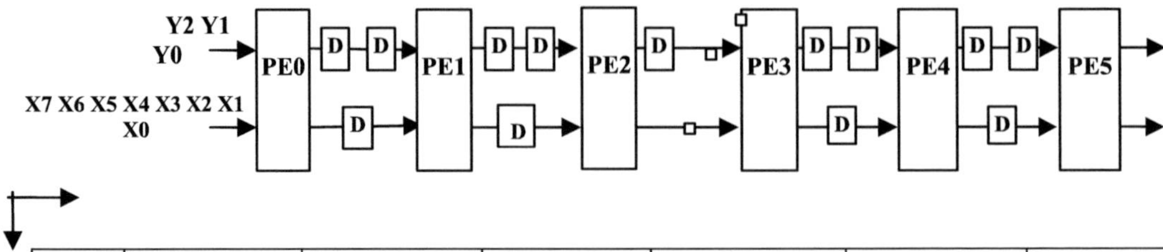


| time | PE0 | PE1 | PE2 | PE3 | PE4 | PE5 |
|---|---|---|---|---|---|---|
| 1 | X0-Y0 | | | | | |
| 2 | X1-Y1 | | | | | |
| 3 | X2-Y2 | X1-Y0 | | | | |
| 4 | $L_{max}$ | X2-Y1 | | | | |
| 5 | | X3-Y2 | X2-Y0 | | | |
| 6 | | $L_{max}$ | X3-Y1 | | | |
| 7 | | | X4-Y2 | X3-Y0 | | |
| 8 | | | $L_{max}$ | X4-Y1 | | |
| 9 | | | | X5-Y2 | X4-Y0 | |
| 10 | | | | $L_{max}$ | X5-Y1 | |
| 11 | | | | | X6-Y2 | X5-Y0 |
| 12 | | | | | $L_{max}$ | X6-Y1 |
| 13 | | | | | | X7-Y2 |
| 14 | | | | | | $L_{max}$ |

Fig. 5. Design-1 and its space-time diagram indicating the sequence of events in the 6 PE's.

The functional block of the PE is shown in Fig. 6, in which the control circuit is not included. Two comparators are needed in the PE: one is for equality check of $Y_j$ and $X_i$ and the other together with two multiplexers are for determining $L_{max}$ and $I_p$. If $Y_j$ and $X_i$ are equal, a counter is incremented each time until an unsuccessful comparison occurs. Sequences $X_i$ and $Y_j$ can be generated by the buffer shown in Fig. 7, which is organized in two levels the upper level of the buffer holds the incoming symbols to be compressed. The contents of the upper level are copied into the lower level whenever the "load" line goes high. The lower level is used to provide data to the PE's in the correct sequence.

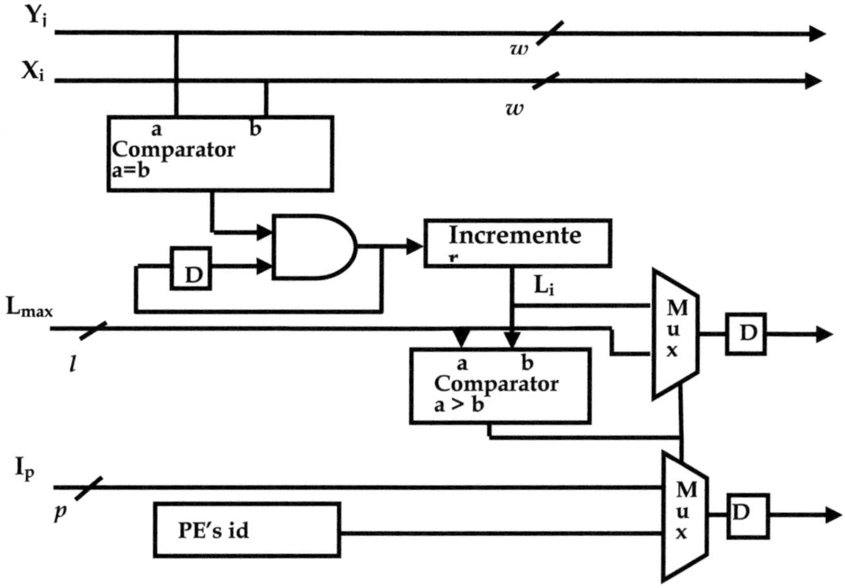


Fig. 6. The functional block of design-1 PE.

The operation of the buffer is as follows. When the longest match length is found, the same number of symbols are shifted into the in upper buffer from the source and then the symbols in the upper buffer are copied to the lower buffer in parallel to generate the next sequence to the processor array. In the Design- 1 array, The number of clock cycles needed to produce a codeword is *2 (n-Ls)*, so the utilization rate of each PE is *Ls/ [(2 (n-Ls)]*, which is low since the PE is idle from the moment when *Li* is determined until the time the codeword is produced. The reason is that it seems impossible to compress subsequent input symbols before the present compression process is completed, because the number of input symbols needed to be shifted into the buffer is equal to the longest match length which is not available before the completion of the present compression process. Therefore, the design with more than $L_s$ pipeline stages must have some idle PEs before the present codeword is produced.

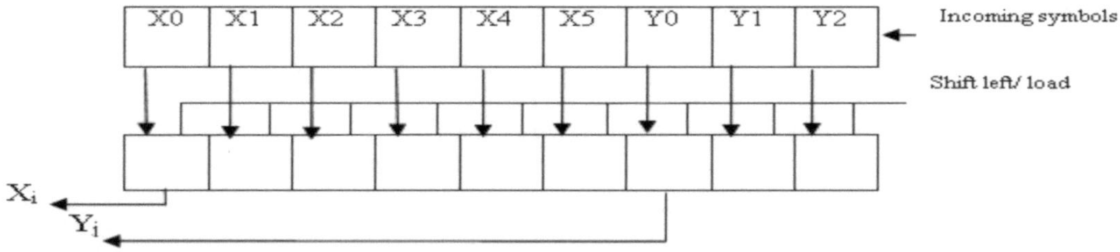


Fig. 7. the buffer.

### 3.2 Design-2:

The Design-2 was first proposed in (Hwang & Wu, 2001). The space-time diagram and its array architecture are given in Fig. 8. It consists of $L_s$ process elements. The match element $Y_j$s stay in the PEs, and $X_i$ and $L_i$ both flow leftwards with delays of 1 and 2 clock cycles, respectively. The first $L_i$ from the leftmost PE will be obtained after 2* $L_s$ clock cycles. After that, one $L_i$ will be obtained every clock cycle. The block diagram of the Design-2 PE is shown in Fig. 9.

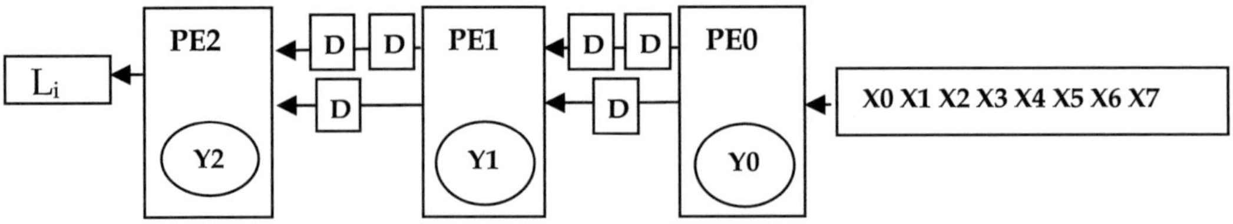


| Li | PE2 | PE1 | PE0 | Time |
|---|---|---|---|---|
| | | | L0<br>X0-Y0 | 1 |
| | | | L1<br>X1-Y0 | 2 |
| | | L0<br>X1-Y1 | L2<br>X2-Y0 | 3 |
| | | L1<br>X2-Y1 | L3<br>X3-Y0 | 4 |
| | L0<br>X2-Y2 | L2<br>X3-Y1 | L4<br>X4-Y0 | 5 |
| L0 | L1<br>X3-Y2 | L3<br>X4-Y1 | L5<br>X5-Y0 | 6 |
| L1 | L2<br>X4-Y2 | L4<br>X5-Y1 | | 7 |
| L2 | L3<br>X5-Y2 | L5<br>X6-Y1 | | 8 |
| L3 | L4<br>X6-Y2 | | | 9 |
| L4 | L5<br>X7-Y2 | | | 10 |
| L5 | | | | 11 |

Fig. 8. Design- 2 space- time diagram and array.

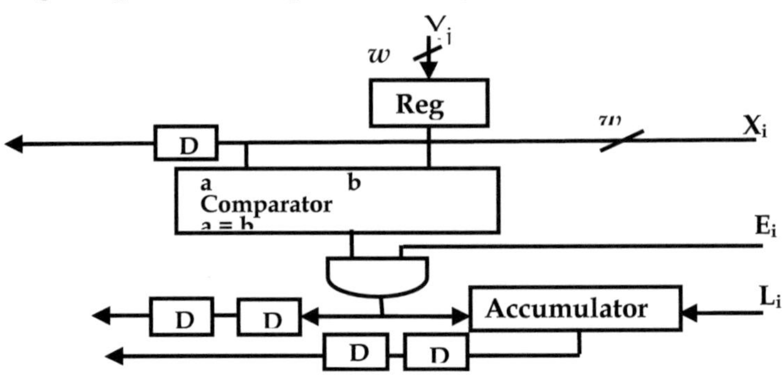


Fig. 9. The structure of Design- 2 PE.

### 3.3 Design-3:

Design-3 was proposed in (Ranganathan & Henriques, 1993). The space-time diagram and the resulting array are given in Fig. 10. The value of $Y_i$ stays in the PE. The buffer element $X_i$ moves systolically from right to left with delay of 2 clocks. $L_i$ propagates from right to left with 1 clock cycle. The first $L_i$ from the leftmost PE will be obtained after $L_s$ clock cycles. After that, the subsequent ones will be obtained every clock cycle. The structure of Design-3 PE is shown in Fig. 11. MRB is needed to determine $L_{max}$ and $Ip$.

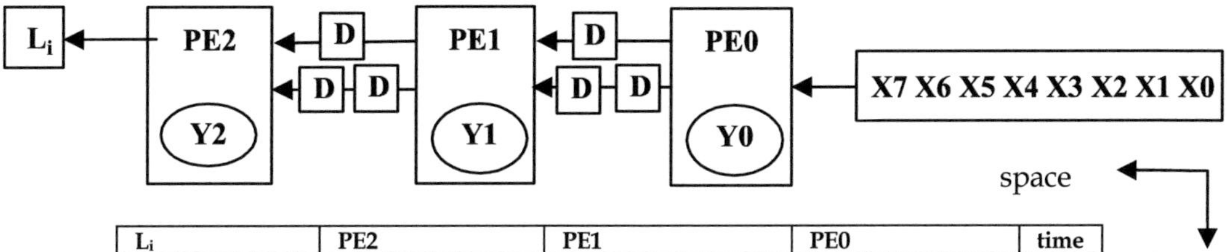


| $L_i$ | PE2 | PE1 | PE0 | time |
|---|---|---|---|---|
| | | | X5-Y0 $L_5$ | 1 |
| | | X6-Y1 $L_5$ | X4-Y0 $L_4$ | 2 |
| | X7-Y2 $L_5$ | X5-Y1 $L_4$ | X3-Y0 $L_3$ | 3 |
| $L_5$ | X6-Y2 $L_4$ | X4-Y1 $L_3$ | X2-Y0 $L_2$ | 4 |
| $L_4$ | X5-Y2 $L_3$ | X3-Y1 $L_2$ | X1-Y0 $L_1$ | 5 |
| $L_3$ | X4-Y2 $L_2$ | X2-Y1 $L_1$ | X0-Y0 $L_0$ | 6 |
| $L_2$ | X3-Y1 $L_1$ | X1-Y1 $L_0$ | | 7 |
| $L_1$ | X2-Y2 $L_0$ | | | 8 |
| $L_0$ | | | | 9 |

Fig. 10. The space-time diagram and the resulting array of Design-3.

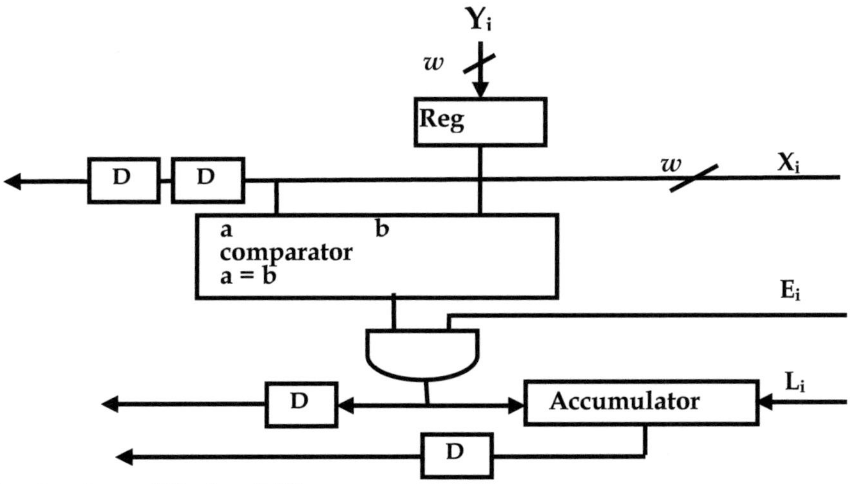


Fig. 11. The structure of Design-3 PE.

### 3.4 The Interleaved Design:

From the dependency graph shown in Fig. 4, the interleaved design is obtained by projecting all the nodes in a particular raw to a single processor element. This design was first proposed in (Hwang & Wu, 2001). The space–time diagram and the resulting array of the interleaved design are given in Fig. 12. The $Y_j$s which need to be accessed in parallel do not change during the encoding step. The special buffer is needed to generate the interleaving symbols of $X_i$ and $X_{i+[n-Ls/2]}$ as shown in Fig. 13. The first $L_i$ will be obtained after $L_s$ clock cycles from the leftmost PE and subsequent ones will be obtained every one clock cycle.

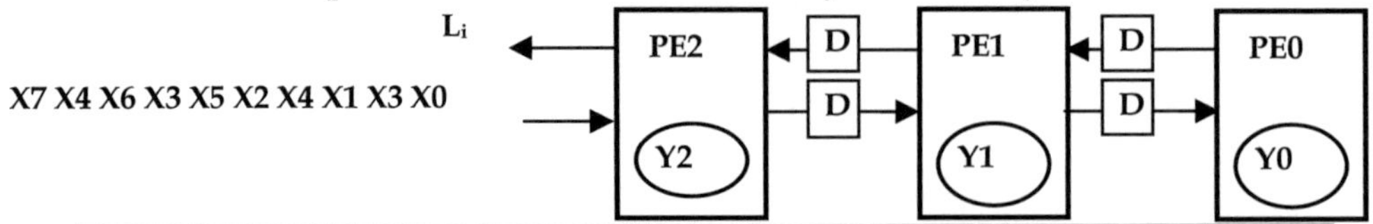


| $L_i$ | PE2 | PE1 | PE0 | time |
|---|---|---|---|---|
| | | | X0-Y0<br>$L_0$ | 1 |
| | | X1-Y1<br>$L_0$ | X3-Y0<br>$L_3$ | 2 |
| | X2-Y2<br>$L_0$ | X4-Y1<br>$L_3$ | X1-Y0<br>$L_1$ | 3 |
| $L_0$ | X5-Y2<br>$L_3$ | X2-Y1<br>$L_1$ | X4-Y0<br>$L_4$ | 4 |
| $L_3$ | X3-Y2<br>$L_1$ | X5-Y1<br>$L_4$ | X2-Y0<br>$L_2$ | 5 |
| $L_1$ | X6-Y2<br>$L_4$ | X3-Y1<br>$L_2$ | X5-Y0<br>$L_5$ | 6 |
| $L_4$ | X4-Y1<br>$L_2$ | X6-Y1<br>$L_5$ | | 7 |
| L2 | X7-Y2<br>$L_5$ | | | 8 |
| $L_5$ | | | | 9 |

Fig. 12. The space-time diagram and the resulting array of interleaved design.

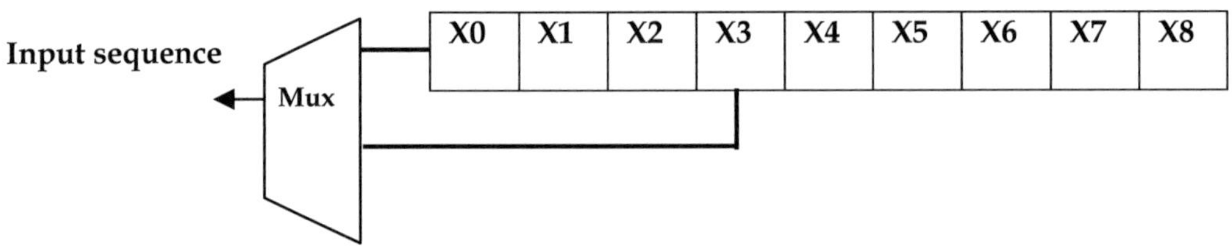


Fig. 13. buffer design for generating the interleaving symbols.

Before the encoding process, the $Y_i$s are preloaded which take $L_s$ extra cycles. During the encoding process, the time to preload new source symbols depend on how many source symbols were compressed in the previous compression step, $L_{max}$. The block diagram of the processor element is shown in Fig. 14.

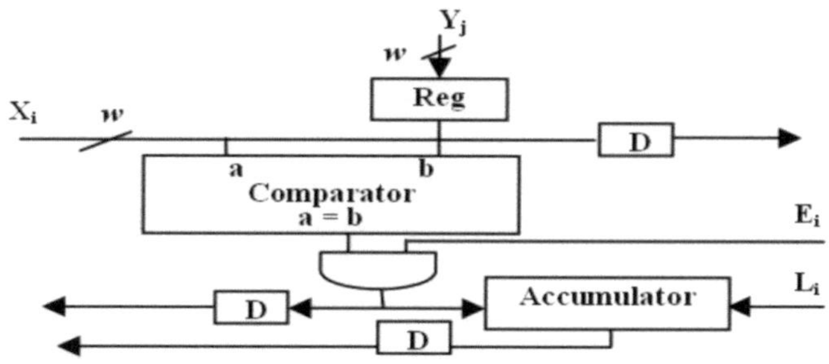


Fig. 14. The block diagram of interleaved design PE.

Match results block MRB is needed to determine $L_{max}$ among the serially produced $L_i$s. MRB is shown in Fig. 15. The PEs do not need to store their ids to record the position of the $L_i$s. A special counter is needed to generate the sequence which interleaves the position of the first half of $L_i$s and the position for the second half as shown in Fig. 16. The compression time of the interleaved design is $n$ clock cycles.

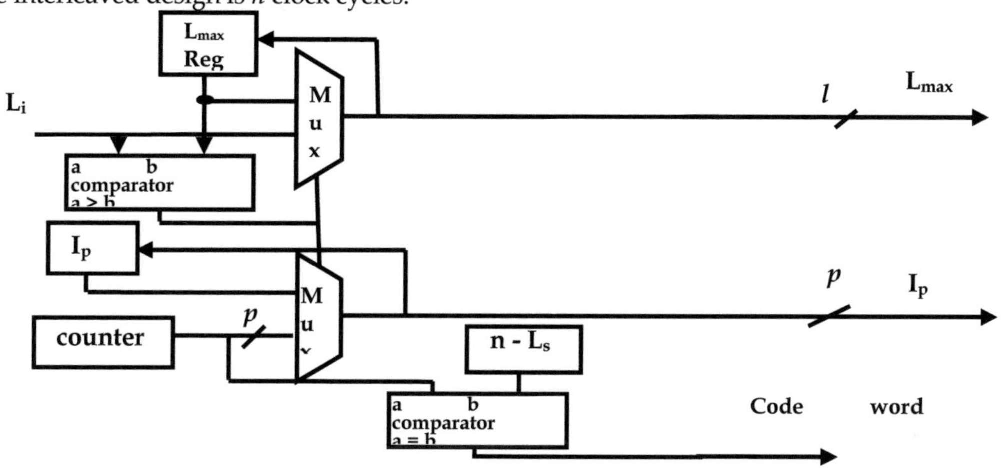


Fig. 15. the match results block

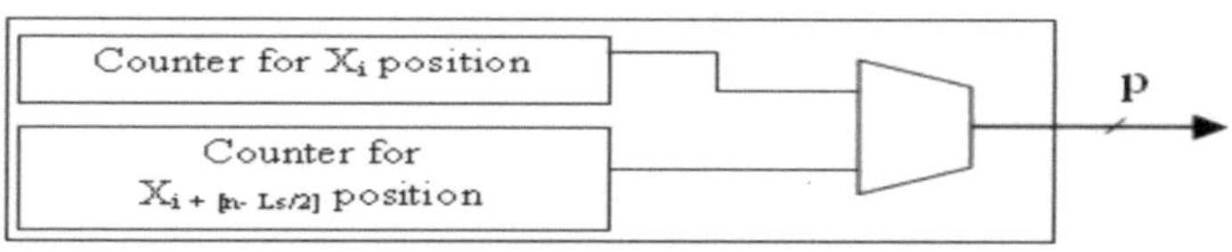


Fig. 16. Special position counter in MRB for interleaved Design.

### 3.5 Proposed Design (Design- P)

From the dependence graph shown in Fig. 4, all the nodes in a particular row are projected to a single processor element (Abd El Ghany, 2007). This produces an array of length $Ls$. The space- time diagram and the resulting array of Design-P are given in Fig. 17, where D represents a unit delay on the signal line between two processing elements.

As shown in Fig. 17, the architecture consists of $L_s$ processing elements which are used for the comparison and L-encoder which is used to produce the matching length. Consequently, the look-ahead buffer symbols $Y_j$s which do not change during the encoding step, stay in PEs.

The dictionary element $X_i$ moves systolically from left to right with a delay of 1 clock cycle. The match signal $E_i$ of the processing element moves to the L-encoder. The output $L_i$ of the encoder is the matching length resulting from the comparisons at step *i-1*. The first $L_i$ will be obtained after one clock cycle and the subsequent ones will be obtained every clock cycle. Before the encoding process, the $Y_i$s are preloaded to be processed and this takes $L_s$ extra cycles. During the encoding process, the time to preload new source symbols depends upon how many source symbols were compressed in the previous compression step, $L_{max}$.
The functional block of the PE is shown in Fig. 18. Only one equality comparator is needed for comparing $Y_j$ and incoming $X_i$. The comparator result $E_i$ (match signal) propagates to L-encoder. The block diagram of L- encoder is shown in Fig. 19. According to $E_i$s (match signals), L-encoder computes the match length $L_i$ corresponding to position *i*.

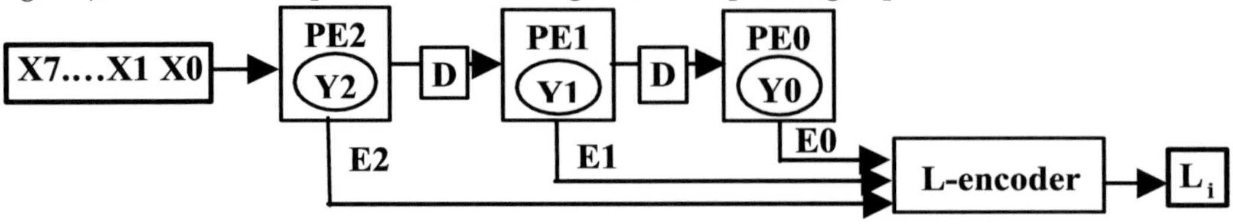


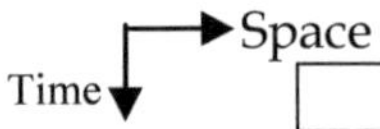


| | PE2 | PE1 | PE0 | $L_i$ |
|---|---|---|---|---|
| 1 | X2-Y0 | X1-Y1 | X0-Y0 | |
| 2 | X3-Y0 | X2-Y1 | X1-Y0 | L0 |
| 3 | X4-Y0 | X3-Y1 | X2-Y0 | L1 |
| 4 | X5-Y0 | X4-Y1 | X3-Y0 | L2 |
| 5 | X6-Y0 | X5-Y1 | X4-Y0 | L3 |
| 6 | X7-Y0 | X6-Y1 | X5-Y0 | L4 |
| 7 | | | | L5 |

Fig. 17. Architecture of Design-P.

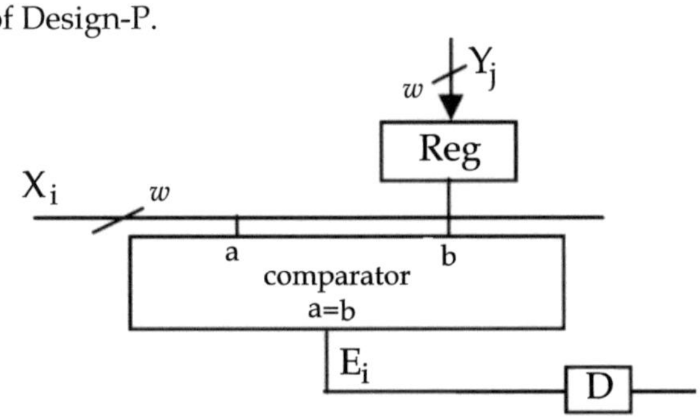


Fig. 18. The functional block of Design-P PE.

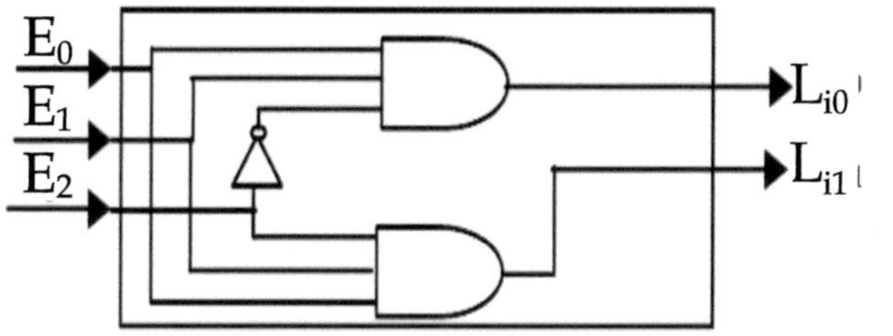


Fig. 19. L-encode

As shown in Fig. 17, it is clear that the maximum matching length is not produced by the L-encoder. So, a match results block (MRB) is needed, as shown in Fig. 20, to determine $L_{max}$ among the serially produced $L_i$s. Also, the PEs need not store their ids to record the position of the $L_i$s *(Ip)*. Since *p = [log2(n-Ls)]* bits are required to represent *Ip*, only a *p-* bit counter is required to provide the position *i* associated with each $L_i$, since the time when $L_i$ is produced corresponds to its position. MRB uses a comparator to compare the current input $L_i$ and the present longest match length $L_{max}$ stored in the register. If the current input $L_i$ is larger than $L_{max}$, then $L_i$ is loaded into the register and the content of the position counter is also loaded into another register which is used to store the present *Ip*. Another comparator is used to determine whether the whole window has been searched. It compares the content of the position counter with $n- L_s$, whose output is used as the codeword - ready signal. During the searching process, $L_i$ might be equal to $L_s$ when $I< n- L_s$, i.e., the content in the look-ahead buffer can be fully matched to a subset of the dictionary, and hence searching the whole window is not always necessary. An extra comparator is used to determine whether $L_{max}$ is equal to $L_s$, and hence the string matching process is completed. Therefore, encoding a new set of data could start immediately. This will reduce the average compression time. The number of clock cycles needed to produce a codeword is $[(n-L_s) + 1]$ clock cycles, so the utilization rate of each PE is $(n-L_s) / [(n-L_s) + 1]$, which almost equals to one. This result is consistent since the PE is busy once $L_i$ is determined until the time at which the codeword is produced.

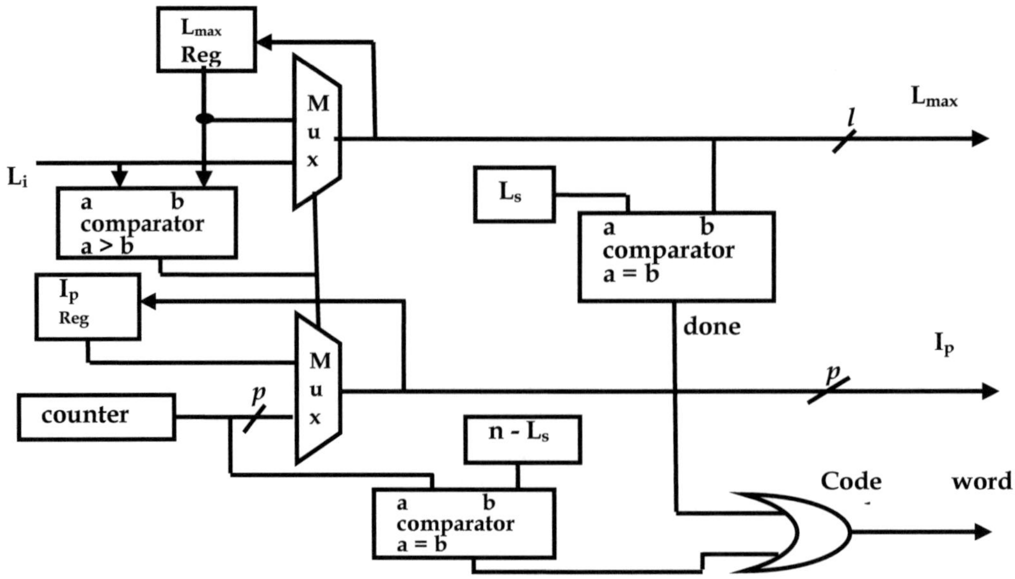


Fig. 20. The match results block (MRB) for design-P.

Parallel compression can be achieved by using an appropriate number of Design- P modules. For example, two modules of Design– P can be used, as shown in Fig. 21. The input sequence of the first module (Xi) is obtained from the first position of Buffer. The input sequence of the second module ($X_{i+[(n-Ls)/2]}$) is obtained starting at *((n –Ls)/2 )* position in the Dictionary. Note that the MRB now needs to determine $L_{max}$ among LI, LII that are produced at the same time. So, the MRB could be modified. The speed is two times the Design –P array.

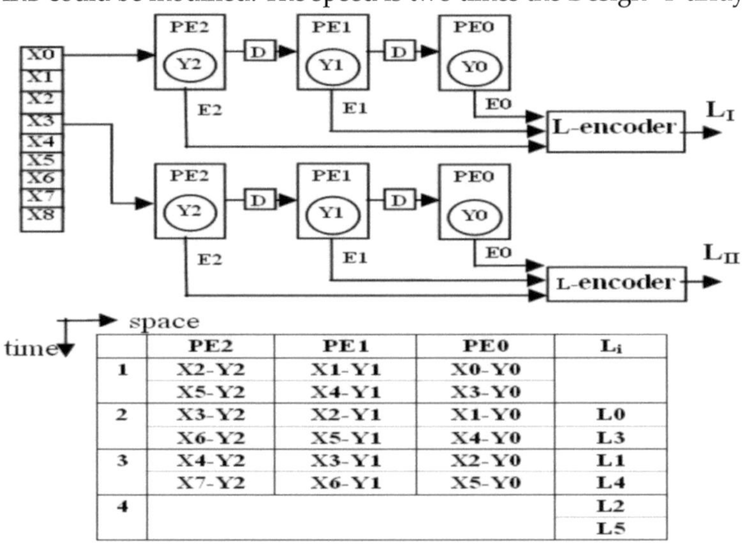


| | PE2 | PE1 | PE0 | Li |
|---|---|---|---|---|
| 1 | X2-Y2 | X1-Y1 | X0-Y0 | |
| | X5-Y2 | X4-Y1 | X3-Y0 | |
| 2 | X3-Y2 | X2-Y1 | X1-Y0 | L0 |
| | X6-Y2 | X5-Y1 | X4-Y0 | L3 |
| 3 | X4-Y2 | X3-Y1 | X2-Y0 | L1 |
| | X7-Y2 | X6-Y1 | X5-Y0 | L4 |
| 4 | | | | L2 |
| | | | | L5 |

Fig. 21. Parallel compression.

## 4. The design comparison

The comparison of four designs is given in Table 2. The Design-1 contains *n- Ls* processing elements, which are always active, resulting in a large area and high- power consumption. It is also slower than the others. Design-P has the maximum utilization rate, minimum latency time (high compression speed) and minimum area for LZ.

| | Interleaved Design | Design-P | Design-1 | Design-2 | Design-3 |
|---|---|---|---|---|---|
| **Number of PEs** | $L_s$ | $L_s$ | $n - L_s$ | $L_s$ | $L_s$ |
| **Utilization** | $(n-L_s)/ n$ | $(n-L_s)/ (n-L_s+ 1)$ | $L_s /2(n-L_s)$ | $(n-L_s)/ (n+L_s-1)$ | $(n-L_s)/ n$ |
| **Latency** | $n$ | $n- L_s+ 1$ | $2 (n -L_s)+1$ | $n+L_s-1$ | $n$ |
| **DFFs per PE** | $2w+l+1$ | $2w + 1$ | $3w+l+2p+1$ | $2w+2l+2$ | $3w+l+1$ |
| **accumulator Per PE** | 1 | --- | 1 | 1 | 1 |
| **Counter per MRB** | 2 | 1 | --- | 2 | 2 |
| **Multiplexer per MRB** | 3 | 2 | --- | 3 | 3 |
| **Multiplexer per buffer** | 1 | --- | --- | --- | --- |
| **Equality comparator per MRB** | 1 | 2 | --- | 1 | 1 |

Table 2. The comparison between Design-P and Design-i.

## 5. FPGA Implementation

In this section, the proposed architecture for LZ is implemented on FPGA. As shown in Fig. 22, the architecture consists of 3 major components: systolic-array LZ component (SALZC), block RAM, and host controller. The length of window (n) is assumed to be 1K, and the length of look-ahead buffer ($L_s$) is assumed to be 16. SALZ component contains 16 PEs and implements the most cost effective array architecture (Design -P). Full - custom layout is straight forward since the array is very regular. Only a single cell (PE) was hand - laid out. The other 15 PEs are copies of it. Since the array is systolic, routing also is simplified. Block RAM that is used as the data buffer (Dictionary) is not included in SALZ component. Thereby, the dictionary length can be increased by directly replacing the block RAM with a larger one. The dictionary length is a parameter to cover a broad range of applications, from text compression to lossless image compression.

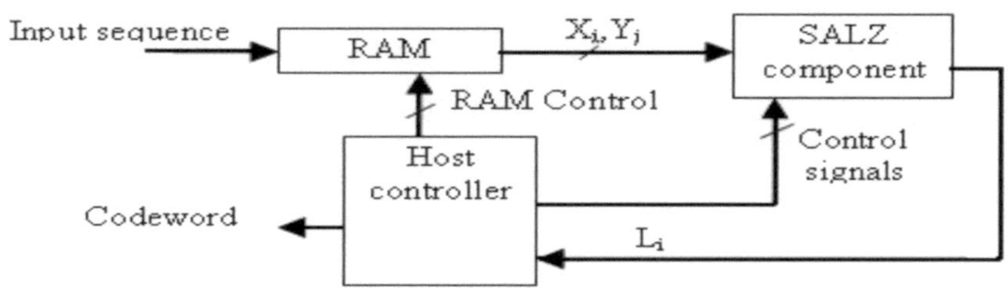


Fig. 22. LZ compression chip

The implementation of the proposed design (Design-P) and interleaved design (Design-i) are carried out using XILINX (Spartan II XC200) FPGA, for $n$= 1 k, $L_s$=16, $w$ =8. The implementation results are shown in Table 3. The number of components and their percentage as compared with the available components on the chip are calculated.
The compression rate of a compressor is defined as the number of input bits which can be compressed in one second. The compression rate (Rc) can be estimated as follows:

$$Rc = clk \times [(LsW)/(n-L_s+1)] \qquad (2)$$

Where clk is the operating frequency. Note that only estimated $Rc$ can be obtained, since it depends on the input data. It is not possible to predict exactly how many words will be compressed ($L_s$ at most) and how many clock cycles will be required $((n - L_s + 1)$ at most) for every compression step. In the proposed implementation, if the window length $(n)$ is 1k, $L_s$ =16, $w$ =8, and $clk$ = 105 MHz, The $Rc$ is 13 M bit per second.

| | Number of Slices | | Number of Slice Flip Flops | | Number of 4 input LUTs | | Number of BRAMs | | Maximum Frequency |
|---|---|---|---|---|---|---|---|---|---|
| **Design-P** | 310 | 13% | 408 | 8% | 419 | 8% | 2 | 14% | 105 MHz |
| **Design-i** | 471 | 20% | 511 | 10% | 650 | 13% | 2 | 14% | 79 MHz |

Table 3. The implementation results of Design-P and Design-i

In order to use the parallel scheme to increase the compression rate, the host controller could be modified and an appropriate number of LZ compressor components could be connected in parallel, as shown in Fig. 23. Note that, the MRB now needs to determine $L_{max}$ among $L_I$, $L_{II}$ and $L_{III}$. e.g., ten components could be implemented in one chip of large size to achieve a compression rate about 130 M bits per second. Moreover, by modifying the host controller and including, e.g., dictionaries, the proposed design can be used for other string-matching based LZ algorithms, such as LZ78 and LZW. The Design-P is flexible.

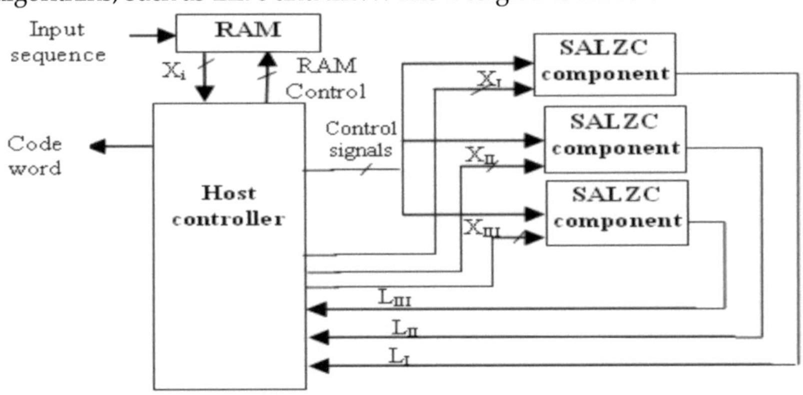


Fig. 23. Multiple SALZC system.

## 6. Conclusions

In this chapter, a parallel algorithm for LZ based data compression is described by transforming a data-dependent algorithm to a data - independent regular algorithm. To further improve the latency, a control variable to indicate early completion is used. The proposed implementation is area and speed efficient. The compression rate is increased by more than 40% and the design area is decreased by more than 30%. The design can be integrated into real - time systems so that data can be compressed and decompressed on - the - fly.

## 7. References


Abd El Ghany, M. A.; Salama, A. E. & Khalil, A. H. "Design and Implementation of FPGA-based Systolic Array for LZ Data Compression" *in Proc. IEEE International Symposium on Circuits and Systems* ISCAS'07, May 2007

Arias, M.; Cumplido, R. & Feregrino C., (2004) "On the Design and Implementation of an FPGA-based Lossless Data Compressor.", *ReConFig'04,* Colima, Mexico, Sep., 2004

Bodden, E.; Clasen, M.; Kneis, J. & Schluter, R., (2004) "Arithmetic coding revealed" pp. 8-57, May 2004

Chang, J.; Jih, H. J & Liu, J. W., (1994) "A lossless data compression processor," in *Proc. 4th VLSI Design/CAD Workshop,* Aug. 1994, pp.134-137

Deorowicz, S., (2003) "Universal lossless data compression algorithms" *Dissertation, Silesian University,* pp 92-119, 2003

Gallager, R. (1978)"Variations on a theme by Huffman," *IEEE Trans. Inform. Theory,* vol. IT-24, pp. 668-674, 1978

Golomb, S., (1966) "Run-length encoding," *IEEE Trans. Inform. Theory,* Vol. IT-12, pp. 399-401, July 1966

Howard, P. G. & Vetter, J. S., (1992) "Practical Implementations of Arithmetic Coding" *Brown University, Department of Computer Science, Technical Report No.* (CS-91-45), April 1992

Huffman, D. A. (1952) "A method for the construction of minimum-redundancy codes" *Proc. IRE,* Vol. 40, pp. 1098-1101, September, 1952.

Hwang, S. -A & Wu, C. -W., (2001) "Unified VLSI Systolic Array Design for LZ Data compression," *IEEE Trans. VLSI Systems,* vol. 9, pp. 489- 499, August 2001

Jung, B. & Burleson, W. P., (1998) "Efficient VLSI for Lempel-Ziv compression in wireless data communication networks," *IEEE Trans. VLSI Syst.* Vol. 6, pp. 475-483, Sept. 1998

Lin, K. -J. & Wu, C.-W., (2000) "A low-power CAM design for LZ data compressor," *IEEE Transactions on Computers,* Vol.49, No.10, pp. 1139-1145, Oct. 2000

Ranganathan, N. & Henriques, S., (1993) "High-Speed VLSI Designs for Lempel-Ziv-Based Data Compression," *IEEE Trans. Circuits and Systems. II: Analog and Digital Signal Processing,* vol. 40, pp.96-106, Feb. 1993

Park, H. & Prasanna, V.K. (1993) "Area efficient VLSI architectures for Huffman coding", *IEEE Trans. Analog and Digital Signal Processing,* Vol.40, pp.568-575,Sep.1993

Said, A., (2003), "Fast Arithmetic Coding," in *Lossless Compression Handbook,* 2003

Said, A., (2004) " Introduction to Arithmetic coding - Theory and Practice" *Imaging Systems Laboratory,* HP Laboratories Palo Alto, April 2004

Salomon, D., (2004) "Data Compression" *The complete reference,* Computer Science Department, California State University, Northridge, pp. 22-205, 2004

Sandoval, M. M. & Uribe, C. F. (2005) "A hardware Architecture for Elliptic Curve Cryptography and Lossless Data Compression," *IEEE Computer Society,* May 2005

Welch, T., (1984) "A technique for high-performance data compression," *IEEE computer*, Vol. 17, pp. 8-19, 1984
Ziv, J. & Lempel, A., (1977) "A universal algorithm for sequential data compression," *IEEE Trans. Inform. Theory*, Vol. IT-23, pp. 337-343, 1977
Ziv, J. & Lempel, A., (1978) "Compression of individual sequences via variable rate coding," *IEEE Trans. Inform. Theory*, Vol. IT-24, pp. 530-536, 1978

6

# Design of Simple and High Speed Scheme to Protect Mass Storages

Ming-Haw Jing, Yan-Haw Chen, Zih-Heng Chen,
Jian-Hong Chen and Yaotsu Chang
*I-Shou University*
*Taiwan, R.O.C.*

## 1. Introduction

The computer industry has entered a stage of unprecedented improvement in CPU performance. However, the speed of file system management of huge information is commonly considered as the main factor that affects the computer performance; for example, the I/O bandwidth is limited by magnetic disks. The capacity and cost of magnetic disks per megabyte have been continually improved, but the rotation speed and seek time are improved very slowly. Recently, many computers have become I/O bound in the applications of video, audio, commercial database, etc. If such an I/O crisis can be resolved, the computer system performance will be improved. In 1988, Patterson et al. proposed the redundant array of independent disks (RAID) system which allows the data to be separated into several disks (Patterson et al., 1988). We can access the data in parallel so that the throughput of I/O systems will be improved. On the other hand, more disks in RAID system have a higher risk of losing data because of high component failure rates. As a result, the safety and reliability have become the major issues in the RAID system.

When designing a highly available and reliable RAID system, the method of bit wise parity checking is mostly used to correct errors and to enhance reliability of the RAID system. However, the parity checking method is limited so that only single disk failure can be tolerated. In 1995, Blaum et al. proposed a method called even-odd code, which tolerates up to two disk failures in the RAID system (Blaum et al., 1995). Even-odd code is the first known scheme for tolerating single or double disk failures, providing an optimal solution with regard to both storage and performance. However, the major problem concerning the even-odd code is a variety of modes of operations when solving erasures or up to 2 disk failures. In practical, it is not easy to be integrated into a VSLI. On the other hand, a small write problem is difficult to be solved with the even-odd code (Liao & Jing, 2002).

In 1997, Plank proposed a tutorial by using the Reed-Solomon (RS) code to provide error correction in the RAID system (Plank, 1997). In 2000, Jing et al. also proposed a simple algorithm, called RS-RAID system, to combine the RS codes with the RAID system (Jing et al. 2000). In this chapter, we aim to improve RS codes codec to design a fast error and erasure correction for RS-RAID system, and to solve the small write problem in RS codes. In a RS decoder, there are various algorithms to solve the error locator polynomial, which affect the complexity and performance in hardware design such as the Berlekam-Massey algorithm, Euclidean algorithm, and Peterson-Gorenstein-Zierler (PGZ) algorithm (Wicker, 1995). The PGZ algorithm is mostly applied to correct less than six or seven errors because it is very simple with enhanced error tolerant capability. This chapter contributes to simplify the PGZ algorithm for single error or double erasure disks correction in the RS-RAID system by using the support of a set of combinational circuits. Its error and erasure correction become faster without the use of Chien search to find the root of the error locator polynomial, as well as the Forney method to find the error magnitudes from evaluator polynomial. Hence, this straightforward algorithm is then suitable for VLSI design.

This chapter is organized as follows: The history of RAID system is presented in Section 2. The simple RS encoder and decoder are described in Section 3. The design of small write modules of RS-RAID system is shown in Section 4. The RS-RAID system is proposed in Section 5. Finally, the result and conclusion are given in Section 6.

## 2. The Redundant Array of Independent Disks

A landmark paper, titled "A case for redundant arrays of inexpensive disks (RAID)", was presented by Patterson, Katz and Gibson in 1988 (Patterson et al., 1988). RAID systems can be configured into various ways to get a compromised result on data access speed, system reliability and size of storage. The general trade-off is to increase data access speed by writing the data into more places, which increases the amount of storage available by a factor *N*. On the other hand, more disks cause lower reliability on the disk system, leading to data redundancy and the need for additional algorithms to enhance the reliability of valuable data. There are several levels in the RAID system, such as RAID-0, RAID-1, RAID-10, RAID-2, RAID-3, RAID-4, RAID-5, RAID-6, and RAID-7. The mostly used versions for the trade-off are RAID-0, RAID-10, RAID-5, and RAID-6.

### 2.1 The RAID-0

RAID-0, as shown in Fig. 1, strips all data across multiple drives in a disk array. This is a high I/O performance solution, since it can simultaneously support many small/individual and large means of access with all disks transferring in parallel. Thus, very high data transfer rates (both reads and writes) may be achieved. RAID-0 is very suitable for I/O time critical or real time applications, such as video on demand (VoD) systems. However, RAID-0 maximizes the access speed and space available while being low in reliability. Because RAID-0 provides no data protection, the probability of disk failure increases with increasing number of disk drives. Any failing single drive will break the entire disk array.

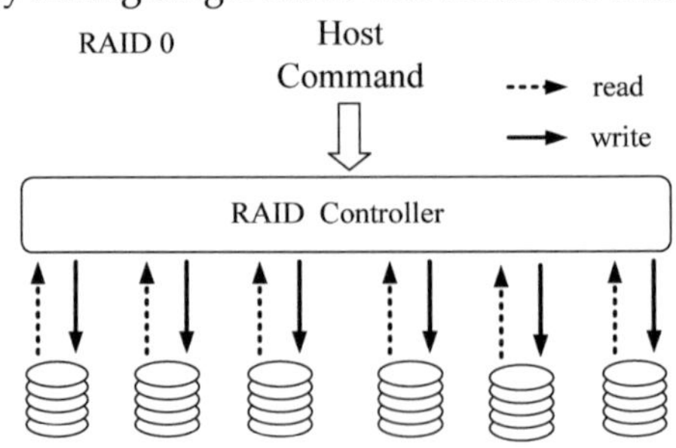


Fig. 1. The hierarchy of RAID-0

### 2.2 The RAID-1

RAID-1 writes data to two drives simultaneously in a replicated way, as shown in Fig. 2. If one drive fails, the data can still be retrieved from the counterpart of the RAID set. This process is also called "disk mirroring". Mirroring refers to the 100% duplication of data from one disk to another so that it is the most expensive RAID (double hardware storage required). It offers the advantage in reliability only. RAID-1 increases the reliability of protection of single disk failure, but doubles the cost for the available storage. RAID-1 is very suitable for both reliability and performance applications, such as OS disk and accountant data.

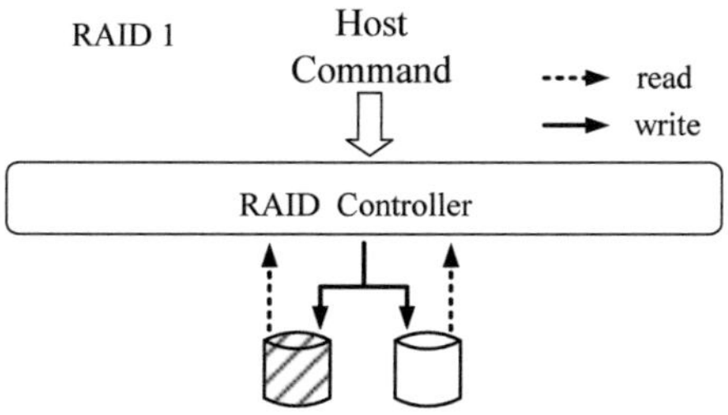


Fig. 2. The hierarchy of RAID-1

### 2.3 The RAID-10

RAID-10 is a combination of RAID-0 and RAID-1, where the data are striped and mirrored as shown in Fig. 3. This provides a higher speed and reliability, but possesses the same cost problem as RAID-1. Again, it can only tolerate single disk failure in each disk pair.

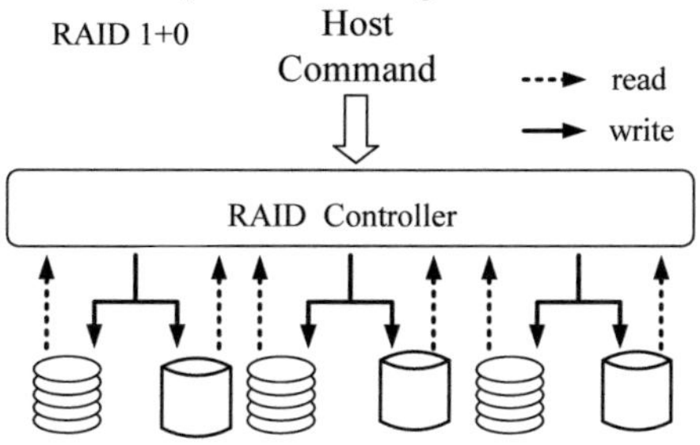


Fig. 3. The hierarchy of RAID-10

### 2.4 The RAID-5

RAID-5 uses a parity encoder to produce parity information and to provide data recovery at a low cost. The architecture of RAID-5 is shown in Fig. 4. Although one disk is added, data are striped over all disks so that large files can be fetched with high bandwidth. To balance the disk access load, a rotating parity is used. Many small random blocks can be accessed in parallel without hot spots/bottlenecks in any single disk. When a single disk fails, the data can still be reconstructed from the parity information.

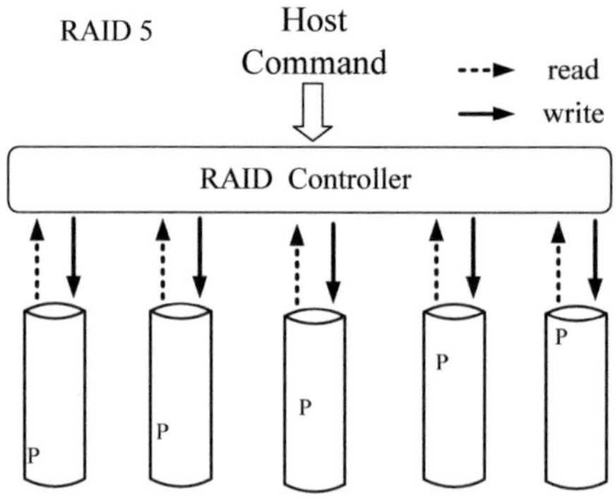


Fig. 4. The hierarchy of RAID-5

### 2.5 The RAID-6

Fig. 5 shows the model of RAID-6. RAID-6 is different from RAID-5 as it has two additional disks to recover the loss of two disks. This capability provides a higher fault tolerant capacity for disk array. The popular techniques for RAID-6 are even-odd and RS codes, which will be discussed later.

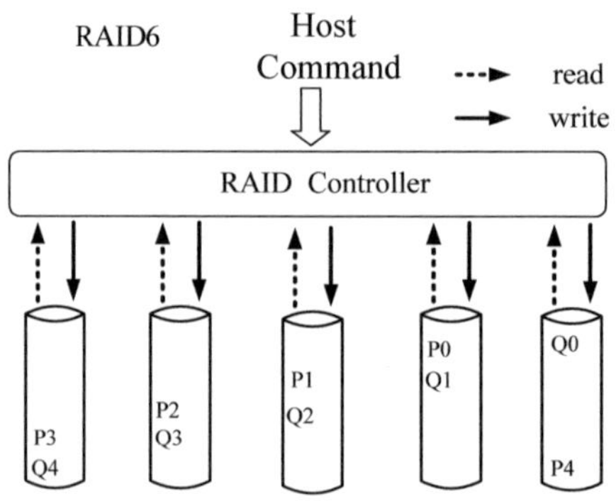


Fig. 5. The hierarchy of RAID-6

## 3. The Design of Reed-Solomon Codes for Error and Erasure Correction

The RS codes have been widely used in error control coding, especially in the applications of communication, satellite, and storage (Wicker, 1994). The RS codes have maximum distance separable (MDS) and hence can extend the largest possible minimum distance for codes of their size and dimension. In addition, RS codes are good at correcting burst errors. In the following, we discuss the basic definition of the encoder and illustrate those algorithms to correct one error or two erasure conditions using the PGZ algorithm (Wicker, 1995).

### 3.1 The Reed-Solomon Codes Encoder

The $(n, k)$ RS codes over GF($2^m$) have the capability to correct $2t = n-k$ erasures or $t$ errors, where $n$ is the total length of a codeword, $k$ is the number of information symbols in GF($2^m$), and $t$ is the number of errors that the RS codes can correct. Consider the construction of a $t$-error-correcting RS code with a length of $2^m - 1$. $2t$ consecutive powers of $\alpha$ are required as zeros of the generator polynomial $g(x)$ for the $t$-error-correcting RS code. The generator polynomial is the production of the associated minimal polynomials:

$$g(x) = \prod_{j=1}^{2t} (x + \alpha^j), \text{for } \alpha \in GF(2^m). \tag{1}$$

We define each codeword as a polynomial $C(x) = c_0 + c_1 x + \ldots + c_{n-1} x^{n-1}$. Let a message polynomial can be expressed in terms of $I(x) = i_0 + i_1 x + \ldots + i_{k-1} x^{k-1}$. The $I(x)$ can be divided by a generator polynomial $g(x)$ to obtain the remainder polynomial $d(x)$, such that an encoded codeword is

$$C(x) = I(x) \cdot x^{2t} + d(x). \tag{2}$$

### 3.2 The Reed-Solomon Codes Decoder

Since the discovery of RS codes, the efficient decoding algorithm has been highly used for the high-speed data process. Peterson provided the first decoding algorithm for binary BCH codes (Peterson, 1960). Then Peterson's algorithm was improved and extended to non-binary codes by Gorenstein and Zierler (Gorenstein & Zierler, 1961), Chien (Chien, 1964), and Forney (Forney, 1965). In the following, we discuss how to solve two erasures or one error using the PGZ algorithm, and propose a fast error and erasure correction algorithm based on the PGZ algorithm. From the example, further design for tolerating more errors or erasures may be developed when needed.

#### 3.2.1 The Syndrome Evaluation Algorithm

The syndrome evaluation is the first procedure in the error detection. Assume that a received codeword polynomial $R(x) = r_0 + r_1 x + \cdots + r_{n-1} x^{n-1}$ can be expressed in terms of the sum of the codeword polynomial $C(x)$ and the error polynomial $e(x) = e_0 + e_1 x + \cdots + e_n x^n$, denoted as

$$R(x) = C(x) + e(x), \tag{3}$$

and the syndromes are

$$S_k(x) = R(\alpha^k) = C(\alpha^k) + e(\alpha^k) \text{ for } 1 \le k \le 2t. \tag{4}$$

The $\alpha^k$ is the root of $C(x)$, so $C(\alpha^k) = 0$; consequently, the syndrome is actually a form of evaluation for the error pattern $e(x)$. If there is an error $e(x)$, the syndrome will be nonzero.

#### 3.2.2 The Design of Single Random Error Correction

In the applications of high speed storage, the requirement for single random error or double erasure correction is commonly applied. The PGZ algorithm is applied to find the error locator polynomial $\sigma(x) = 1 + \sigma_1 x + \cdots + \sigma_t x^t$. We represent the syndromes with $t$ errors in the received word as follows:

$$S_k = \sum_{i=1}^{t} Y_i X_i^k, \text{ for } 1 \le k \le 2t, \tag{5}$$

where $X_i$ is the error locator for the $i$th error and $Y_i$ is the magnitude of the $i$th error. If a random error $e_i$ has been introduced into the received word as $r_i = c_i + e_i$, the syndromes from equation (4) can be represented as

$$S_1 = R(\alpha) = e_i \cdot \alpha^i \tag{6}$$

and

$$S_2 = R(\alpha^2) = e_i \cdot \alpha^{2i} . \tag{7}$$

From equations (6) and (7), the $e_i$ can directly affect the syndromes $S_1$ and $S_2$. With single error, the error magnitude $e_i$ is substituted by $Y_i$ and the error location $\alpha^i$ is substituted by $X_i$. Rearranging the equations (6) and (7), we have

$$S_1 = Y_i \cdot X_i \tag{8}$$

and

$$S_2 = Y_i \cdot X_i^2 . \tag{9}$$

Finally, the direct solution of the error location $X_i$ and magnitude $Y_i$ are obtained from equations (8) and (9) as

$$X_i = \frac{S_2}{S_1} = S_2 \cdot S_1^{-1} \tag{10}$$

and

$$Y_i = \frac{S_1^2}{S_2} = S_1^2 \cdot S_2^{-1} . \tag{11}$$

### 3.2.3 The Design of Single or Double Erasure Correction

In the definition, the erasure means that the error location has been known. Starting from the case of double erasures, we assume those magnitudes as $Y_i$ and $Y_j$, on the $i$th and $j$th locations in the codeword, respectively, and the effected syndromes are

$$S_1 = Y_i \cdot \alpha^i + Y_j \cdot \alpha^j \tag{12}$$

and

$$S_2 = Y_i \cdot \alpha^{2i} + Y_j \cdot \alpha^{2j} . \tag{13}$$

By solving equations (12) and (13), the magnitudes can be obtained from the syndromes as

$$Y_i = \frac{S_1\alpha^j + S_2}{\alpha^{2i} + (\alpha^{i+j})} \tag{14}$$

and

$$Y_j = \frac{S_1\alpha^i + S_2}{\alpha^{2j} + (\alpha^{i+j})} . \tag{15}$$

In the event of one erasure error, $Y_i \neq 0$ and $Y_j = 0$; the syndromes become $S_1 = Y_i \cdot \alpha^i$ and $S_2 = Y_i \cdot \alpha^{2i}$. We obtain the location or $Y_i$ as

$$Y_i = \frac{S_1 + S_2}{\alpha^{2i} + \alpha^i} . \tag{16}$$

For this event, we can also use the same equation of solving double erasure errors by setting $Y_j = 0$ and $j = 0$, such that $\alpha^j = 1$; therefore, equation (16) can be substituted by equation (14). Thus, only one set of erasure module is needed.

## 4. The Design of Reed-Solomon Codes with Small Write Capability

In the design of highly reliable systems for banks, stock markets and hospitals, RAID-6 systems are normally applied. A problem that will affect the system is the frequent transactions or updating of data/information. Those frequent writing is a small amount of bytes compared with a block of record in kilo-bytes. This is called the small write problem which is an important factor that influences the performance of a RAID system. The small write problem is caused by the frequent modifications of partial codewords, and the parity bytes of each codeword also need to be updated. In other words, to update the parities, block data reading is needed for the task of partial data updating in RAID systems.
As shown in Fig. 6, in the RAID-5, assume the D0 is modified, so that the parity should be updated, too. For example, an inefficient method fetches the unused/whole data and encodes them again, causing a great delay and a serious problem on writing a small amount of data. Another smart algorithm is as follows: first, read the old D0 and old parity P and then perform exclusive-OR operation with the new data D0′ to obtain the new party P′. Second, write the new data D0′ and new parity P′ back. In this proposed algorithm, we need 2 reads and 2 writes operation to update D0.

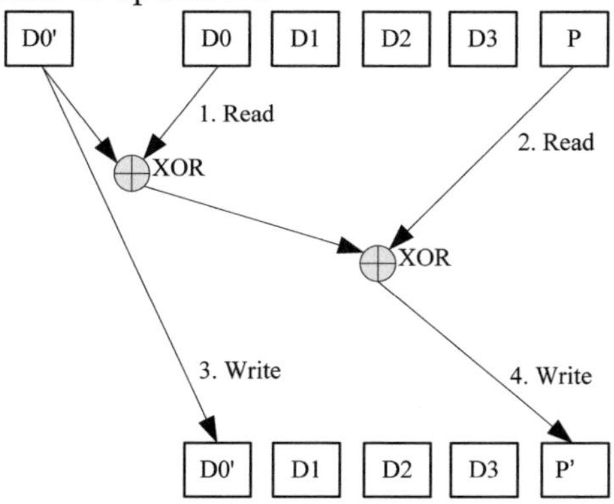


Fig. 6. The data updating for single parity

On the other hand, the RAID-6 systems have 2 parities, and the modification of parities might need to fetch a block of data to calculate the new parity. This is another inefficient method that fetches more data and performs encoding again. The proposed algorithm has limited times of access so that only the changed data can be read and the calculation of the parities is performed, such as the $c_0'$ and $c_1'$, which may be different from the original $c_0$ and $c_1$ in the encoder. Since the advance of VLSI, the proposed IP has absolutely become a combinational circuit to perform the calculation which will provide a high speed performance in the case of low delay and a simple interface to the current RAID systems, as presented in the following sections.

### 4.1 The Algorithm of Small Write Encoder

Regarding RS-RAID, according to the design of RS codes in Section 3.1, if a symbol/data in a set of codeword $C(x)$ has been modified, the original parity symbols $c_0$ and $c_1$ have to be re-encoded. Assuming the new symbol $c_i' \in C(x)$, where $2 \le i < k$, is an updated parity in the codeword $C(x)$. Take $c_i'$ as the coefficient of the new input, the encoder should generate the

correspondence parity symbols $c_0'$ and $c_1'$ to construct a new set of codeword from the original parity symbols $c_0$ and $c_1$. The fast algorithm is explained as follows.
First, the codeword C($x$) can be expressed in terms of

$$C(\alpha)=\sum_{i=0}^{n-1} c_i\alpha^i = 0 \tag{17}$$

and

$$C(\alpha^2)=\sum_{i=0}^{n-1} c_i\alpha^{2i} = 0\,. \tag{18}$$

We also know the $c_0$ and $c_1$ are parity check symbols, thus the equations (17) and (18) can be expressed in terms of

$$c_0\alpha^0 + c_1\alpha^1 = c_j\alpha^j + \sum_{i=2,i\neq j}^{n-1} c_i\alpha^i \tag{19}$$

and

$$c_0\alpha^0 + c_1\alpha^2 = c_j\alpha^{2j} + \sum_{i=2,i\neq j}^{n-1} c_i\alpha^{2i}\,. \tag{20}$$

where $j$ is the index or the location, $c_j$ is the original coefficient and $c_j'$ is the new coefficient of the updated codeword.
Secondly, the new coefficients $c_0'$ and $c_1'$ can be expressed in terms of the equations $c_0' = c_0 + \Delta_0$ and $c_1' = c_1 + \Delta_1$ . In a similar manner, $c_j' = c_j + \Delta_j$ , where $\Delta_j$ stands for the differences between the original and new coefficients of the $j$th symbol in the codeword. Since $\Delta_j$ is known, we need to solve $\Delta_0$ and $\Delta_1$ so that we can substitute $\Delta_0$, $\Delta_1$ and $\Delta_j$ into equations (19) and (20); therefore, we have

$$(c_0+\Delta_0)\alpha^0 + (c_1+\Delta_1)\alpha^1 = (c_j+\Delta_j)\alpha^j + \sum_{i=2.i\neq j}^{n-1} c_i\alpha^i \tag{21}$$

and

$$(c_0+\Delta_0)\alpha^0 + (c_1+\Delta_1)\alpha^2 = (c_j+\Delta_j)\alpha^{2j} + \sum_{i=2.i\neq j}^{n-1} c_i\alpha^{2i}\,. \tag{22}$$

To solve the $\Delta_0$ and $\Delta_1$, subtract equation (19) from equation (21) and use the same way on equations (20) and (22); we obtain

$$\Delta_0\alpha^0 + \Delta_1\alpha^1 = \Delta_j\alpha^j \tag{23}$$

and

$$\Delta_0\alpha^0 + \Delta_1\alpha^2 = \Delta_j\alpha^{2j}\,. \tag{24}$$

From the equations (23) and (24), it is found that we do not need the whole codeword to generate the new set of parity symbols. This is the key to calculate the new parity symbols on line. To solve $\Delta_0$ and $\Delta_1$, the set of equations in equations (23) and (24) can be solved simultaneously, and we have

$$\Delta_1 = (c_j' - c_j)\frac{(\alpha^j + \alpha^{2j})}{(\alpha + \alpha^2)}\,. \tag{25}$$

Finally, the new parity check coefficient $c_1'$ can be expressed in terms of

$$c_1' = (c_j' - c_j)\frac{(\alpha^j + \alpha^{2j})}{(\alpha + \alpha^2)} + c_1\,. \tag{26}$$

Extending this representation to the new parity check coefficient $c_0'$, we obtain

$$c_0' = (c_j' - c_j)\alpha^j + (c_j' - c_j)\frac{(\alpha^j + \alpha^{2j})\alpha}{(\alpha + \alpha^2)} + c_0\,. \tag{27}$$

This proves the decoder without a sequential stream of data. If all the elements are over GF($2^8$), equations (26) and (27) can be rearranged to obtain

$$c_1' = (c_j' - c_j)(\alpha^j + \alpha^{2j})\alpha^{229} + c_1 \tag{28}$$

and

$$c_0' = (c_j' - c_j)(\alpha^j + (\alpha^j + \alpha^{2j})\alpha^{230}) + c_0\,. \tag{29}$$

By observing equations (28) and (29), we have a combinational circuit to construct a VLSI module to finally realize this function.

## 5. The RS-RAID System Design

Based on the explanations in Sections 3 and 4, the basic modules of RS codes are included to develop a reliable disk system, or RS-RAID system. The RS-RAID system design not just tolerates up to two or more disks failure but also corrects error(s) and erasures transparently. Transparency features high speed and real-time processes without complicated software control. This section will discuss the design of this RS-RAID system from its operation to system architecture.

### 5.1 System Design

In regard to modern mass storage systems, there are usually ten or more disks in the RAID system with less reliability or a higher risk of data loss. A reliable storage system must satisfy the following requirements:

1. High-performance disk failure recovery: It not just features high-speed access but also tolerates up to two or more disks failure.
2. Low recovery time: When one or more disks are not returning data within a limited period of time, the system control assumes that the disk(s) is/are slow disk(s) and solves its original information from the existing data/codeword. This strategy must be realized with low access or recovery time and speed up the system performance.
3. High confidence on individual disk: The disk can identify whether its data are reliable or not.

Aiming to meet the above requirements, we first use CRC 32 as part of the major checking data to judge the health of data disks. The rate of miss checking using CRC 32 is comparatively low. Secondly, a Reed-Solomon Product Code (RS-PC) is proposed with the support of CRC 32 checking bits to construct a highly reliable RS-RAID. The RS-PC is a combination of two $(n, k)$ RS codes, denoted by inner-codes $C_{row}$ and outer-codes $C_{col}$. The $C_{row}$ and $C_{col}$ codes are presented as the parity symbols of line blocks in row and column directions, as shown in Fig. 7. The codes $C_{row}$ and $C_{col}$ are combined for double protection, which is a "check-on-check" of the RS-PC to enhance the error-correcting capability. Since the two parity symbols are utilized as the line blocks in rows and columns, the architecture of RS-RAID is then partitioned into dual levels, namely the system level and disk level, as shown in Fig. 8.

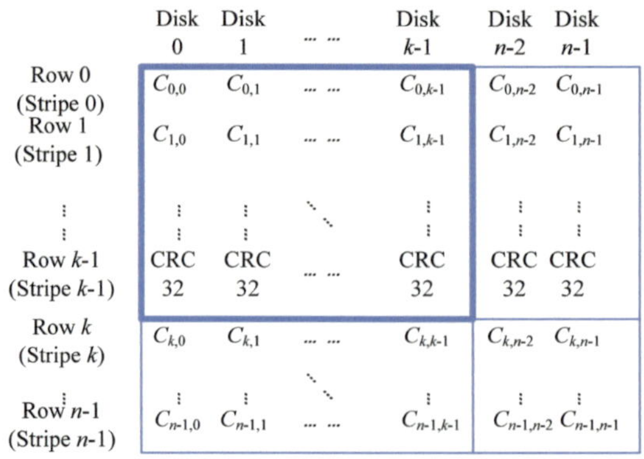


Fig. 7. The format of Reed-Solomon product code

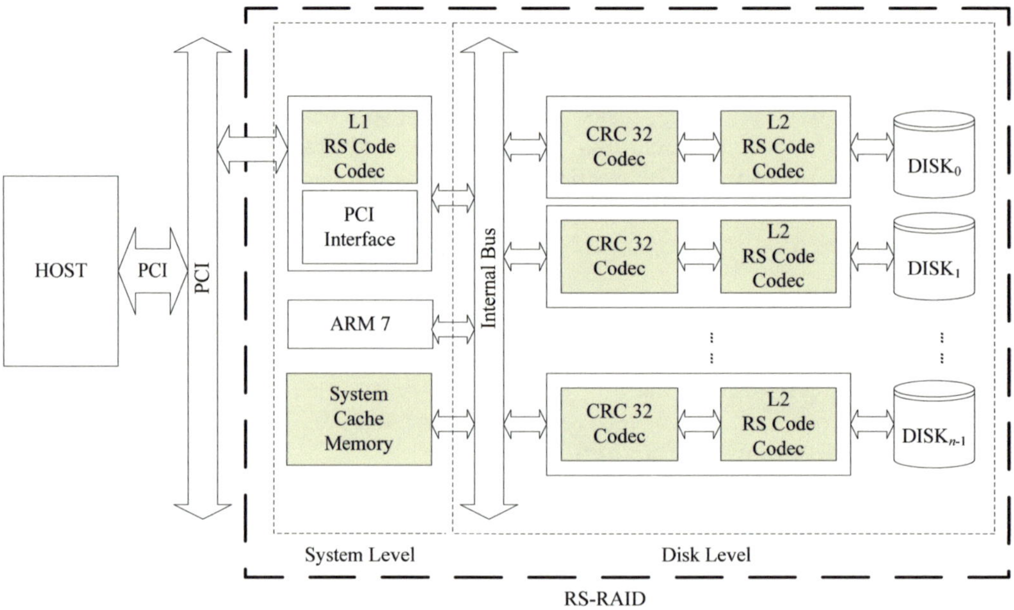


Fig. 8. The architecture of RS-RAID

In this design, all disks are considered as large logical/unified storage. The host can access the data in RS-RAID through the IDE or SCSI interface. At the system level, there are $n$ disks, and all data are encoded and decoded by L1 (level one) RS-code codec through the PC interface. This design guarantees the reliability of data reading from the large logical disk. System Cache memory, which temporarily stores the data encoded from L1 RS-code codec, is used to buffer the currently used data. Cache buffer will improve the RS-RAID performance in frequent access to/from the system.

At the disk level, each disk has $n$ stripes space. When the data are read from a disk, they are decoded by L2 (level two) RS-code codec and then checked by CRC 32 codec. If the amount of errors is too many for the correcting capability of L2 RS-code codec, this situation will be detected by CRC 32 codec. This guarantees the data reading from individual disk in a reliable condition. This system has advantages such as high capacity, throughput and reliability, because all encoding/decoding processes are operating in real time.

### 5.2 System Operation

For easier explanations, the operation of the system is based on the concept of the error correction design. The operations in dual levels can enhance the system reliability and increase the number of errors tolerated in the system.

#### 5.2.1 The System Level

At the system level, the L1 RS-code codec can be partitioned into the encoder and the decoder parts, as shown in Fig. 9. When bulk write from the host is performed, the information of stripe $u$ can be expressed in terms of $I_u(x)=\{i_{k-1},i_{k-2},\ldots,i_0\}$ and encoded into a inner-code $C_{cow_u}(x)=\{c_{u,n-1},c_{u,n-2},\ldots,c_{u,0}\}$ for each tripe of data, where $0\le u<n$, $n$ is the number of total disks in system, and $k$ is the number of data disks. When the frequently rewritten data are sent to the system cache sequentially from the host, the $c_0'$ and $c_1'$ become new parity symbols and must be updated in real time, as shown in Fig. 9.

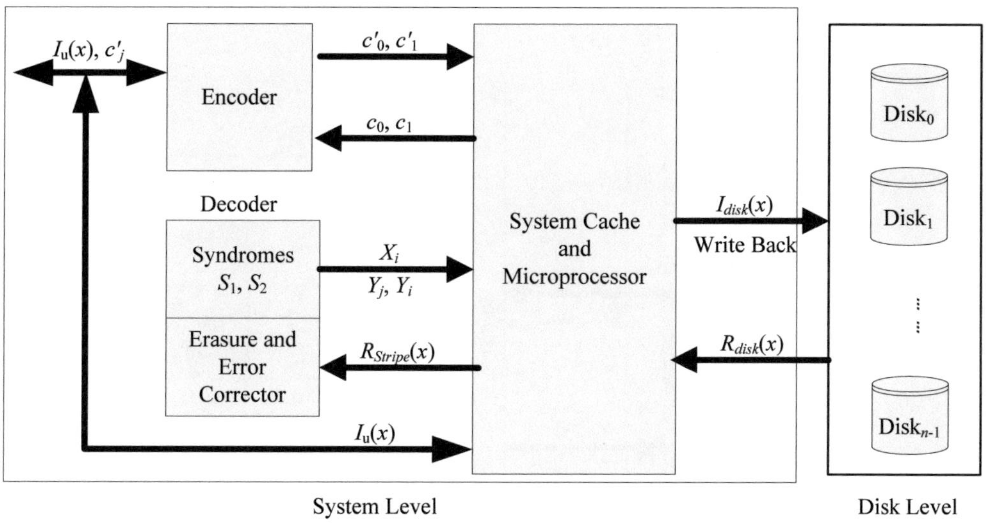


Fig. 9. The RS codes codec block diagram of system level

Before being written back to disks, all data are temporarily stored into system cache. During write back, the data are firstly encoded into the outer-code $C_{col_v}(x)=\{c_{n-1,v},c_{n-2,v},\ldots,c_{0,v}\}$ for each disk, where $0\le v<n$, and $n$ is the stripes of a disk.

When read from an unreliable disk or communication channel, the received data from disk $R_{disk}(x)=\{R_{n-1},R_{n-2},\ldots,R_0\}$ are decoded into $I_{disk}(x)=\{I_{n-1},I_{n-2},\ldots,I_0\}$ and stored as inner-code $C_{row}$ in system cache. When read from cache, the inner-code $C_{row}$ can be represented in terms of stripe $R_{stripe_u}(x)=\{r_{u,n-1},r_{u,n-2},\ldots,r_{u,0}\}$, where $0 \le u < n$, and $n$ is the total number of disks. Decoding $R_{stripe}(x)$, from the previous research in (Jing et al. 2001), the procedure is as follows:

A. $R_{stripe_u}(x)$ is firstly sent to the error corrector and generates its syndromes $S_1$ and $S_2$ for error checking and correction purposes.

B. When a random error occurs, the corrector will use the syndromes to calculate its magnitude $Y_i$ on position $X_i$.

C. With erasure(s), the corrector firstly sets one or both of $X_i$ and $X_j$ as the already known position(s) of erasure(s) to solve their correlated error magnitudes $Y_i$ and $Y_j$.

When an error or erasure(s) is found, the corrector will correct the $R_{stripe_u}(x)$ using $S_1$ and $S_2$ immediately after completion of reading. The timing of this procedure is shown in Fig. 10. With such high-speed correction, we consider this operation as a real-time correction process.

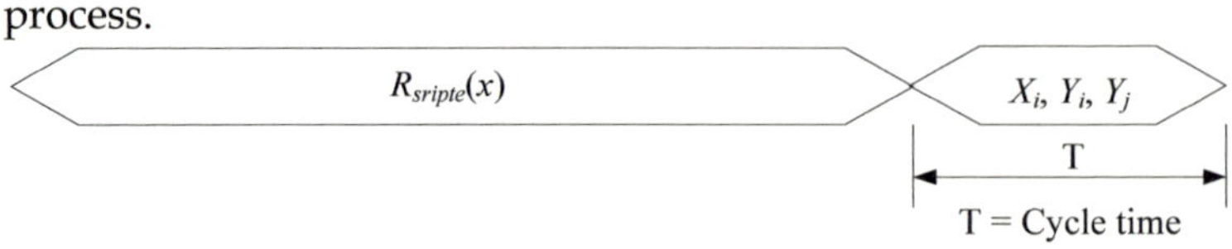


Fig. 10. The RS codes codec block diagram of system level

### 5.2.2 The Disk Level

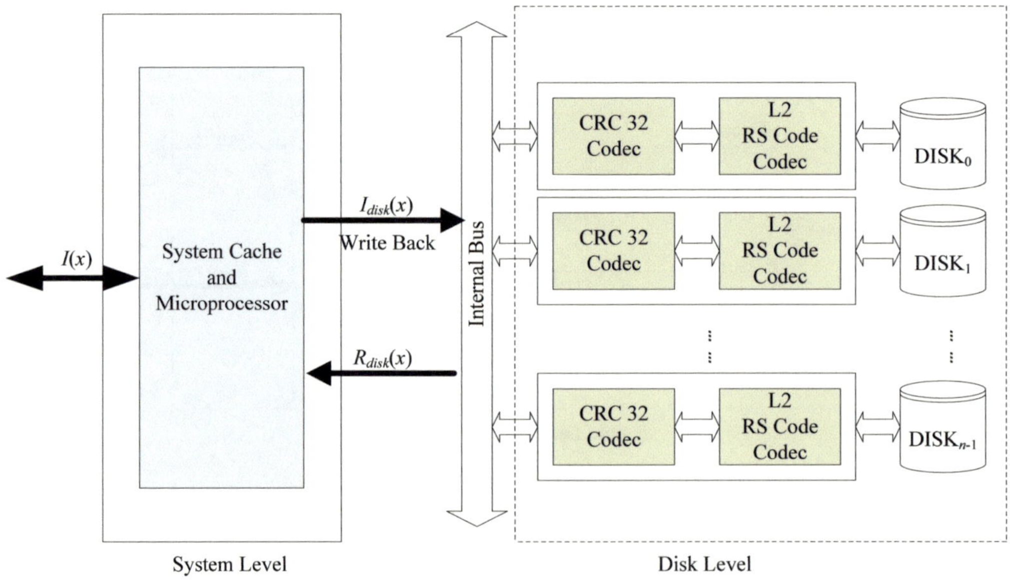


Fig. 11. The RS codes codec block diagram of system level

At the disk level as shown in Fig. 11, when the bulks are written from cache into disks, the encoding procedure at the disk level is as follows:

1. The data $I_{disk}(x)=\{I_{n-1},I_{n-2},\ldots,I_0\}$ in cache is written into disks.

2. Each disk receives its own data *I* which is then encoded by CRC 32 codec.
3. The encoded data stream from CRC 32 codec are encoded again by L2 RS-codes codec and stored in the disks.
Thus, the RS-PC encoding is finished.
When a system reads data from disks into cache, all data will be checked by CRC 32 codec and decoded by L2 RS-codes codec. The decoding procedure at the disk level is as follows:
1. The data in each disk are decoded and corrected by its own L2 RS-codes codec.
2. The decoded data stream from each L2 RS-codes codec are decoded again by its own CRC 32 codec.
Finally, if the quantity of errors is greater than the error-correcting capacity of L2 RS-codes codec, the CRC 32 codec can detect the errors and report to the system level, so this disk is marked as an erasure at the system level. This strategy will enhance the system reliability and increase the data access speed with less possibility to retry failure disk(s). This design provides support of double protection for the RAID system in real time.

## 6. Conclusion

This paper provides an example of coding to implement a RS code in redundant array of independent disks system in correcting single random error and double erasures. There are new directions such as the small write module and higher correction capabilities for the design of a RS-RAID system. As a result, the proposed RS-RAID system has the following advantages:
1. Expandable design: As the design of RAID-6, this paper does not only propose a solution for dual disks failure, but also adopt the PGZ algorithm to correct less than six or seven errors.
2. Integrated concept: This system presents a unified RSPC concept to partite the system into dual levels of abstract/structure. Thus, the modules at the disk level mainly deal with burst or random errors in disks, and the control of the system level does the correction for multiple failures of the system. On the other hand, each disk may be a surface of disk so that a fault tolerant hard disk is produced.
3. Real-time updating capability: In regard to the applications for banks, stock markets, hospitals or military purposes, the system requires frequent transactions or updating of data/information. The small write module may support the system cache with a real time requirement and solve the frequent update operations in the RAID system with very low overhead.
4. Suitability for co-design: The proposed algorithm is suitable for both hardware and software designs of the modules in the applications of RS codes by using the finite field. The math of finite field belongs to modern algebra which has been largely applied to the applications of error correction code and cryptography. This suggests that the hardware modules will be integrated into the math processor in CPU of the future versions. The reliable control may be easily integrated into microcontrollers and general processors.
5. More applications: With the advantages from the expandability to the co-design of the system, this concept may extend its applications to most memory systems such as the flash memory, DRAM, and so on.

## 7. Acknowledgments

This work is supported in part by the Nation Science Council, Taiwan, under grant NSC 91-2213-E-214-010.

## 8. References

Blaum, M.; Brady, J. ; Bruck, J. & Menon, J. (1995). EVENODD: An Efficient Scheme for Tolerating Double Disk Failures in RAID Architectures. *IEEE Transaction on Computers,* Vol. 44, No. 2, pp. 192-202, ISSN: 0018-9340

Chien, R.T. (1964). Cyclic Decoding Procedure for the Bose-Chaudhuri- Hocquenghem Codes. *IEEE Transaction on Information Theory,* Vol. IT-10, No. 10, pp. 357-363, ISSN: 0018-9448

Forney, G.D. (1965). On Decoding BCH Codes. *IEEE Transaction on Information Theory,* Vol. IT-11, No. 4, pp. 549-557, ISSN: 0018-9448

Gorenstein, D. & Zierler, N. (1961). A Class of Error Correcting Codes in $p^m$ Symbols. *Journal of the Society of Industrial and Applied Mathematics,* Vol. 9, No. 2, pp. 207-214, ISSN: 0368-4245

Jing, M.H.; Chen, Y.H. & Yuan, K.Y. (2000). The Comparison of Evenodd Code and RS Code for RAID Applications, *Asia Pacific Conference on Multimedia Technology and Application*, pp. 261-268, December, 2000, Kaohsiung, Taiwan

Jing, M.H.; Chen, Y.H. & Liao, J.E. (2001). A Fast Error and Erasure Correction Algorithm for a Simple RS-RAID, *Proceedings of the 2001 International Conferences on Info-tech and Info-net*, pp. 333-338, ISBN: 0-7803-7010-4, October, 2001, Beijing, China

Liao, J.E & Jing, M.H. (2002). *The Research and Implementation of High-Speed RAID Using Reed-Solomon Codes,* Master's thesis, Department of Information Engineer, I-Shou University, Kaohsiung, Taiwan

Patterson, D.A.; Gibson, G. & Katz, R.H. (1988). A Case for Redundant Arrays of Inexpensive Disks (RAID), *Proceedings of the 1988 ACM SIGMOD international conference on Management of data,* pp. 109-116, ISBN: 0-89791-268-3, June, 1988, ACM, Chicago, Illinois

Peterson, W.W. (1960). Encoding and Error-Correction Procedures for the Bose-Chaudhuri Codes. *IRE Transaction on Information Theory,* Vol. IT-6, No. 4, pp. 459-470, ISSN: 0096-1000

Plank, J.S. (1997). A Tutorial on Reed-Solomon Coding for Fault-Tolerance in RAID-like Systems. *Software - Practice and Experience,* Vol. 27, No. 9, pp. 995-1012, ISSN: 0038-0644

Wicker, S.B. & Bhargava, V.K. (1994). *Reed-Solomon Codes and Their Applications,* IEEE Press, ISBN: 0-7803-5391-9, NJ

Wicker, S.B. (1995). *Error Control Systems for Digital Communication and Storage,* Prentice Hall, ISBN: 0-13-308941-X, US

# Administration and Monitoring Service for Storage Virtualization in Grid Environments

Salam Traboulsi
*Institut de recherche en informatique de Toulouse IRIT*
*Université Paul Sabatier Toulouse III*
*31062 Toulouse Cedex 3, France*
*Traboulsi.salam@gmail.com*

## 1. Introduction

A grid is collection of computers and storage resources maintained to serve the needs of some community (Foster et al., 2002). It addresses collaboration, data sharing, cycle sharing and other patterns of interaction that involve distributed resources.
Actually, the de facto building block is for high performance storage systems. In grid context, the scale and the reliability have key issues as many independently failing and unreliable components need to be continuously accounted for and managed over time (Porter & Katz, 2006). Manageability also becomes of paramount importance, since nowadays the grid commonly consists of hundred or even thousands of storage and computing nodes (Foster et al., 2002). One of the key challenges faced by high performance storage system is scalable administration and monitoring of system state.
A monitoring system captures subset of interactions amongst the myriad of computational nodes, links, and storage devices. These interactions are interpreted in order to improve performance in grid environment.
On a grid scale basis, ViSaGe aims at providing to the grid users a transparent, reliable and powerful storage system underpinned by a storage virtualization layer. ViSaGe is based on three services, namely as: administration and monitoring service, storage virtualization service and distributed file system. The virtualization service incorporates storage resources distributed on the grid in virtual spaces. These virtual spaces will be attributed by the distributed file system various qualities of service and data placement policies.
In this paper, we present our scalable distributed system: Admon. Admon consists of an administration module that manages virtual storage resources according to their workloads based on the information collected by a monitoring module. It is known that the performance of a system depends deeply on the characteristics of its workload. Usually, the node's workload is associated to the service response time of a storage application. As the workload increases, the service response time becomes longer. However, the utilization percentage of system resources (CPU load, the Disk load and Network load) must be taken into more consideration. Therefore, Admon traces ViSaGe's applications and collects system resources (CPU, Disk, Network...) percentage of utilization. It is characterized by an

automatic instrumentation. It is an auto-manager monitoring system. In this paper, we demonstrate Admon efficiency due to nodes workload and user constraint like CPU usage workload.
The remainder of this paper is composed as follows: Section 2 presents the existing monitoring systems and motivates the need of Admon. Section 3 illustrates ViSaGe and grid environment, followed by Admon architecture, in Section 4, where we delve into details of Admon functionalities and API. In Section 5, we show a performance experiment tests for an Admon evaluation in a storage virtualization system. Finally, we conclude the paper in Section 6 and some future work is also presented.

## 2. Related work

In a distributed system such as ViSaGe, the storage management is principally funded on automatic decisions to improve performance. These decisions identify nodes which can be accessed efficiently. Therefore, analyzing node's workload is primary to make an adequate decision. Moreover, this workload is mainly supported by the monitoring systems. Several existing monitoring systems are available for monitoring grid resources (computing resources, storage resources, networks) and grid applications. Examples of existing monitoring systems are: Network Weather Service (NWS) (Wolski et al., 1999), Relational grid Monitoring Architecture (R-GMA) (Cooke et al., 2004), NetLogger (Gunter et al., 2000), etc.
Network Weather Service (NWS) is a popular distributed system for producing short term performance forecasts based on historical performance measurements. NWS is specific to monitor grid computing and network resources. It provides CPU percentage availability rather than CPU usage of a particular application. It supposes that nodes are available for the entire application. This conclusion is very limited to be used to achieve high throughput in a storage virtualization system like ViSaGe.
Relational grid Monitoring Architecture (R-GMA) is based on a relational model. It is an implementation of GGF Grid Monitoring Architecture (GMA). It is being used both for information about the grid and for application monitoring. R-GMA collected information was used only to find out about what services are available at any time.
Netlogger is a monitoring and a performance analysis tool for grids. It provides tracing services for distributed applications to detect bottlenecks. However, performance analysis is carried out in post mortem. In ViSaGe, we don't need a system for studying the application's state, but a system that analyzes the availability of grid resources.
The aforementioned monitoring systems are designed to produce and deliver measurements on grid resources and application efficiently. Nevertheless, none of these systems presents the whole of the pertinent characteristics for a virtualization system like ViSaGe. ViSaGe needs a monitoring system providing a full view of node's workload in order to choose better nodes according to its target (replicating data, distributing workload …) and during nodes workload variations. Therefore, our monitoring system, Admon, traces applications, and collects information about storage resources, grid resources and networks. It is considered as an intersection point between all the aforementioned monitoring systems. It should use its monitoring knowledge for choosing the accurate node. The choice will be according to a prediction model in order to place data, efficiently, during runtime execution.

## 3. ViSaGe Architecture

A grid consists of three levels: node level represents storage node and computing node, site level represents site's administrator of the grid, and grid's level represents grid's administrator. The components of our storage virtualization system are distributed on this architecture (Fig.1) which brought an additional service for improving storage quality, and the access to the data.

- At the node level, we have :
  1. The virtualization service (Vrt).
  2. The distributed file system service (Visagefs).
  3. The administration and monitoring service (Admon).
- At the upper levels (the site level and the grid level), we found the tools of the administration and monitoring service (Admon).

ViSaGe aggregates distributed storage resources. It proposes for providing a self adaptive storage management system. The ViSaGe storage virtualization layer allows simplifying the management of sharing storage resources: flexible and transparent access to the data, high performance (data replication, links configuration, etc).

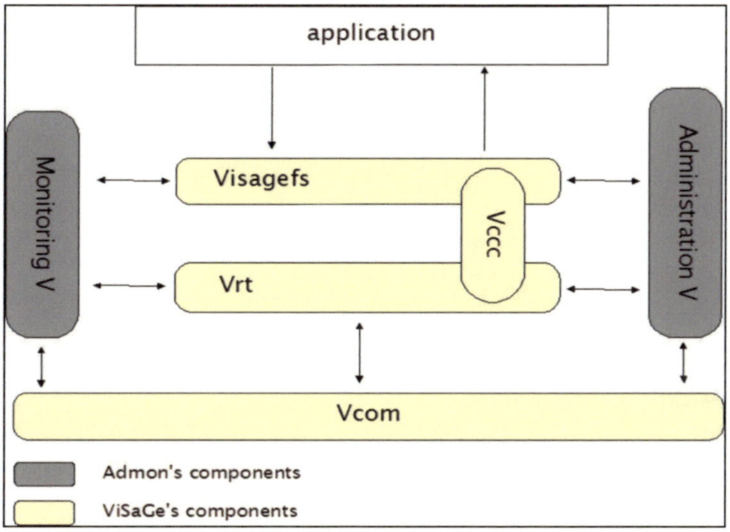


Fig. 1. ViSaGe's Architecture

The traditional application (like creation file, reading/writing data) uses the virtual storage resource through our file system, and thus reached data by means of virtualization layer. Furthermore, to handle the dynamic and the inherent nature of the grid, and to control the virtualization (storage resources attribution, virtual storage resources creation/destruction or modification), our storage virtualization system proposes the administration and the monitoring layer, Admon. Therefore, Admon's design must be strongly related to grid environment. Next, we present the hierarchical architecture and the fundamental concept of this system.

## 4. Administration and Monitoring Service

The Admon's components (Fig.2) are distributed throughout the grid. These components are:

1. An intelligent administration and monitoring agent, distributed among the storage and computing resources.
2. The administration and monitoring tools (server types), installed on site and grid controllers.

These components rely on a send/request protocol to monitor and manage the state of grid nodes (Foster et al., 2002).

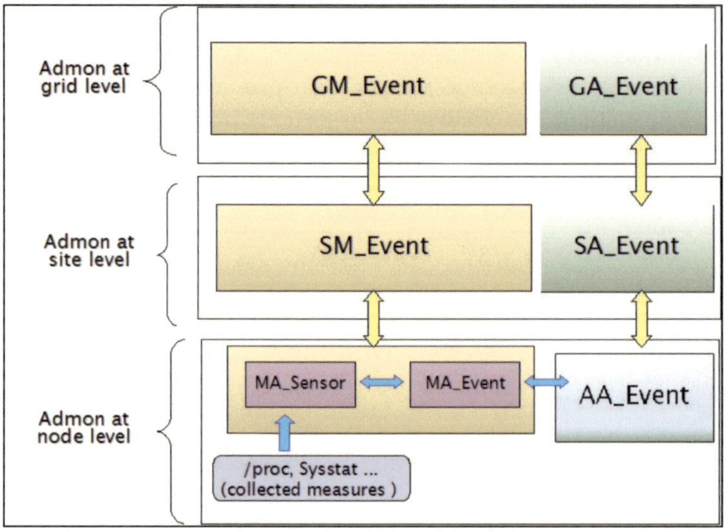


Fig. 2. Admon's Architecture

### 4.1 The administration components

The administration service manages the grid resources. It consists of (Fig.2): administration agent (AA_event), site's administration tool (SA_Event) and grid's administration tool (GA_event).

a) The administration agent:

In order to facilitate the deployment, the configuration and the update of the resources, an administration agent runs at the storage and computing elements. It constitutes a means of communication with the site's administration tool, and the other layers' interfaces of our storage virtualization system. It receives or sends events for instance when a node asks to be integrated into the site, its administration agent contacts the administration tool of its site to send its identity.

b) The site's administration tool:

It is a centralized tool for the site management, able to send to the grid's administration tool the information concerning the site that it manages. For example:

1. The storage elements configuration within the site, to allow the resource sharing.
2. The management of the available physical resources to be shared.
3. Sending and receiving messages from the grid's administration tool.

c) The grid's administration tool:
At the grid's level, the Admon's administration part is represented by the administration tool which runs in front of the grid owner. It manages grid user requests, and the information concerning the grid components in order to make decisions according to the nodes state.

### 4.2 The monitoring components

The Monitoring service collects information and sends notifications to the administrator. It consists of (Fig.2): monitoring agent (MA_sensor and MA_event), site's monitoring tool (SM_event) and grid's monitoring tool (GM_event).
a) The monitoring agent:
The intelligent monitoring agent is launched on all single machines where the processes of the application are executed. Distributed among the computing and storage elements, it allows collecting relevant information by the mean of MA_sensor and observing the behaviour of its node by the mean of MA_event. This information is represented by: CPU usage percent, Memory usage percent, Input/Output throughput to storage devices, Network throughput and event log.
The monitoring information is collected by the system command as "top". We usually poll at 100 ms intervals. Since the kernel events are not time-stamped, the data obtained this way represents all events in this interval. We use a simple statistical method to send the collected information when a significant change occurred. In order to no overload the grid, our agent monitoring is autonomous. It changes its interval of polling.
*Event log analysis:* for studying the node stability it is very important to collect the times-tamping of interest events to the logical volume of this node. This information will be sent to Admon grid's tool, by the mean of site's tool, in order to analyze the storage virtual state.
The adopted method for collecting relevant information is no disrupted of the running application, which means that our system is a non intrusive system.
b) The site's monitoring tool:
It is introduced as an intermediate monitoring process between the grid's monitoring tool and the monitoring agent. These monitoring tools are used to forward data from the monitoring agent to the grid's monitoring tool. The introspection mechanism, adopted by the monitoring agent to the node level, leverages the collected and optimized information of each observed node. Thus, it will have a global vision concerning the state of the components of the corresponding site.
c) The grid's monitoring tool:
The grid's monitoring tool incorporates the synthesized information by the monitoring tools of each site into the grid information system. This information describes the state of each site in the grid and represents the significant behaviours of the various components.
The synthesized information consists of:

- Site's state: overloaded or failing sites.
- Network's state: overloaded or broken links.

This collected information makes it possible to notify the grid's administration tool in order to make appropriate management decisions, and helps to have a global vision concerning the state of virtual storage resources created.

The collection of traces and logs creates a complete view of what the system is being ordered to be achieved. The next step should allow combining the system's knowledge with the statistically gathered data, for evaluating the stability state of the virtual storage resources.

## 5. Experimental results

In a data storage distributed system, the major concern is the data access performance. Many works focus on the data access performance has been concentrated on a static value and is not related to nodes load. However, whole system's performance is affected not only by the behavior of each single application, but also by the resulting execution of several different applications combined together. We have implemented Admon to study the service response time of ViSaGe's application influencing the system resources utilization. It traces applications and collects system resources' percentages (CPU, Disk, Network…) of utilization. The contribution of our work is to uncover which nodes are dedicated or not to ViSaGe. The Admon's performance metrics are represented by the CPU, Disk and Network. Admon sets the maximum value of performance metrics; constraint for achieving an experiment and making an adequate decision. This solution is used by Admon to identify grid dedicated node.
Here we present a use case study in order to show the Admon automatic instrumentation due to its decision. This decision improves data storage management and performance in our data storage system. Before on going on our experiment, we choose the CPU load (CPU < 70) like a constraint. This constraint is like a user demand to improve experiment performance.

### 5.1 Experimental setup

In our experimental, we choose the meshing AMIBE 3D. The European consortium EADS-CCR makes use of AMIBE drive electromagnetic simulations. We used grid platform, which gathered 4 sites distributed in France (IRIT, SEANODES, EADS-CCR, and CS-SI). For our preliminary experiments, we used 4 nodes (node1, node2, node3 and node4) distributed in these sites, where nodes are connected through gigabit Ethernet network.
The meshing full process encompasses three phases, each one being data dependent from its elder. First step is the 1D meshing which is started with a structural description. This job will run on a single node and generates one directory filled with one file per face to mesh. After completion, ViSaGe administration tools replicate data from current logical volume to all of the involved sites with at least one replica per site. Having 1D stage data replicated, we can launch the 2D stage on the reserved ViSaGe nodes for our application. We use a job scheduler (torque) to dispatch AMIBE 2D jobs on a face per face basis. On each run, a new directory is filled with an intermediate files. The final AMIBE 3D job is to collect and compound all those intermediate 2D files in one final set of 3D files. Thereby, although 2D data sets now span over a wide range of local storage resources. In AMIBE, before launching, an edge length must be determined. We used an AMIBE executable version where this value is set to 50. Modifying this value will modify performance result. However, in our experiment, we fix this value to 3. The reason from that is to show the administration and monitoring efficiency and utility by using AMIBE.

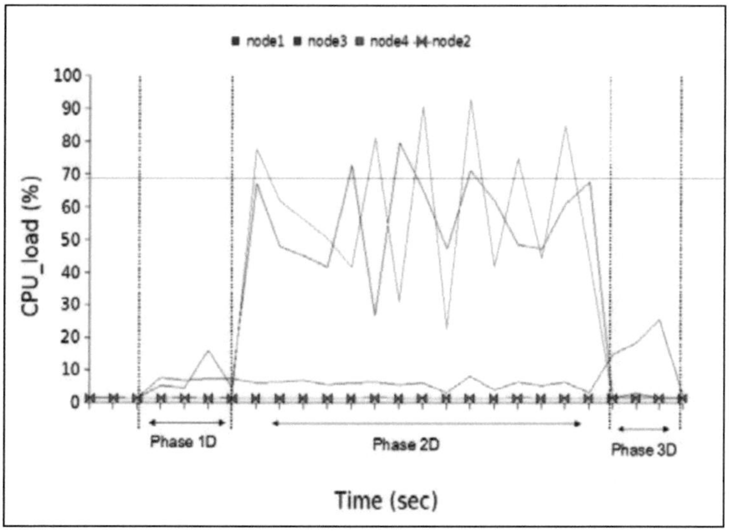


Fig. 3. nodes dedicated to ViSaGe

### 5.2 Results and discussion

We installed on node1 the Admon grid tools and site tools. On the three other nodes, we installed the Admon agents. The site monitoring tools know the nodes of its site where ViSaGe turns. For AMIBE, we used 3 nodes: one node for 1D or 3D and two other nodes for 2D phase. The CPU load worse case is fixed to 70 %.

We started by mounting the ViSaGe file system (Visagefs) on node1.

Before starting 2D stage, the Admon administration contacts the monitoring part to ask about computing nodes state reserved for the task. The grid scheduler has not all control over nodes tasks will be delegated. In our case study we have three nodes. The Admon administration chooses nodes according to their workload.

The first test (Fig.3) showed the CPU's nodes state in our experiment. This figure (Fig.3) shows the normal case of our test: all the nodes are dedicated to ViSaGe. We conclude that CPU usage percentage, in the 2D phase reaches highest percentage. Here, I must mention that the 2D phase is computing of 2D faces followed by storage of information in order to initialize the next step: we had CPU usage and I/O usage. That's mean, if the node2 is loaded node and it was choose in the 2D phase. We will have an experiment failure or increasing of service time.

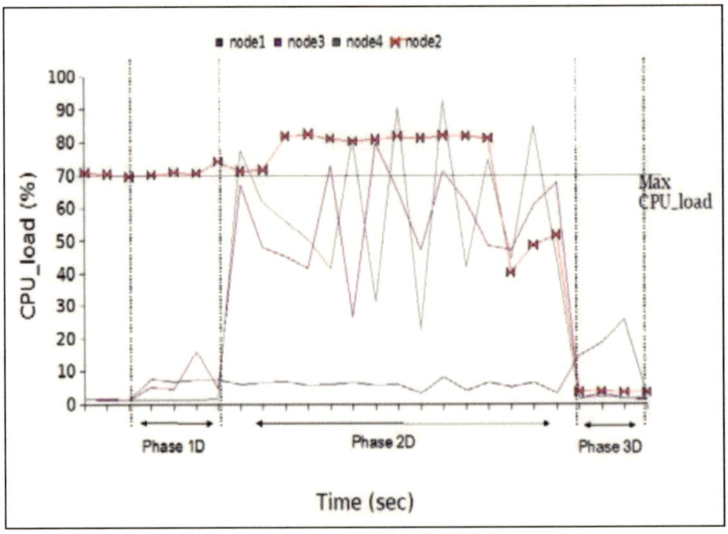


Fig. 4. node2 is dedicated to the grid

In the other hand, the second test, represented by the figure 4, shows from the workload of node2 (in terms of CPU load), that node2 is dedicated to the grid- that mean that this node is used by another applications (local or on the grid).
Before the launching the 2D phase, we launch on the node2 applications simulating the use of this node by a virtual user. The application of this user uses the nodes CPU, stores and sends requests to the disk (read or write data). The goal of this operation is to increase the load of the CPU in a progressive way in order to stabilize it on a maximum value. The monitoring agent collects the percentages of CPU node and sends this significant change to the monitoring tools. The monitoring tools, starting from the information collected by each monitoring agent, test the node's state. For ongoing on the 2D phase, Admon administration doesn't choose this node - "node2" for the 2D stage.
The other two nodes, (node3 and node4), aren't detected in term of dedicated node to the grid, Admon launches commands to mount the Visagefs. For adding these nodes in the same virtual space, Admon contacts the Vrt (the visage virtualization layer). The Vrt replicates data in order to launch the 2D phase.
We finalize our experiment by the 3D phase that synthesizes information on the node1.

## 6. Conclusion

In this paper, we have described a non-intrusive, scalable administration and monitoring system for high performance grid environment. It is a fundamental building block for achieving and analyzing the performance of the storage virtualization system in a huge and heterogeneous grid storage environment. It offers a very flexible and simple model that collects nodes state information and requirements needed by the other services of our virtualization storage system improving storage distributed data performance. It is based on a multi-tiered hierarchical architecture the start-up of the monitoring and administration system.

Future work will focus on developing interactive jobs with the storage virtualization system, in order to study the relation between different system resources (CPU, disk, networks) and tracing events, where Admon allows changing the storage distributed protocols (for instance, replication) during runtime execution. Therefore, this work will be difficult since we have many parameters that must be taken into consideration. However, this mechanism will allow generalizing I/O workload model in order to improve applications throughput during workload variations in grid environments.

## 7. References

Foster and al. (2002), *The Anatomy of the Grid: Enabling Scalable Virtual Organizations,* Intl J. High-Performance Computing Applications, vol. 15, no. 3, 2001, pp. 200-222, June 2002.

Porter, G. & Katz, R.H. (2006). Effective Web Service Load Balancing Through Statistical Monitoring. *Communication of the ACM, March 2006.*

Wolski, R; Spring, N.T. & Hayes, J. (1999). The Network Weather Service: A Distributed Resource Performance Forecasting Service for Metacomputing. *Future Generation Computing Systems, Metacomputing Issue,* 15(5-6): 157-768, Oct. 1999.

Gunter, D.; Tierney, B.; Crowley, B.; Holding, M. & Lee, J. (2000). NetLogger: A Toolkit for Distributed System Performance Analysis, *In Proceedings of the IEEE Mascots 2000,* Aug. 2000.

Cooke, A. et al. (2004). *The Relational Grid Monitoring Architecture: Mediating information about the grid,* 2004

8

# Power-Aware Memory Allocation for Embedded Data-Intensive Signal Processing Applications

Florin Balasa[1], Ilie I. Luican[2], Hongwei Zhu[3] and Doru V. Nasui[4]
[1]*Dept. of Computer Science, Southern Utah University, Cedar City, UT 84721*
[2]*Dept. of Computer Science, University of Illinois at Chicago, Chicago, IL 60607*
[3]*ARM, Inc., San Jose, CA 95134*
[4]*American Int. Radio, Inc., Rolling Meadows, IL 60008*

**Abstract**
Many signal processing systems, particularly in the multimedia and telecommunication domains, are synthesized to execute data-intensive applications: their cost related aspects – namely power consumption and chip area – are heavily influenced, if not dominated, by the data access and storage aspects. This chapter presents a power-aware memory allocation methodology. Starting from the high-level behavioral specification of a given application, this framework performs the assignment of of the multidimensional signals to the memory layers – the on-chip scratch-pad memory and the off-chip main memory – the goal being the reduction of the dynamic energy consumption in the memory subsystem. Based on the assignment results, the framework subsequently performs the mapping of signals into the memory layers such that the overall amount of data storage be reduced. This software system yields a complete allocation solution: the exact storage amount on each memory layer, the mapping functions that determine the exact locations for any array element (scalar signal) in the specification, and, in addition, an estimation of the dynamic energy consumption in the memory subsystem.

## 1. Introduction

Many multidimensional signal processing systems, particularly in the areas of multimedia and telecommunications, are synthesized to execute data-intensive applications, the data transfer and storage having a significant impact on both the system performance and the major cost parameters – power and area.

In particular, the memory subsystem is, typically, a major contributor to the overall energy budget of the entire system (8). The *dynamic* energy consumption is caused by memory accesses, whereas the *static* energy consumption is due to leakage currents. Savings of dynamic energy can be potentially obtained by accessing frequently used data from smaller on-chip memories rather than from the large off-chip main memory, the problem being how to optimally assign the data to the memory layers. Note that this problem is basically different from caching for performance (15), (22), where the question is to find how to fill the cache such that the needed data be loaded in advance from the main memory. As on-chip storage, the scratch-pad memories (SPMs) – compiler-controlled static random-access memories, more energy-efficient than the hardware-managed caches – are widely used in embedded systems, where caches incur a significant penalty in aspects like area cost, energy consumption, hit latency, and real-time guarantees. A detailed study (4) comparing the tradeoffs of caches as compared to SPMs found in their experiments that the latter exhibit 34% smaller area and 40% lower power consumption than a cache of the same capacity. Even more surprisingly, the runtime measured in cycles was 18% better with an SPM using a simple static knapsack-based allocation algorithm. As a general conclusion, the authors of the study found absolutely no advantage in using caches, even in high-end embedded systems in which performance is important. [1] Different from caches, the SPM occupies a distinct part of the virtual address space, with the rest of the address space occupied by the main memory. The consequence is that there is no need to check for the availability of the data in the SPM. Hence, the SPM does not possess a comparator and the miss/hit acknowledging circuitry (4). This contributes to a significant energy (as well as area) reduction. Another consequence is that in cache memory systems, the mapping of data to the cache is done during the code execution, whereas in SPM-based systems this can be done at compilation time, using a suitable algorithm – as this chapter will show.

The energy-efficient assignment of signals to the on- and off-chip memories has been studied since the late nineties. These previous works focused on partitioning the signals from the application code into so-called *copy candidates* (since the on-chip memories were usually caches), and on the optimal selection and assignment of these to different layers into the memory hierarchy (32), (7), (18). For instance, Kandemir and Choudhary analyze and exploit the temporal locality by inserting local copies (21). Their layer assignment builds a separate hierarchy per loop nest and then combines them into a single hierarchy. However, the approach lacks a global view on the lifetimes of array elements in applications having imperfect nested loops. Brockmeyer *et al.* use the steering heuristic of assigning the arrays having the lowest access number over size ratio to the lowest memory layer first, followed by incremental reassignments (7). Hu *et al.* can use *parts* of arrays as copies, but they typically use cuts along the array dimensions (18) (like rows and columns of matrices). Udayakumaran and Barua propose a dynamic allocation model for SPM-based embedded systems (29), but the focus is global and stack data, rather than multidimensional signals. Issenin *et al.* perform a data reuse analysis in a multi-layer memory organization (19), but the mapping of the signals into the hierarchical data storage is not considered. The energy-aware partitioning of an on-chip memory in multiple banks has been studied by several research groups, as well. Techniques of an exploratory nature analyze possible partitions, matching them against the access patterns of the application (25), (11). Other approaches exploit the properties of the dynamic energy cost and the resulting structure of the partitioning space to come up with algorithms able to derive the optimal partition for a given access pattern (6), (1).

Despite many advances in memory design techniques over the past two decades, existing computer-aided design methodologies are still ineffective in many aspects. In several previous works, the reduction of the dynamic energy consumption in hierarchical memory subsystems is addressed using in part enumerative approaches, simulations, profiling, heuristic explorations of the solution space, rather than a formal methodology. Also, several models of mapping the multidimensional signals into the physical memory were proposed in the past (see (12) for a good overview).

[1] Caches have been a big success for desktops though, where the usual approach to adding SRAM is to configure it as a cache.

However, they all failed
(a) to provide efficient implementations,
(b) to prove their effectiveness in hierarchical memory organizations, and
(c) to provide quantitative measures of quality for the mapping solutions.
Moreover, the reduction of power consumption and the mapping of signals in hierarchical memory subsystems were treated in the past as completely separate problems.
This chapter presents a power-aware memory allocation methodology. Starting from the high-level behavioral specification of a given application, where the code is organized in sequences of loop nests and the main data structures are multidimensional arrays, this framework performs the assignment of of the multidimensional signals to the memory layers – the on-chip scratch-pad memory and the off-chip main memory – the goal being the reduction of the dynamic energy consumption in the memory subsystem. Based on the assignment results, the framework subsequently performs the mapping of signals into the memory layers such that the overall amount of data storage be reduced. This software system yields a complete allocation solution: the exact storage amount on each memory layer, the mapping functions that determine the exact locations for any array element (scalar signal) in the specification, metrics of quality for the allocation solution, and also an estimation of the dynamic energy consumption in the memory subsystem using the CACTI power model (31). Extensions of the current framework to support dynamic allocation are currently under development.
The rest of the chapter is organized as follows. Section 2 presents the algorithm that assigns the signals to the memory layers, aiming to minimize the dynamic energy consumption in the hierarchical memory subsystem subject to SPM size constraints. Section 3 describes the global flow of the memory allocation approach, focusing on the mapping aspects. Section 4 discusses on implementation and presents experimental results. Finally, Section 5 summarizes the main conclusions of this research.

## 2. Power-aware signal assignment to the memory layers

The algorithms describing the functionality of real-time multimedia and telecommunication applications are typically specified in a high-level programming language, where the code is organized in sequences of loop nests having as boundaries linear functions of the outer loop iterators. Conditional instructions are very common as well, and the multidimensional array references have linear indexes (the variables being the loop iterators).[2]
Figure 1 shows an illustrative example whose structure is similar to the kernel of a motion detection algorithm (9) (the actual code containing also a *delay* operator – not relevant in this context). The problem is to automatically identify those parts of arrays from the given application code that are more intensely accessed, in order to steer their assignment to the energy-efficient data storage layer (the on-chip scratch-pad memory) such that the dynamic energy consumption in the hierarchical memory subsystem be reduced.
The number of storage accesses for each array element can certainly be computed by the simulated execution of the code. For instance, the number of accesses was counted for every pair of possible indexes (between 0 and 80) of signal $A$ (see Fig. 1). The array elements near the

[2] Typical piece-wise linear operations can be transformed into affine specifications (17). In addition, pointer accesses can be converted at compilation to array accesses with explicit index functions (16). Moreover, specifications where not all loop structures are *for* loops and not all array indexes are affine functions of the loop iterators can be transformed into affine specifications that captures all the memory references amenable to optimization (20). Extensions to support a larger class of specifications are thus possible, but they are orthogonal to the work presented in this chapter.

```
optDelta[0] = 0 ;                          // int A[81][81]: input;
for ( i=16; i<=64; i++ )
  for ( j=16; j<=64; j++ )
  { Delta[i][j][0] = 0 ;
    for ( k=i-16; k<=i+16; k++ )
      for ( l=j-16; l<=j+16; l++ )
        Delta[i][j][33*k-33*i+l-j+545] = A[i][j] - A[k][l]
                  + Delta[i][j][33*k-33*i+l-j+544] ;
    optDelta[49*i+j-799] = Delta[i][j][1089] + optDelta[49*i+j-800];
  }
opt[0] = optDelta[2401];
```

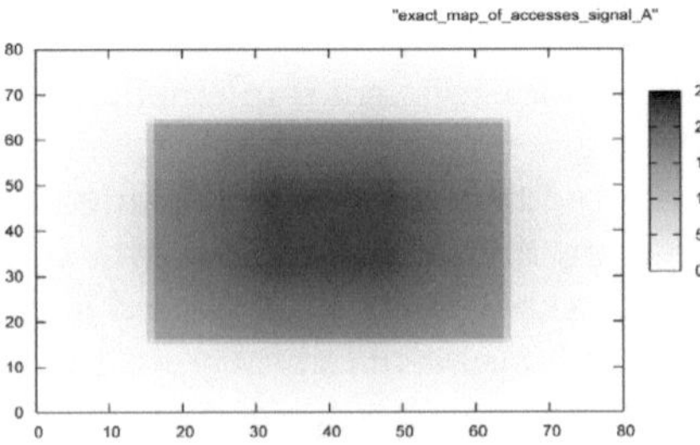


Fig. 1. Code derived from a motion detection (9) kernel ($m = n = 16$, $M = N = 64$) and the exact map of memory *read* accesses (obtained by simulation) for the 2-D signal $A$.

center of the index space are accessed with high intensity (for instance, $A[40][40]$ is accessed 2,178 times; $A[16][40]$ is accessed 1,650 times), whereas the array elements at the periphery are accessed with a significantly lower intensity (for instance, $A[0][40]$ is accessed 33 times and $A[0][0]$ only once).

The drawbacks of such an approach are twofold. First, the simulated execution may be computationally ineffective when the number of array elements is very significant, or when the application code contains deep loop nests. Second, even if the simulated execution were feasible, such a scalar-oriented technique would not be helpful since the addressing hardware of the data memories would result very complex. An address generation unit (AGU) is typically implemented to compute arithmetic expressions in order to generate sequences of addresses (26); a set of array elements is not a good input for the design of an efficient AGU.

Our proposed computation methodology for power-aware signal assignment to the memory layers is described below, after defining a few basic concepts.

Each *array reference* $M[x_1(i_1,\ldots,i_n)] \cdots [x_m(i_1,\ldots,i_n)]$ of an $m$-dimensional signal $M$, in the scope of a nest of $n$ loops having the iterators $i_1,\ldots, i_n$ , is characterized by an *iterator space* and an *index* (or *array*) *space*. The iterator space signifies the set of all iterator vectors $\mathbf{i} = (i_1,\ldots,i_n) \in \mathbf{Z}^n$ in the scope of the array reference, and it can be typically represented by a so-called **Z**-polytope (a polyhedron bounded and closed, restricted to the set $\mathbf{Z}^n$): $\{ \mathbf{i} \in \mathbf{Z}^n \mid \mathbf{A} \cdot \mathbf{i} \geq \mathbf{b} \}$. The index space is the set of all index vectors $\mathbf{x} = (x_1, \ldots, x_m) \in \mathbf{Z}^m$ of the array reference. When the indexes of an array reference are linear mappings with integer coefficients of the loop iterators, the index space consists of one or several *linearly bounded lattices* (27): $\{ \mathbf{x} = \mathbf{T} \cdot \mathbf{i} + \mathbf{u} \in \mathbf{Z}^m \mid \mathbf{A} \cdot \mathbf{i} \geq \mathbf{b}\ ,\ \mathbf{i} \in \mathbf{Z}^n \}$. For instance, the array reference $A[i+2*j+3][j+2*k]$ from the loop nest

```
        for (i=0; i<=2; i++)
          for (j=0; j<=3; j++)
            for (k=0; k<=4; k++)
              if ( 6*i+4*j+3*k ≤ 12 )   ···
A[i+2*j+3][j+2*k] ···
```

has the iterator space $P = \left\{ \begin{bmatrix} i \\ j \\ k \end{bmatrix} \in \mathbf{Z}^3 \;\middle|\; \begin{bmatrix} 1 & 0 & 0 \\ 0 & 1 & 0 \\ 0 & 0 & 1 \\ -6 & -4 & -3 \end{bmatrix} \begin{bmatrix} i \\ j \\ k \end{bmatrix} \geq \begin{bmatrix} 0 \\ 0 \\ 0 \\ -12 \end{bmatrix} \right\}$. (The inequalities $i \leq 2$, $j \leq 3$, and $k \leq 4$ are redundant.)

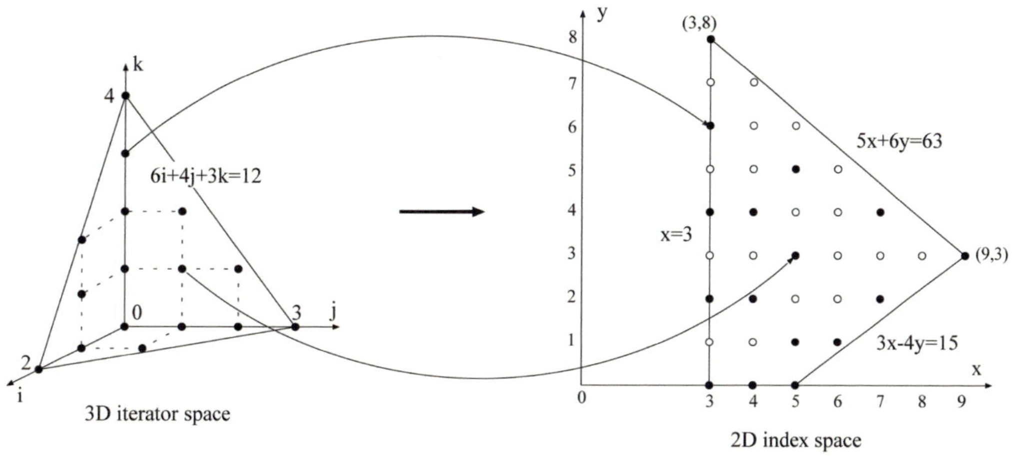


Fig. 2. The mapping of the iterator space into the index space of the array reference $A[i+2*j+3][j+2*k]$.

The $A$-elements of the array reference have the indices $x$, $y$: $\left\{ \begin{bmatrix} x \\ y \end{bmatrix} = \mathbf{T}\cdot\mathbf{i}+\mathbf{u} = \begin{bmatrix} 1 & 2 & 0 \\ 0 & 1 & 2 \end{bmatrix} \begin{bmatrix} i \\ j \\ k \end{bmatrix} + \begin{bmatrix} 3 \\ 0 \end{bmatrix} \middle| \begin{bmatrix} i \\ j \\ k \end{bmatrix} \in P \right\}$. The points of the index space lie inside the **Z**-polytope $\{\ x \geq 3\ ,\ y \geq 0\ ,\ 3x-4y \leq 15\ ,\ 5x+6y \leq 63\ ,\ \ x,y \in \mathbf{Z}\}$, whose boundary is the image of the boundary of the iterator space $P$ (see Fig. 2). However, it can be shown that only those points $(x,y)$ satisfying also the inequalities $-6x+8y \geq 19k-30$, $x-2y \geq -4k+3$, and $y \geq 2k \geq 0$, for some positive integer $k$, belong to the index space; these are the black points in the right quadrilateral from Fig. 2. In this example, each point in the iterator space is mapped to a distinct point of the index space; this is not always the case, though.

*Algorithm 1: Power-aware signal assignment to the SPM and off-chip memory layers*

**Step 1** *Extract the array references from the given algorithmic specification and decompose the array references for every indexed signal into* disjoint *lattices.*

```
for (k=0; k<=10; k++)
  for (l=0; l<=5; l++)        M[k][l]= ... ;
for (j=0; j<=5; j++)
  for (i=0; i<=2j; i++)   ... = M[i][j];
for (i=1; i<=5; i++)
  for (j=0; j<=i-1; j++) ... = M[2*i][j+1];
```

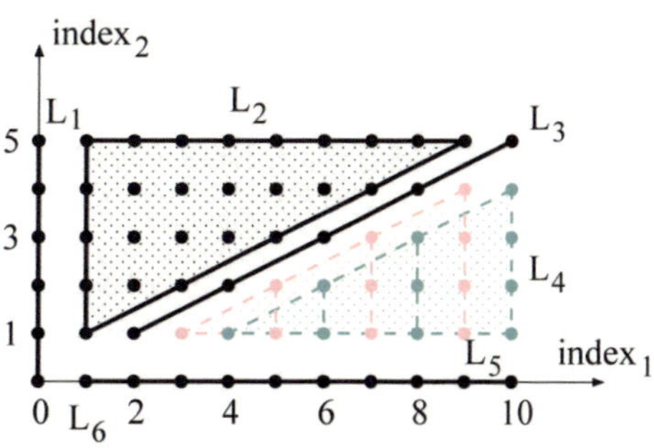


Fig. 3. The decomposition of the array space of signal $M$ in 6 disjoint lattices.

The motivation of the decomposition of the array references relies on the following intuitive idea: the disjoint lattices belonging to many array references are actually those parts of arrays more heavily accessed during the code execution. This decomposition can be analytically performed, using intersections and differences of lattices – operations quite complex (3) involving computations of Hermite Normal Forms and solving Diophantine linear systems (24), computing the vertices of **Z**-polytopes (2) and their supporting polyhedral cones, counting the integral points in **Z**-polyhedra (5; 10), and computing integer projections of polytopes (30). Figure 3 shows the result of such a decomposition for the three array references of signal $M$. The resulting lattices have the following expressions (in non-matrix format):

$L_1 = \{x = 0,\ y = t \mid 5 \geq t \geq 0\}$
$L_2 = \{x = t_1,\ y = t_2 \mid 5 \geq t_2 \geq 1\ ,\ 2t_2 - 1 \geq t_1 \geq 1\}$
$L_3 = \{x = 2t,\ y = t \mid 5 \geq t \geq 1\}$
$L_4 = \{x = 2t_1 + 2,\ y = t_2 \mid 4 \geq t_1 \geq t_2 \geq 1\}$
$L_5 = \{x = 2t_1 + 1,\ y = t_2 \mid 4 \geq t_1 \geq t_2 \geq 1\}$
$L_6 = \{x = t,\ y = 0 \mid 10 \geq t \geq 1\}$

**Step 2** *Compute the number of memory accesses for each disjoint lattice.*

The total number of memory accesses to a given linearly bounded lattice of a signal is computed as follows:

*Step 2.1* Select an array reference of the signal and intersect the given lattice with it. If the intersection is not empty, then the intersection is a linearly bounded lattice as well (27).

*Step 2.2* Compute the number of points in the (non-empty) intersection: this is the number of memory accesses to the given lattice (as part of the selected array reference).

*Step 2.3* Repeat steps 2.1 and 2.2 for all the signal's array references in the code, cumulating the numbers of accesses.

For example, let us consider one of signal $A$'s lattices[3] $\{\ 64 \geq x\ ,\ y \geq 16\}$ obtained in *Step 1*. Intersecting it with the array reference $A[k][l]$ (see the code in Fig. 1), we obtain the lattice $\{i = t_1,\ j = t_2,\ k = t_3,\ l = t_4 \mid 64 \geq t_1,\ t_2,\ t_3,\ t_4 \geq 16,\ t_1 + 16 \geq t_3 \geq t_1 - 16,\ t_2 + 16 \geq t_4 \geq t_2 - 16\}$. The size of this set is 2,614,689 , which is the number of memory accesses to the given lattice as part of the array reference $A[k][l]$. Since the given lattice is also included in the other array reference[4] in the code – $A[i][j]$, a similar computation yields 1,809,025 accesses to the same lattice as part of $A[i][j]$. Hence, the total amount of memory accesses to the given lattice is 2,614,689+1,809,025=4,423,714.

Figure 4 displays a computed map of memory accesses for the signal $A$, where $A$'s index space is in the horizontal plane $xOy$ and the numbers of memory accesses are on the vertical axis $Oz$. This computed map is an approximation of the exact map in Fig. 1 since the accesses within each lattice are considered uniform, equal to the average values obtained above. The advantage of this map construction is that the (usually time-expensive) simulation is not needed any more, being replaced by algebraic computations. Note that a finer granularity in the decomposition of the index space of a signal in disjoint lattices entails a computed map of accesses closer to the exact map.

**Step 3** *Select the lattices having the highest access numbers, whose total size does not exceed the maximum SPM size (assumed to be a design constraint), and assign them to the SPM layer. The other lattices will be assigned to the main memory.*

---

[3] When the lattice has **T**=**I** – the identity matrix – and **u**=**0**, the lattice is actually a **Z**-polytope, like in this example.

[4] Note that in our case, due to *Step 1*, any disjoint lattice is either included in the array reference or disjoint from it.

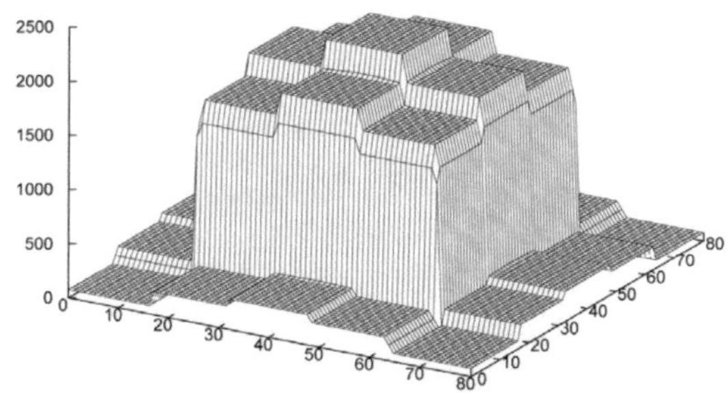

Fig. 4. Computed 3D map of memory *read* accesses for the signal $A$ from the illustrative code in Figure 1.

Storing on-chip all the signals is, obviously, the most desirable scenario in point of view of dynamic energy consumption, which is typically impossible. We assume here that the SPM size is constrained to smaller values than the overall storage requirement. In our tests, we computed the ratio between the dynamic energy reduction and the SPM size after mapping; the value of the SPM size maximizing this ratio was selected, the idea being to obtain the maximum benefit (in energy point of view) for the smallest SPM size.

## 3. Mapping signals within memory layers

This design phase has the following goals: (a) to map the signals (already assigned to the memory layers) into amounts of data storage as small as possible, both for the SPM and the main memory; (b) to compute these amounts of storage after mapping on both memory layers (allocation solution) and be able to determine the memory location of each array element from the specification (assignment solution); (c) to use mapping functions simple enough in order to ensure an address generation hardware of a reasonable complexity; (d) to ascertain that any scalar signals (array elements) *simultaneously alive* are mapped to distinct storage locations.
Since the mapping models (13) and (28) play an important part in this section, they will be explained and illustrated below.
To reduce the size of a multidimensional array mapped to memory, the model (13) considers all the possible *canonical*[5] linearizations of the array; for any linearization, the largest distance at any time between two live elements is computed. This distance plus 1 is then the storage "window" required for the mapping of the array into the data memory. More formally, $|W_A| = \min \max \{ \, dist(A_i, A_j) \, \} + 1$, where $|W_A|$ is the size of the storage window of a signal $A$, the minimum is taken over all the canonical linearizations, while the maximum is taken over all the pairs of $A$-elements ($A_i$,$A_j$) simultaneously alive.
This mapping model will be illustrated for the loop nest from Fig. 5(a). The graph above the code represents the array (index) space of signal $A$. The points represent the $A$-elements $A[index_1][index_2]$ which are produced (and consumed as well) in the loop nest. The points to the left of the dashed line represent the elements produced till the end of the iteration ($i = 14$, $j = 4$), the black points being the elements still alive (i.e., produced and still used as

[5] For instance, a 2-D array can be typically linearized concatenating the rows or concatenating the columns. In addition, the elements in a given dimension can be mapped in the increasing or decreasing order of the respective index.

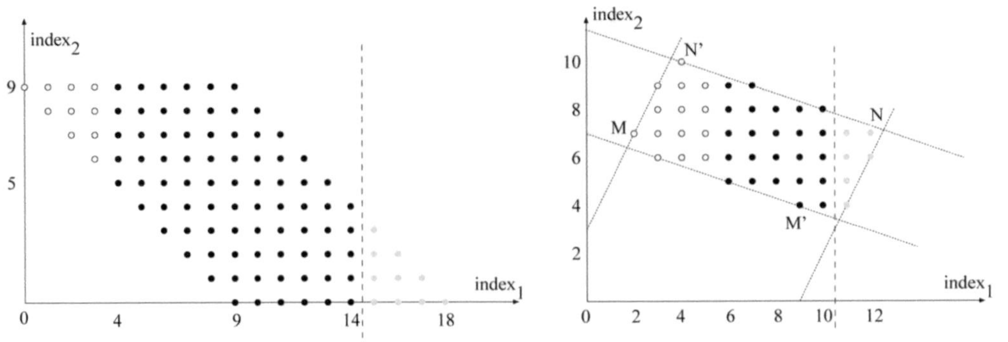


```
                              // All the A-elements are
for (i=0; i<=28; i++)         // consumed in this loop nest
  for (j=0; j<=9; j++) {
    if ( i+j >= 9  && i+j <= 18 )  A[i][j] = 1 ;
    if ( i+j >= 19 && i+j <= 28 )  ... = A[i-10][j] ;
  }
```

(a)

```
                              // All the A-elements are
for (i=2; i<=16; i++)         // consumed in this loop nest
  for (j=2*i-18; j<=2*i+3; j++) {
    if ( i+3*j >= 21 && i+3*j <= 34 )  A[i][j] = 1 ;
    if ( i+3*j >= 49 && i+3*j <= 62 )  ... = A[i-4][j-8] ;
  }
```

(b)

Fig. 5. (a-b) Illustrative examples having a similar code structure. The mapping model by array linearization yields a better allocation solution for the former example, whereas the bounding window model behaves better for the latter one.

operands in the next iterations), while the circles representing $A$-elements already 'dead' (i.e., not needed as operands any more). The light grey points to the right of the dashed line are $A$-elements still unborn (to be produced in the next iterations).

If we consider the array linearization by column concatenation in the increasing order of the columns (($A[index_1][index_2]$, $index_1$=0,18), $index_2$=0,9), two elements simultaneously alive, placed the farthest apart from each other, are $A[9][0]$ and $A[9][9]$. The distance between them is 9×19=171. Now, if we consider the array linearization by row concatenation in the increasing order of the rows (($A[index_1][index_2]$, $index_2$=0,9), $index_1$=0,18), the maximum distance between live elements is 99 (e.g., between $A[4][5]$ and $A[14][4]$). For all the canonical linearizations, the maximum distances have the values {99, 109, 171, 181}. The best canonical linearization for the array $A$ is the concatenation row by row, increasingly. A memory window $W_A$ of 99+1=100 successive locations (relative to a certain base address) is sufficient to store the array without mapping conflicts: it is sufficient that any access to $A[index_1][index_2]$ be redirected to $W_A[(10 * index_1 + index_2) \bmod 100]$.

In order to avoid the inconvenience of analyzing different linearization schemes, another possibility is to compute a maximal bounding window $W_A = (w_1, \ldots, w_m)$ large enough to encompass at any time the simultaneously alive $A$-elements. An access to the element $A[index_1] \ldots [index_m]$ can then be redirected without any conflict to the window location $W_A[index_1 \bmod w_1] \ldots [index_m \bmod w_m]$; in its turn, the window is mapped, relative to a base address, into the physical memory by a typical canonical linearization, like row or column concatenation for 2-D arrays. Each window element $w_k$ is computed as the maximum difference in absolute value between the $k$-th indexes of any two $A$-elements ($A_i$,$A_j$) simultaneously alive, plus 1. More formally, $w_k = \max\{\, |x_k(A_i) - x_k(A_j)| \,\} + 1$, for $k = 1, \ldots, m$. This ensures that any two array elements simultaneously alive are mapped to distinct memory locations. The amount of data memory required for storing (after mapping) the array $A$ is the volume of the bounding window $W_A$, that is, $|W_A| = \Pi_{k=1}^{m} w_k$.

In the illustrative example shown in Fig. 5(a), the bounding window of the signal $A$ is $W_A = (11\ ,\ 10)$. It follows that the storage allocation for signal $A$ is 100 locations if the linearization model is used, and $w_1 \times w_2$=110 locations when the bounding window model is applied. However, in the example shown in Fig. 5(b), where the code has a similar structure, the bounding window model yields a better allocation result – 30 storage locations, since the 2-D window of $A$ is $W_A = (5\ ,\ 6)$, whereas the linearization model yields 32 locations (the best canonical linearization being the row concatenation in the increasing order of rows).

Our software system incorporates both mapping models, their implementation being based on the same polyhedral framework operating with lattices, used also in Section 2. This is advantageous both from the point of view of computational efficiency and relative to the amount of allocated data storage – since the mapping window for each signal is the smallest one of the two models. Moreover, this methodology can be applied independently to the memory layers, providing a complete storage allocation/assignment solution for distributed memory organizations.

Before explaining the global flow of the algorithm, let us examine the simple case of a code with only one array reference in it: take, for instance, the two nested loops from Fig. 5(b), but without the second conditional statement that consumes the $A$-elements. In the bounding window model, $W_A$ can be determined by computing the integer projections on the two axes of the lattice of $A[i][j]$, represented graphically by all the points inside the quadrilateral from Fig. 5(b). It can be directly observed that the integer projections of this polygon have the sizes: $w_1 = 11$ and $w_2 = 7$. In the linearization model, denoting $x$ and $y$ the two indexes, the distance between two $A$-elements $A_1(x_1, y_1)$ and $A_2(x_2, y_2)$, assuming row concatenation in the increasing order of the rows, is: $dist(A_1, A_2) = (x_2 - x_1)\Delta y + (y_2 - y_1)$, where $\Delta y$ is the range of the second index (here, equal to 7) in the array space.[6] Then, the $A$-elements at a maximum distance have the minimum and, respectively, the maximum index vectors relative to the lexicographic order. These array $A$-elements are represented by the points $M = A[2][7]$ and $N = A[12][7]$ in Fig. 5(b), and $dist(M, N)$ = (12-2)×7 +(0-0)=70. Similarly, in the linearization by column concatenation, the array elements at the maximum distance from each other are still the elements with (lexicographically) minimum and maximum index vectors, *provided an interchange of the indexes is applied first.* These are the points $M' = A[9][4]$ and $N' = A[4][10]$ in Fig. 5(b). More general, the maximum distance between the points of a live lattice in a canonical linearization is the distance between the (lexicographically) minimum and maximum index vectors, providing an index permutation is applied first. The distance between the array elements $A_i(x_1^i, x_2^i, \ldots, x_m^i)$ and $A_j(x_1^j, x_2^j, \ldots, x_m^j)$ is:

$dist(A_i, A_j) = (x_1^j - x_1^i)\Delta x_2 \cdots \Delta x_m + (x_2^j - x_2^i)\Delta x_3 \cdots \Delta x_m + \cdots + (x_{m-1}^j - x_{m-1}^i)\Delta x_m + (x_m^j - x_m^i)$ where the index vector of $A_j$ is lexicographically larger than of $A_i$ ($\Delta x_i$ is the range of $x_i$).

*Algorithm 2: For each memory layer* (SPM and main memory) *compute the mapping windows for every indexed signal having lattices assigned to that layer.*

**Step 1** *Compute underestimations of the window sizes on the current memory layer for each indexed signal, taking into account only the live signals at the boundaries between the loop nests.*

Let $A$ be an $m$-dimensional signal in the algorithmic specification, and let $\mathcal{P}_A$ be the set of disjoint lattices partitioning the index space of $A$. A high-level pseudo-code of the computation

[6] To ensure that the distance is a nonnegative number, we shall assume that $[x_2\ y_2]^T \succ [x_1\ y_1]^T$ relative to the lexicographic order. The vector $\mathbf{y} = [y_1, \ldots, y_m]^T$ is larger lexicographically than $\mathbf{x} = [x_1, \ldots, x_m]^T$ (written $\mathbf{y} \succ \mathbf{x}$) if $(y_1 > x_1)$, or $(y_1 = x_1$ and $y_2 > x_2), \ldots,$ or $(y_1 = x_1, \ldots, y_{m-1} = x_{m-1}$, and $y_m > x_m)$.

of $A$'s preliminary windows is given below. Preliminary window sizes for each canonical linearization according to DeGreef's model (13) are computed first, followed by the computation of the window size underestimate according to Tronçon's model (28) in the same framework operating with lattices. The meaning of the variables are explained as comments.

**for** ( *each canonical linearization* $\mathcal{C}$ ) {
**for** ( *each disjoint lattice* $L \in \mathcal{P}_A$ ) // compute the (lexicographically) minimum and maximum ...
compute $x^{min}(L)$ and $x^{max}(L)$ ; // ... index vectors of $L$ relative to $\mathcal{C}$
**for** ( *each boundary* $n$ *between the loop nests* $n$ *and* $n+1$ ) { // the start of the code is boundary 0
let $\mathcal{P}_A(n)$ be the collection of disjoint lattices of $A$, which are alive at the boundary $n$ ;
// these are disjoint lattices produced *before* the boundary and consumed *after* it
let $X_n^{min} = \min_{L \in \mathcal{P}_A(n)} \{x^{min}(L)\}$ and $X_n^{max} = \max_{L \in \mathcal{P}_A(n)} \{x^{max}(L)\}$ ;
$|W_\mathcal{C}(n)| = dist(X_n^{min}, X_n^{max}) + 1$ ; // The distance is computed in the canonical linearization $\mathcal{C}$
}
$|W_\mathcal{C}| = \max_n \{ |W_\mathcal{C}(n)| \}$ ; // the window size according to (13) for the canonical linearization $\mathcal{C}$
} // (possibly, an underestimate)
**for** ( *each disjoint lattice* $L \in \mathcal{P}_A$ )
**for** ( *each dimension k of signal A* )
compute $x_k^{min}(L)$ and $x_k^{max}(L)$ ; // the extremes of the integer projection of $L$ on the $k$-th axis
**for** ( *each boundary* $n$ *between the loop nests* $n$ *and* $n+1$ ) { // the start of the code is boundary 0
let $\mathcal{P}_A(n)$ be the collection of disjoint lattices of $A$, which are alive at the boundary $n$ ;
**for** ( *each dimension k of signal A* ) {
let $X_k^{min} = \min_{L \in \mathcal{P}_A(n)} \{x_k^{min}(L)\}$ and $X_k^{max} = \max_{L \in \mathcal{P}_A(n)} \{x_k^{max}(L)\}$ ;
$w_k(n) = X_k^{max} - X_k^{min} + 1$ ; // The $k$-th side of $A$'s bounding window at boundary $n$
}
}
**for** ( *each dimension k of signal A* ) $w_k = max_n\{w_k(n)\}$ ; // $k$-th side of $A$'s window over all boundaries
$|W| = \Pi_{k=1}^m w_k$ ; // the window size according to (28) (possibly, an underestimate)

*Step 1* finds the exact values of the window sizes for both mapping models only when every loop nest either produces or consumes (but not both!) the signal's elements. Otherwise, when in a certain loop nest elements of the signal are both produced *and* consumed (see the illustrative example from Fig. 5(a)), then the window sizes obtained at the end of *Step 1* may be only underestimates since an increase of the storage requirement can happen *inside* the loop nest. Then, an additional step is required to find the exact values of the window sizes in both mapping models.

**Step 2** *Update the mapping windows for each indexed signal in every loop nest producing and consuming elements of the signal.*

The guiding idea is that local or global maxima of the bounding window size $|W|$ are reached immediately before the consumption of an $A$-element, which may entail a shrinkage of some side of the bounding window encompassing the live elements. Similarly, the local or global maxima of $|W_C|$ are reached immediately before the consumption of an $A$-element, which may entail a decrease of the maximum distance between live elements. Consequently, for each $A$-element consumed in a loop nest which also produces $A$-elements, we construct the disjoint lattices partially produced and those partially consumed until the iteration when the $A$-element is consumed. Afterwards, we do a similar computation as in *Step 1* which may result in increased values for $|W_C|$ and/or $|W|$.
Finally, the amount of data memory allocated for signal $A$ on the current memory layer is $|W_A| = \min\{\,|W|\,,\min_C\{\,|W_C|\,\}\,\}$, that is, the smallest data storage provided by the bounding window and the linearization mapping models. In principle, the overall amount of data memory after mapping is $\sum_A |W_A|$ – the sum of the mapping window sizes of all the signals having lattices assigned to the current memory layer. In addition, a post-processing step attempts to further enhance the allocation solution: our polyhedral framework allows to efficiently check weather two multidimensional signals have disjoint lifetimes, in which case the signals can share the largest of the two windows. More general, an incompatibility graph (14) is used to optimize the memory sharing among all the signals at the level of whole code.

## 4. Experimental results

A hierarchical memory allocation tool has been implemented in C++, incorporating the algorithms described in this chapter. For the time being, the tool supports only a two-level memory hierarchy, where an SPM is used between the main memory and the processor core. The dynamic energy is computed based on the number of accesses to each memory layer. In computing the dynamic energy consumptions for the SPM and the main (off-chip) memory, the CACTI v5.3 power model (31) was used.
Table 1 summarizes the results of our experiments, carried out on a PC with an Intel Core 2 Duo 1.8 GHz processor and 512 MB RAM. The benchmarks used are: (1) a motion detection algorithm used in the transmission of real-time video signals on data networks; (2) the kernel of a motion estimation algorithm for moving objects (MPEG-4); (3) Durbin's algorithm for solving Toeplitz systems with $N$ unknowns; (4) a singular value decomposition (SVD) updating algorithm (23) used in spatial division multiplex access (SDMA) modulation in mobile communication receivers, in beamforming, and Kalman filtering; (5) the kernel of a voice coding application – essential component of a mobile radio terminal.
The table displays the total number of memory accesses, the data memory size (in storage locations/bytes), and the dynamic energy consumption assuming only one (off-chip) memory layer; in addition, the SPM size and the savings of dynamic energy applying, respectively, a previous model steered by the total number of accesses for whole arrays (7), another previous model steered by the most accessed array rows/columns (18), and the current model, versus the single-layer memory scenario; the CPU times. The energy consumptions for the motion estimation benchmark were, respectively, 1894, 1832, and 1522 $\mu$J; the saved energies relative to the energy in column 4 are displayed as percentages in columns 6-8. Our experiments show that the savings of dynamic energy consumption are from 40% to over 70% relative to the energy used in the case of a flat memory design. Although previous models produce energy savings as well, our model led to 20%-33% better savings than them.
Different from the previous works on power-aware assignment to the memory layers, our framework provides also the mapping functions that determine the exact locations for any

| Application parameters | #Memory accesses | Mem. size | Dyn. energy 1-layer [$\mu J$] | SPM size | Dyn. energy saved (7) | Dyn. energy saved (18) | Dyn. energy saved | CPU [sec] |
|---|---|---|---|---|---|---|---|---|
| Motion detection M=N=32, m=n=4 | 136,242 | 2,740 | 486 | 841 | 30.2% | 44.5% | 49.2% | 4 |
| Motion estimation M=32, N=16 | 864,900 | 3,624 | 3,088 | 1,416 | 38.7% | 40.7% | 50.7% | 23 |
| Durbin algorithm N =500 | 1,004,993 | 1,249 | 3,588 | 764 | 55.2% | 58.5% | 73.2% | 28 |
| SVD updating n =100 | 6,227,124 | 34,950 | 22,231 | 12,672 | 35.9% | 38.4% | 46.0% | 37 |
| Vocoder | 200,000 | 12,690 | 714 | 3,879 | 30.8% | 32.5% | 39.5% | 8 |

Table 1. Experimental results.

array element in the specification. This provides the necessary information for the automated design of the address generation unit, which is one of our future development directions. Different from the previous works on signal-to-memory mapping, our framework offers a hierarchical strategy and, also, two metrics of quality for the memory allocation solutions: (a) the sum of the *minimum* array windows (that is, the optimum memory sharing between elements of same arrays), and (b) the minimum storage requirement for the execution of the application code (that is, the optimum memory sharing between all the scalar signals or array elements in the code) (3).

## 5. Conclusions

This chapter has presented an integrated computer-aided design methodology for power-aware memory allocation, targeting embedded data-intensive signal processing applications. The memory management tasks – the signal assignment to the memory layers and their mapping to the physical memories – are efficiently addressed within a common polyhedral framework.

## 6. References

[1] F. Angiolini, L. Benini, and A. Caprara, "An efficient profile-based algorithm for scratch-pad memory partitioning," *IEEE Trans. Computer-Aided Design*, vol. 24, no. 11, pp. 1660-1676, Nov. 2005.
[2] D. Avis, "lrs: A revised implementation of the reverse search vertex enumeration algorithm," in *Polytopes – Combinatorics and Computation*, G. Kalai and G. Ziegler (eds.), Birkhauser-Verlag, 2000, pp. 177-198.
[3] F. Balasa, H. Zhu, and I.I. Luican, "Computation of storage requirements for multi-dimensional signal processing applications," *IEEE Trans. VLSI Systems*, vol. 15, no. 4, pp. 447-460, April 2007.
[4] R. Banakar, S. Steinke, B.-S. Lee, M. Balakrishnan, and P. Marwedel, "Scratchpad memory: A design alternative for cache on-chip memory in embedded systems," in *Proc. 10th Int. Workshop on Hardware/Software Codesign*, Estes Park CO, May 2002.
[5] A.I. Barvinok, "A polynomial time algorithm for counting integral points in polyhedra when the dimension is fixed," *Mathematics of Operations Research*, vol. 19, no. 4, pp. 769-779, Nov. 1994.
[6] L. Benini, L. Macchiarulo, A. Macii, E. Macii, and M. Poncino, "Layout-driven memory synthesis for embedded systems-on-chip," *IEEE Trans. VLSI Systems*, vol. 10, no. 2, pp. 96-105, April 2002.
[7] E. Brockmeyer, M. Miranda, H. Corporaal, and F. Catthoor, "Layer assignment techniques for low energy in multi-layered memory organisations," in *Proc. ACM/IEEE Design, Automation & Test in Europe*, Munich, Germany, Mar. 2003, pp. 1070-1075.
[8] F. Catthoor, S. Wuytack, E. De Greef, F. Balasa, L. Nachtergaele, and A. Vandecappelle, *Custom Memory Management Methodology: Exploration of Memory Organization for Embedded Multimedia System Design*, Boston: Kluwer Academic Publishers, 1998.
[9] E. Chan and S. Panchanathan, "Motion estimation architecture for video compression," *IEEE Trans. on Consumer Electronics*, vol. 39, pp. 292-297, Aug. 1993.
[10] Ph. Clauss and V. Loechner, "Parametric analysis of polyhedral iteration spaces," *J. VLSI Signal Processing*, vol. 19, no. 2, pp. 179-194, 1998.

[11] S. Coumeri and D.E. Thomas, "Memory modeling for system synthesis," *IEEE Trans. VLSI Systems*, vol. 8, no. 3, pp. 327-334, June 2000.
[12] A. Darte, R. Schreiber, and G. Villard, "Lattice-based memory allocation," *IEEE Trans. Computers*, vol. 54, pp. 1242-1257, Oct. 2005.
[13] E. De Greef, F. Catthoor, and H. De Man, "Memory size reduction through storage order optimization for embedded parallel multimedia applications," *Parallel Computing*, special issue on "Parallel Processing and Multimedia," Elsevier, vol. 23, no. 12, pp. 1811-1837, Dec. 1997.
[14] G. De Micheli, *Synthesis and Optimization of Digital Circuits*, McGraw-Hill, 1994.
[15] J.Z. Fang and M. Lu, "An iteration partition approach for cache or local memory thrashing on parallel processing," *IEEE Trans. Computers*, vol. 42, no. 5, pp. 529-546, 1993.
[16] B. Franke and M. O'Boyle, "Compiler transformation of pointers to explicit array accesses in DSP applications," in *Proc. Int. Conf. Compiler Construction*, 2001.
[17] C. Ghez, M. Miranda, A. Vandecapelle, F. Catthoor, D. Verkest, "Systematic high-level address code transformations for piece-wise linear indexing: illustration on a medical imaging algorithm," in *Proc. IEEE Workshop on Signal Processing Systems*, pp. 623-632, Lafayette LA, Oct. 2000.
[18] Q. Hu, A. Vandecapelle, M. Palkovic, P.G. Kjeldsberg, E. Brockmeyer, and F. Catthoor, "Hierarchical memory size estimation for loop fusion and loop shifting in data-dominated applications," in *Proc. Asia-S. Pacific Design Automation Conf.*, Yokohama, Japan, Jan. 2006, pp. 606-611.
[19] I. Issenin, E. Brockmeyer, M. Miranda, and N. Dutt, "Data reuse analysis technique for software-controlled memory hierarchies," in *Proc. Design, Automation & Test in Europe*, 2004.
[20] I. Issenin and N. Dutt, "FORAY-GEN: Automatic generation of affine functions for memory optimization," *Proc. Design, Automation & Test in Europe*, 2005.
[21] M. Kandemir and A. Choudhary, "Compiler-directed scratch-pad memory hierarchy design and management," in *Proc. 39th ACM/IEEE Design Automation Conf.*, Las Vegas NV, June 2002, pp. 690-695.
[22] N. Manjiakian and T. Abdelrahman, "Reduction of cache conflicts in loop nests," *Tech. Report CSRI-318*, Univ. Toronto, Canada, 1995.
[23] M. Moonen, P. V. Dooren, and J. Vandewalle, "An SVD updating algorithm for subspace tracking," *SIAM J. Matrix Anal. Appl.*, vol. 13, no. 4, pp. 1015-1038, 1992.
[24] A. Schrijver, *Theory of Linear and Integer Programming*, New York: John Wiley, 1986.
[25] W. Shiue and C. Chakrabarti, "Memory exploration for low-power embedded systems," in *Proc. 35th ACM/IEEE Design Automation Conf.*, June 1998, pp. 140-145.
[26] G. Talavera, M. Jayapala, J. Carrabina, and F. Catthoor, "Address generation optimization for embedded high-performance processors: A survey," *J. Signal Processing Systems*, Springer, vol. 53, no. 3, pp. 271-284, Dec. 2008.
[27] L. Thiele, "Compiler techniques for massive parallel architectures," in *State-of-the-art in Computer Science*, P. Dewilde (ed.), Kluwer Acad. Publ., 1992.
[28] R. Tronçon, M. Bruynooghe, G. Janssens, and F. Catthoor, "Storage size reduction by in-place mapping of arrays," in *Verification, Model Checking and Abstract Interpretation*, A. Coresi (ed.), 2002, pp. 167-181.
[29] S. Udayakumaran and R. Barua, "Compiler-decided dynamic memory allocation for scratch-pad based embedded systems," in *Proc. Int. Conf. on Compilers, Architecture, and Synthesis for Embedded Systems*, pp. 276-286, New York NY, Oct. 2003.

[30] S. Verdoolaege, K. Beyls, M. Bruynooghe, and F. Catthoor, "Experiences with enumeration of integer projections of parametric polytopes," in *Compiler Construction: 14th Int. Conf.*, R. Bodik (ed.), vol. 3443, pp. 91-105, Springer, 2005.
[31] S. Wilton and N. Jouppi, "CACTI: An enhanced access and cycle time model," *IEEE J. Solid-State Circ.*, vol. 31, pp. 677-688, May 1996.
[32] S. Wuytack, J.-P. Diguet, F. Catthoor, and H. De Man, "Formalized methodology for data reuse exploration for low-power hierarchical memory mappings," *IEEE Trans. VLSI Systems*, vol. 6, no. 4, pp. 529-537, Dec. 1998.

9

# High Throughput Architecture for High Performance NoC

Mohamed A. Abd El Ghany,
Magdy A. El-Moursy* and Mohammed Ismail**
*Electronics Engineering Dept., German University in Cairo, Cairo, Egypt*
*Electronics Research Institute, Cairo, Egypt, Mentor Graphics Corporation, Cairo, Egypt**
*Electrical Engineering Dept., The Ohio State University, Columbus, USA. The RaMSiS Group, KTH, Sweden***

## 1. Introduction

As the number and functionality of intellectual property blocks (IPs) in System on Chips (SoCs) increase, complexity of interconnection architectures of the SoCs have also been increased. Different researches have been published in high performance SoCs; however, the system scalability and bandwidth are limited. Network on Chip (NoC) is emerging as the best replacement for the existing interconnection architectures. NoC is composed of network of interconnects and number of temporary storage elements called switches. The temporary storage element of different NoC architectures has different number of ports. The main component of the port is the virtual channels. The virtual channels consist of several buffers controlled by a multiplexer and an arbiter which grants access for only one buffer at a time according to the request priority. When the number of buffers is increased, the throughput increases. High throughput and low latency are the desirable characteristics of a multi processing system. More research is needed to enhance performance of NoC components (network of interconnects and the storage elements). Many NoC architectures have been proposed in the past, e.g., SPIN (Guerrier & Greiner, 2000), CLICHÉ (Kumar et al., 2002), Folded Torus (Dally & Towles, 2001), Octagon (Karim et al., 2002) and Butterfly fat-tree (BFT) (Pande et al., 2003a). Among those, the butterfly fat tree (BFT) has found extensive use in different parallel machines and shown to be hardware efficient (Grecu et al., 2004a). The main advantage of the butterfly fat tree is that the number of storage elements in the network converges to a constant irrespective of the number of levels in the tree network. In the SPIN architecture, redundant paths contained within the fat tree structure are utilized to reduce contention in the network. CLICHÉ (*Chip-Level Integration of Communicating Heterogeneous Elements*) is simplest from a layout perspective and the local interconnections between resources and storage elements are independent of the size of the network. In the Octagon architecture, the communication between any two nodes takes at most two hops within the basic Octagon unit.
After the NoC design paradigm has been proposed (Dally & Towles, 2001) ; (Kumar et al., 2002) ; (Guerrier & Greiner, 2000) ; (Karim et al., 2002) ; (Pande et al., 2003) ; (Benini &

Micheli, 2002) ; (Grecu et al., 2004a), many researches on architectural and conceptual aspects of NoC have been reported such as topology selection (Murali & Micheli, 2004), quality of service (QoS) (Bolotin et al., 2004), design automation (Bertozzi et al., 2005) ; (Liang et al., 2004) ; ( Pande et al., 2005a), performance evaluation (Pande et al., 2005b) ; (Salminen et al., 2007) ; (Grecu et al., 2007a) and test and verification (Grecu et al., 2007b) ; (Kim et al., 2004) ; (Murali et al., 2005). These researches have taken a top-down approach (a high level analysis of NoC) and they didn't touch the issues on a circuit level. However, a little research has reported on design issues in implementation of NoC in the perspective of circuit level (Lee et al., 2003) ; (Lee et al., 2004) ; (Lee & Kim et al., 2005) ; (Lee et al., 2006) ; (Lee; Lee & Yoo, 2005). Although, they were implemented and verified on the silicon, they were only focusing on implementation of limited set of architectures.

In large-scale NoC, power consumption should be minimized for cost-efficient implementations. Although different researches have been published in NoCs, they were only focusing on performance and scalability issues rather than power efficiency. Scaling with power reduction is the trend in future technologies. Lowering supply voltage is the most effective way to reduce power consumption. With lowering supply voltage, the threshold voltage ($V_{TH}$) has to be decreased to achieve high performance requirements. Reducing $V_{TH}$ causes significant increase in the leakage component. Different researches have been published in power minimization of high performance CMOS circuits (Khellah & Elmasry, 1999) ; (Kao & Chandrakasan, 2000) ; (Kursun & Friedman, 2004).

In this chapter, different tradeoffs in designing efficient NoC including both elements of the network (interconnects network and storage elements) are described. Building high performance NoC is presented. In addition, a high throughput architecture is proposed. The proposed architecture to achieve high throughput can improve the latency of the network. The circuit implementation issues are considered in the proposed architecture. The switch structure along with the interconnect architecture are shown in Fig. 1 for 2 IPs and 2 switches. The proposed architecture is applied to different NoCs topologies. The efficiency and performance are evaluated. To the best of our knowledge, this is the first in depth analysis on circuit level to optimize performance of different NoC architectures.

This chapter is organized as follows: In Section 2, the proposed port architecture is presented. The new High Throughput architecture is described in Section 3. In Section 4, power characteristics for different high throughput architectures are provided. The performance and overhead analysis of the proposed architecture are provided in Section 5. In Section 6, the proposed design of low power NoC switch is described. Finally, conclusions are provided in Section 7.

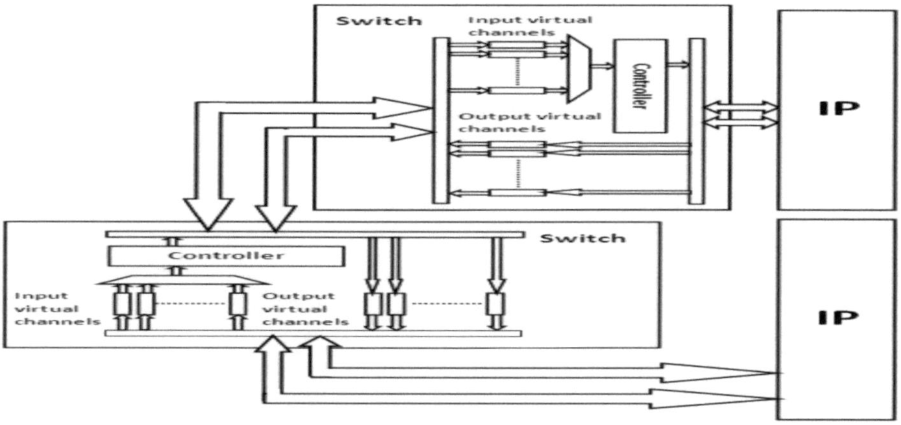


Fig. 1. proposed high throughput architecture.

## 2. Port architecture

The switch of different architectures has different number of ports. Each port of the switch includes input virtual channels, output virtual channels, a header decoder, controller, input arbiter and output arbiter as shown in (Pande et al., 2003a). When the number of virtual channel is increased, the throughput increases. The input arbiter is used to allow only one virtual channel to access a physical port. The input arbiter consists of a priority matrix and grant circuits (Pande et al., 2003b).

The priority matrix stores the priorities of the requests. The grant circuits generate the granted signals to allow only one virtual channel to access a physical port. The messages are divided into fixed length flow control units (flits). When the granted virtual channel stores one whole flit, it sends a full signal to controller. If it is a header flit, the header decoder determines the destination. The controller checks the status of destination port. If it is available, the path between input and output is established. All subsequent flits of the corresponding packet are sent from input to output using the established path. The flits from more than one input port may simultaneously try to access a particular output port. The output arbiter is used to allow only one input port to access an output port.

Virtual channels consist of several buffers controlled by a multiplexer and an arbiter which grants access for only one virtual channel at a time according to the request priority. Once the request succeeds, its priority is set to be the lowest among all other requests. In the proposed architecture, rather than using one multiplexer and one arbiter to control the virtual channels, two multiplexer and two arbiters are employed as shown in Fig. 2. The virtual channels are divided into two groups, each group controlled by one multiplexer and one arbiter. Each group of virtual channels is supported by one interconnect bus as described in Section 3. However looks trivial, this port architecture has a great influence on the switch frequency and the throughput of the network.

Let us consider an example with the number of virtual channels of 8 channels. In the NoC architecture, 8x8 input arbiter and 8x1 multiplexer are needed to control the input virtual channels as shown in Fig. 2 (a). The 8x8 input arbiter consists of 8x8 grant circuit and 8x8 priority matrix. In the proposed architecture, two 4x4 input arbiters, two 4x1 multiplexers, 2x1 multiplexers and 2x2 grant circuit are integrated to allow only one virtual channel to access a physical port as shown in Fig. 2 (b). The 4x4 input arbiter consists of 4x4 grant circuit and 4x4 priority matrix. The values of the grant signals are determined by the priority matrix. The number of grant signals equals to the number of requests and the number of selection signals of the multiplexer. The area of 8x8 input arbiter is larger than the area of two 4x4 input arbiters. Also, the area of 8x1multiplexer is larger than the area of two 4x1 multiplexers. Consequently, the required area to implement the proposed switch with the proposed architecture is less than the required area to implement the conventional switch. In order to divide a 4x1 multiplexer into three 2x1 multiplexers, the 4x4 input arbiter should be divided into three 2x2 input arbiters. The grant signals generated by three 2x2 input arbiter (6 signals) aren't the same grant signals generated by the 4x4 input arbiter (4 signals). Therefore, the 4x4 input arbiter can't be replaced by three 2x2 input arbiters unless the number of interconnect buses is increased to be equal the number of virtual channels groups. By increasing the number of interconnect buses, the metal resources and power dissipation are increased as described in Section 5.

Without circuit optimization in BFT architecture, the change in the maximum frequency of the switch with the number of virtual channels is shown in Fig. 3. When the number of virtual channels is increased beyond four, the maximum frequency of the switch is decreased. The throughput is saturated when the number of virtual channels is increased beyond four (Pande et al., 2005b) for different number of ports. On the other hand, the average message latency increases with the number of virtual channels. To keep the latency low while preserving the throughput, the number of virtual channels is constrained to four (Pande et al., 2003b),(Pande et al., 2005b). Throughput is a parameter that measures the rate in which message traffic can be sent across a communication network. It is defined by (Pande et al., 2005b):

$$TP = \frac{(number\ of\ messages\ completed) * (message\ length)}{(number\ of\ IP\ blocks) * (total\ time)} \quad (1)$$

The throughput is proportional to the number of completed messages. The number of completed messages increases with the number of virtual channels. Total transfer time of messages decreases with the frequency of the switch. Therefore the throughput can be improved by increasing the number of virtual channels or by increasing the frequency of switch (Lee & Bagherzadeh, 2006). The HT-BFT switch is smaller than the BFT switch. Therefore, the maximum frequency of the switch is improved. The change in the maximum frequency of the proposed switch with the number of virtual channels is shown in Fig. 3 for HT-BFT architecture. The number of virtual channels could be increased up to eight without significant reduction in the operating frequency.

The frequency of the network switch is characterized with different number of virtual channels for different network topologies and the proposed architectures as shown in Fig. 4. As compared to the conventional architectures, the operating frequency of the proposed architectures is decreased when the number of virtual channels is higher than eight rather than four. As shown in Fig. 3 and Fig. 4, doubling the number of virtual channels does not degrade the frequency of the switch (rather than 4 virtual channels, 8 virtual channels could be used). However, a severe increase in the number of virtual channels (more than 8) could degrade performance. Increasing the number of virtual channels would increase the traffic going through the links (interconnects) between the switches, increasing the contention on the bus and increasing the latency which each flit will experience. In order to improve throughput, the links (interconnects) connecting the switches with each other should be increased. Since the number of virtual channels could be doubled (from four to eight), doubling the number of virtual channels between switches is proposed.

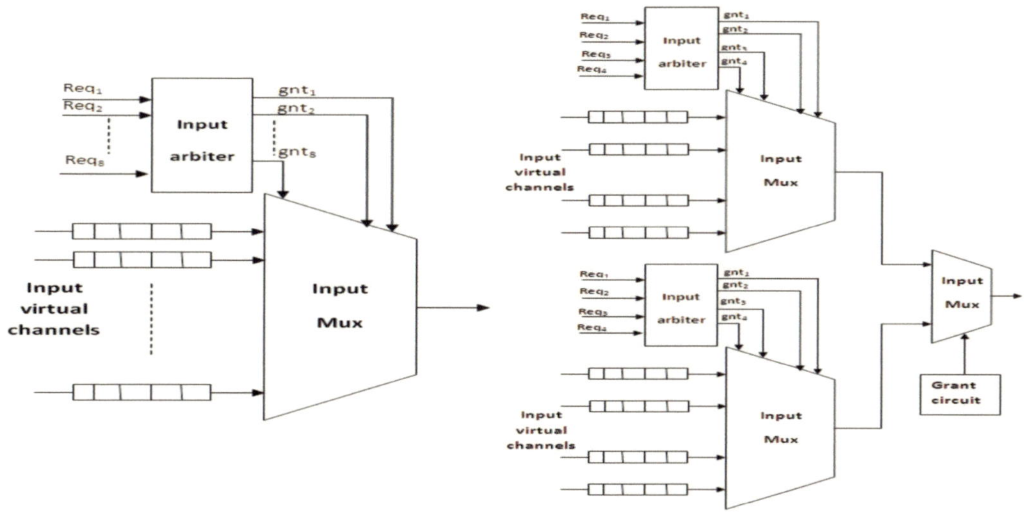


(a) (b)

Fig. 2. (a) Circuit diagram of switch port, (b) circuit diagram of High Throughput switch port.

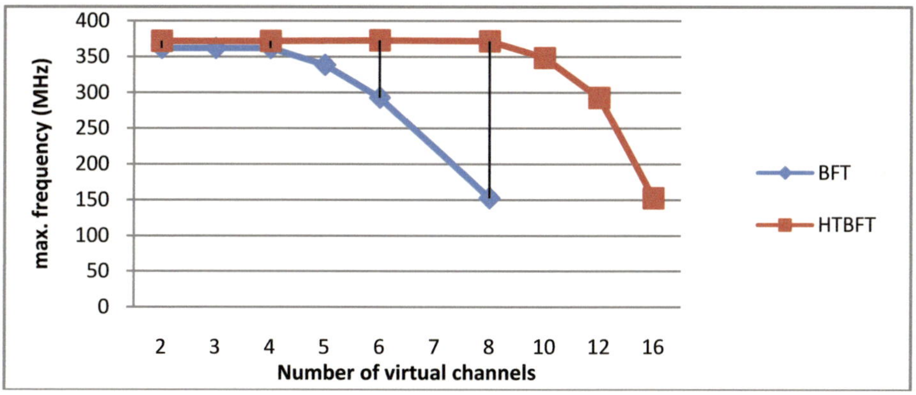


Fig. 3. Maximum frequency of a switch with different number of virtual channels for BFT and HTBFT.

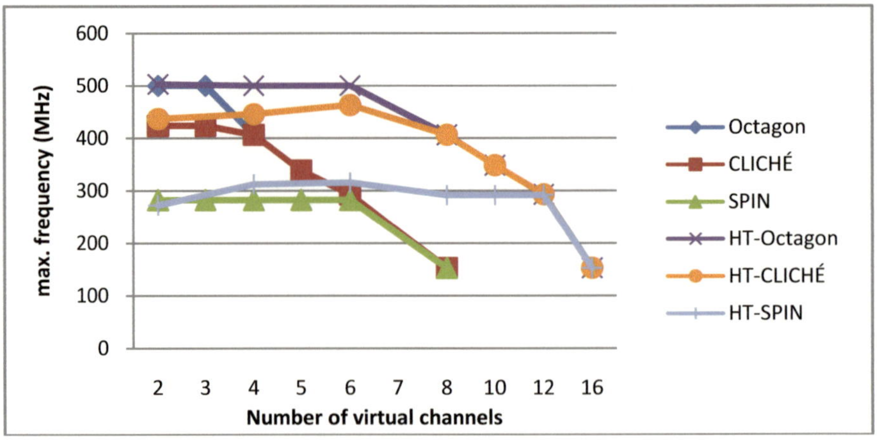


Fig. 4. Maximum frequency of a switch with different number of virtual channels for different NoC architectures.

Let us consider an example of BFT architecture. The area required to implement the BFT switch and HT-BFT switch is shown with different number of virtual channels in Fig. 5. The HT-BFT architecture decreases the area of switch by 18%. Consequently, a system with eight virtual channels achieves high throughput, high frequency and low latency while the area of design is optimized. The architectures of different NoC topologies to achieve high throughput network is discussed in Section 3.

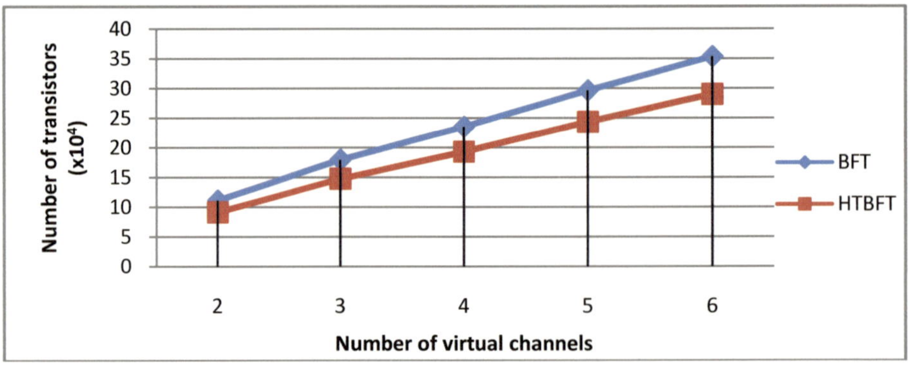


Fig. 5. Area of a switch for different number of virtual channels.

## 3. High Throughput architecture

A novel interconnect template to integrate IP blocks using NoC architecture is proposed as shown in Fig. 1. In the proposed architecture, rather than using a single interconnect bus between each two elements of NoC (IP block and switch or two switches), two buses are employed. The number of virtual channels can be doubled to get higher throughput. Each bus will support half number of virtual channels to maintain the average latency.

Increasing the number of buses between two switches could improve the throughput by optimizing the design of the switch on the circuit level as shown in Section II. However, using two buses to connect two switches implies a consumption of the metal resources and may be silicon area for the repeaters within long interconnect bus. The overhead of the proposed architecture is discussed in Section 5. Applying the proposed high throughput architecture on different NoC topologies is presented in the following subsections.

### 3.1 High Throughput BFT

The interconnect template of butterfly fat-tree topology was proposed in (Pande et al., 2003a). This structure assumes a 4-ary tree with switches connected 4 down links and 2 up links. Each group of 4 leaf nodes needs one switch. At the next level, half as many switches are needed (every 4 switches on the lower level need 2 switches at the next level). This relation continues with each succeeding level.

A novel interconnect template to integrate IP blocks using HT-BFT architecture is proposed as shown in Fig. 6 (a). In the proposed HT-BFT architecture (Abd El Ghany et al., 2009a), rather than using a single interconnect bus between each two switches, two buses are employed. Each group of 4 IPs (no. 0, no. 1, no.2 and no.3) needs one switch (no.4). Each switch in the first level (no. 4) connects to each switch in the second level (no. 5) by 2 buses as shown in Fig. 6 (a). Each bus will support half number of virtual channels. Therefore, the throughput can be improved while preserving the average latency.

### 3.2 High Throughput CLICHÉ

The mesh-interconnect topology called CLICHÉ (Chip-Level Integration of Communicating Heterogeneous Elements) was proposed in (Kumar et al., 2002). The architecture consists of m x n mesh of switches interconnecting the IP blocks. Every switch is connected to four switches and one IP block. At the edges, the switches, except those at the corners, are connected to three switches and one IP block. The number of switches equals to the number of IP blocks. The interconnect template to integrate IP blocks using High Throughput CLICHÉ (HT-CLICHÉ) architecture is shown in Fig. 6 (b) (Abd El Ghany et al., 2009b). The interconnect bus between each two switches consists of two unidirectional links.

### 3.3 High Throughput Octagon

The interconnect template of Octagon topology was proposed in (Karim et al., 2002). The basic unit of Octagon topology consists of eight nodes and 12 bidirectional buses. Each node is associated with an IP block and a switch. Communication between any two nodes takes at most two hops within the basic Octagon unit. The Octagon is extended to multidimensional space for a system of more than eight nodes. The interconnect template to integrate IP blocks using High Throughput Octagon (HT-Octagon) architecture is shown in Fig. 6 (c). For the basic unit of HT-Octagon architecture, number of bidirectional buses equals to 24 rather than 12 bidirectional buses in conventional Octagon architecture.

### 3.4 High Throughput SPIN

The interconnect template called SPIN (Scalable, Programmable, Integrated Network) was proposed in (Guerrier & Greiner, 2000). This structure assumes a 4-ary tree with switches connected 4 down links and 4 up links. Each group of 4 leaf nodes needs one switch. At the next level, the same number of switches are needed (every 4 switches on the lower level need 4 switches at the next level). This relation continues with each succeeding level. The main rationale behind this approach is utilization of the redundant buses by the routers in order to reduce contention in the network. Therefore, SPIN trades area overhead and extra power dissipation for higher throughput. The interconnect template to integrate IP blocks using High Throughput SPIN (HT-SPIN) architecture is shown in Fig. 6 (d). In the proposed HT-SPIN architecture, the double number of buses is needed to connect between each two switches or between an IP block and a switch. Due to the higher usage of on-chip resources by the interswitch links, applying the high throughput architecture on SPIN topology is not efficient for insignificant improvement of throughput as described in Section 5. The power characteristics for different high throughput architectures are provided in Section 4.

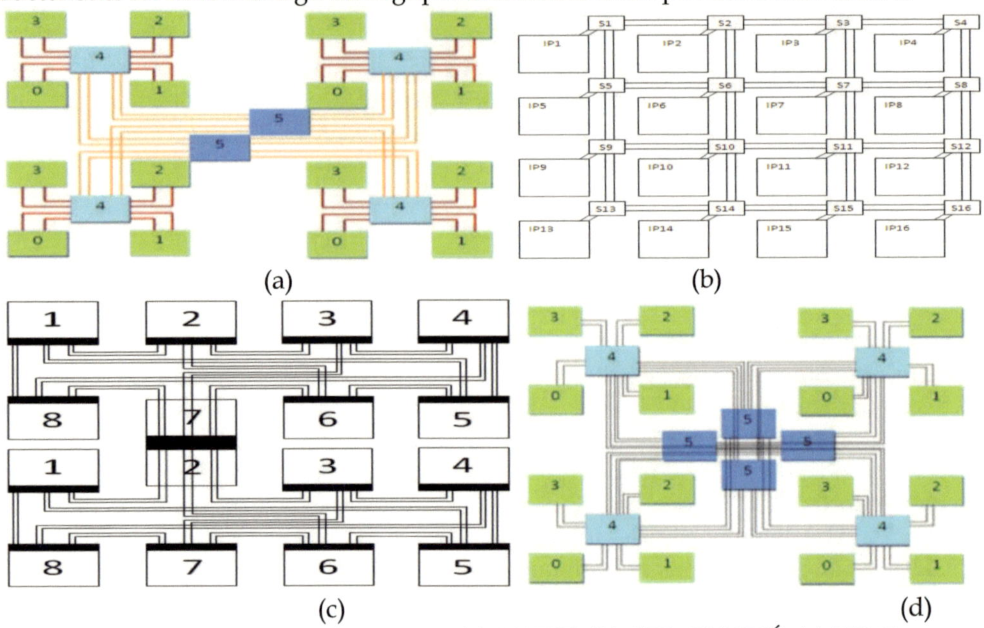


Fig. 6. proposed interconnect architectures. (a) HTBFT. (b) HT- CLICHÉ. (c) HT-Octagon. (d) HT-SPIN.

## 4. Power Characteristics

Power dissipation is a primary concern in high speed, high complexity integrated circuits (IC). Power dissipation increases rapidly with the increase in frequency and transistor density in integrated circuits. To achieve power efficient NoC, power dissipation need to be characterized for different topologies. Communication network on chip contains three primary parts; network switch, interswitch links (interconnects), and repeaters within interswitch links as shown in Fig. 7. Including different sources of power consumption in NoC, the total power dissipation of on chip network is defined as follows:

$$P_{total} = P_{switches} + P_{line} + P_{rep} \quad (2)$$

$$P_{switches} = P_{switching} + P_{leakage} \quad (3)$$

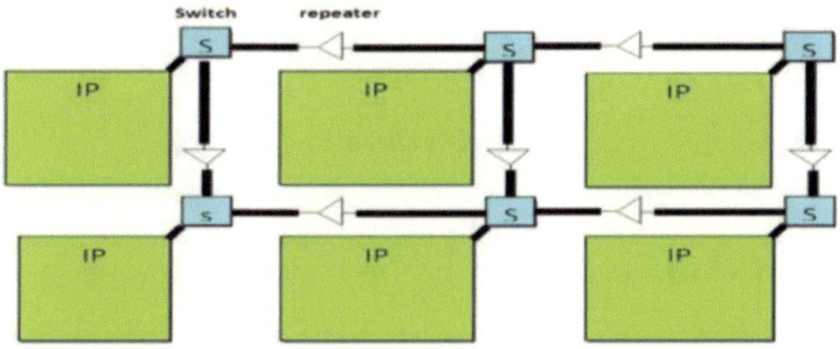


Fig. 7. communication networks on chip

where $P_{switches}$ is the total power dissipation of these switches forming the network. $P_{switches}$ is the summation of switching (including dynamic and short circuit) power and leakage power of switches. $P_{line}$is the total power dissipation of interswitch links. $P_{rep}$ is the total power dissipation of the repeaters which are required for long interconnects. The number of repeaters depends on the length of the interswich link. According to the topology of NoC interconnects, the interswitch wire lengths, the number of repeaters and the number of switches can be determined a priori.

The power consumption of interswitch links $P_{line}$and the power consumption of repeaters are defined by (El-Moursy & Friedman, 2004)

$$P_{line} = C\, V_{dd}^2 f \tag{4}$$

$$P_{rep} = P_{rep-dyn} + P_{rep-SC} + P_{rep-leakage} \tag{5}$$

$$P_{rep-dyn} = N_{rep}\, H_{opt}\, C_o V_{dd}^2\, f \tag{6}$$

where $P_{rep-dyn}$ is the total dynamic power dissipation of repeaters, $N_{rep}$ is the number of repeaters, $H_{opt}$ is the optimal repeater size and $C_o$is the input capacitance of a minimum size repeater. $P_{rep-SC}$ is the total short-circuit power of repeaters. $P_{rep-leakage}$ is the total leakage power dissipation of repeaters. $P_{rep-leakage}$ and $P_{rep-SC}$ are negligible as compared to the total dynamic power dissipation of repeaters [32 ]. The closed form equations for the power dissipation of different high throughput NoC architectures are described in the following subsections.

### 4.1 High Throughput Butterfly Fat Tree

In the HT-BFT, the interconnection is performed on levels of switching. The number of switch levels can be expressed as $levels = log_2 N - 3$, where N is the number of IP blocks. The total number of switches in the first level is $N/4$. At each subsequent level, the number of required switches reduces by a factor of 2 as shown in Fig. 6 (a). The interswitch wire length and total number of switches are given by the following expression (Grecu et al., 2004b):

$$l_{a+1,a} = \frac{\sqrt{Area}}{2^{levels-a}} \tag{7}$$

$$N_{switches-HTBFT} = \frac{N}{4}\left(\frac{1-(1/2)^{levels}}{1-1/2}\right) \tag{8}$$

where $l_{a+1,a}$ is the length of the wire spanning the distance between level *a* and *a+1* switches, where *a* can take integer values between 0 and (*levels-1*). In the HT-BFT, The total length of interconnect and the total number of repeaters can be determined from the following equations:

$$l_{tot-HTBFT} = \frac{\sqrt{area}}{2^{((\log_2 N)-3)}} N \times (levels) \times 2N_{wires} \quad (9)$$

$$N_{repeater-HTBFT} = N\, 2N_{wires} \left( \left\lfloor \frac{l_{1,0}}{K_{opt}} \right\rfloor + \frac{1}{2} \left\lfloor \frac{l_{2,1}}{K_{opt}} \right\rfloor + \frac{1}{4} \left\lfloor \frac{l_{3,2}}{K_{opt}} \right\rfloor + \dots\dots + \frac{1}{2^{N-1}} \left\lfloor \frac{l_{levels,levels-1}}{K_{opt}} \right\rfloor \right) \quad (10)$$

Where $K_{opt}$ is the optimal length of the global interconnect (Li et al., 2005). Using the number of switches, the total length of interconnect and the total number of repeaters, the total power dissipation of HT-BFT architecture ( $P_{tot-HTBFT}$ ) can be calculated using the following expression:

$$P_{tot-HTBFT} = \frac{N}{4} \left( \frac{1-(1/2)^{((\log_2 N)-3)}}{1-1/2} \right) (6\, P_{port}) + \frac{\sqrt{area}}{2^{((\log_2 N)-3)}} N \times ((\log_2 N) - 3) \times 2N_{wires}\, c\, V_{dd}^2 f + \left( \left\lfloor \frac{l_{1,0}}{K_{opt}} \right\rfloor + \frac{1}{2} \left\lfloor \frac{l_{2,1}}{K_{opt}} \right\rfloor + \frac{1}{4} \left\lfloor \frac{l_{3,2}}{K_{opt}} \right\rfloor + \dots\dots + \frac{1}{2^{N-1}} \left\lfloor \frac{l_{((\log_2 N)-3),\ ((\log_2 N)-2)}}{K_{opt}} \right\rfloor \right) N\, 2N_{wires}\, H_{opt}\, C_o V_{dd}^2 f \quad (11)$$

### 4.2 High Throughput CLICHÉ Architecture

In HT-CLICHÉ architecture, the number of switches is equal to the number of IPs as shown in Fig. 6 (b). The interswitch wire lengths can be determined from the following expression:

$$l_{HTCLICHE} = \frac{\sqrt{Area}}{\sqrt{N}} \quad (12)$$

The number of horizontal interswitch links between switches equals to $2\sqrt{N}(\sqrt{N}-1)$, and the number of vertical interswich links between switches equals to $2\sqrt{N}(\sqrt{N}-1)$. According to the technology node, the optimal length of global interconnect can be obtained (Li et al., 2005). Therefore, the total length of interconnect and the number of repeaters for HT-SPIN can be calculated by:

$$l_{tot-HTCLICHE} = 4\sqrt{area}\ (\sqrt{N}-1)\ N_{wires} \quad (13)$$

$$N_{repeaters-HTCLICHE} = 4 \left\lfloor \frac{\sqrt{area}}{\sqrt{N}\, K_{opt}} \right\rfloor \sqrt{N}\,(\sqrt{N}-1)\ N_{wires} \quad (14)$$

Using the number of ports, number of switches, total length of interconnects and number of repeaters, the total power consumption of the HT-CLICHÉ architecture can be determined by the following expression:

$$P_{tot-HTCLICHE} = 5\, N\, P_{port} + 4\sqrt{area}\ (\sqrt{N}-1)\ N_{wires}\, c\, V_{dd}^2 f + 4 \left\lfloor \frac{\sqrt{area}}{\sqrt{N}\, K_{opt}} \right\rfloor \sqrt{N}\,(\sqrt{N}-1)\ N_{wires}\, H_{opt}\, C_o V_{dd}^2 f \quad (15)$$

### 4.3 High Throughput Octagon Architecture

For HT-Octagon architecture, there are four types of interswitch wire length as shown in Fig. 6 (c) : First (connecting nodes 1-5 and 4-8), second (connecting nodes 2-6 and 3-7, third (connecting nodes 1-8 and 4-5), forth (connecting nodes 1-2, 2-3, 3-4, 5-6, 6-7 and 7-8). the interswitch wire lengths can be defined by:

$$l_1 = \frac{3L}{4} \tag{16}$$

$$l_2 = 13\, w_l\, N_{wires} + \frac{L}{4} \tag{17}$$

$$l_3 = 13\, w_l\, N_{wires} \tag{18}$$

$$l_4 = \frac{L}{4} \tag{19}$$

Where L is the length of four nodes; it equals to $\left(4 * \sqrt{\frac{area}{N}}\right)$. $w_l$ is the summation of the global interconnect width and space. Considering the interswitch wire lengths and the optimal length of global interconnect, the total length of interconnect and number of repeaters can be obtained by:

$$l_{tol-HTOctagon} = (7\,L + 104\, w_l\, N_{wires})\, N_{wires}\, N_{oct-units} \tag{20}$$

$$N_{repeaters-HTOctagon} = \left(4\left\lfloor\frac{3L/4}{K_{opt}}\right\rfloor + 4\left\lfloor\frac{13\, w_l\, N_{wires} + L/4}{K_{opt}}\right\rfloor + 4\left\lfloor\frac{13\, w_l\, N_{wires}}{K_{opt}}\right\rfloor + 12\left\lfloor\frac{L/4}{K_{opt}}\right\rfloor\right) N_{wires}\, N_{oct-unit} \tag{21}$$

Where $N_{oct-units}$ is the number of basic octagon unit. The total power dissipation of the HT-Octagon architecture can be determined by the following expression:

$$P_{tot-HTOctagon} = 3\,N\,P_{port} + \left(\left(28\left(\sqrt{\frac{area}{N}}\right) + 104\, w_l\, N_{wires}\right) N_{wires}\, N_{oct-units}\right) c\, V_{dd}^2 f + \left(\left(4\left\lfloor\frac{3\left(\sqrt{\frac{area}{N}}\right)}{K_{opt}}\right\rfloor + 4\left\lfloor\frac{13\, w_l\, N_{wires} + \left(\sqrt{\frac{area}{N}}\right)}{K_{opt}}\right\rfloor + 4\left\lfloor\frac{13\, w_l\, N_{wires}}{K_{opt}}\right\rfloor + 12\left\lfloor\frac{\left(\sqrt{\frac{area}{N}}\right)}{K_{opt}}\right\rfloor\right) N_{wires}\, N_{oct-unit}\right) H_{opt}\, C_o V_{dd}^2\, f \tag{22}$$

## 4.4 High Throughput SPIN Architecture

An interconnect template to integrate IP blocks using SPIN architecture was proposed as shown in Fig. 6 (d). In large SPIN, the total number of switches is $3N/4$ (Guerrier & Greiner, 2000). The interswitch wire length can be determined using eq. (7). In the HT-SPIN, The total length of interconnect and the number of repeaters are defined by:

$$l_{tot-HTSPIN} = 1.75\sqrt{area}\, N\, N_{wires} \tag{23}$$

$$N_{repeaters-HTSPIN} = \left(\left\lfloor\frac{\sqrt{area}}{8K_{opt}}\right\rfloor + \left\lfloor\frac{\sqrt{area}}{4K_{opt}}\right\rfloor + \left\lfloor\frac{\sqrt{area}}{2K_{opt}}\right\rfloor\right) N\; 2N_{wires} \tag{24}$$

The total power dissipation of the network architecture depends on the main three parameters; the number of switches, the total length of interconnect and the number of repeaters. The total power consumption of the HT-SPIN architecture ($P_{tot-HTSPIN}$) can be determined by:

$$P_{tot-HTSPIN} = \frac{3N}{4}\left(8\,P_{port}\right) + 1.75\sqrt{area}\,N\,N_{wires}\,c\,V_{dd}^2 f + \left(\left\lfloor\frac{\sqrt{area}}{8K_{opt}}\right\rfloor + \left\lfloor\frac{\sqrt{area}}{4K_{opt}}\right\rfloor + \left\lfloor\frac{\sqrt{area}}{2K_{opt}}\right\rfloor\right) N\,2N_{wires}H_{opt}\,C_o V_{dd}^2\,f \quad (25)$$

### 4.5 Power Dissipation for Different NoC Architectures

According to the equations (11), (15), (22) and (25), the total power dissipation of the network can be considered as a function of the number of IP blocks. The change in the power consumption with the number of IP blocks for different network architectures is shown in Fig. 8. The power consumption for different NoC architectures increases by different rates with the number of IP blocks. The SPIN and Octagon architectures have much higher rates of power dissipation. The BFT architecture consumes the minimum power as compared to other NoC architectures.

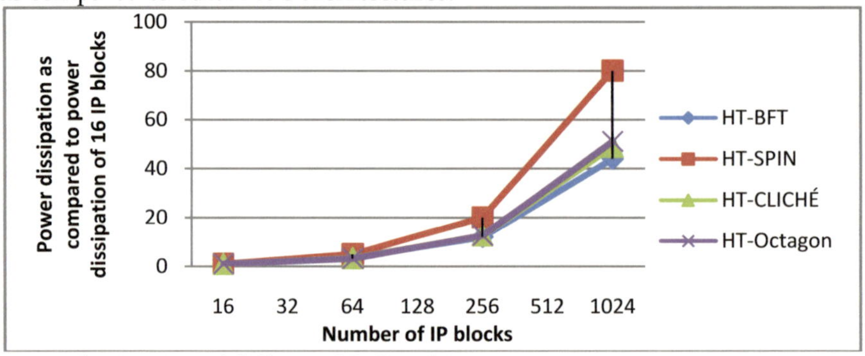


Fig. 8. power dissipation of different NoC architectures

The percentage of the power dissipation of the interswitch links and repeaters is shown in Fig. 9. For the SPIN and architecture, the power dissipation of the interswitch links and repeaters equals to 25% of the total power dissipation of the architecture. For the BFT, CLICHÉ and Octagon architectures, the percentage of power dissipation of the interswitch links and repeaters decreases with the number of IP blocks.

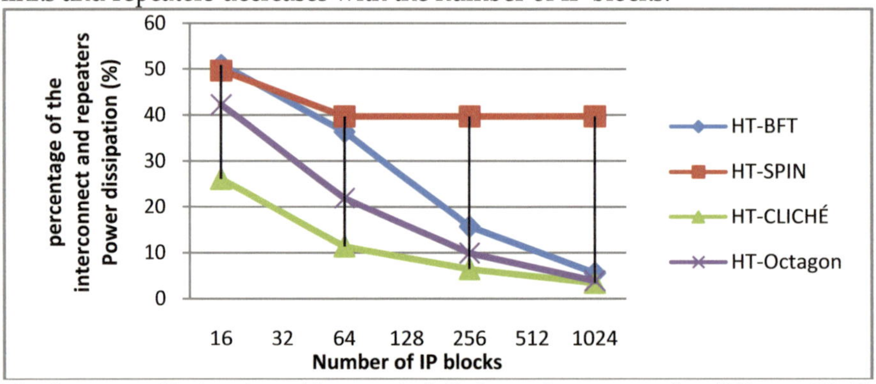


Fig. 9. power dissipation of interswitch links and repeaters for different NoC architectures.

The overhead analysis and simulation results are provided in Section 5.

## 5. Performance and Overhead analysis

The proposed high throughput architectures are implemented using the Application Specific Integrated Circuit (ASIC) by Leonardo Spectrum synthesis tool, used for 90nm technology node. Under uniform traffic assumption, the throughput for different NoC architectures is calculated. The comparative analysis focuses on the frequency of the switch, the throughput, the area of the switch and the power consumption is presented in the following subsections.

### 5.1 Improvement of the Throughput

The proposed high throughput architecture trades the double number of virtual channels for higher throughput while preserving the average latency. Therefore, the throughput of using eight virtual channels in the HT-BFT is double the throughput of four virtual channels in BFT. The average latency of HT-BFT with 8 virtual channels equals to the average latency of BFT with 4 virtual channels. Considering the uniform traffic, the Maximum frequency of the switch and the number of completed messages for HT-BFT, the throughput of HT-BFT is determined. The variation of throughput with the number of virtual channels for HT-BFT and BFT is shown in Fig. 10. In our architecture, when the number of virtual channels is increased beyond eight, the throughput saturates. The architecture increases the throughput of the network by 38%. The percentage of increasing of throughput for different high throughput architectures is presented in Table 1. The maximum improvement in the throughput is obtained in HT-CLICHÉ and HT-BFT. The increase in the throughput for HT-SPIN is the minimum as compared to other high throughput architectures.

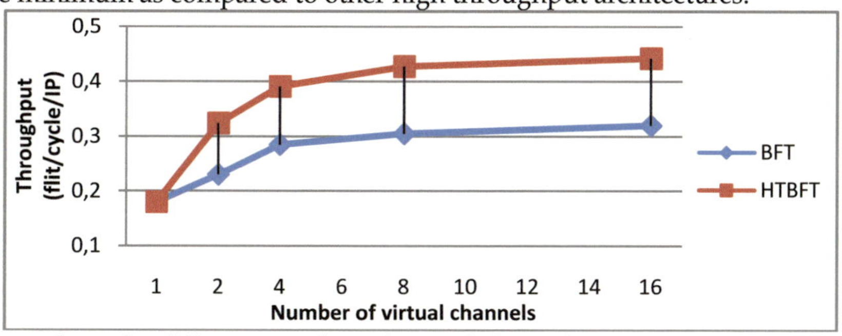


Fig. 10. Throughput for different number of virtual channels.

| architecture | The percentage of increase in throughput (%) |
|---|---|
| HT-BFT | 38 |
| HT-CLICHÉ | 40 |
| HT-Octagon | 17 |
| HT-SPIN | 12 |

Table 1. the percentage of increase in the throughput for different high throughput architectures

### 5.2 Overhead of High Throughput Architectures

With the advance in technology, the number of metal levels increases reaching twelve (ITRS, 2007). Metal resources on chip increase. Considering a chip size of 20 *mm* x 20 *mm (Area)*, technology node of 90 *nm*, and a system of 256 IP blocks, the length of interswitch links for different NoC architectures is obtained. Given the optimal global interconnect width $W_{opt}$ of 935 *nm*, optimal global interconnect spacing $S_{opt}$ of 477 *nm* (Li et al., 2005), the global interconnect pitch is $W_{opt}$ + $S_{opt}$. Assuming all of global interconnects have the same line width and line spacing, then the number of global interconnects $N_{gi}$ per layer equals to

$$N_{gi} = \frac{\sqrt{Area}}{W_{\mathrm{opt}} + S_{\mathrm{opt}}}$$

According to the NoC architecture, the total length of interswitch links are calculated. Using the critical interconnect length of 2.54 *mm*, optimal repeater size of 174 (Li et al., 2005), the number of repeaters is determined. The extra area and power required to implement different high throughput NoC architectures are presented in the following subsections.

#### 5.2.1 HT-BFT

It is possible to organize the butterfly fat tree so that it can be laid out in *O(N)* active area(IPs and switches) and *O(log(N))* wiring layers (Dehon, 2000). The basic strategy for wiring is to distribute tree layers in pair of wire layers – one for horizontal wiring $H_{a+1,a}$ and one for vertical wiring $V_{a+1,a}$. The length of horizontal part $H_{a+1,a}$ equals to the length of vertical part $V_{a+1,a}$ given that the chip is squared. More than one tree layer can share the same wiring trace. High throughput architecture has the same number of switches, but the number of wires and repeaters will be doubled. The length of interswitch wire depends on the number of levels in BFT, which depends on the system size as shown in eq (7).

In the circuit implementation of HT-BFT, a bus between each two switches has 12 wires, 8 for data and 4 for control signals. Considering a system of 256 IP blocks, the length of $H_{a+1,a}$ and $V_{a+1,a}$ are calculated. The number of BFT levels is seven. Using the critical interconnect length, the number of repeaters equals to 960 repeaters. The area of repeaters required to implement the HT-BFT interswitch links equals to 20880 $\mu m^2$ (it equals to the double area of repeaters required for BFT interswitch links). The power consumption of repeaters and switches required to implement the BFT and HT-BFT is presented in Table 2. The power consumption required to implement HT-BFT is increased by 7% as compared with the power consumption of BFT.

| Architecture | No. of repeaters | Power dissipation of repeaters and interswitch links (*mw*) | Power dissipation of switches (*mw*) | Total power dissipation (*mw*) | Percentage of power dissipation of repeaters and interswitch links (%) |
|---|---|---|---|---|---|
| BFT | 960 | 1458.24 | 15663.68 | 17121.92 | 8.5 |
| HT-BFT | 1920 | 2916.48 | 15674.84 | 18591.32 | 15.7 |

Table 2. power consumption of repeaters and switches for BFT and HT-BFT

The horizontal wiring is distributed in the metal layer no. 11 and the vertical wiring is distributed in the metal layer no. 12. The total length of horizontal wires needed equals to 4800 *mm* (it is 5 % of the total metal resources available in the metal 11). The same for total length of vertical wires, it requires 5 % of the total metal resources available in the metal 12.

For the proposed design, the double number of interswitch links is required to achieve the communication between each two switches. Therefore, the total metal resources required to implement the proposed architecture will be 10%. The metal resources of HT-BFT architecture equals to the double metal resources of BFT architecture. The extra metal resources required to achieve the proposed architecture is negligible as compared to the metal resources.

The percentage of the metal resources and power consumption of interswitch links and repeaters for different technology node is shown in Table 3. With the advance in technology, the available metal resources in the same die size are increased. Therefore, the number of IPs could be increased. The number of switches is also increased. The required metal resources to implement the BFT and HT-BFT are increased by fewer rates than the rates of increase of the available metal resources with the advance in technology. The extra metal resources and power consumption required to implement the HT-BFT decreases. The extra power consumption required to achieve the proposed architecture is 1% of the total power consumption of the BFT architecture. Also, the extra metal resources required for HT-BFT is 3% of the metal resources. The HT-BFT is more efficient with the advance in technology.

| Technology node | No. of IPs | No. of levels | Percentage of power consumption of interswitch links and repeaters for BFT | Percentage of power consumption of interswitch links and repeaters for HT-BFT (*mw*) | Percentage of BFT metal resources | Percentage of HT-BFT metal resources |
|---|---|---|---|---|---|---|
| **130 nm** | 500 | 6 | 10.26% | 20.5% | 4.95 % | 9.89 % |
| **90 nm** | 1000 | 7 | 4.49% | 8.98% | 4.02 % | 8.04 % |
| **65 nm** | 2500 | 9 | 1.32% | 2.64% | 2.55 % | 5.1 % |
| **45 nm** | 7500 | 10 | 0.59% | 1.19% | 2.97 % | 5.94 % |

Table 3. metal resources and power consumption of interswitch links and repeaters for HT-BFT and BFT

### 5.2.2 HT-CLICHÉ

The CLICHÉ architecture with N IP blocks can be laid out in *O(N)* active area(IPs and switches) and $O(\sqrt{N})$ interswitch links. In the circuit implementation of HT-CLICHÉ, a bus between each two switches has 20 wires, 16 for data and 4 for control signals. Considering a system of 256 IP blocks, the architecture consists of 16x16 mesh of switches interconnecting the IPs. The length of horizontal links and vertical links equal to 1.25 mm. They are smaller than the critical interconnect length. Therefore, no repeaters are needed within the interswitch links. The power dissipation of the network is presented in Table 4 for CLICHÉ and HT-CLICHÉ. The extra power dissipation required to implement HT-CLICHÉ for 256 IPs equals to 5%.

| Architecture | Power consumption of interswitch links and repeaters (*mw*) | Power consumption of switches (*mw*) | Total power dissipation (*mw*) | Percentage of power dissipation of repeaters and interswitch links (%) |
|---|---|---|---|---|
| CLICHÉ | 1398 | 24448 | 25846 | 5.4 |
| HT-CLICHÉ | 2796 | 24471 | 27267 | 10.25 |

Table 4. power consumption for CLICHÉ and HT-CLICHÉ architectures

Using the equation no. 12, the total length of interswitch links is calculated. Distributing the horizontal and vertical interswitch links into metal 11 and metal 12 respectively, the metal resources required to implement the horizontal wires equals to 7 % of the total metal resources available in the metal 11. Also, the metal resources required to the vertical wires equals to 7 % of the total metal resources available in the metal 12. Therefore, the total metal resources required to implement the HT-CLICHÉ architecture will be 14%. The increasing percentage of the metal resources for HT-CLICHÉ is negligible as compared to the metal resources.

Since the interswitch links is short enough, there is no need for repeaters within the interconnects, the power and metal resources consumed by CLICHÉ and HT-CLICHÉ are shown in Table 5 for different technology nodes. With the advance in technology, the power dissipation required to implement the HT-CLICHÉ is increased by less than 2% of the total power consumption of the CLICHÉ architecture. The percentage of metal resources for HT-CLICHÉ is increased by 35% as compared with the metal resources of CLICHÉ. The HT-CLICHÉ trades extra metal resources for higher throughput.

| Technology node | No. of IPs | Percentage of power consumption of interswitch links and repeaters for CLICHÉ (%) | Percentage of power consumption of interswitch links and repeaters for HT-CLICHÉ (%) | Percentage of CLICHÉ metal resources (%) | Percentage of HT-CLICHÉ metal resources (%) |
|---|---|---|---|---|---|
| 130 nm | 361 | 7.6 | 14.1 | 21 | 43 |
| 90 nm | 729 | 4.8 | 9.1 | 22 | 44 |
| 65 nm | 1849 | 2.7 | 5.2 | 28 | 57 |
| 45 nm | 5625 | 1.4 | 2.7 | 36 | 71 |

Table 5. Power consumption of interswitch links and repeaters for HT-CLICHÉ and CLICHÉ

### 5.2.3 HT- Octagon

The HT-Octagon architecture has the same number of switches, but the number of wires and repeaters will be doubled. A bus between each two switches has 12 wires, 8 for data and 4 for control signals. Considering a system of 256 IP blocks, the length of interswitch links is obtained. According to the critical interconnect length (Li et al., 2005), the number of repeaters equals to 7680 repeaters. The power consumption required to implement the Octagon and HT-Octagon architectures is presented in Table 6. Due to the extra interswitch

links required to implement HT-Octagon architecture, the power consumption is increased by 6% as compared with the power consumption of Octagon topology.
By distributing the wiring of HT-Octagon architecture into the metal 11, the total length of wires needed equals to 7057.92 *mm*. The architecture consumes 8 % of the total metal resources available in the metal 11. In the proposed design, the double number of interswitch links is utilized to implement HT-Octagon architecture. Therefore, the total metal resources required to implement the proposed architecture will be 16%.

| Architecture | Power consumption of interswitch links and repeaters (*mw*) | Power consumption of switches (*mw*) | Total power dissipation (*mw*) | Percentage of power dissipation of repeaters and interswitch links (%) |
|---|---|---|---|---|
| **Octagon** | 1094.12 | 19861.04 | 20955 | 5.2 |
| **HT-Octagon** | 2188.24 | 19844.08 | 22072.3 | 9.9 |

Table 6. power consumption of switches for Octagon and HT-Octagon

The percentage of power consumption and metal resources required to implement the Octagon and HT-Octagon networks in different technologies are shown in Table 7. By increasing the number of IP blocks with the advance in technology, the extra power consumption required to implement the proposed architecture is decreased. The extra power consumption is 2% of the total power consumption of the Octagon architecture. The percentage of extra metal resources for HT-Octagon is 25% of the available metal resources.

| Technology node | No. of IPs | Percentage of power consumption of interswitch links and repeaters for Octagon (%) | Percentage of power consumption of interswitch links and repeaters for HT-Octagon (%) | Percentage of Octagon metal resources (%) | Percentage of HT-Octagon metal resources (%) |
|---|---|---|---|---|---|
| **130 nm** | 361 | 7.6 | 14.1 | 13 | 26 |
| **90 nm** | 729 | 4.78 | 9.1 | 13 | 26 |
| **65 nm** | 1849 | 2.8 | 5.4 | 17 | 35 |
| **45 nm** | 5625 | 1.6 | 3.1 | 25 | 50 |

Table 7. Power consumption of interswitch links and repeaters for HT-Octagon and Octagon

### 5.2.4 HT-SPIN

By applying the high throughput architecture on SPIN topology, the length of interswitch links and number of repeaters are calculated by eq. (22) and eq. (23) respectively. Considering a system of 256 IP blocks, the number of repeaters equals to 12288 repeaters. The area of repeaters required to implement the HT-SPIN interswitch links equals to 267264 $\mu m^2$ (it equals to the double area of repeaters required for SPIN interswitch links). The horizontal wires and vertical wires are distributed into metal 11 and metal 12 respectively. The length of horizontal wires needed consumes 28 % of the total metal resources available in the metal 11. The vertical wires needed consume 28 % of the total metal resources available in the metal 12. The total metal resources required to implement the proposed HT-

SPIN architecture will be 56%.The power consumption of interswitch links, repeaters and switches required to implement the SPIN and HT-SPIN is presented in Table 8. The extra power dissipation required by the interswitch links and repeaters for HT-SPIN architecture (with 256 IPs) equals to 15% as compared with the total power dissipation.

| Architecture | No. of repeaters | Power dissipation of repeaters and interswitch links (*mw*) | Power dissipation of switches (*mw*) | Total power dissipation (*mw*) | Percentage of power dissipation of repeaters and interswitch links (%) |
|---|---|---|---|---|---|
| **SPIN** | 12288 | 10612.99 | 32263.68 | 42876.67 | 24.75 |
| **HT-SPIN** | 24576 | 21225.98 | 32280.96 | 53506.94 | 39.67 |

Table 8. power consumption of repeaters and switches for SPIN and HT-SPIN

For different technologies, the power consumption and metal resources required to implement the SPIN and HT-SPIN are shown in Table 9. With the advance in technology, the extra power consumption required to achieve the proposed HT-SPIN architecture is 15% of the total power consumption of the architecture. The percentage of extra metal resources needed is more than 100% of the metal resources. Therefore, the overhead in the HT-SPIN is high. Applying the high throughput architecture on the SPIN topology is not recommended.

| Technology node | No. of IPs | Percentage of power consumption of interswitch links and repeaters for SPIN (%) | Percentage of power consumption of interswitch links and repeaters for HT-SPIN (%) | Percentage of SPIN metal resources (%) | Percentage of HT-SPIN metal resources (%) |
|---|---|---|---|---|---|
| **130 nm** | 400 | 41.2 | 58.4 | 21 | 42 |
| **90 nm** | 800 | 33.6 | 50.3 | 30 | 59 |
| **65 nm** | 2000 | 32.6 | 49.1 | 59 | 118 |
| **45 nm** | 6000 | 28.1 | 43.8 | 126 | 253 |

Table 9. Power consumption of interswitch links and repeaters for HT-SPIN and SPIN

Since the proposed architecture increases the power dissipation, a low power NoC switch is proposed in Section 6.

## 6. Low power noc switch design

The switch of BFT has six ports, four children ports and two parent ports. Each port can be used as either input port or output port. If the port considers as input port, the input virtual channels, header decoder and crossbar are active. If the port considers as output port, the output virtual channels are active.

In the proposed design, only one part (input part or output part) is activated as shown in Fig. 11. The stand-by transistors (M1) disconnect the input circuit from the supply voltage during the output mode. The stand-by transistors (M2) disconnect the output circuit from the supply voltage during the input mode. There is no need for the new control signals to control the stand-by transistors (M1 and M2). The acknowledgment signals (Ack_in and Ack_out) developed by the control unit are used to control the stand-by transistors M1 and M2 respectively. Using the number of virtual channels ($N_{VC}$), The number of stand-by transistors equals to $3 + 2N_{VC}$. The number of virtual channels is limited (it is not more 16 virtual channels (Abd El Ghany et al., 2009a)). By comparing the number of stand-by transistors with the total number of transistors required to implement the NoC port (as described is Section 2), the number of stand-by transistors is less than 1% of the total number of transistors. Therefore, the area overhead in the proposed design is negligible as compared to the area of NoC switch. The total power dissipation can be reduced by using power gating technique.

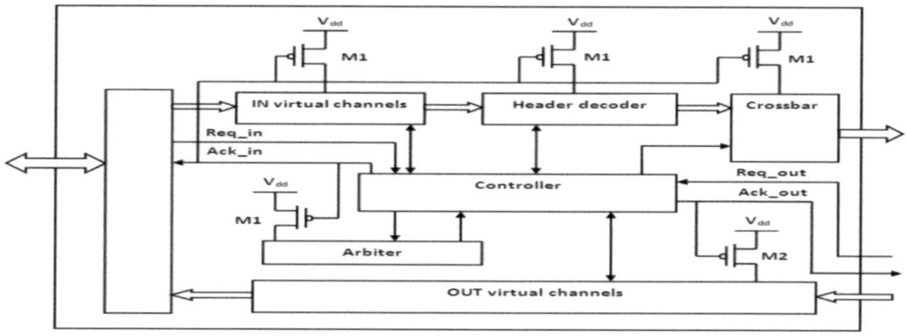


Fig. 11. proposed design for low power NoC port.

Using the Cadence tools and 90nm technology node, the proposed low power NoC switch is implemented. The power dissipation of BFT switch is determined. The total power dissipation of the BFT switch equals to 41.29 $mW$. The total power dissipation of the port during the input mode equals to 6.79 $mW$. The total power dissipation of the port during the output mode equals to 6.57 $mW$. In the proposed BFT switch design of one virtual channel, the power dissipation of the main components of the port for the active mode and sleep mode is obtained as shown in Table 10. According to the mode of operation, the activation of the component is determined. In the Input mode, the input FIFO, header decoder and crossbar are activated, while the output FIFO is switched to sleep mode. The power dissipation of the port will be 5.68 $mW$. In the output mode, the output FIFO is activated while the input FIFO, the header decoder and cross bar are switched to sleep mode. The power dissipation of the port equals to 3.79 $mW$. Therefore, the average power dissipation of the proposed switch equals to 29,59 $mW$. The average power dissipation of the proposed BFT switch is decreased by 28.32 % as compared to the average power dissipation of the conventional BFT switch.

| Component | power dissipation in active mode (*mW*) | power dissipation in sleep mode (*μW*) | Percentage of reduction in power dissipation (%) |
|---|---|---|---|
| **Input FIFO** | 3.618 | 0.1029 | 97.15 |
| **Header decoder** | 0.955 | 0.2157 | 77.41 |
| **Crossbar** | 0.473 | 0.1274 | 73.07 |
| **Output FIFO** | 3.562 | 0.1003 | 97.18 |

Table 10. the power dissipation of the main components of the BFT switch

The power consumption of BFT switch increases with the number of virtual channels as shown in Fig. 12. Applying the leakage power reduction technique on the BFT with different number of virtual channels, the power reduction increases with the number of virtual channels. The percentage of power reduction equals to 28 % when the number of virtual channels equals to one. The percentage of power reduction of BFT switch with 12 virtual channels equals to 45%. Increasing the number of virtual channels can improve the throughput in an on- chip interconnect network. By optimizing the design on the circuit levels, the high throughput can be provided by eight virtual channels (Abd El Ghany et al., 2009a). Using the leakage power reduction technique, the power consumption of BFT switch with 8 virtual channels is reduced by 44 %.
With the advance in technology, the number of IPs implemented in the same system size is increased. The effect of power gating technique on the HT-BFT is presented in Fig. 13. The power consumption of HT-BFT architecture using the leakage power reduction technique (HT-BFT-PR) is less than the power consumption of the conventional BFT architecture.

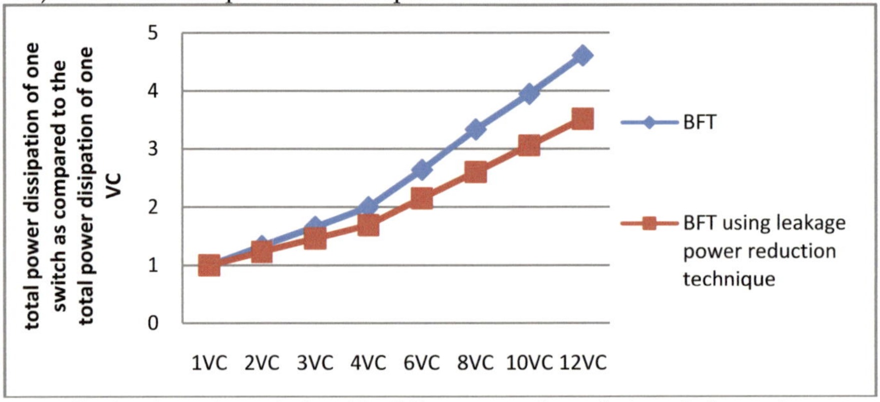


Fig. 12. power dissipation of a switch with different number of virtual channels.

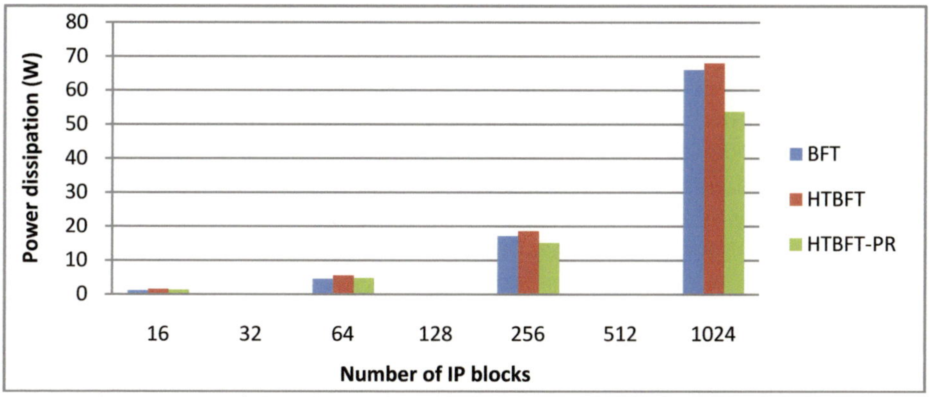


Fig. 13. power dissipation of the HT-BFT using the power reduction technique

The power consumption $P_{switches}$ of switches for different high throughput architectures is obtained as shown in Table 11. The power consumption of these switches is more than 80% of the total power consumption of the on chip network. Switching off the power supply is an efficient technique to reduce the total power dissipation of NoC. The minimum power consumption can be obtained by using the BFT architecture as presented in Table 11. Using the leakage power reduction technique, the power consumption for different NoC architectures is determined. The overall power consumption, includes the power consumption of the interswitch links and repeaters, is decreased up to 33%.

| Network architecture | Total power (*mW*) | $P_{switches}$ | | Total power using power reduction technique (*mW*) | Percentage of power reduction |
|---|---|---|---|---|---|
| | | *mW* | % | | |
| **HT-BFT** | 18591.32 | 15674.84 | 84 | 15104.44 | 19% |
| **HT-SPIN** | 53506.94 | 32280.96 | 60 | 46312.7 | 13% |
| **HT-CLICHÉ** | 26148.64 | 24471 | 94 | 18608.16 | 29% |
| **HT-Octagon** | 22072.32 | 19884.08 | 90 | 16253.04 | 26% |

Table 11. the total power consumption of different network architectures with 256 IPs

## 7. Conclusions

In this chapter, the high throughput NoC architecture is proposed to increase the throughput of the switch in NoC. The proposed architecture can also improve the latency of the network. The proposed high throughput interconnect architecture is applied on different NoC architectures. The architecture increases the throughput of the network by more than 38% while preserving the average latency. The area of high throughput NoC switch is decreased by 18% as compared to the area of BFT switch. The total metal resources required to implement the proposed high throughput NoC is increased by less than 10 % as compared to the metal resources required to implement the conventional NoC design.

The power characterization for different high throughput NoC architectures is developed. The extra power consumption required to achieve the proposed high throughput NoC architecture is less than 15% of the total power consumption of the NoC architecture. Low power switch design is proposed. The power reduction technique is applied to different high

throughput NoC architectures. The technique reduces the overall power consumption of the network by up to 29%.
The relation between throughput, number of virtual channels and switch frequency is analyzed. The simulation results demonstrate the performance enhancements in terms of throughput, number of virtual channels, switch frequency and power dissipation. It is shown that optimizing the circuit can increase the number of virtual channels without degrading the frequency. The throughput of different NoC architectures is also improved with the proposed architecture. The minimum power consumption and the minimum area can be obtained by using HT-BFT as compared to other high throughput NoC architectures. The extra metal resources required to achieve the proposed HT-BFT is negligible as compared to the metal resources of the network. The extra power consumption required to achieve the proposed HT-BFT is eliminated by using the leakage power reduction technique.

## 8. References


Abd El Ghany, M. A.; El-Moursy, M. & Ismail, M. (2009a) "High Throughput Architecture for High Performance NoC" *Proceedings of IEEE International Symposium on Circuits and Systems (ISCAS)*, May, 2009 (in publication)

Abd El Ghany, M. A.; El-Moursy, M. & Ismail, M. (2009b) "High Throughput Architecture for CLICHÉ Network on Chip" *Proceedings of the IEEE International SoC Conference*, September, 2009

Benini, L. & Micheli, G. de (2002) "Networks on chips: A new SoC paradigm," *IEEE Computer*, vol. 35, no. 1, pp. 70–78, Jan. 2002

Bertozzi, D.; Jalabert, A. & Murali, S. *et al.*, (2005) "NoC synthesis flow for customized domain specific multiprocessor systems-on-chip," *IEEE transactions on Parallel and Distributed Systems*, vol. 16, no. 2, pp. 113–129, February 2005

Bolotin, E.; Cidon, I.; Ginosar, R. & Kolodny, A. (2004) "QNoC: QoS architecture and design process for network on chip," *Journal of Systems Architecture*, vol. 50, no. 2–3, pp. 105–128, February 2004

Dally, W. J. & Towles, B. (2001) "Route packets, not wires: on-chip interconnection networks", *In Proceedings of Design Automation Conference*, pp 684–689, June 2001

Dehon, A. (2000) "Compact, Multilayer layout for butterfly fat-tree", *In Proceedings of The 12th ACM Symposium on Parallel algorithm Architectures*, pp. 206- 215, July 2000

El-Moursy, M. A. & Friedman, E. G. (2004) "optimum wire sizing of RLC interconnect with repeaters", *Integration, the VLSI journal*, vol. 38, no. 2, pp. 205-225, 2004

Grecu, C.; Pande, P. P.; Ivanov, A. & Saleh, R. (2004a) "Structured Interconnect Architecture: A Solution for the Non-Scalability of Bus-Based SoCs," *Proceedings of Great Lakes Symposium on VLSI*, pp. 192-195, April 2004

Grecu, C.; Pande, P. P.; Ivanov, A. & Saleh, R. (2004b) "Ascalable Communication-Centric SoC Interconnect Architecture", *In Proceedings of IEEE International Symposium On Quality Electronic Design*, pp. 22- 24, March, 2004

Grecu, C.; Pande, P.; Ivanov, A.; Marculescu, R.; Salminen, E. & Jantsch, A. (2007a) "Towards open network-on-chip benchmarks," *In Proceedings of the International Symposium on Network on Chip*, pp. 205, May 2007

Grecu, C.; Ivanov, A.; Saleh, R. & Pande, P. (2007b) "Testing network-on-chip communication fabrics," *IEEE transactions Computer-Aided Design of Integrated Circuits and Systems*, vol. 26, no. 10, pp. 2201–2014, December 2007

Guerrier, P. & Greiner, A. (2000) "A generic architecture for on-chip packet-switched interconnections", *In Proceedings of Design, Automation and Test in Europe Conference and Exhibition*, pp. 250–256, March 2000

ITRS 2007 Documents, http://itrs.net/Links/2007ITRS/Home2007.htm

Kao, J. T. & Chandrakasan, A. P. (2000) "Dual-Threshold Voltage Techniques for Low-Power Digital Circuits ", *IEEE Journal of Solid-State Circuits*, vol. 35(7), pp. 1009- 1018, July 2000

Karim, F.; Nguyen, A. & Sujit Dey, (2002) "An Interconnect Architecture for Networking Systems on Chips," *IEEE Micro*, vol. 22, no. 5, pp. 36-45, September 2002

Khellah, M. M. & Elmasry, M. I. (1999) " Power minimization of high-performance submicron CMOS circuit using a dual-V/sub dd/ dual-V/sub th/ (DVDV) approach" *In Proceeding of the International symposium on Low Power Electronics and Design* , pp. 106-108, 1999

Kim, J.-S.; Hwang, M.-S & Roh, S. *et al.*, (2004) "On-chip network based embedded core testing," *In Proceedings of the IEEE International SoC Conference*, pp. 223–226, September 2004

Kumar, S. et al., (2002) "A Network on Chip Architecture and Design Methodology," *In Proceedings of the IEEE Computer Society Annual Symposium on VLSI*, pp. 117-124, 2002

Kursun, V. & Friedman, E. G. (2004) "Sleep switch dual threshold voltage domino logic with reduced standby leakage current," *IEEE transactions on VLSI systems*, 12(5), pp. 485-496, May 2004

Lee, S.-J.; Song, S.-J. & Lee, K. et al. (2003) "An 800MHz Star-Connected On-Chip Network for Application to Systems on a chip", *IEEE Digest of International Solid State Circuits Conference*, vol. 1, pp. 468-489, February, 2003

Lee, K.; Lee, S.-J. & Kim, S.-E. et al. (2004) "A 51mW 1.6GHz On-Chip Network for Low power Heterogeneous SoC Platform", *IEEE Digest of International Solid State Circuits Conference*, vol. 1, pp.152-518, February, 2004

Lee, S.-J.; Kim, K. & Kim, H. et al. (2005) "Adaptive Network-on-Chip with Wave-Front Train Serialization Scheme", *IEEE Digest of Symposium on VLSI Circuits*, pp. 104-107, June, 2005

Lee, S.-J.; Lee, K. & Yoo, H.-J. (2005)"Analysis and Implementation of Practical Cost-Effective Network-onChips", *IEEE Design & Test of Computers Magazine* (Special Issue for NoC), September 2005

Lee, K.; Lee, S.-J. & Yoo, H.-J. (2006) "Low-Power Networks-on-Chip for High-Performance SoC Design", *IEEE Transactions on Very Large Scale Integration Systems*, vol. 14, no.2, pp.148-160, February 2006

Lee, S. & Bagherzadeh, N. (2006) "Increasing the Throughput of an Adaptive Router in Network-on Chip(NoC)", *In Proceedings of 4th International Conference on Hardware/Software Codesign and System Synthesis CODES+ISSS'06*, pp. 82-87, Oct. 2006

Liang, J.; Laffely, A.; Srinivasan, S. & Tessier, R. (2004) "An architecture and compiler for scalable on-chip communication," *IEEE transactions on VLSI Systems*, vol. 12, no. 7, pp. 711-726, July 2004

Li, X.-C.; Mao, J.-F.; Huang, H.-F. & Liu, Y. (2005) "Global interconnect width and spacing optimization for latency, bandwidth and power dissipation," *IEEE Transactions on Electron Devices*, vol. 52, no. 10, pp. 2272–2279, Oct. 2005

Murali, S. & De Micheli, G. (2004) "SUNMAP: A Tool for Automatic Topology Selection and Generation for NoCs", *IEEE Proceedings of Design Automation conference*, pp. 914-919, June 2004

Murali, S.; Theocharides, T. & Vijaykrishnan, N. *et al.*, (2005) "Analysis of error recovery schems for networks on chips," *IEEE Design and test*, vol. 22, no. 5, pp. 434–442, October 2005

Pande, P. P.; Grecu, C.; Ivanov, A. & Saleh, R. (2003a) "Design of a Switch for Network on Chip Applications," *In Proceedings of The 2003 International Symposium on Circuits and Systems*, vol. 5, pp. 217-220, May 2003

Pande, P. P.; Grecu, C.; Ivanov, A. & Saleh, R. (2003b) "High-Throughput Switch-Based Interconnect for Future SoCs", *the 3rd IEEE International workshop on SoC for real-time Applications,* pp 304-310, July 2003

Pande, P. P.; Grecu, C.; Ivanov, A. & Saleh, R. (2005a) "Design, synthesis, and test of networks on chips," *IEEE Design and Test of Computer*, vol. 22, no. 5, pp. 404–413, Aug. 2005

Pande, P. P.; Grecu, C.; Jones, M.; Ivanov, A. & Saleh, R. (2005b) "Performance Evaluation and Design Trade-Offs for Network-on-Chip Interconnect Architectures", *IEEE Transaction on Computers*, vol. 54, no. 8, Aug. 2005

Salminen, E.; Kulmala, A. & H¨am¨al¨ainen, T. (2007) "On network-on-chip comparison," *In Proceedings of the Euromicro conference on Digital System Design Architecture,* August 2007, pp. 503–510

# Non-volatile memory interface protocols for smart sensor networks and mobile devices

Octavian Postolache, Pedro Silva Girão and José Miguel Dias Pereira
*Instituto de Telecomunicações*
*Portugal*

## 1. Introduction

Data acquisition, storage and transmission are mandatory requirements for different applications in the area of smart sensors and sensor networks.
Different architectures and scenarios can be considered. Thus for smart sensors architectures (Frank, 2002) based on the IEEE1451.X standard (IEEE, 2007) the acquired data can be processed at the smart sensor level using data of the so-called standard template TEDS (Honeywell, 2009) stored in a non-volatile memory (Brewer & Gill, 2008). The auto-identification of the smart sensor (Yurish & Gomes, 2003) unit from a sensor network is based on the Basic TEDS that also represents part of the stored information.
Considering smart sensor architectures (Song & Lee, 2008), the communication between the sensor processing unit (e.g. microcontroller) and one or multiple non-volatile memory units (e.g. Flash EEPROM memory units) is done using different communication protocols, such as SPI, I2C, 1-wire (Kalinsky & Kalinsky, 2002); (Paret & Fenger, 1997); (Linke, 2008). These protocols are thus frequently used in smart sensor implementations (IEEE, 2004)(Ramos et al., 2004).
As the name implies, smart sensors networks are networks of smart sensors, that is, of devices that have an inbuilt ability to sense information, process the information and send selected information to an external receiver (including to other sensors). A "smart sensor" is a transducer (or actuator) that provides functions beyond what is necessary to generate a correct representation of a sensed or controlled quantity. This means that such nodes require memory capabilities to store data temporarily or permanently.
In an increasingly number of applications, the nodes are required to change their spatial position (mobile nodes), which leads to wireless networks. The sensor network nodes data management and advanced data processing are carried out by a host unit characterized by high data processing capabilities, non-volatile data storage capabilities and data communication capabilities. One kind of solutions that materialize the host unit is mobile devices (e.g. phones and PDAs) with special operating systems (e.g. WindowsCE, Symbian, BalckBerry OS) and internal and extended data storage memory capabilities (CF card memory, SD card memory). Specific protocols, *CompactFlash* and *Secure-Digital* (Compact Flash, 2009) (SD Association, 2009) are associated with memory card interfaces that are used to perform the communication between the host unit processor and the memory units. In wireless sensors networks, special attention is granted to the memory read/write operations

time interval and the associated power consumption considering the mobile device autonomy requirements.
Considering the importance of non-volatile memory and the communication protocols associated with memory units as parts of smart sensors, sensor networks and distributed mobile systems (e.g. wearable sensing system for physiological parameter measurements), the proposed chapter briefly reviews some non-volatile memory solutions more used in those contexts.

## 2. Non-volatile Memory, Smart Sensors and Mobile Devices

A non-volatile memory is an important part of a smart sensor. Non-volatile memory is a general term for all forms of a solid state memory that do not need to have their memory contents periodically refreshed. This includes all forms of read-only memory (ROM) such as programmable read-only memory (PROM), erasable programmable read-only memory (EPROM), electrically erasable programmable read-only memory (EEPROM), and flash memory. It also includes the random access memory (RAM) that is powered by a battery.
Regarding smart sensors, the non-volatile memory stores a table of parameters that identify the transducer and are held in the transducer on an EEPROM for interrogation by external electronics. The table's contents can be the one defined by the IEEE committee associated with IEEE1451 standard for smart sensors (Ulivieri et al., 2009). The transducer parameters table is also known as TEDS (Transducer Electronic Datasheet) and according with the above mentioned standard, brings plug-and-play capabilities to transducers. TEDS-compatible measurement systems can auto-detect and automatically configure these "smart sensors" for measurement, reducing setup time and eliminating transcription errors that commonly occur during sensor configuration.
Different IEEE1451 family members include the TEDS module as part of particular smart sensor architecture implementations. Figure 1 presents the TEDS module localization according to IEEE1451.2, IEEE1451.3, IEEE1451.4, IEEE1451.5 and IEEE1451.6. Figure 1 shows that the TEDS that is localized at the transducer's level sends the specific transducer information to the Network Capable Information Processor (NCAP) using different kinds of interfaces. The smart transducers communicate with the NCAP using the mixed mode interface that joins the analogue signal line and the memory communication lines according to IEEE1451.4, using CAN (*Controller Area Network*) (Pfeiffer et al., 2003) interface according to IEEE1451.6, using digital point-to-point according to IEEE1451.2, using distributed bus interfaces such as I2C (Pardo et al., 2006) according to IEEE1451.3 or using wireless interfaces such as Bluetooth (Flittner, 2007) or ZigBee (Higuera, 2009) according to IEEE1451.5. Additionally, an IEEE1451 standard extension for smart sensors with RFID (IEEE1451.7) is under discussion.
From the different individuals in the IEEE1451 standard family one of the more implemented is the mixed mode transducer interfaces IEEE1451.4. The IEEE 1451.4 standard defines a mechanism for adding self-identification technology to traditional analogue sensors and actuators (IEEE, 2009) and it is described in details in the next section.

### IEEE1451.4

IEEE 1451.4 (dot 4 from now on) defines a mechanism for adding self-describing behaviour to traditional transducers with an analogue signal interface. The dot 4 defines the concept of a transducer that supplies both analogue and digital interface, namely, *mixed-mode interface* (Fig.2) where the TEDS non-volatile memory localization is better highlighted. In this case, the non-volatile memory interface will materialize the digital interface associated with IEEE1451.4.

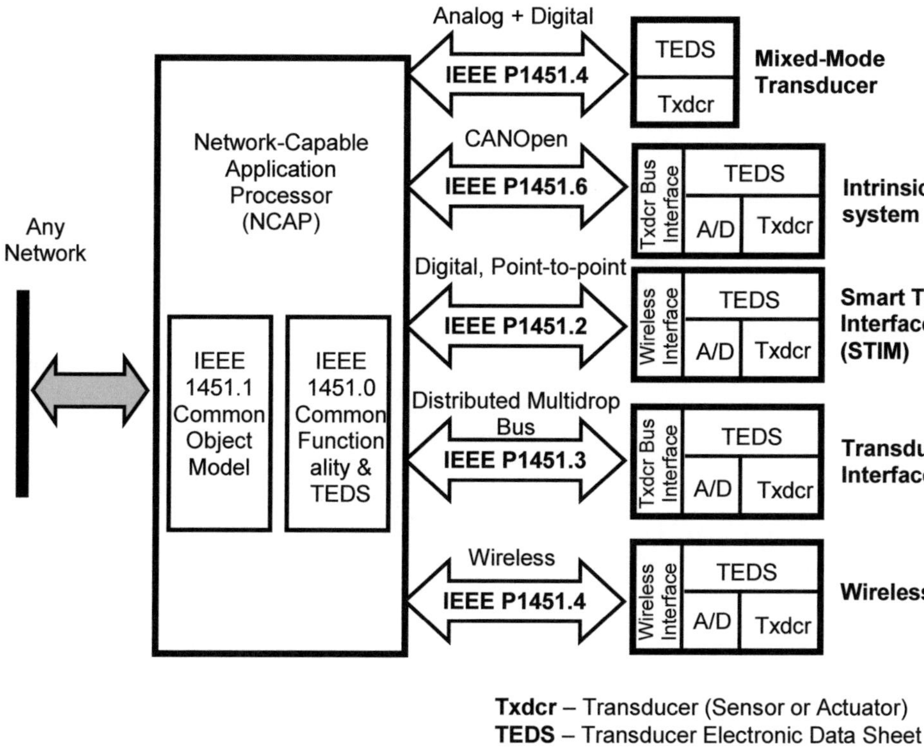


Fig. 1. TEDS on IEEE 1451 family of smart transducer interface standards network (Txdcr - transducer sensor or actuator)

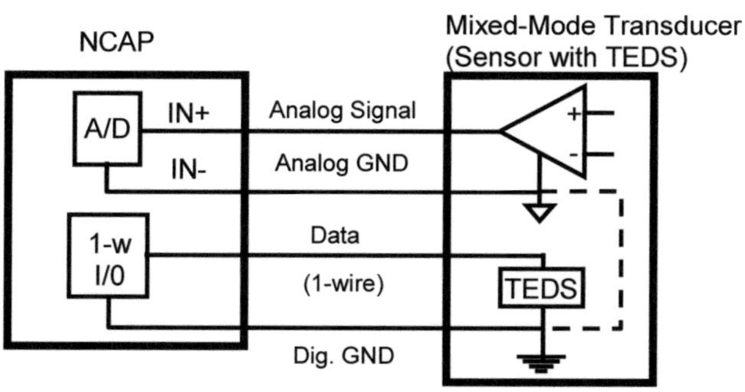


Fig. 2. Non-volatile memory for TEDS associated with *mixed-mode interface* for smart sensors (NCAP - network capable application processor)

The memory interfaces that are mainly used in the IEEE1451.4 implementation are 1-wire and I2C. In the following paragraph a brief description of the 1-wire and 2-wire (I2C) memory interface protocols particularly used in smart sensor implementation will be presented.

## 3. Memory Interfaces Protocols for Smart Sensors

The 1-wire interface provides advantages over other industry interfaces such as $I^2C$ or SPI™ in applications where contacts between the host controller and the memory device are limited or must be minimized, and/or where factory-programmed unique device serialization is required or valuable. 1-wire devices require a total of two contacts for total device operation, compared to four contacts for $I^2C$ memory or five contacts for SPI memory.

### 3.1 1-wire interface protocol for smart sensor memories

1-wire protocol was developed by Dallas Semiconductor in order to permit digital communications over twisted-pair cables with 1-wire components over a 1-wire network.
A 1-wire bus uses only one wire for signalling and power. Communication is asynchronous and half-duplex, and it follows a strict master-slave scheme. One or several slave devices can be connected to the bus at the same time. Only one master should be connected to the bus.
1-wire bus electronics implements an open-drain (wired-AND) master/slave multidrop architecture with resistor pull-up to a nominal supply at the master. A block diagram of 1-wire network is presented in Fig. 3.

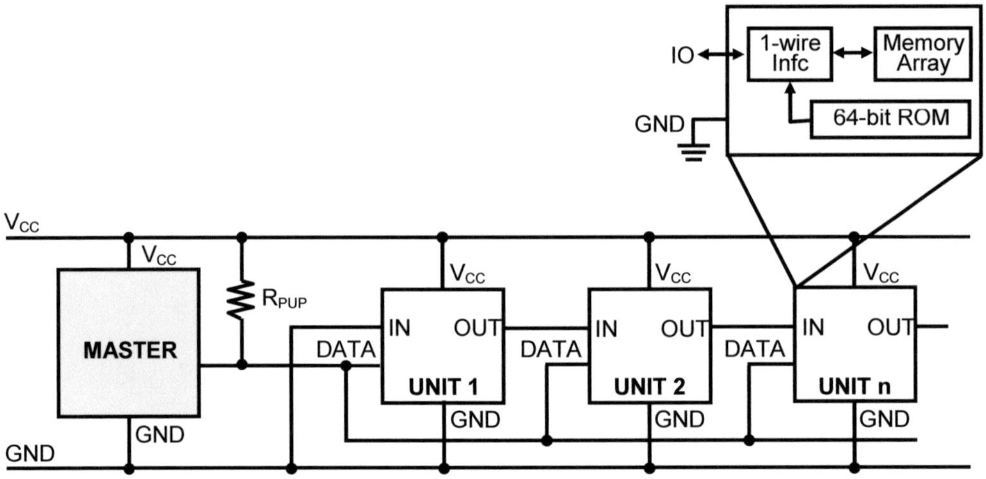


Fig. 3. - 1-wire network of non-volatile memories

The 1-wire network has three main components: a bus master with controlling software, wiring and associated connectors (e.g. Esensors connectors) and 1-wire devices (unit1, unit2, unit3,..unitn) that can be sensors, actuators and memories (e.g. DS2430A from Maxim). The

protocol uses conventional CMOS/TTL logic levels (maximum 0.8V for logic "zero" and a minimum 2.2V for logic "one") with operation specified over a supply voltage range of 2.8V to 6V. System clock is not required; each 1-wire part is self-clocked by an internal oscillator synchronized to the falling edge of the master.
Signalling on the 1-wire bus is divided into time slots of 60us. One data bit is transmitted on the bus per time slot. Units are allowed to have a time base that differs significantly from the nominal time base. This however, requires the timing of the master to be very precise, to ensure correct communication with slaves with different time bases.

**Addressing**

All 1-wire devices have a unique address laser-registered into the chip. Dallas Semiconductors guarantees that the address is unique. The individual address is expressed by a 64-bit serial number that is stored in the device memory. It is composed of eight bytes divided into three main sections as presented in Table 1.

| Family code | ID | CRC8 |
|---|---|---|
| 8 bits | 48 bits (unique within family) | 8 bits |

Table 1. - 1-wire address format. Left to right: increasing time, increasing bit order

Starting with the least significant bit (LSB), the first byte stores the 8-bit family codes that identify the device type. For the particular case of 1-wire memories the family codes are presented in Table 2.

| 1-wire memory | Family code |
|---|---|
| 1k memory iButton | 08 |
| 4k memory iButton | 06 |
| 16k memory iButton | 0A |
| 64k memory iButton | 0C |
| 4k EEPROM | 23 |
| 1k EEPROM | 2D |
| 256 EEPROM | 14 |
| 1k EEPROM protected with SHA-1 | 33 |

Table 2. - 1 wire address family code for several memory devices

The next six bytes store a customizable 48-bit individual address or ID that guaranteed unique within a family. A few types of chips have sequences of IDs reserved for special manufacturing runs, but in general, there are no special characteristics to the ID. The last byte, the most significant byte (MSB), contains a cyclic redundancy check (CRC) with a value based on the data contained in the first seven bytes. This allows the master to determine if an address was read without error.
With a $2^{48}$ serial number pool, conflicting or duplicate node addresses on the net are never a problem. For maximum data security the 1-wire memories can implement US government-certified Secure Hash Algorithm (SHA-1).

### Basic bus signals

As mentioned before, 1-wire memory interface protocol uses a single wire (plus ground) to accomplish both communication and power transmission. A single bus master can feed multiple slaves over a single twisted-pair cable. Thus, the master initiates every communication on the bus down to the bit-level. This means that for every bit that is to be transmitted, regardless of direction, the master has to initiate the bit transmission. This is always done by pulling the bus low, which will synchronize the timing logic of all units.

### 1-wire bus commands and operations

The communication between the master and slaves uses a set of five basic commands of the 1-wire bus: "Write 1", "Write 0", "Read", "Reset" and "Presence".

- ***Write 1***- The master pulls the bus low for 1 to 15 μs. It then releases the bus for the rest of the time slot (Fig.4).

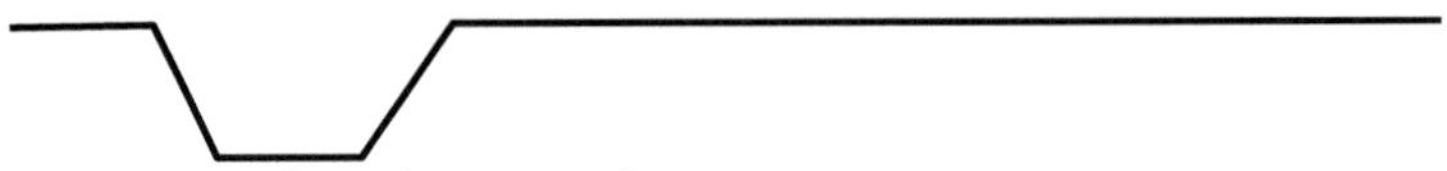

Fig. 4. - Write 1 – command on the 1-wire bus

- ***Write 0*** - The master pulls the bus low for a period of at least 60 μs, with a maximum length of 120 μs (Fig.5).

Fig. 5. - Write 0 – command on the 1-wire bus

- ***Read*** - The master pulls the bus low for 1 to 15 μs. The slave then holds the bus low if it wants to send a '0'. If it wants to send a '1', it simply releases the line. The bus should be sampled 15μs after the bus was pulled low. As seen from the master's side, the "Read" signal is in essence a "Write 1" signal. It is the internal state of the slave, rather than the signal itself that dictates whether it is a"Write 1" or "Read" signal (Fig. 6).

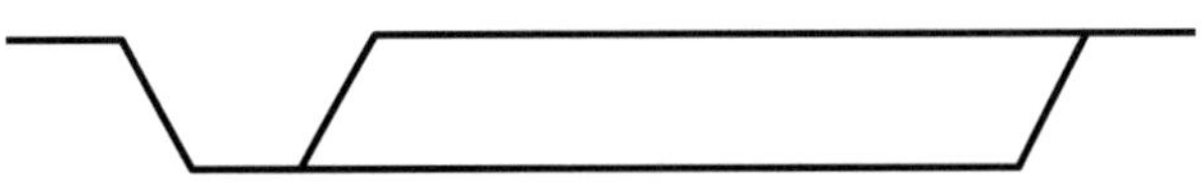

Fig. 6. - Read command on the 1-wire bus

- ***Reset & Presence*** - The master pulls the bus low for at least 8 time slots or 480μs and then releases it. This long low period is called the "Reset" signal. If there is a slave present, it should then pull the bus low within 60μs after it was released by the master and hold it low for at least 60μs. This response is called a "Presence" signal. If no presence signal is issued on the bus, the master must assume that no device is present on the bus, and further communication is not possible (Fig.7).

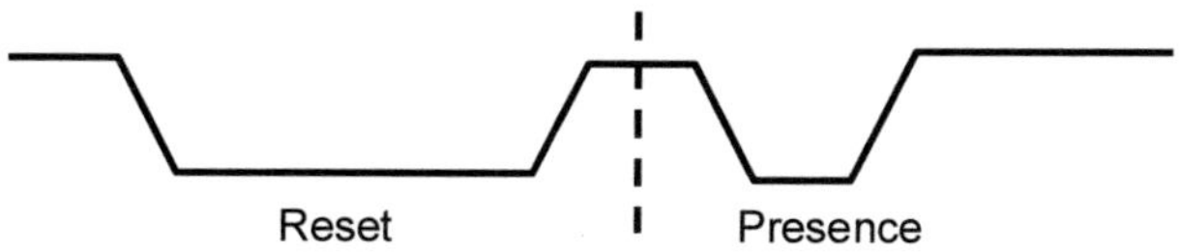


Fig. 7 .- Reset & Presence – command on the 1-wire bus

The communication between the master and slave is performed using the 1-wire commands according with the flowchart that is presented in Fig.8.

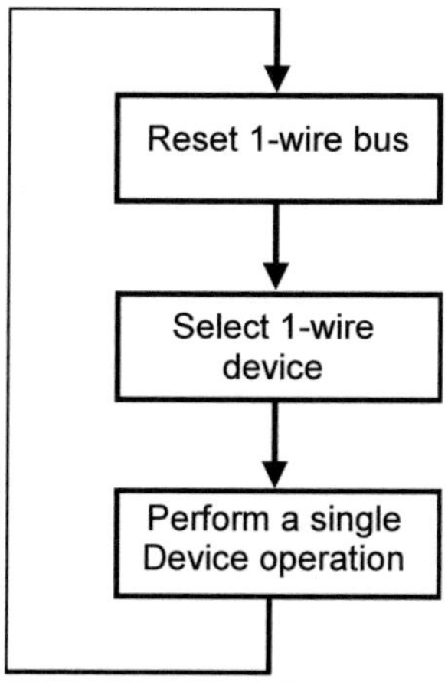


Fig. 8. - 1-wire master-slave communication flowchart

The first step of the communication is materialized by the „reset" command that is delivered by the master synchronizing the entire 1-wire bus. One of the unit1, unit2, ...., unit n (slave devices) is selected for the next communication. The selection of the specific slave is done using the serial number of the device or using a binary search algorithm (Maxim, 2002). Once a specific device has been selected, all other devices drop out and ignore subsequent communications until the next reset is carried out.

Because each device type performs different functions and serves a different purpose, each has a unique protocol once it has been selected. For the particular case of a non-volatile memory, a set of particular commands are mentioned:

- ***Write Scratchpad [0F$_h$]*** - applies to the data memory and the writable addresses in the register page. After issuing the Write Scratchpad command, the master must first provide the 2-byte target address, followed by the data to be written to the scratchpad;
- ***Read Scratchpad command [AAh]*** - allows verifying the target address and the integrity of the scratchpad data. After issuing the command code, the master begins reading. The master should read through the end of the scratchpad, after which it receives an inverted CRC16, based on data as it was sent by the 1-wire memory.
- ***Copy Scratchpad command [55h]*** - is used to copy data from the scratchpad to the data memory and the writable sections of the register page.
- ***Read Memory command [F0h]*** - is the general function to read from the 1-wire memory. After issuing the command, the master must provide a 2-byte target

address, which should be in the range of 0000h to 0A3Fh. If the target address is higher than 0A3Fh, for the particular case of DS28EC20 (1-wire memory), the upper four address bits are changed to "0". After the address is transmitted, the master reads data starting at the (modified) target address and can continue until address 0A3Fh. If the master continues reading, the result is FFh. The Read Memory command sequence can be ended at any point by issuing a reset pulse.

- ***Extended read memory [A5h]-*** works essentially the same way as Read Memory, except for the 16-bit CRC that the DS28EC20 generates and transmits following the last data byte of a memory page. The Extended Read Memory command sequence can be ended at any point by issuing a reset pulse.

### Master host computer interfacing

In a 1-wire network associated with smart sensors the master is generally a microcontroller. An example of DS28EC20 connection to the microcontroller as part of an IEEE1451.4 implementation is presented in Fig. 9. It presents the advantage of compactness but requires 1-wire implementation protocol at the microcontroller level. 1-wire protocol implementation for Atmel microcontroller (Atmel, 2004) and PIC microcontroller (Maxim, 2003) are referred in the literature.

Using a serial 1-wire line driver, the 1-wire memory device can be connected to the UART port of the microcontroller reducing the design time. A solution in this field is the MAXIM's DS2480B chip. It connects directly to UARTs and 5V RS232 systems. Interfacing to RS232C (±12V levels) requires a passive clamping circuit and one 5V to ±12V level translator such as MAX232. Internal timers relieve the host of the burden of generating the time-critical 1-wire communication waveforms. The DS2480B can be set to communicate at four different data rates, including 115.2kbps, 57.6kbps, and 19.2kbps, with 9.6kbps being the power-on default. Command codes received from the host's crystal controlled UART serve as a reference to continuously calibrate the on-chip timing generator. The various control functions of the DS2480B are optimized for MicroLAN 1-wire networks and support the special needs EPROM-based add-only memories and EEPROM devices as well as the other 1-wire devices (e.g. ibutton, 1-wire thermometers).

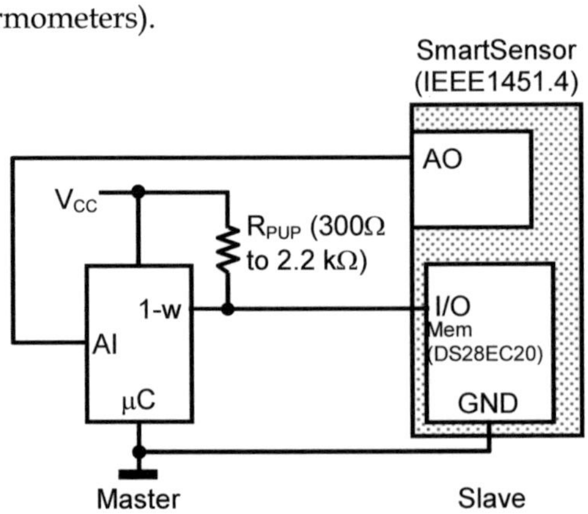


Fig. 9. - The interfacing of memory as part of IEEE1451.4 smart sensor to the microcontroller (μC)

Referring to the implementation of 1-wire software that works under Windows OS, an 1-wire *Software Development KIT (SDK)* can be used to develop applications associated with IEEE1451.4 smart sensor data management. The 1-wire SDK includes 1-wire API for .NET, API examples in VB.NET and C#, along with TMEX API examples in C, C++, Pascal (Borland Delphi), and Microsoft Visual Basic that assures high degree of flexibility and reduced time of software design and implementation.

### 3.2 2-wire (I2C) interface protocol for smart sensor memories

In the early 1980's, Philips Semiconductors developed a simple bi-directional 2-wire bus for developing networks of integrated circuits (IC), including memories. This bus is called the Inter-Integrated Circuit or I2C-bus. At present, Philips' IC range includes more than 150 CMOS and bipolar I2C-bus compatible types for performing communication functions between intelligent control devices (e.g. microcontrollers), general-purpose circuits (e.g. LCD drivers, remote I/O ports, memories) and application-oriented circuits (e.g. digital tuning and signal processing circuits for radio and video systems).
Taking into account the capabilities of I2C bus on device interfacing, it was considered as an interesting solution for smart sensors (SmartS) interfacing, including those compatibles with the IEEE1451 protocol. An example of I2C network, including a set of memories as part of IEEE1451.4 smart sensor network implementation, is presented in Fig. 10.

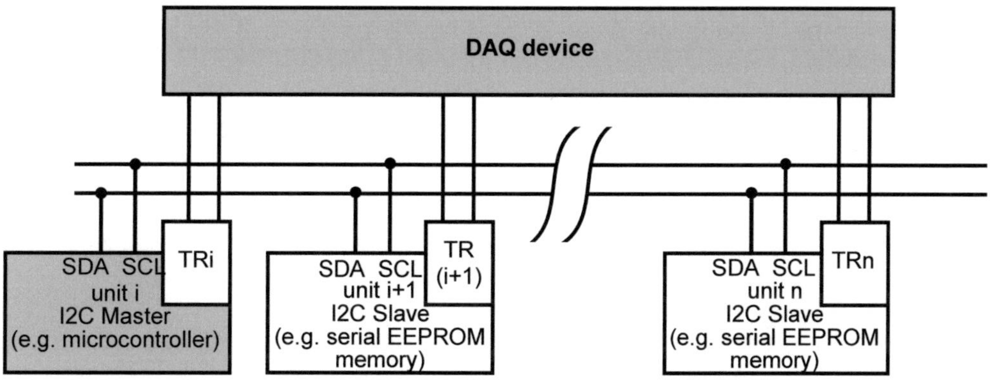


Fig. 10. - I2C device network including 1 master device and n - slave devices ( TRi, TR(i+1), TRn - analog transducers, DAQ device - analog signal acquisition devices)

Each device has a particular address. I2C bus supports two addressing schemes: 7-bit address and 10-bit address. Up to 1024 devices are allowed to be connected to the bus. The 7-bit address scheme has shorter message length and requires less complex hardware. Devices with 7 and 10 bit addresses can be mixed in the same system.
The bus can operate in three modes with different data rates. Data on the bus can be transferred at rates of up to 100kbit/s in the standard-mode, up to 400 kbit/s in the fast-mode, or up to 3.4 Mbit/s in the high-speed mode. The number of interfaces connected to the bus is dependent on the bus capacitance limit of 400pf (Phillips, 2000).

**Basic bus signals**

The I2C bus wires are called SDA (Serial DAta line) and SCL (Serial CLock line). They are both bi-directional and assure the communication between the network devices through the SDA and SCL signals (Fig.11). As can be observed, the communication signals are characterized by: the start bit, the 7 bits (B6...B0) I2C device address, the RD/nWR bit associated with master-slave read or write operations signalling, the ACKNOWLEDGE bit, the 8 (D7...D0) data bits, and the STOP bit.

The SCL signal is an explicit clock signal on which the communication synchronizes and is imposed by the master unit. When the slave unit is not able to follow with the clock rate given by the master a mechanism clock stretching is activated on the slave level (Leens, 2009).

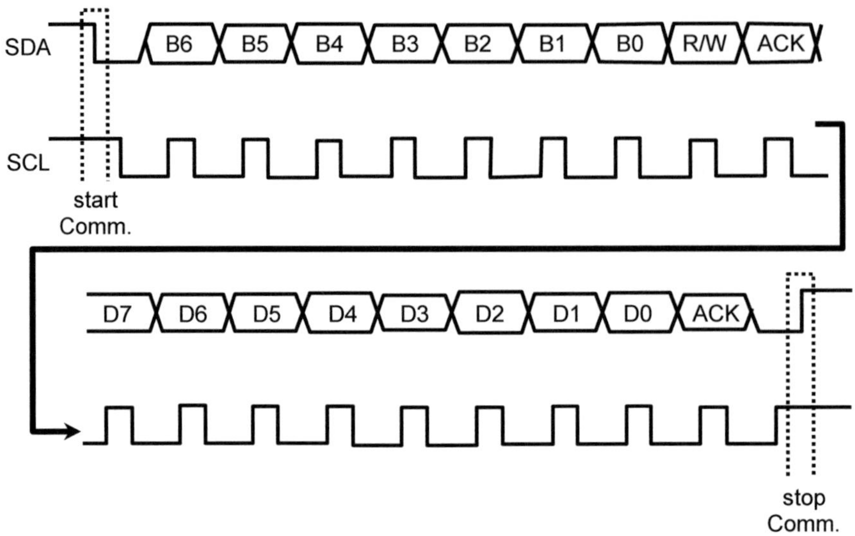


Fig. 11. - The SDA and SCL signals associated with the I2C bus communication

The I2C bus does not support plug-n-play or interrupt functions that are important for many sensor networks or memory networks. To save energy, some sensor nodes should be in sleep mode most of the time and woken up by a timer or sensing event. For each transported information, the microcontroller should initiate the request and provide the clock to the sensors. To get the updated information from the sensor, the microcontroller has to poll each sensor node connected on the bus very often to make sure it will not miss new information or unexpected events. These features make I2C unsuitable for the applications which have strict requirement for the power efficiency and emergency processing. Although the sensor node could be clipped to or from the system easily, the microcontroller can not detect an event or configure the system during operation. This limits the application of I2C in sensor networks which are usually dynamically reconfigurable and/or demand high energy-efficiency.

### Commands and operations

Every device connected to the bus has its own unique address and can act as a receiver and/or transmitter, depending on its own functionality.
The I2C bus is a multi-master bus. Thus, more than one device with I2C interface are capable of initiating a data transfer. The I2C protocol specification states that the unit that initiates a data transfer on the bus is considered the *Bus Master*. Consequently, at that time, all the other units are regarded to be *Bus Slaves*. The master can send data to a slave or receive data from a slave. Slaves do not transfer data between themselves.
Considering the particular scenario of a microcontroller as master of I2C bus that includes memories associated with smart sensor TEDS as bus slaves, the commands and operation associated with master-slave, slave-master communication are next presented.
First, the master will send out a START signal. This acts as an "Attention" signal sent to the bus units. All of the units connected to the bus will listen for incoming data. Then, the master sends the ADDRESS of the device it wants to access, along with an indication of whether the access is a Read or Write operation ("1" logic for read operation and "0" for write operation).
Having received the address, all ICs will compare it with their own address. If it does not match, they simply wait until the STOP command from the master.
Considering that the received address by the slave matches its proper address, the response is materialized by the ACKNOWLEDGE signal. Once the master unit receives the ACKNOWLEDGE, it can start transmitting or receiving *DATA* according to the RD/nWR bit.
When all the data transmission is done the master will send the *STOP* command. This is the signal that the bus has been released and that the connected units may expect another transmission to start any moment.
Referring to memories as I2C bus units, there are several important manufactures of very broad range of memory capacities with I2C bus interface. As common used memories in smart sensor implementation can be mentioned the Microchip memories, that are characterized by capacities from 16 bytes, for the 24C00, up to 32k bytes, for the 24C256 family.

## 4. Memory Interfaces Protocols for Mobile Devices

Mobile devices must have memories that assure the capability to store applications and data files. However, data logging tasks are always related to the utilization of memory extension cards, such as CompactFlash memories (CF card) or Secure Digital memories (SD card). Considering the importance of mobile devices external memories, two of the communications protocols associated with this kind of memories are now described.

### 4.1 Compact Flash memory protocol

CompactFlash® (CF) has established itself as a dominant flash memory card technology in applications where small form factor, low-power dissipation and ease-of-design are crucial considerations. Introduced by SanDisk Corporation in 1994, CF Storage Cards provide the capability to transfer all types of digital information and software between different types of digital systems and are compatible with future CF designs, eliminating interoperability restrictions. As a result, CF is a powerful solution that can be found in digital SLR cameras, PDAs (e.g. iPAQ 2700 series), embedded systems, single-board computers and data recorders.

CF based data storage is used especially at the master device level such as PDAs (Postolache, 2006) or touch panel computers (e.g. TPC2106T) (Postolache, 2007).

Two types of CF non-volatile memory cards are considered:

- Type I cards or CF, dimensionally characterized by 43mm (1.7") x 36mm (1.4") x 3.3mm (0.13"));
- Type II cards or CF2, dimensionally characterized by 43mm (1.7") x 36mm (1.4") x 5mm (0.19").

CompactFlash cards are designed with flash technology [(Kingmax Digital Inc., 2009)]. According to the CompactFlash card specification version 4.1 it can be characterized by data storage capacities up to 137GB. However, the current commercial CF solutions have data storage capacities up to only 64GB (e.g. Pretec CF memory).

The CF classification by speed is:

- original CF;
- CF High Speed (using CF+/CF2.0);
- CF3.0 standard.

Compact Flash supports data rates up to 133MB/sec. However, values associated with current commercially CF devices are up to only 45Mb/s (e.g. 8GB ScanDisk Extreme).

### CF electrical interface

The internal configuration of the CF protocol associated to CF non-volatile memory cards includes a CF controller connected through I/O digital lines to a host interface that can be associated with PDAs, laptop computers, tablet PC, etc. The CF block diagram and the CF connector pin-out are presented in Fig. 12.

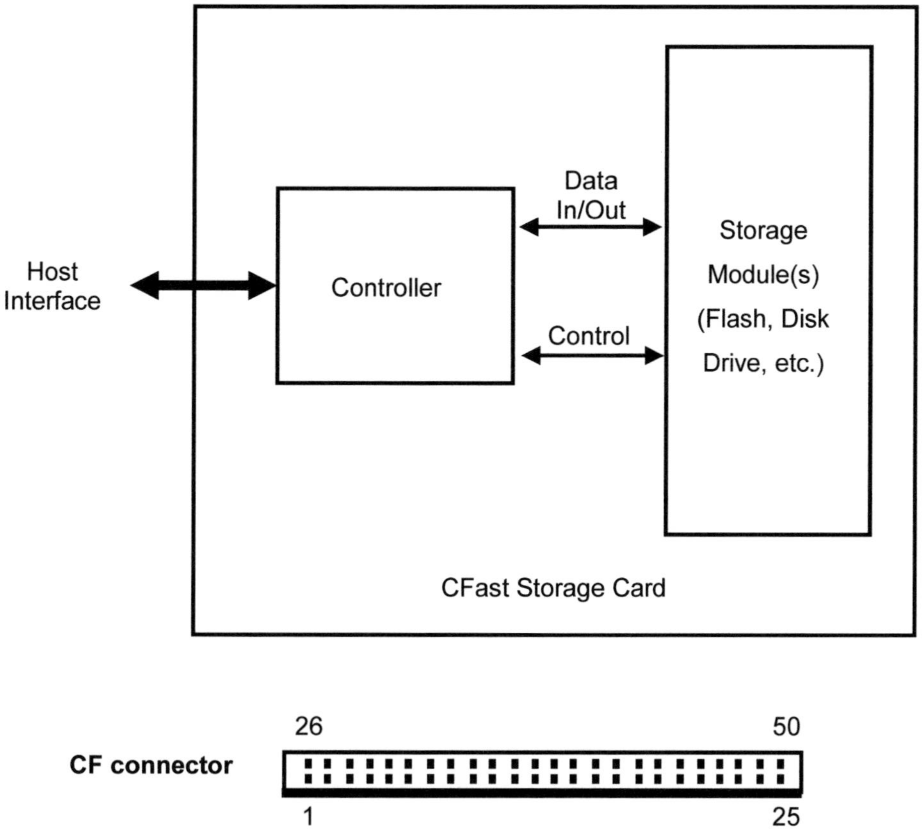


Fig. 12. - Compact Flash block diagram and CF connector pin-out

Pins 13 and 38 correspond to power supply, which according to the standard can be either 3.3 volts or 5 volts. Pins 1 and 50 correspond to GND. The data stored on the CF can be accessed through 8 or 16 bit data bus associated to the CF connector. The data and address bits for 8 and 16 bits memory access bus are shown in Table 3.

| | | | | | | | | |
|---|---|---|---|---|---|---|---|---|
| Pins | 21 | 22 | 23 | 2 | 3 | 4 | 5 | 6 |
| Data lines | D00 | D01 | D02 | D03 | D04 | D05 | D06 | D07 |
| Pins | 47 | 48 | 49 | 27 | 28 | 29 | 30 | 31 |
| Data lines | D08 | D09 | D10 | D11 | D12 | D13 | D14 | D15 |

Table 3. - CF pins and data line correspondence for 8bit and 16 bit data bus for memory access.

The address bus (A0 to A10 lines) pin assignment is given in Fig. 13.

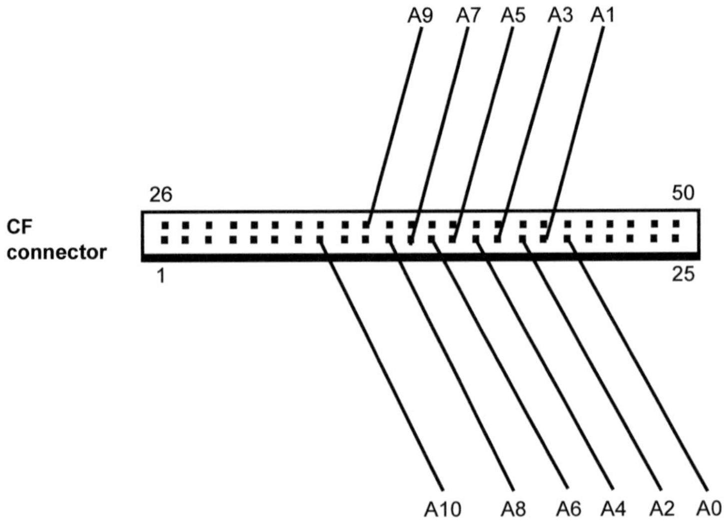


Fig. 13. - CF's connector address bus pin out

### 4.2 Secure digital (SD) memory protocol

The SD card standard is a standard for removable memory storage designed and licensed by the SD Card Association (Compact Flash, 2009). It is the result of the collaboration between three manufacturers, Toshiba, SanDisk, and MEI (Panasonic) and is specifically designed to meet the security, capacity, performance, and environment requirements inherent in newly emerging audio and video consumer electronic devices as well as an important component of smart sensing networks that include smart mobile devices such as smart phones and PDAs, assuring data logging capabilities for individual nodes.

At the same time, the SD standard is not limited to removable memory storage devices and has been adapted to many different classes of devices, including 802.11 cards, Bluetooth devices, and modems.

The SD Memory Card includes a content protection mechanism that complies with the security of the SDMI (Secure Digital Music Initiative) standard and is faster and capable of higher memory capacity. Nowadays, SD high-capacity (SDHC) cards start at 4GB and going up to 32GB.

In what concerns the operating rate of the SD card working in the default mode, typical values are up to 12.5 MB/sec interface speed for a variable clock rate 0 - 25 MHz, while for high-speed working mode are reported values of up to 25 MB/sec interface speed for a variable clock rate from 0 - 50 MHz.

#### SD electrical interface

A block diagram of an SD card interface associated with a SD card non-volatile memory is presented in Fig. 14 and the corresponding pin-out, together with the SD function are presented in Table 4.

The SD card is clocked by an internal clock generator. The interface driver unit synchronizes the DAT and CMD signals from external CLK to the internal used clock signal. The card is controlled by the six line SD card interface containing the signals: CMD, CLK,DAT0~DAT3.

For the identification of the SD card in a stack of SD card, a card identification register (CID) and a relative and address register (RCA) is foreseen [(Kingmax Digital Inc., 2009)].
An additional register, (CSD), contains different types of operation parameter.

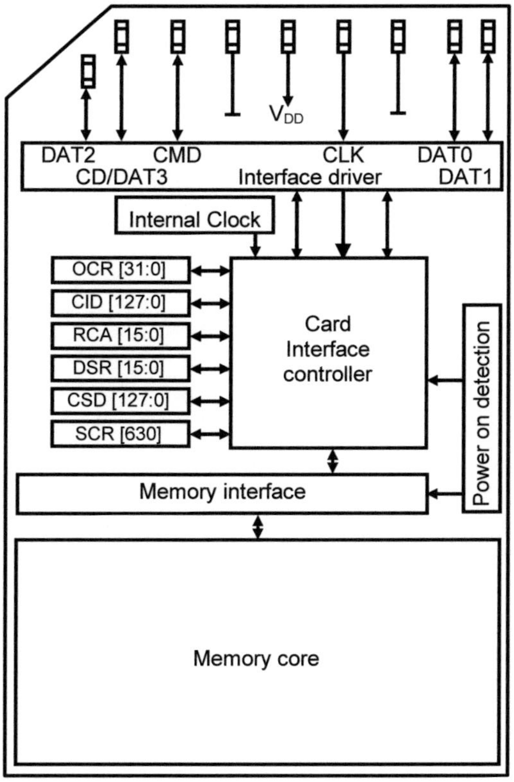


Fig. 14. - SD card block diagram

| Pin | Name | SD function |
|---|---|---|
| 1 | DATA3/CS | Data Line 3 |
| 2 | CMD/DI | Command Line |
| 3 | VSS1 | Ground |
| 4 | VDD | Supply Voltage |
| 5 | CLK | Clock (SCK) |
| 6 | VSS2 | Ground |
| 7 | DAT0/D9 | Data Line 0 |
| 8 | DAT1/IRQ | Data Line 1 |
| 9 | DAT2/NC | Data Line 2 |

Table 4. - SD pin out

The card has its own power on detected unit. No additional master reset signal is required to setup the card after power on. It is protected against short circuit during insertion and removal while the SD card system is powered up
The communication using the SD card lines to access either the memory field or the register is defined by the SD card standard. Different protocols are supported by SD cards.

**SD 1 bit protocol**
It is a synchronous serial protocol with one data line, used for bulk data transfers, one clock line for synchronization, and one command line, used for sending command frames. The SD 1-bit protocol explicitly supports bus sharing. A simple single-master arbitration scheme allows multiple SD cards to share a single clock and DAT0 line.

**SD 4 bit protocol**
It is nearly identical to the SD 1-bit protocol. The main difference is that bulk data transfers use a 4-bit parallel bus instead of a single wire. With proper design, this has the potential to quadruple the throughput for bulk data transfers. Both the SD 1-bit and 4-bit protocols by default require a Cyclic Redundancy Check (CRC) protection of bulk data transfers.
Cyclic Redundancy Check is a simple method for detecting the presence of simple bit-inversion errors in a transmitted block of data. In SD 4-bit mode, the input data is multiplexed over the four bus (DAT) lines and the 16-bit CRC is calculated independently for each of the four lines, which imply an increased software complexity of CRC calculation. Hardware implementation of 4-bit parallel CRC calculation represents an interesting alternative and can be materialized using an Application Specific Integrated Circuit (ASIC) or field programmable gate arrays (FPGA).

**SPI mode – SD card protocol**
It is distinct from the 1-bit and 4-bit protocols in that the protocol operates over a generic and well-known bus interface, Serial Peripheral Interface (SPI). SPI is a synchronous serial protocol that is extremely popular for interfacing peripheral devices with microcontrollers (Leens, 2009). Most modern microcontrollers, including the MSP430, support SPI natively at relatively high data rates. The SPI communications mode supports only a subset of the full SD Card protocol. However, most of the unsupported command sets are simply not needed in SPI mode. A fully-functional SD Card implementation can be realized using only SPI.
This flexibility of electrical interfaces is a significant advantage to a designer. A designer may opt for a fast parallel interface, or depending on the application, may prefer a slower implementation using SPI. Due to the popularity of the SPI protocol and its efficient implementation on the MSP430, we mention here only the SPI mode of the SD Card protocol. Minor differences in the initialization sequence exist between the two major modes. For more information, the interested reader should consult the full SD Card Specification available from the SD Card Association.

## 5. References

Atmel (2004). AVR318: Dallas 1-Wire master 8-bit Microcontrollers, on-line at: *www.atmel.com/dyn/resources/prod_documents/doc2579.pdf, Sept-2004*

Brewer, J. & Gill, M. (2008). *Nonvolatile Memory Technologies with Emphasis on Flash: A Comprehensive Guide to Understanding and Using Flash Memory Devices,* Wiley-IEEE Press, February 2008

Compact Flash Org. (2009). CF+ & CompactFlash Specification Revision 4.1, on line at http://www.compactflash.org/spec_download.htm, May 2009

Flittner P. (2007). CSR (Bluetooth Subgroup Chair) Thurston Brooks, 3eTI, *IEEE P1451.5 Wireless Sensor Interface Working Group Bluetooth Subgroup. Proposal* on-line at: grouper.ieee.org/groups/1451/5/.../P1451.5_Bluetooth2.pdf

Frank, R. (2002). *Understanding Smart Sensors,* Artech House Publishers, April 2002

Higuera J.; Polo J.; Gasulla M. (2009). A Zigbee wireless sensor network compliant with the IEEE1451 standard, *Proceedings of IEEE Sensors Applications Symposium,* SAS 2009, pp.309-313, 2009

Honeywell (2009). "TEDS - plug and play sensor configuration", on-line at http://www.sensotec.com/pnpterms.shtml, June 2009

IEEE Std 1451.4-2004 (2004), Standard for a Smart Transducer Interface for Sensors and Actuators- Mixed-Mode Communication Protocols and Transducer Electronic Data Sheet (TEDS) Formats, *IEEE Standards Association,* Piscataway, NJ, sub classe 5.1.1, 2004

IEEE STD 1451.0-2007 (2007). Standard for a Smart Transducer Interface for Sensors and Actuators - Common Functions, Communication Protocols, and Transducer Electronic Data Sheet (TEDS) Formats, IEEE Instrumentation and Measurement Society, TC-9, The Institute of Electrical and Electronics Engineers, Inc., New York, N.Y. 10016, SH99684, October 5, 2007

IEEE Standard Association (2009). IEEE Standard 1451.4-2004 Tutorials, on-line at: http://standards.ieee.org/regauth/1451/Tutorials.html, 2009

Kalinsky D. & Kalinsky R. (2002). Introduction to Serial Peripheral Interface, on-line at http://www.embedded.com/story/OEG20020124S0116, January '02

Kingmax Digital Inc. (2009). SD Card Specification" on line at:: *downloads.amilda.org/MODs/SDCard/SD.pdf*

Leens F. (2009). An introduction to I2C and SPI protocols, *Instrumentation and Measurement Magazine,* vol.12, No. 1, pp. 8-13, February 2009

Linke B. (2008). Overview of 1-Wire® Technology and Its Use, on-line at http://www.maxim-ic.com/appnotes.cfm/an_pk/1796, June 2008

Maxim Inc. (2002), 1-Wire Search Algorithm, on-line at http://www.maxim ic.com/appnotes.cfm/an_pk/187, March 2002

Maxim Inc. (2003), *1-Wire Communication with a Microchip PICmicro Microcontroller* on-line at http://www.maximic.com/appnotes.cfm/an_pk/2420, Sept. 2003

Pardo A.; Camara L.; Cabre J.; Perera A.; Cano X.; Marco S.; Bosch J. (2006). Gas measurement systems based on IEEE1451.2 standard, *Sensors and Actuators B: Chemical,* Vol.116, Issues 1-2, pp. 11-16, July 2006

Paret D.& Fenger, C. (1997). *The I2C Bus: From Theory to Practice,* Wiley, John & Sons, *1997*

Pfeiffer O.; Ayre A.; Keydel C. (2003) *Embedded Networking with CAN and CANopen,* Annabooks Publisher, 2003

Phillips Semiconductor (2000). The I2C-BUS specification, Version 2.1, 2000, online at: *i2c2p.twibright.com/spec/i2c.pdf.* 2000

Postolache O.; Postolache G.; Girão P. M. (2006). Non-invasive mobile homeostasis Instrument", Proc *IEEE International Workshop on Medical Measurements and Applications*, Benevento, Italy,.Vol. I, pp. 94 – 98, May 2006

Postolache O.; Dias Pereira J. M.; Girão P. M. (2007). Optical Fiber Based Turbidity Sensing System, Proc *IMEKO TC19 Symp*, Iasi, Romania, Vol. II, pp. 71 - 75, September, 2007

Ramos H.; Pereira J.M.; Viegas V.; Postolache O.; Girão P. M. (2004). A Virtual Instrument to Test Smart Transducer Interface Modules (STIMs), *IEEE Transactions on Instrumentation and Measurement*, vol. 53, no. 4, pp. August 2004

SD Association (2009). SD Card Compact and Powerful, Ideal for Small Products, on-line at: http://www.sdcard.org/developers/tech/sdcard/, May 2009

Song E. Y. & Lee K (2008). Understanding IEEE 1451-Networked smart transducer interface standard, *IEEE Instrumentation & Measurement Magazine*, Vol.11, No. 2, pp.11-17, February 2008

Ulivieri N.; Distante C.; Luca T.; Rocchi S.; Siciliano P. (2006). IEEE1451.4: A way to standardize gas sensor, *Sensors and Actuators B: Chemical*, Volume 114, Issue 1, pp. 141-151, March 2006

Yurish, S. & Gomes M. (2003). *Smart Sensors and MEMS,* NATO Science Series Mathematics, Physics and Chemistry, September 2003

# Electronic Nose System and Artificial Intelligent Techniques for Gases Identification

Iman Morsi
*Arab Academy for Science and Technology,*
*Electronics and Communications Department*
*Alexandria-Egypt*

## 1. Introduction

Electronic nose is the intelligent design to identify food flavors, cosmetics and different gas odors, depending on sensors. The continuous developing of these sensors permit advanced control of air quality, as well as, high sensitivity to chemical odors. Accordingly, a group of scientists have worked on developing the properties of sensors, while others have modified ways of manufacturing ultra low-cost design (Josphine & Subramanian , 2008); (Wilson et al., 2001).
In the design of an electronic nose, sampling, filtering and sensors module, signal transducers, data preprocessing, feature extraction and feature classification are applied. (Getino et al., 1995) is used as an integrated sensor array for gas analysis in combustion atmosphere in the presence of humidity and variation in temperature from 150-350°C. The sensor array exposed to a gas mixture formed by $N_2$, $O_2$, $CO_2$, $H_2S$ , HCL and water vapour with a constant flow rate of 500 ml/ min was studied. (Marco et al., 1998). The gas identification with tin oxide sensor array is investigated, in addition, the several undesirable characteristics such as slow response, non-linearties, long term drifts are studied. Correction of the sensor's drift with adaptive self organizing maps permit success in gas classification problems.(Wilson et al., 2001) is introduced as a review of three commonly used gas sensors which are, solid state gas sensor, chemical sensors and optical sensors. Comparisons are deducted among them in terms of their ability to operate at low power, small size and relatively low cost with numerous interference and variable ambient conditions.(Dong Lee & Sik Lee, 2001) depended on solid state gas sensor, thus the pollutants of environment are controlled relative to the sensing mechanism, the sensing properties of solid - state gas sensors to environmental gases, such as No, Co and volatile organic compounds.(Guardado et al. , 2001) is used as a neural network efficiency for the detection of incipient fault in power transformers. The NN was trained according to five diagnosis criteria and then tested by using a new set of data.
This study shows that NN rate of successful diagnosis is dependent on specific criterion under consideration with values in the range of 87-100 %.( Zylka & Mazurek, 2002) introduced a rapid analysis of gases by means of a portable analyzer fitted with

electrochemical gas sensor. The analyzer, which was built, is controlled by a microprocessor and the system incorporates only two gases which are Co and $H_2$.
The drawback is the lack of sensors selectivity which is disadvantageous in most applications.(Belhovari et al., 2004; Belhovari et al., 2005) used sensors array with gas identification and Gaussian mixture models. Some problems are studied such as drift problem and slow response is introduced. Robust detection is applied through a drift counteraction approach which is based on extending the training data set using a simulated drift. (Belhovari et al., 2006) gas identification is introduced using sensors array, and different neural networks algorithms. Different classifiers are used MLP, RBF, KNN, GMM and PPCA are compared with each other using the same gas data set allowed performance up to 97%. Electronic gas sensors based on tin oxide films are used for the identification of gases, detection of toxic contaminants and separation of mixture of gases (Kolen, 1994); (Belhovari et al., 2005); (Marco et al., 1998); (Getino et al., 1995); (Becker et al., 2000); (Amigoni et al., 2006).
The problem here is to identify or to discriminate different gases such as, methane, propane, butane, carbon dioxide and hydrogen. Using different concentrations. Taguchi gas sensors (TGS) are used, which is a metal oxide semiconductor sensor, based on tin oxide that has been commercially available from Figaro engineering company (Figaro sensor.com "on – line"). In the design of electronic nose systems, power consumption directly related to temperature operation, selectivity, sensitivity, and stability typically has the most influence on the choice of metal oxide films for a particular application (Fleming, 2001); (Carullo, 2006). For electronic nose applications (Morsi-b, 2008); (Luo et al, 2002); (Bourgeois et al., 2003); (Carullo, 2006) metal oxide semiconductors are largely hampered by their power consumption demands. Thermal isolation and intermittent operation of the heaters reduce the power consumption of the sensors themselves to facilitate their use of importable applications. However, it also presents significant obstacles in terms of noise, drift, aging, and sensitivity to environmental parameters. The Feed Forward Back Propagation of Neural Network using the multilayer perceptron is used to separate between them. Fuzzy logic is used to discriminate different gases and to detect the concentration of each gas. Electronic nose design provides rapid responses, ease of operation and sufficient detection limits. Data quality objectives (DQOs) of gases must be considered as a part of technology development and a focus should be made on the most urgent problems.

**Organization of the chapter**

1. Introduction.
2. Experimental setup.
3. Results and analysis.
4. Surface response modeling algorithms and analysis of variance (ANOVA).
5. Separation of butane and propane as a gas mixture using an artificial intelligent technique of Neural Networks.
6. On-line identification of gases using artificial intelligent techniques of Fuzzy Logic.
7. Conclusion.
8. Acknowledgement.
9. References.

## 2. Experimental Setup

The analysis and the characterization of gases are acquired by building a prototype of multi-sensors monitoring system (electronic nose), which are TGS 822, TGS 3870, TGS 4160 and TGS 2600, from Figaro sensor industry, temperature sensor, humidity sensor and supply voltage equal to 5 V. However, current monitoring methods are costly and time intensive, likewise limitations and analytical techniques exist. Clearly, a need exists for accurate, inexpensive, long-term monitoring using sensors. TGS 822 is tin dioxide ($Sno_2$) as semiconductor. The sensor's conductivity increases, depending on the gas concentration. It has high sensitivity to the vapors of organic solvents, as well as, combustible gases. TGS 2600 is comprised of metal oxide semiconductor layer formed on an alumina substrate of a sensing chip together with an integrated heater. TGS 3870 is a metal oxide semiconductor gas sensor, embedding a micro-bead gas sensing structure. TGS 4160 is a hybrid sensor unit composed of a carbon dioxide sensitive element and a thermistor. All presented sensors have features of long life, low cost, small size, simple electrical circuit, low power consumption and are available in commercial application. The experimental equipment consists basically of the gas bottle mass flow controllers, sensor chamber with volume 475 $cm^3$, supply voltage of 5 V and a heating system (Morsi, 2007); (Morsi-a, 2008).Gases used in the experiment are carbon dioxide, hydrogen, methane, propane, butane and a mixture of propane and butane. All measurements are presented at 45% relative humidity. All sensors are connected as an array and covered by a chamber, which has "in" and "outlet" ports. The input is connected with the mass flow controllers to control the concentration of input gas after purging with humidified air. All sensors are subjected to variation in temperatures from ambient temperatures and up (Clifford et al., 2005); (Fleming, 2001). Four variable resistances are connected in series to the four sensors, placed out of chamber, then are followed by the microcontroller, to control and monitor the output of each sensor (Smulko, 2006). The output of the microcontroller is monitored and recorded every 20 sec. Different gases concentrations are applied 100 ppm, 400 ppm, 700 ppm, 1000 ppm with different environmental temperatures between 20°C to 50°C with different variable resistances for each sensor $R_L$ = 1 kΩ, 3 kΩ, 5 kΩ, and 7 kΩ . Variable load resistance is used to control the conductivity and to increase the selectivity of each gas than other gases. Sensitivity is used to refer either to the lowest level of chemical concentration that can be detected or to the smallest increment of concentration that can be detected in the sensing environment. While selectivity refers to the ratio of the sensor's ability to detect what is of interest over the sensor's ability to detect what is not of interest as the interferents. Sensors for use in electronic nose need partial selectivity, mimicking the responses of the olfactory receptors in the biological nose (Belhovari et al., 2006). Figure (1) shows the electronic nose gas system. The hardware requirements for the system implementation include a microcontroller Pic 16 F 877A with embedded (A/D) converter. It is chosen for the implementation of this task due to the on chip memory resources, as well as, its high speed. The output data is transferred to a PC via a serial port RS 232 with a Baud rate of 2400 from the microcontroller. The software is developed in C language and is complied, assembled, and downloaded to the system. The output volt of each sensor is collected, stored in memory and transferred to a microcontroller to be ready for the processing work and the temperature is also monitored via a temperature sensor and is recorded (Ishida et al., 2005); (Weigong et al., 2006);(Smulko,2006).

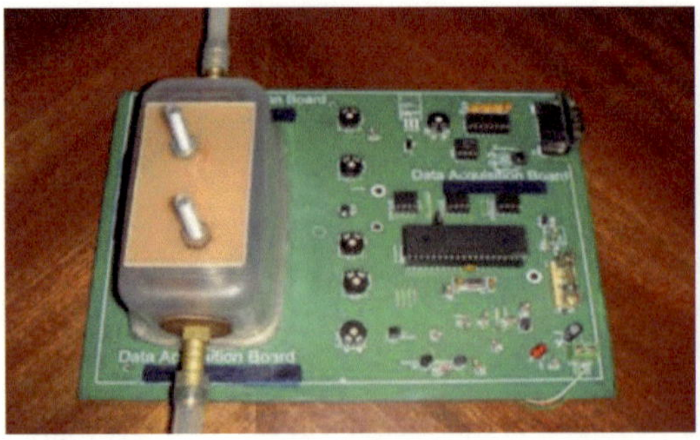

Fig. 1-a. Electronic nose of gas detection with chamber

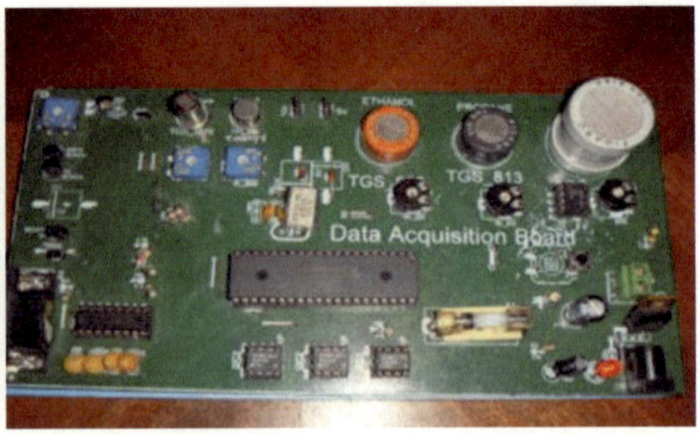


Fig. 1-b. Electronic nose of gas detection without chamber

Measurements using the electronic nose gas system detector have been done according to three parts: measurement part, mathematical analysis part, and presentation part. The system is supported by a collection of methods to improve the uncertainty and reliability. Different processing techniques like self calibration, self validation and statistical analysis methods are included. Data averaging standard deviation calculation are used to test and evaluate the performance of the whole measuring system in order to minimize error (Morsi, 2007); (Morsi - a, 2008).

## 3. Results and Analysis:

The design of electronic nose depends on physical connectivity of the sensors, relating to the data management, computing management and knowledge discovery management, which are associated with the sensors and the data they generate, and how they can be addressed within an open computing environment. Eventually, the issue relates to the integrated analysis of the sensor data depending on the variation of gases respectively. Moreover, there is a correlation and interaction of data.

Hence, the use of standardized data access and integration techniques to asses and integrate such data is essential. Furthermore, if the analysis is to proceed over large data sets, it is essential to provide high performance computing resources to allow rapid computation to proceed. Measurements have been done using the described experimental setup. The gas is injected inside the chamber and the concentration in ppm is controlled through the mass flow controller. Extensive measurements are performed and data collected from gas sensor via microcontroller undergoes a processing stage. Due to variation in temperature from 20°C to 50°C, the load resistance is adjusted to 1 kΩ , 3 kΩ, 5 kΩ and 7 kΩ, respectively and the gas concentrations are adjusted to 100 ppm, 400 ppm, 700 ppm and 1000 ppm respectively. There is an output voltage of each sensor relative to the variation of these parameters. The extensive numbers of measured values have been extracted at each resistance with different concentrations. The measurement values of different parameters with different gases at $R_L$ = 7 kΩ are described by figs 2 till 13 as a specimen deducted from enormous measured data due to different variable resistances with different concentrations (Morsi –a , 2008) .

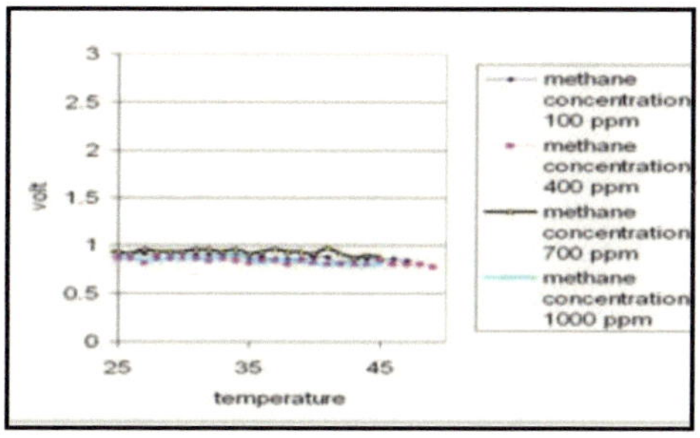


Fig. 2. Methane gas with TGS 3870 at $R_L$ 7 kΩ

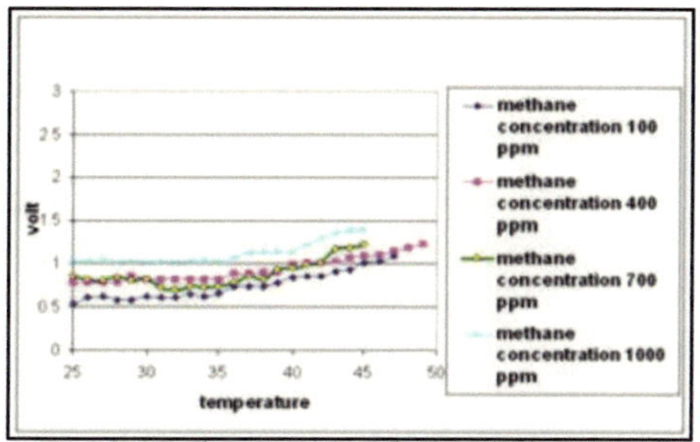


Fig. 3. Methane gas with TGS 822 at $R_L$ 7 kΩ

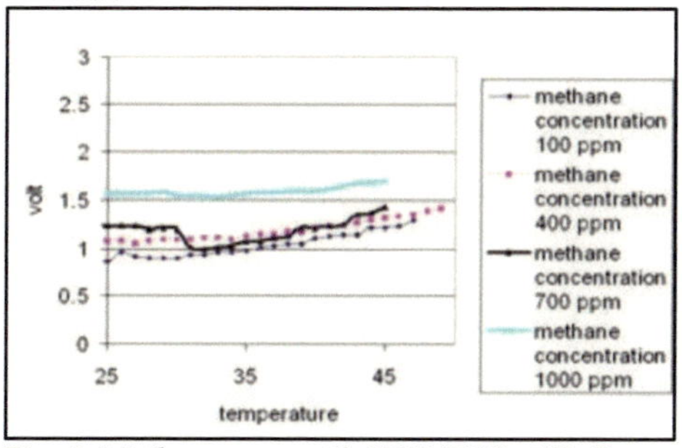


Fig. 4. Methane gas with TGS 2600 at $R_L$ 7 kΩ

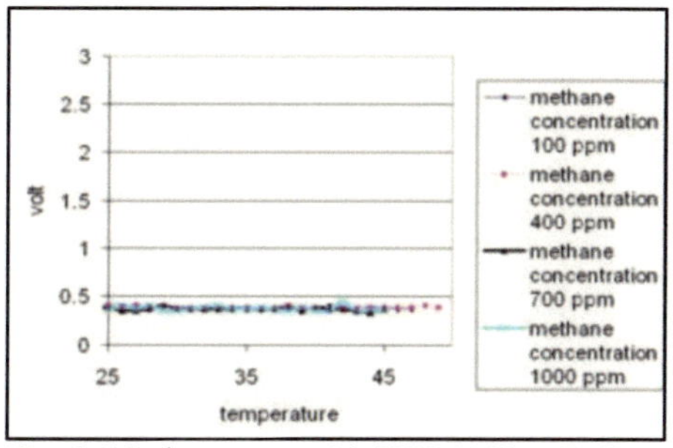


Fig. 5. Methane gas with TGS 4160 at $R_L$ 7 kΩ

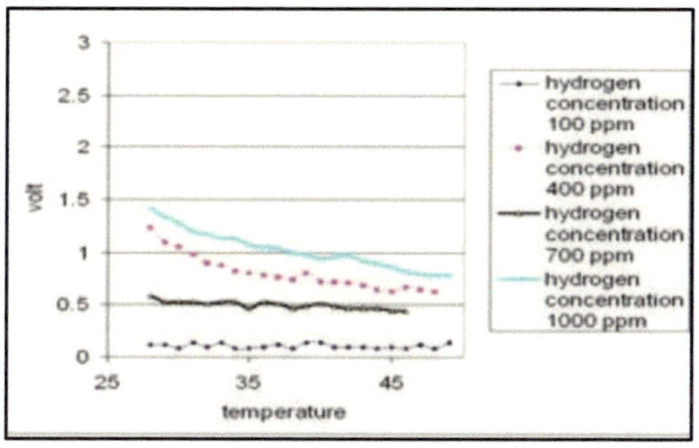


Fig. 6. Hydrogen gas with TGS 3870 at $R_L$ 7 kΩ

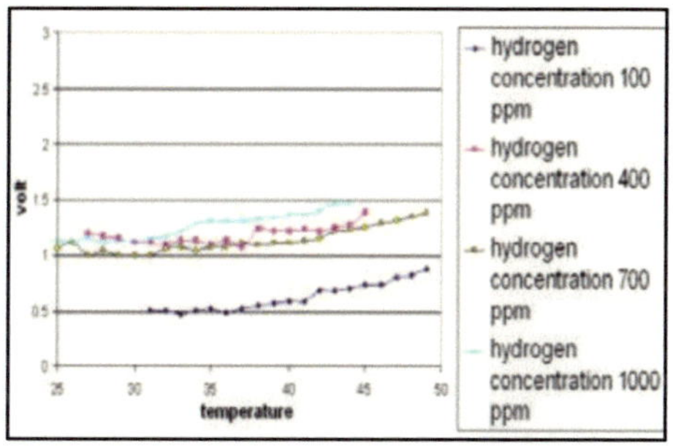


Fig. 7. Hydrogen gas with TGS 822 at $R_L$ 7 kΩ

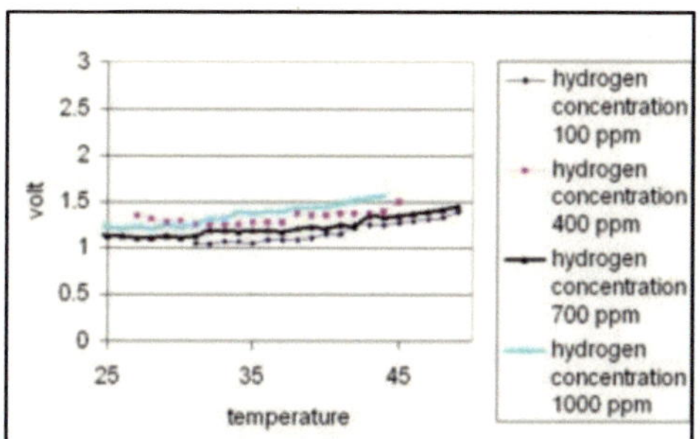


Fig. 8. Hydrogen gas with TGS 2600 at $R_L$ 7kΩ

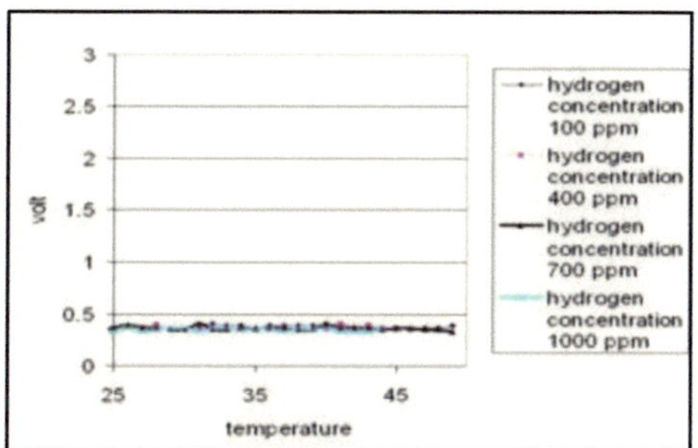


Fig. 9. Hydrogen gas with TGS 4160 at $R_L$ 7 kΩ

Figures 14, 15 and 16 show resistances fluctuations with different sensors, different gases and constant concentration at 700 ppm (Morsi - a, 2008).

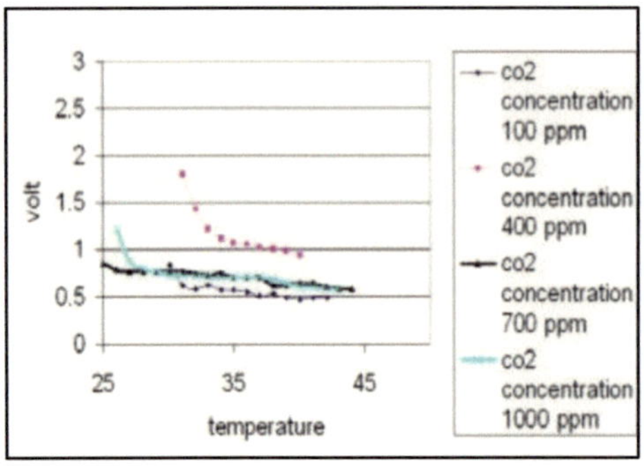


Fig. 10. Carbon dioxide gas with TGS 3870 at $R_L$ 7 kΩ

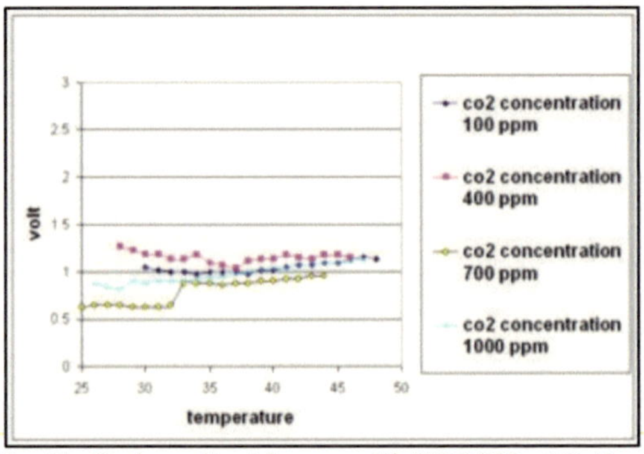


Fig. 11. Carbon dioxide gas with TGS 822 at $R_L$ 7 kΩ

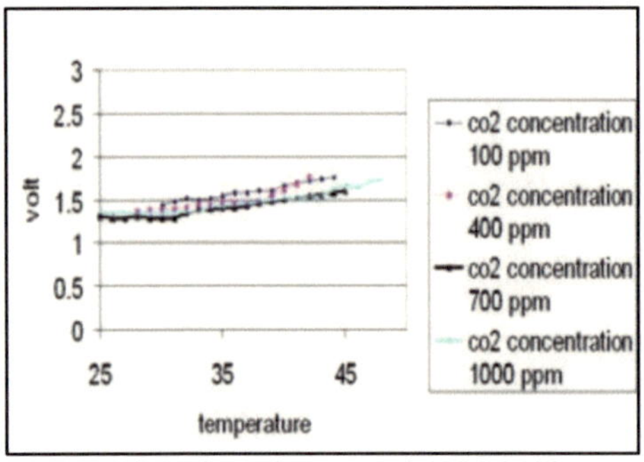


Fig. 12. Carbon dioxide gas with TGS 2600 at $R_L$ 7 kΩ

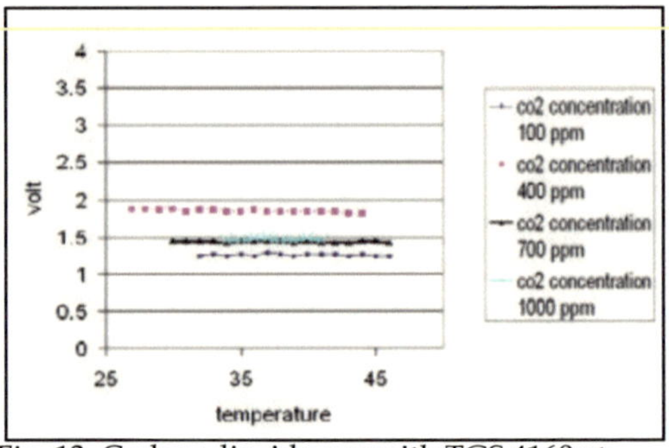


Fig. 13. Carbon dioxide gas with TGS 4160 at $R_L$ 7 kΩ

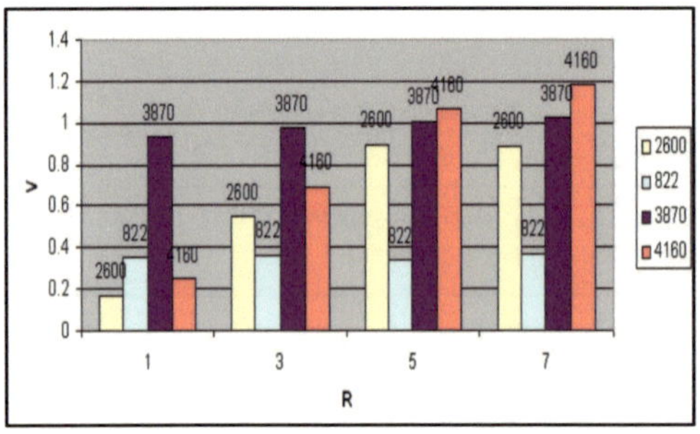


Fig. 14. Methane gas at concentration 700 ppm

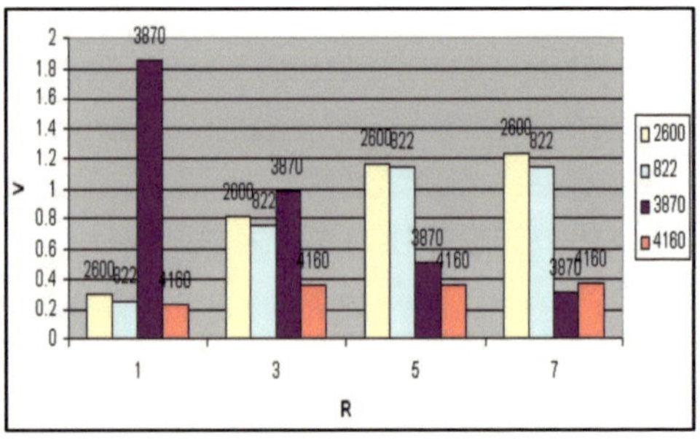


Fig. 15. Hydrogen gas at Concentration 700 ppm

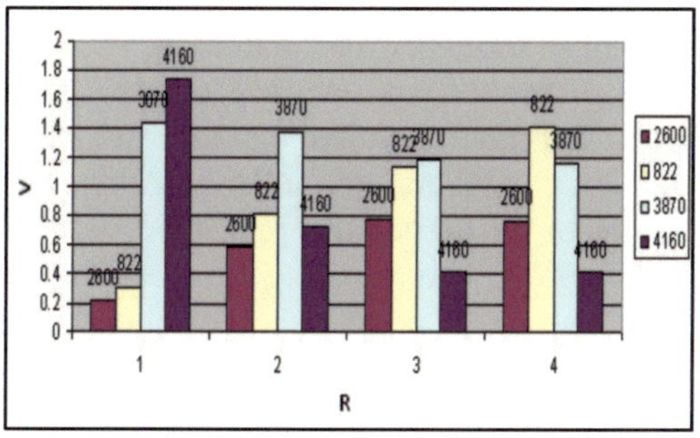


Fig. 16. Carbon dioxide gas at concentration 700 ppm

The Electronic nose system used for gas detection depends on the resistance variation of the gas sensor, which given the possibility increases the selectivity and sensibility. The portable and cheap electronic nose is based on commercially available gas sensors. The stability of the sensors, as well as, their sensitivity depends on the ratio between the change in sensor resistance in the presence or absence of the gas, which was experimentally characterized. Moreover, the method can reduce the number of gas sensors to limit power consumption and maintenance costs. From figs 14 , 15 and 16 it can be noticed that, by increasing load resistance from 1 kΩ to 7 kΩ, the output volt of TGS 822, TGS 2600 is directly proportional (i.e. increase with load resistance), However, TGS 3870 is inversely proportional by increasing load resistance incase of hydrogen and carbon dioxide. TGS 4160 remains constant with average output volt in the range (0.2-0.4) V incase of hydrogen, but incase of carbon dioxide TGS 4160 gives variation in the output voltage from (0.4 - 1.8) V. This variation is inversely proportional to the load resistance variation, which concludes that this sensor is preferable to detect carbon dioxide than other gases.

It can also illustrate the sensitivity of each sensor due to the resistance fluctuation. The output results include non-linear response, drift and slow response time. The main problem is the drift, which causes significant temporal variations of the sensor response when exposed to the same gas under identical conditions (Clifford et al., 2005); (Fleming, 2001). It is noticed that response times depend on many parameters, such as the material type, operating temperature, thickness of the semiconductor, variable resistance, humidity as well as gas concentration. The sensor array reacts slowly and takes an average of 10 min to reach the stationary state. This time is a combination of the time to fill the chamber and the sensor response time. To achieve robust and fast identification of combustion gases with an array of sensors, a recent study suggested three main methods for reducing response time:

1. Increasing operating temperature.
2. Reducing the film thickness.
3. Using variable resistance to reduce the number of sensors and the power consumption of the system.

## 4. Surface Response Modeling Algorithms and Analysis of Variance (ANOVA)

In the system design, surface response models investigated are very useful in understanding the functional relationships between a set of independent factors.
The relationship can be expressed as a mathematical equation which describes the response of the independent factors and a set of parameters. The surface response models depend on observing input and output values of the actual and predicted parameters, which is known by the system model identification (SMI). The resulting empirical models of SMI can be used to: (1) Predict the system behaviour over a specified designed space, (2) Illustrate the mathematical relationships and interactions between input and output of the system (3) Optimize the system performance (4) Select the appropriate factor values that satisfy system performance goals to investigate the performance prediction accuracy of different algorithms, thus the predicted results generated by each empirical model is compared with actual measured results to provide a comparison and identify the advantages of each algorithm.
In the present work, different empirical models are used to detect the response of the surface of each gas. By entering the voltage of each sensor, load resistance and temperature as an input thus predicts the concentration as an output. The following are the used four empirical models:
Linear

$$Y = b_0 + b_1 x_1 + b_2 x_2 + b_3 x_3. \quad (1)$$

Interaction

$$Y= b_0 + b_1 x_1+ b_2 x_2+ b_3 x_3+ b_{12} x_1 x_2+ b_{13} x_1 x_3+ b_{23} x_2 x_3. \quad (2)$$

Pure Quadratic

$$Y= b_0 + b_1 x_1 + b_2 x_2 + b_3 x_3 + b_{11} x_{12} + b_{22} x_{22} + b_{33} x_{33}. \quad (3)$$

Full Quadratic

$$Y = b_0 + b_1 x_1 + b_2 x_2 + b_3 x_3 + b_{12} x_1 x_2 + b_{13} x_1 x_3 + b_{23} x_2 x_3 + b_{11} x_{12} + b_{22} x_{22} + b_{33} x_{23}. \quad (4)$$

Where
Y is the predicting concentration of each gas.
$x_1$, $x_2$, $x_3$ are voltages of each sensor, load resistance, and temperature, respectively.
Bij is the effect of element i on element j or the effect of first input on the second input, i and j have values from 1 to 3.
More than 300 readings for each input are used to detect the error. The concentrations of each gas are stored in matrices, which are related to the output voltage of each sensor through a regression coefficient matrix and the equations can be solved using surface response empirical models to predict the concentrations. Then, the percentage error can be calculated between actual concentration and predicted concentration to determine the best empirical modeling algorithm, which describes the surface response of each gas and has the least error. Table1 shows the percentage error for the different gases with different surface response empirical modeling algorithms (Morsi – a, 2008).

| Empirical Modeling Algorithms \ Gases | The Percentage Error of Carbon Dioxide | The Percentage Error of Hydrogen | The Percentage Error of Methane |
|---|---|---|---|
| Sensor Type | TGS 822 | | |
| Linear | 21.322% | 13.745% | 20.048% |
| Interactions | 19.613% | 0.2439% | 21.175% |
| Pure Quadratic | 17.7612% | 11.2664% | 17.9546% |
| Full Quadratic | 14.2644% | 0.096.029% | 14.426% |
| Sensor Type | TGS 2600 | | |
| Linear | 18% | 9.2% | 2.2% |
| Interactions | 11% | 7.7% | 5.5% |
| Pure Quadratic | 30.5% | 12.95% | 5.8% |
| Full Quadratic | 8% | 5.5% | 5.7% |
| Sensor Type | TGS 3870 | | |
| Linear | 6.41% | 1.66% | 3.47% |
| Interactions | 3.03% | 1.1% | 0.98% |
| Pure Quadratic | 2.08% | 2.3% | 0.28% |
| Full Quadratic | 1.68% | 0.641% | 0.02% |
| Sensor Type | TGS 4160 | | |
| Linear | 6.6534% | 49.925% | 51.572% |
| Interactions | 8.1904% | 53.159% | 51.253% |
| Pure Quadratic | 8.9625% | 45.646% | 44.386% |
| Full Quadratic | 7.0078% | 40.353% | 44.358% |

Table 1. Comparisons of different empirical modeling algorithms with different sensors and different gases.

It can be noticed that, for the three different gases, four different algorithms are used. Thus, full quadratic algorithms can predict the concentration of each gas with less error than other algorithms. From the percentage error, it is clear that in the case of TGS 822, TGS 2600 and TGS 3870 gas sensors provide the least error in the case of methane than hydrogen. It is preferred to use this sensor to detect hydrogen and methane. However, it is unpreferable in the case of carbon dioxide. It is also noticed that in TGS 4160 gas sensor is preferable to be carbon dioxide, where as the highest errors are recorded in the case of hydrogen and methane.

From the above results, it can be concluded that the surface response modeling algorithms provide accurate detection for different concentrations of gases depending on solving regression matrices using different equations while detecting the percentage error between the actual and the predicted measurements. The key challenges for building regression algorithms determine the significant factors that are included in the final mathematical equation and quantify the effects of those factors. Tables 2, 3 and 4 show the ANOVA results for each sensor with different gases. The second column is the degree of freedom (DF). The mean square (MS) is the variance of the data for each factor interaction. The sum of squares (SS) is computed as MS x DF. F-statistic is defined as the ratio of MS to Error. P-value is the smallest probability of rejecting the null hypothesis. Using the analysis of variance (ANOVA), it is possible to identify those effects that are statistically significant. It can be noticed that, the variance is not constant and if the output voltage has a high value, the variance also has a high value for different gases. The resulting algorithm includes only those independent factors that are statistically significant (P-value < 0.05). Quantifying the main and two-way interaction effects of the independent factors are equivalent to using the well- known method of least squares fitting method in order to compute the regression coefficients (Morsi-a, 2008) .

| Source | Sum Sq. | d.f. | Mean Sq. | F | Prob>F |
|---|---|---|---|---|---|
| X1 | 4.98058 | 3 | 1.66019 | 116.18 | 0 |
| X2 | 0.13867 | 3 | 0.04622 | 3.23 | 0.0257 |
| X3 | 0.05372 | 11 | 0.00488 | 0.34 | 0.9738 |
| X1*X2 | 1.89822 | 9 | 0.21091 | 14.76 | 0 |
| X1*X3 | 0.33692 | 33 | 0.01021 | 0.71 | 0.8624 |
| X2*X3 | 0.19688 | 33 | 0.00597 | 0.42 | 0.9972 |
| Error | 1.34323 | 94 | 0.01429 | | |
| Total | 9.95126 | 186 | | | |

Table 2-a. Anova of methane gas with TGS 3870 gas sensor

| Source | Sum Sq. | d.f. | Mean Sq. | F | Prob>F |
|---|---|---|---|---|---|
| X1 | 2.32996 | 3 | 0.77665 | 511.05 | 0 |
| X2 | 0.18818 | 3 | 0.06273 | 41.27 | 0 |
| X3 | 0.01857 | 11 | 0.00169 | 1.11 | 0.3617 |
| X1*X2 | 0.42355 | 9 | 0.04706 | 30.97 | 0 |
| X1*X3 | 0.03739 | 33 | 0.00113 | 0.75 | 0.8291 |
| X2*X3 | 0.06018 | 33 | 0.00182 | 1.2 | 0.2453 |
| Error | 0.14285 | 94 | 0.00152 | | |
| Total | 3.40834 | 186 | | | |

Table 2-c. Anova of methane gas with TGS 2600 gas sensor

| Source | Sum Sq. | d.f. | Mean Sq. | F | Prob>F |
|---|---|---|---|---|---|
| X1 | 10.0555 | 3 | 3.35183 | 341.8 | 0 |
| X2 | 0.6069 | 3 | 0.20229 | 20.63 | 0 |
| X3 | 0.166 | 11 | 0.01509 | 1.54 | 0.1306 |
| X1*X2 | 1.5482 | 9 | 0.17203 | 17.54 | 0 |
| X1*X3 | 0.2412 | 33 | 0.00731 | 0.75 | 0.8293 |
| X2*X3 | 0.1651 | 33 | 0.005 | 0.51 | 0.9847 |
| Error | 0.9218 | 94 | 0.00981 | | |
| Total | 15.7931 | 186 | | | |

Table 2-b. Anova of methane gas with TGS 822 gas sensor

| Source | Sum Sq. | d.f. | Mean Sq. | F | Prob>F |
|---|---|---|---|---|---|
| X1 | 0.00687 | 3 | 0.00229 | 6.03 | 0.0008 |
| X2 | 0.01906 | 3 | 0.00635 | 16.72 | 0 |
| X3 | 0.00246 | 11 | 0.00022 | 0.59 | 0.8346 |
| X1*X2 | 0.04452 | 9 | 0.00495 | 13.02 | 0 |
| X1*X3 | 0.01365 | 33 | 0.00041 | 1.09 | 0.3658 |
| X2*X3 | 0.01377 | 33 | 0.00042 | 1.1 | 0.3545 |
| Error | 0.03572 | 94 | 0.00038 | | |
| Total | 0.13722 | 186 | | | |

Table 2-d. Anova of methane gas with TGS 4160 gas sensor

| Source | Sum Sq. | d.f. | Mean Sq. | F | Prob>F |
|---|---|---|---|---|---|
| X1 | 6.9938 | 3 | 2.33128 | 157.37 | 0 |
| X2 | 0.3428 | 3 | 0.11428 | 7.71 | 0.0001 |
| X3 | 0.1795 | 11 | 0.01631 | 1.1 | 0.369 |
| X1*X2 | 1.2806 | 9 | 0.14229 | 9.6 | 0 |
| X1*X3 | 0.3798 | 33 | 0.01151 | 0.78 | 0.7921 |
| X2*X3 | 0.6352 | 33 | 0.01925 | 1.3 | 0.1647 |
| Error | 1.3925 | 94 | 0.01481 | | |
| Total | 12.7402 | 186 | | | |

Table 3-a. Anova of hydrogen gas with TGS 3870 gas sensor

| Source | Sum Sq. | d.f. | Mean Sq. | F | Prob>F |
|---|---|---|---|---|---|
| X1 | 26.7364 | 3 | 8.91215 | 57.34 | 0 |
| X2 | 2.5009 | 3 | 0.83363 | 5.36 | 0.0019 |
| X3 | 0.6347 | 11 | 0.0577 | 0.37 | 0.9642 |
| X1*X2 | 13 | 9 | 1.44444 | 9.29 | 0 |
| X1*X3 | 2.8352 | 33 | 0.08591 | 0.55 | 0.9722 |
| X2*X3 | 7.7506 | 33 | 0.23487 | 1.51 | 0.0634 |
| Error | 14.6111 | 94 | 0.15544 | | |
| Total | 66.6705 | 186 | | | |

Table 4-a. Anova of carbon dioxide gas with TGS 3870 gas sensor

| Source | Sum Sq. | d.f. | Mean Sq. | F | Prob>F |
|---|---|---|---|---|---|
| X1 | 14.339 | 3 | 4.77966 | 947.25 | 0 |
| X2 | 0.8761 | 3 | 0.29205 | 57.88 | 0 |
| X3 | 0.019 | 11 | 0.00173 | 0.34 | 0.9738 |
| X1*X2 | 2.0629 | 9 | 0.22921 | 45.43 | 0 |
| X1*X3 | 0.2706 | 33 | 0.0082 | 1.63 | 0.0362 |
| X2*X3 | 0.481 | 33 | 0.01457 | 2.89 | 0 |
| Error | 0.4743 | 94 | 0.00505 | | |
| Total | 20.4315 | 186 | | | |

Table 3-b. Anova of hydrogen gas with TGS 822 gas sensor

| Source | Sum Sq. | d.f. | Mean Sq. | F | Prob>F |
|---|---|---|---|---|---|
| X1 | 22.3335 | 3 | 7.4445 | 61.91 | 0 |
| X2 | 1.154 | 3 | 0.38466 | 3.2 | 0.0269 |
| X3 | 0.6538 | 11 | 0.05944 | 0.49 | 0.9025 |
| X1*X2 | 12.6893 | 9 | 1.40992 | 11.73 | 0 |
| X1*X3 | 1.1833 | 33 | 0.03586 | 0.3 | 0.9999 |
| X2*X3 | 2.157 | 33 | 0.06536 | 0.54 | 0.9754 |
| Error | 11.3033 | 94 | 0.12025 | | |
| Total | 55.1715 | 186 | | | |

Table 4-b. Anova of carbon dioxide gas with TGS 822 gas sensor

| Source | Sum Sq. | d.f. | Mean Sq. | F | Prob>F |
|---|---|---|---|---|---|
| X1 | 13.7397 | 3 | 4.5799 | 672.08 | 0 |
| X2 | 0.3778 | 3 | 0.12592 | 18.48 | 0 |
| X3 | 0.074 | 11 | 0.00673 | 0.99 | 0.4632 |
| X1*X2 | 2.0214 | 9 | 0.2246 | 32.96 | 0 |
| X1*X3 | 0.247 | 33 | 0.00748 | 1.1 | 0.3541 |
| X2*X3 | 0.1528 | 33 | 0.00463 | 0.68 | 0.8954 |
| Error | 0.6406 | 94 | 0.00681 | | |
| Total | 19.635 | 186 | | | |

Table 3-c. Anova of hydrogen gas with TGS 2600 gas sensor

| Source | Sum Sq. | d.f. | Mean Sq. | F | Prob>F |
|---|---|---|---|---|---|
| X1 | 18.6028 | 3 | 6.20092 | 232 | 0 |
| X2 | 1.08 | 3 | 0.35999 | 13.47 | 0 |
| X3 | 0.2586 | 11 | 0.02351 | 0.88 | 0.5628 |
| X1*X2 | 7.5837 | 9 | 0.84263 | 31.53 | 0 |
| X1*X3 | 0.6088 | 33 | 0.01845 | 0.69 | 0.8857 |
| X2*X3 | 0.923 | 33 | 0.02797 | 1.05 | 0.4189 |
| Error | 2.5124 | 94 | 0.02673 | | |
| Total | 32.1458 | 186 | | | |

Table 4-c. Anova of carbon dioxide gas with TGS 2600 gas sensor

| Source | Sum Sq. | d.f. | Mean Sq. | F | Prob>F |
|---|---|---|---|---|---|
| X1 | 0.00826 | 3 | 0.00275 | 8.08 | 0.0001 |
| X2 | 0.00037 | 3 | 0.00012 | 0.36 | 0.7818 |
| X3 | 0.00914 | 11 | 0.00083 | 2.44 | 0.0101 |
| X1*X2 | 0.01784 | 9 | 0.00198 | 5.82 | 0 |
| X1*X3 | 0.01671 | 33 | 0.00051 | 1.49 | 0.0714 |
| X2*X3 | 0.01413 | 33 | 0.00043 | 1.26 | 0.1966 |
| Error | 0.03203 | 94 | 0.00034 | | |
| Total | 0.09954 | 186 | | | |

Table .3-d. Anova of hydrogen gas with TGS 4160 gas sensor

| Source | Sum Sq. | d.f. | Mean Sq. | F | Prob>F |
|---|---|---|---|---|---|
| X1 | 0.03518 | 3 | 0.01173 | 18.08 | 0 |
| X2 | 0.03206 | 3 | 0.01069 | 16.47 | 0 |
| X3 | 0.00647 | 11 | 0.00059 | 0.91 | 0.5377 |
| X1*X2 | 0.10369 | 9 | 0.01152 | 17.76 | 0 |
| X1*X3 | 0.03503 | 33 | 0.00106 | 1.64 | 0.0342 |
| X2*X3 | 0.02637 | 33 | 0.0008 | 1.23 | 0.2165 |
| Error | 0.06097 | 94 | 0.00065 | | |
| Total | 0.32414 | 186 | | | |

Table 4-d. Anova of carbon dioxide gas with TGS 4160 gas sensor

## 5. Separation of Butane and Propane as a Gas Mixture Using an Artificial Intelligent Neural Network

The use of natural gas has been increasingly adapted as butane and propane exist in both industry and as a fuel in domestic applications. One of the most important problems in the gas detection field is that there is a strong demand to detect butane and propane as pure gases which are used as fuel; however, both are extracted from the natural gas mixed with each other. The calibration of both gases in the pure case and also as a mixture at different temperatures using electronic nose system is studied. Also, a study is done for the efficiency of feed forward back propagation neural network for the detection of gases using the multilayer pereception (MLP) methods to differentiate between them depending on the data driven from the electronic nose gas system (Morsi - a, 2008).

Butane ($C_4H_{10}$): a normally gaseous straight-chain or branch-chain hydrocarbon is derived from natural gas or from refinery gas streams. It includes isobutane and normal butane and is used for cooking, heating, as a household fuel, propellant or refrigerant, where, it is commonly used in UK. It is slightly toxic by inhalation, as it causes central nervous system depression at high concentrations, and is used in the manufacture of rubber and fuels (Morsi –a, 2008).

Propane ($C_3H_8$): a normally gaseous straight- chain hydrocarbon is a colorless paraffinic gas that boils at a temperature of - 42 °C. It is extracted from natural gas or refinery gas streams. Under normal atmospheric pressure and temperature, it exists in a gaseous state. However, propane is usually liquified through pressurization for transportation and storage. It is primarily used for heating or cooking, as a fuel gas in areas not serviced by natural gas, and as a petrochemical fuel stock. Propane is used in forklifts because it offers the best performance in power, speed and saves money on fuel costs. It is also used in agriculture as an alternative to conventional pesticides and herbicides and in outdoor grills (Morsi –a, 2008).

Neural Networks with feed forward back propagation training algorithm is used to detect each gas with different sensors. It is combined with gas sensors to address these issues. After a processing stage, the resulting feature vector is used to solve separation problem in case of a mixture, by identifying an unknown sample as one from a set of previously known gases. Multi Layer Perceptron MLP improves linear discrimination techniques in case of a mixture, depending on the data driven from each sensor (Morsi –a, 2008); (Guardado et al., 2001).

Gases used are butane and propane and their mixtures. They are injected into a gas chamber. The sensor detects sequentially the variation in the propane and butane gas concentration and its resistance is modified accordingly. Figures 17 till 32 depict the output voltage of sensors TGS 822, TGS 3870, TGS 2600 and TGS 4160 as functions of temperature, with load resistances $R_L$ = 1 kΩ and $R_L$ = 7 kΩ. The relations are given for butane and propane at concentrations of 100 ppm, 400 ppm, 700 ppm and 1000 ppm respectively. It can be noticed that the detection of both gases can be carried out by TGS 822, TGS 3870, TGS 2600, but not by TGS 4160. It is clear noticed from figs 17-20, that for the TGS 822 gas sensor, the conductivity and sensitivity increase for both butane and propane by increasing concentration and load resistance. The sensitivity is directly proportional to the load resistance. For TGS 3870 gas sensor, Figs 21-24, it can be noticed that the sensitivity and conductivity are inversely proportional with load resistance.

By increasing load resistance, the sensitivity and conductivity will decrease. The difference between the relationship of sensitivity, conductivity and load resistance between both sensors, allows the discrimination between propane and butane depending on the variation of the resistance. For the TGS 2600 gas sensor, figs 25 till 28, the voltage increases with the increase of concentrations, temperature and load resistance for both gases.
With TGS 4160 gas sensor, figs 29-32, for both butane and propane, there is no change in the output volt in load resistance, therefore, we can not depend on this sensor discrimination. The calibration of pure gases among their semiconductor sensor, predicts the correct sensor that should be used in classification. Figures 33 and 34 depict the mixture of both propane and butane injected inside the chamber. Propane has a concentration of 600 ppm while butane has a concentration of 400 ppm. It can be noticed that the output of both gases is unstable, which leads to difficulties in discrimination. Neural Networks (NN) have been used extensively in applications where pattern recognition is needed. They are adaptive, capable of handling highly non-linear relationships and generalizing solutions for a new set of data. In fact, NN do not need a predefined correspondence function, which means that there is no need for a physical model. A neuron model is the most basic information processing unit in a neural network. Depending on the problem complexity, they are organized in three or more layers: the input layer, the output layer and one or several hidden layers. Each neuron model receives input signals, which are multiplied by synaptic weights. An activation function transforms these signals into an output signal to the next neuron model. The Back Propagation learning algorithm is used due to its ability of pattern recognition. A sigmoid activation function was also used because of two reasons: it is highly non-linear and has been reported to have a good performance when working with the back propagation learning algorithms [45][46] . In order to avoid slow training, it is decided to use only three layers. During the training process, a vector from a training set ($x_i$) representing a gas pattern is presented to the net. The winning neuron (the closet to the pattern with an Euclidean), and its neighbours, the neighborhood area, change their position, becoming closer to the input pattern according to the following learning rule:

$$W_{ji}^{new} = W_{ji}^{old} + \zeta\ (t).\ nb\ (t,d).\ (x_i - x_{ji}^{old}) \quad (5)$$

where $W_{ji}$ are the weights of the neurons inside, the neighborhood area, j is the index of the neuron, i is the index of pattern , t is the time step, $\zeta$ (t) is the learning rate, nb (t,d) is the neighborhood function, and d is the distance between the neuron and the winner measured over the net. The learning rate and the neighborhood are monotonically decreasing functions along the training (Eberhart et al. 1996); (Wesley, 1997). Both patterns constitute an NN training set. In case NN training is slow or shows little convergence, then both patterns are either poorly correlated or incorrect. This study is performed on pure butane and propane gases, and a mixture of them. The data set is divided in two parts. The first is used to train the net, while the second is used to test it. Training patterns are chosen from different concentrations, different times and different temperatures. A large number of patterns have been selected from the extremes of the concentrated range and from initial parts of the dynamic response to give a larger weight to more early difficult cases. The Neural Network is constructed as a feed forwarded back propagation network that is composed of three layers: input, hidden and output layers. The input layer has three neurons corresponding to the output voltages of each sensor ($x_1$), temperature ($x_2$) and variable resistance ($x_3$).

The hidden layer has five neurons. The hidden layer neurons use a transfer function of tansig which is a hyperbolic tangent sigmoid function used to calculate the layer's output from its net input. One hidden layer with 5 neurons is used which gives the least mean square error (MSE) between the actual and the predicted data. The output layer has one neuron corresponding to the concentration of gas. The predicted performance metric, y, given by the neural network model is as follows.

$$y = \text{Purelin}\left( \sum_{i=1}^{5} w_{2i1}, \text{Tansig}\left( \sum_{j=1}^{3} w_{1ji} \, x_j + \theta_{1j} \right) + \theta_{21} \right) \quad (6)$$

Where: $x_j$ is the input of node j in the input layer.
$W_{1ji}$ is the weight between node j in the input layer to node i in the hidden layer. $\theta_{1i}$ is the bias of node i in the hidden layer. $W_{2i1}$ is the weight between node i in the hidden layer to the node in the output layer. $\theta_{21}$ is the bias of the node in the output layer. The numbers 5 and 4 are the numbers of nodes in the hidden layer and in the input layer, respectively, using a simple linear transformation. All performance data are scaled to provide values between -1 and 1. Scaling is performed for two reasons: to provide commensurate data ranges, so that the regressions are not dominated by any variable that happened to be expressed in large number, and to avoid the asymptotes of the sigmoid function. During the training, the weights of the neural network are iteratively adjusted to minimize the network performance function MSE. The validation set is used to stop training early if the network performance on the validation set fails to improve. Test set is used to provide an independent assessment of the model predictive ability. The percentage error is important; 100% error means a zero prediction accuracy and error close to 0% means an increasing prediction accuracy. For the proposed Neural Network model, the percentage error is found to be 0.662%, 0.031%, 0.162%, 1.5% for sensors TGS 822, TGS 3870, TGS 2600 and TGS 4160, respectively. MLP provides an optimized structure which provides linear discrimination between both gases. Figs 35, 36, 37, and 38 depict the MLP results in separating butane and propane gas by using TGS 822, TGS 3870 , TGS 2600 and TGS 4160 sensors respectively. The sign circle indicates butane gas where as the sign plus indicates propane gas. Table 5 depicts the results of classification for different gases among the different semiconductor sensors. From the presented results, TGS 3870, TGS 2600 and TGS 822 gas sensor can discriminate both gases rather than TGS 4160 which does not give different response with different conditions. This conclusion is obtained from the multiplayer perception of Neural Network. The Neural Network model does not yield a mathematical equation that can be manipulated. However, its strength lies in its ability to accurately predict system performance over the entire design space and its ability to compensate for the inherent information inadequacy by requiring large and well spread training sets. Neural Network with feed forward back propagation is used to detect the concentration of each gas. MLP is able to separate between the mixtures with linear discrimination. TGS 3870 gives the optimum classification with a percentage error of 0.031%, then, TGS 2600 gas sensor can be classified between them with a percentage error 0.162%, then, TGS 822 gas sensor gives percentage error of classification 0.662%. However, TGS 4160 gas sensor failed to discriminate both gases and gives a percentage error of 40%.

Neural Network with MLP method is very robust against sensor nonlinearities, time effects, and error rate depending on the selection of data, which is acquired by different semiconductor gas sensors (Morsi -a, 2008) .

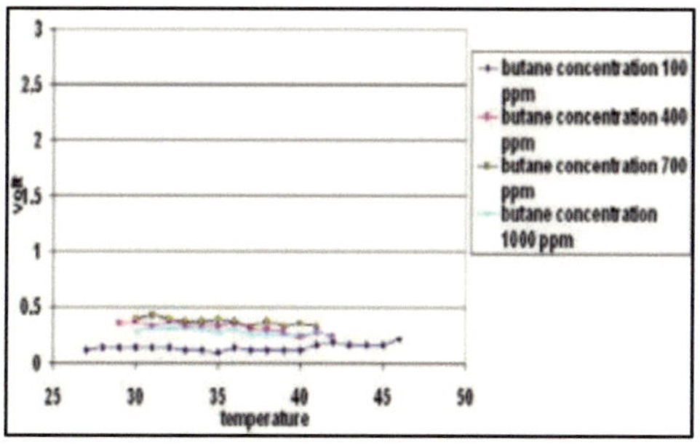


Fig. 17. Butane with TGS 822 at $R_L$ 1 kΩ

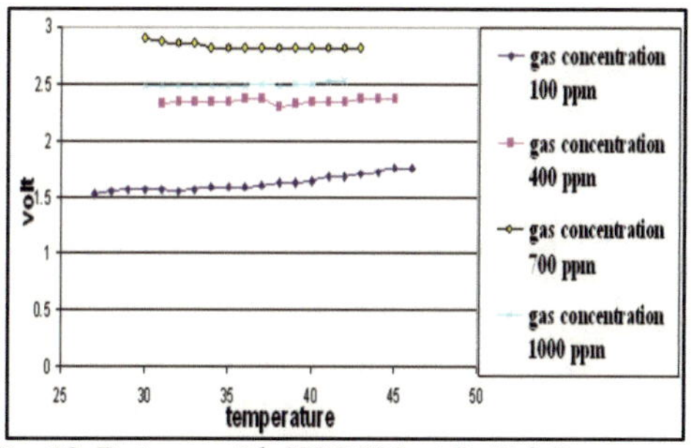


Fig. 18. Butane with TGS 822 at $R_L$ 7 kΩ

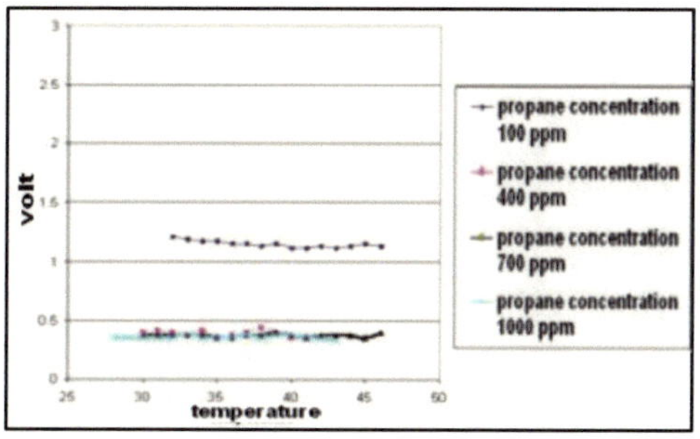


Fig. 19. Propane with TGS 822 at $R_L$ 1 kΩ

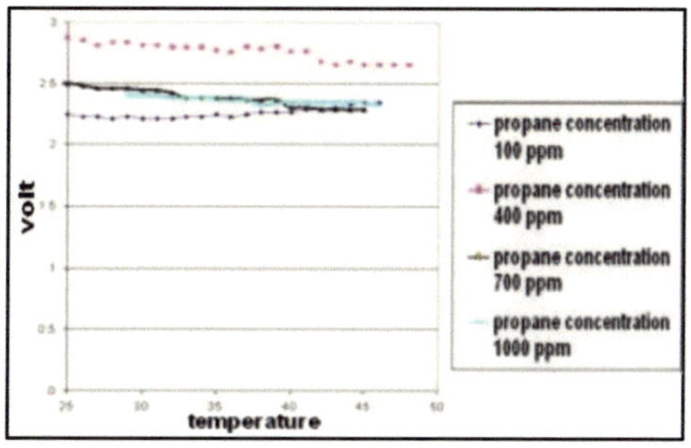


Fig. 20. Propane with TGS 822 at $R_L$ 7 kΩ

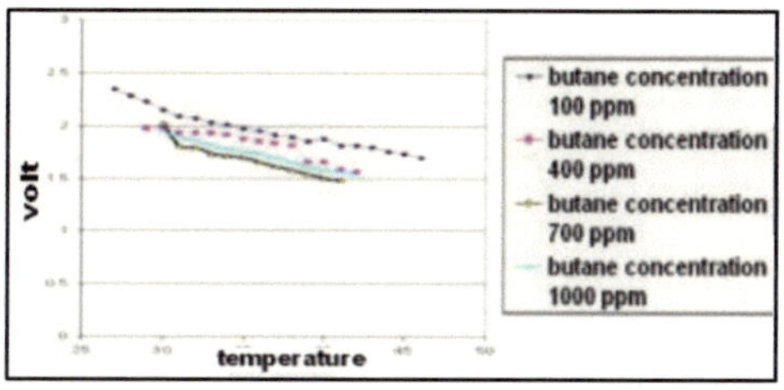


Fig. 21. Butane with TGS 3870 at $R_L$ 1

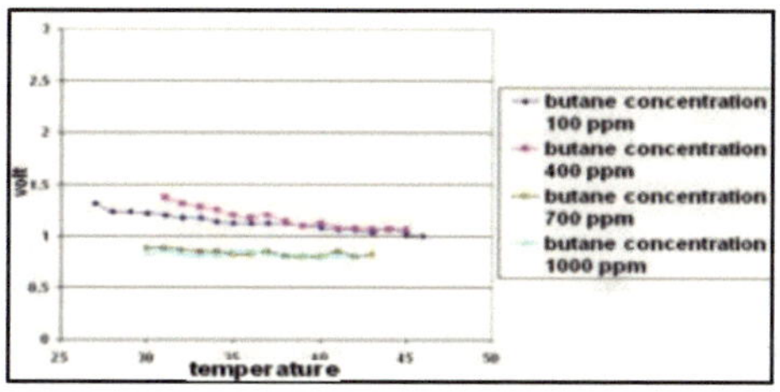


Fig. 22. Butane with TGS 3870 at $R_L$ 7 kΩ

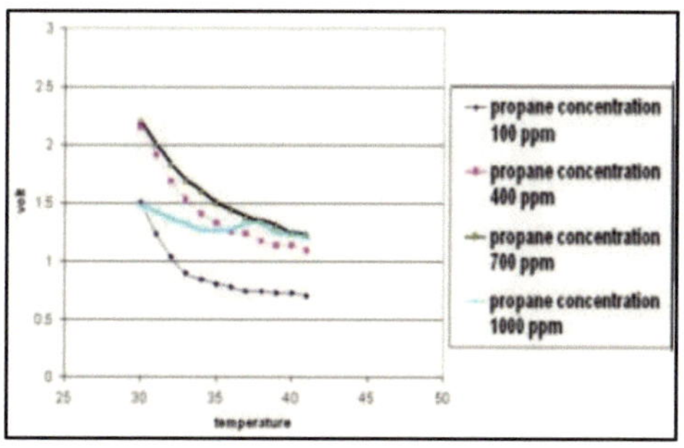


Fig. 23. Propane with TGS 3870 at $R_L$ 1kΩ

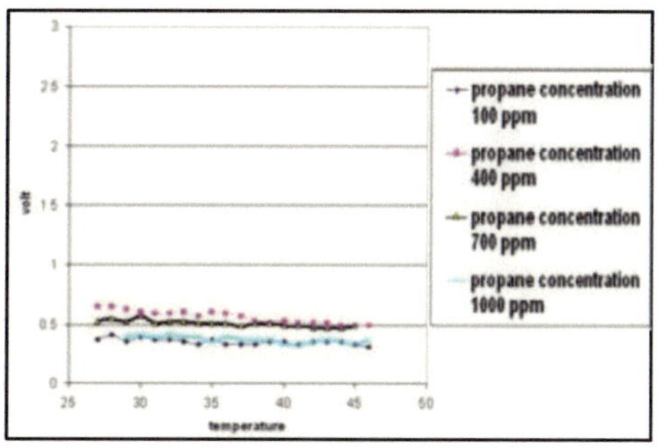


Fig. 24. Propane with TGS 3870 at $R_L$ 7 kΩ

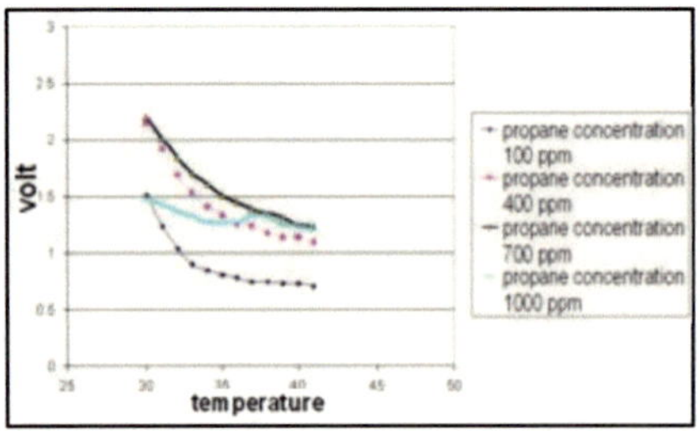


Fig. 23. Propane with TGS 3870 at $R_L$

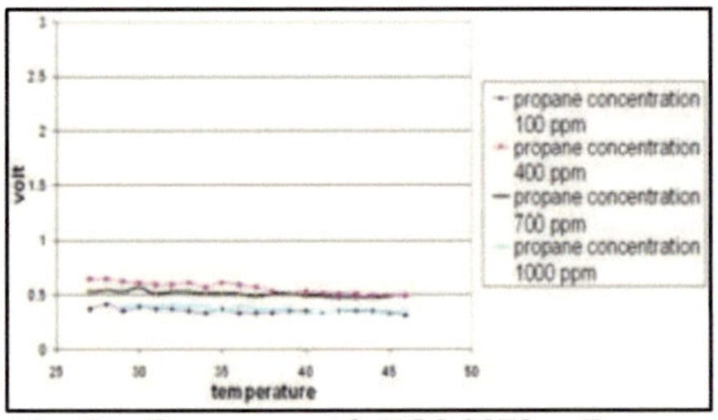


Fig. 24. Propane with TGS 3870 at $R_L$

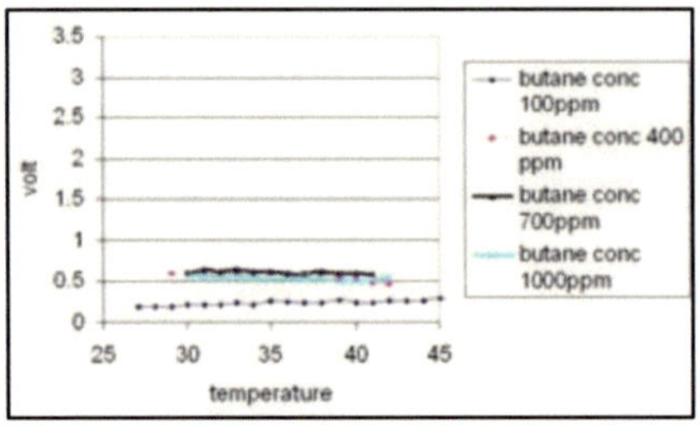


Fig. 25. Butane with TGS 2600 at $R_L$

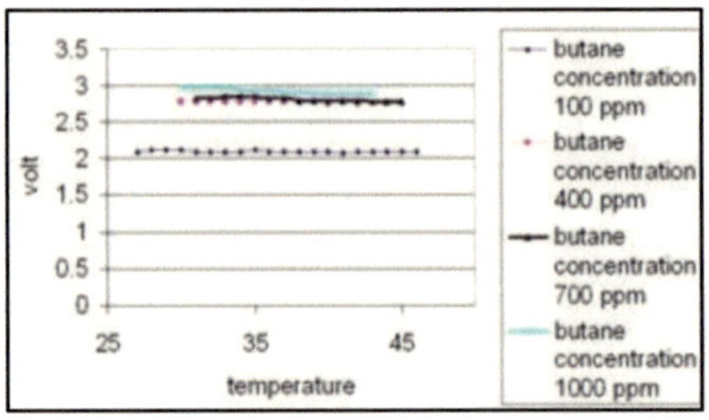


Fig .26. Butane with TGS 2600 at $R_L$ 7

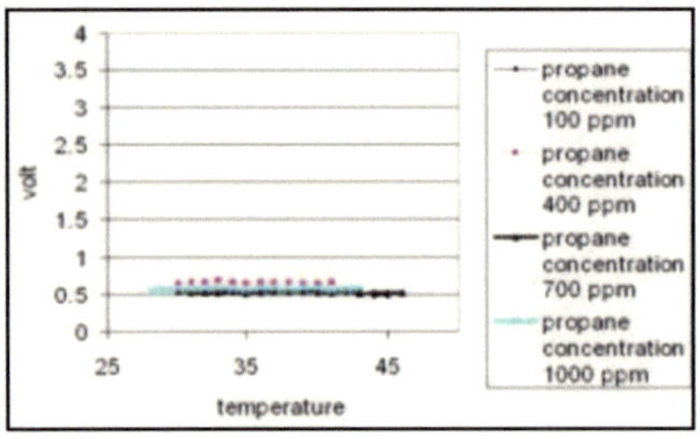


Fig. 27. Propane with TGS 2600 at $R_L$

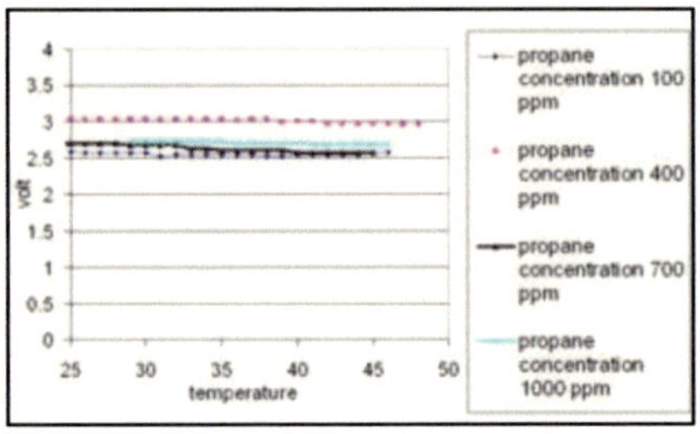


Fig. 28. Propane with TGS 2600 at $R_L$

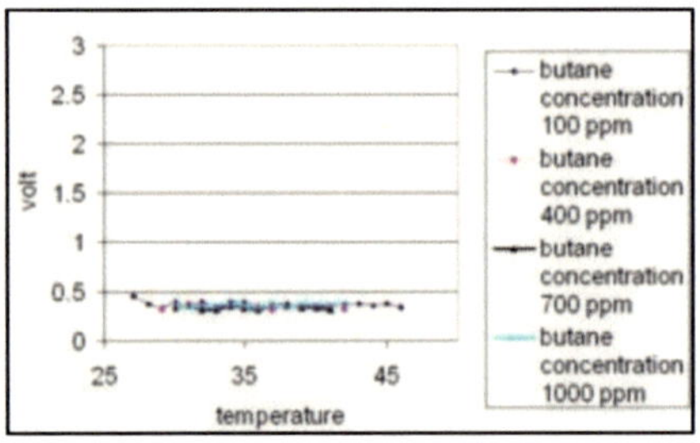


Fig. 29. Butane with TGS 4160 at $R_L$

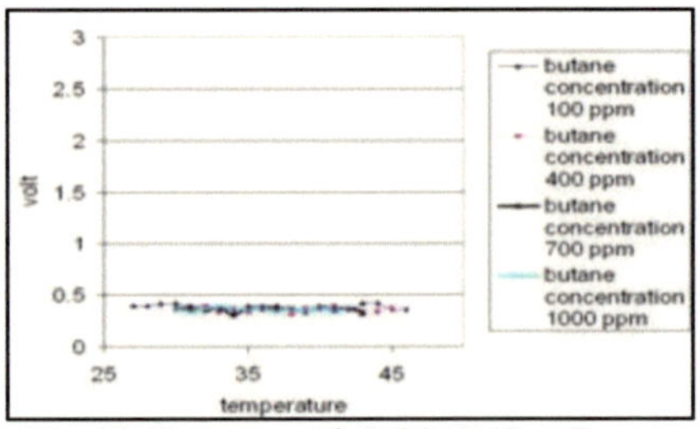


Fig. 30. Butane with TGS 4160 at $R_L$

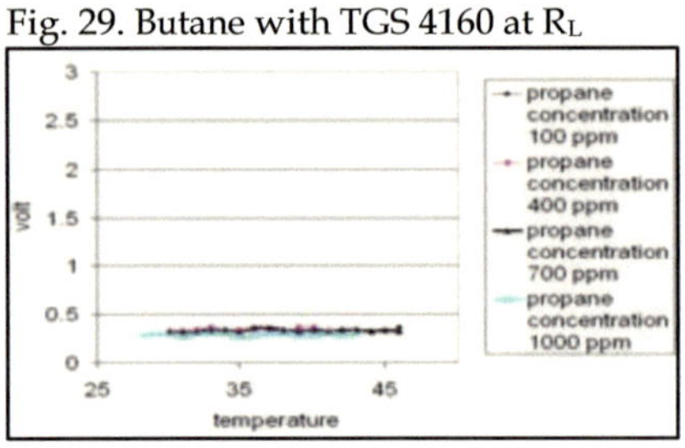


Fig. 31. Propane with TGS 4160 at $R_L$ 1 kΩ

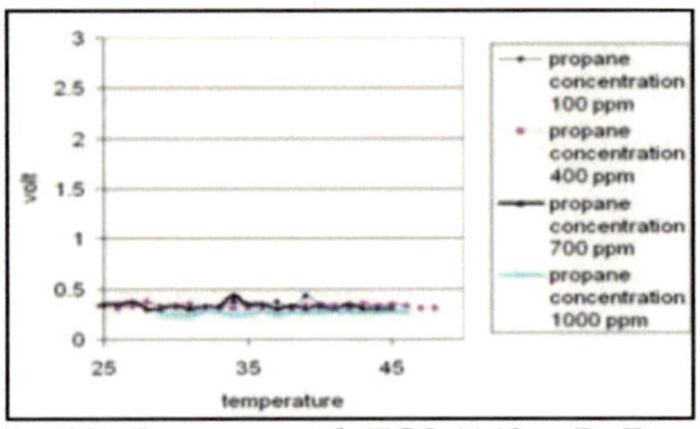


Fig. 32. Propane with TGS 4160 at $R_L$ 7 kΩ

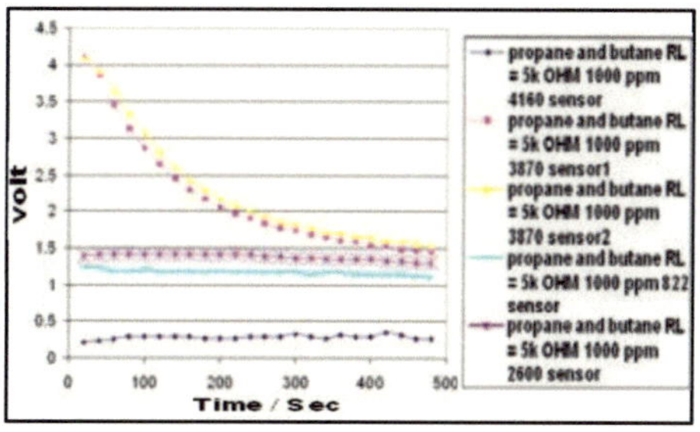


Fig. 33. Mixture of propane and butane at $R_L$ 1 kΩ

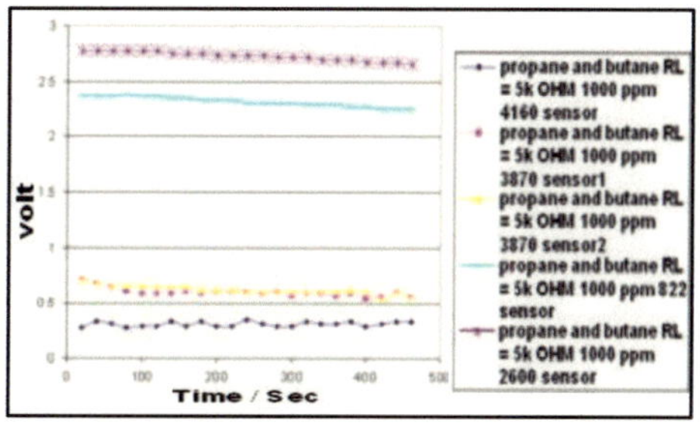


Fig. 34. Mixture of propane and butane at $R_L$ 7 kΩ

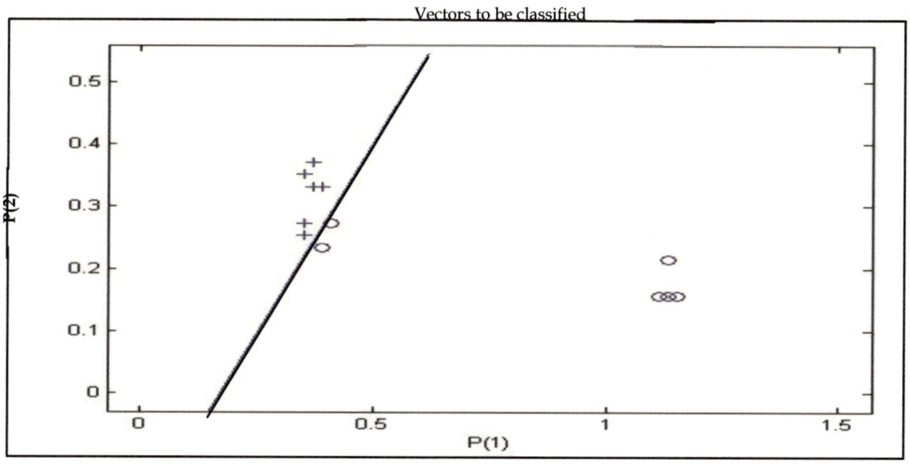


Fig. 35. Separation between propane and butane using NN(MLP) with TGS 822

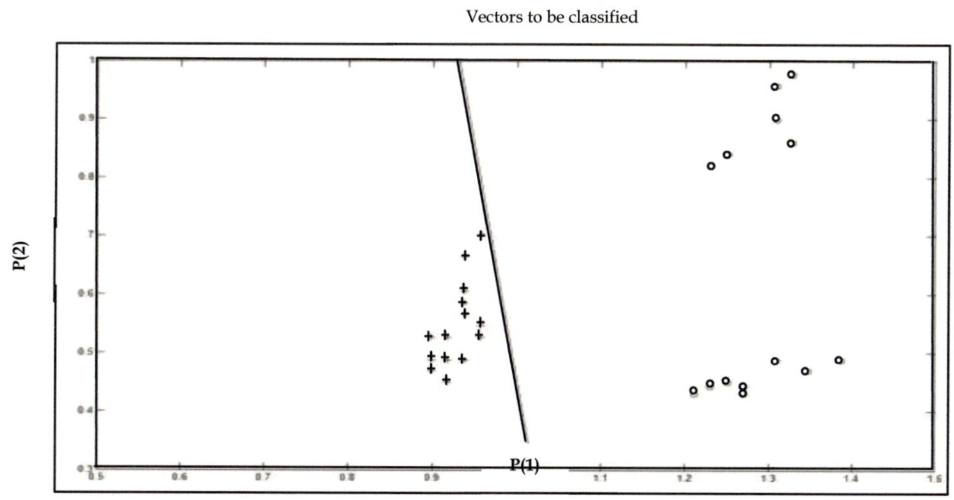


Fig. 36. Separation between propane and butane using NN (MLP) with TGS 3870

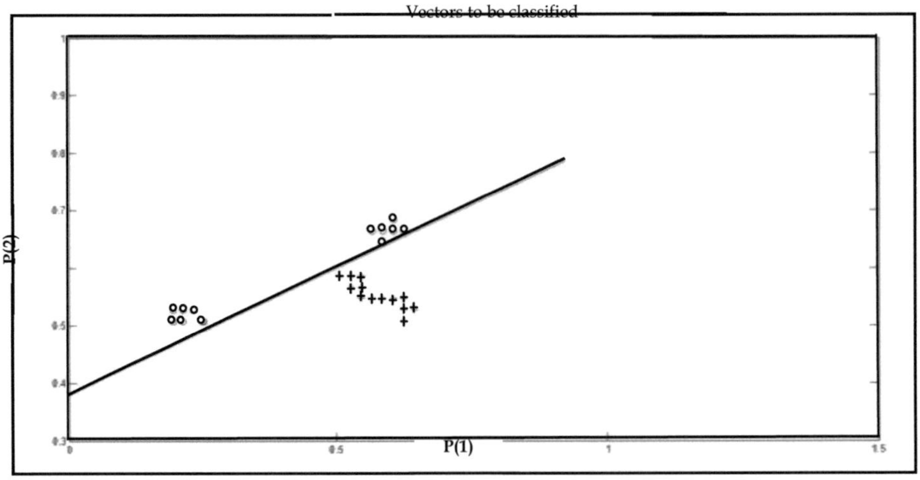


Fig. 37. Separation between propane and butane using NN (MLP) with TGS 2600

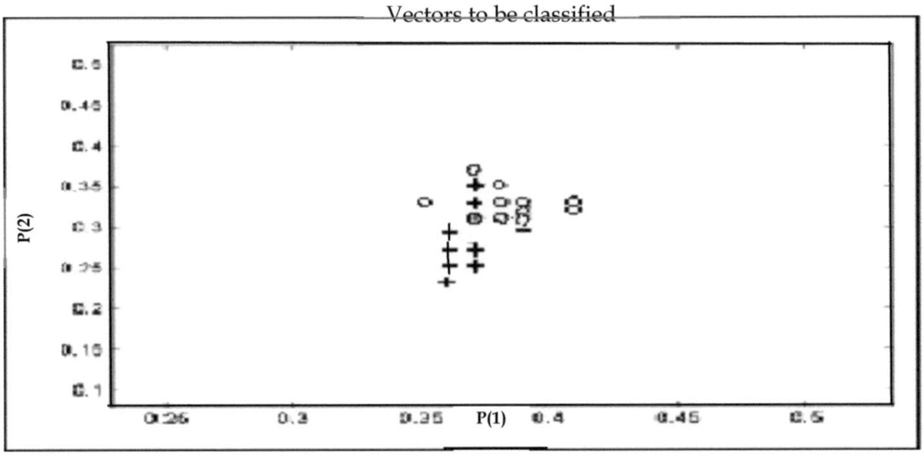


Fig. 38. Separation between propane and butane using NN (MLP) With TGS 4160

| Sensors | No. of inputs | No. of output | Test | Epoch | % Error | Classificatio n | % Unflassificatio n |
|---|---|---|---|---|---|---|---|
| TGS 822 | 3 (100 sample) | 1 (100 sample) | 30 sample | 1000 | 0.662% | 60% | 40% |
| TGS 3870 | 3 (100 sample) | 1 (100 sample) | 30 sample | 1000 | 0.031% | 97% | 3% |
| TGS 2600 | 3 (100 sample) | 1 (100 sample) | 30 sample | 1000 | 0.162% | 96% | 14% |
| TGS 4160 | 3 (100 sample) | 1 (100 sample) | 30 sample | 1000 | 1.5% | 40% | 60% |

Table. 5. The results of classification by using Neural Networks (MLP) for four different sensors.

## 6. On- Line Identification of Gases Using Artificial Intelligent Technique of Fuzzy Logic:

Fuzzy set theory and fuzzy logic theory are the preferred choices for the models. Fuzzy sets introduced were particularly designed to mathematically represent fuzziness and vagueness, and to provide the fundamental concept for handling the imprecision intrinsic to the problems of subjective evaluation and measurement. Fuzzy set is based on possibility instead of probability where as fuzzy logic is based on fuzzy set. Fuzzy logic is unlike classical logical systems in that it aims to modeling the imprecise modes of reasoning that plays an essential role in the remarkable human ability to make rational decisions in gases of uncertainty and imprecision. This ability depends, in turn, on the ability to infer an approximate answer to a question based on a store of knowledge that is inexact, incomplete, or not totally reliable. The whole approach is based on measurements taken from an experimental set up with certain typical commercial sensors. The outputs of sensors are monitored by a microcontroller, and then a proper intelligent processing. Fuzzy logic has been chosen because it gives better results and enhances discrimination techniques among sensed gases. Fuzzy logic systems encode human reasoning to make decisions and control dynamical systems. Fuzzy logic comprises fuzzy sets which are methods of representing nonstatistical uncertainty and approximate reasoning, including the operations used to make inferences. It is a tool for mapping the input features to the output, based on data in the form of "IF - Then" rules. An implementation of a fuzzy expert system depends on Mamdani type fuzzy controller as shown in fig. 39 (Tanaka, 1996); (Timothy, 1995); (Wesley, 1997). The objective of the controller is to discriminate different gases and to detect the concentration of each gas according to the input variables as shown in fig. 40. There are five steps to construct a Mamdani type fuzzy controller:

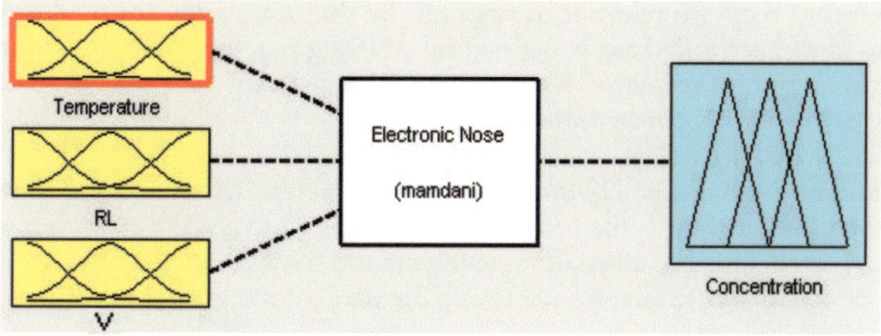

Fig. 39. Mamdani type fuzzy controller

Step 1: Identify and name the input linguistic variables, the output linguistic variables and their numerical ranges. There are three input variables which are temperature, output voltage of the microcontroller, and the variable resistance related to each sensor. The output variable is the concentration of each gas. There are five identified ranges for each variable (Morsi , 2007)

Temperature (°C)

| Linguistic | Range |
|---|---|
| Low | $20 < T < 30$ |
| Moderate | $25 < T < 35$ |
| Medium | $30 < T < 40$ |
| High | $35 < T < 45$ |
| V. High | $40 < T < 50$ |

Variable Resistance (KΩ)

| Linguistic | Range |
|---|---|
| V. Low | $1 < R_L < 3$ |
| Low | $2 < R_L < 4$ |
| Medium | $3 < R_L < 5$ |
| High | $4 < R_L < 6$ |
| V. High | $5 < R_L < 7$ |

Output volt of microcontroller (V)

| Linguistic | Range |
|---|---|
| V. Low | $0.5 < V < 1.5$ |
| Low | $1 < V < 2$ |
| Medium | $1.5 < V < 2.5$ |
| High | $2 < V < 3$ |
| V. High | $2.5 < V < 3.5$ |

The concentration of each gas in (ppm)

| Linguistic | Range |
|---|---|
| V. Low | 100 <concentration < 400 |
| Low | 250 <concentration < 550 |
| Medium | 400 <concentration < 700 |
| High | 550 <concentration < 850 |
| V. High | 700 <concentration < 1000 |

Step 2: Define a set of fuzzy membership functions for each of the input and the output, variables. The low and high values are used to define a triangular membership function. The height of each function is one and the function bounds do not exceed the high and low ranges listed above for each range. The membership functions must cover the dynamic ranges related to the minimum and maximum values of inputs and outputs that represent the universe of discourse.

Step 3: Construct the rule base that will govern the controller's operation. The rule base is represented as a matrix of input and output variables. At each matrix row different input variable ranges with one of the output variable range. All rules are activated and fired in parallel whether they are relevant or not and the duplicate ones are removed to conserve computing time. Each rule base is defined by ANDing together with the inputs to produce each individual output response. For example, If temperature is low AND, if voltage is low AND if, $R_L$ is low THEN concentration is low.

Step 4: The control actions will be combined to form the excited interface. The most common rules combination method is the centroid defuzzification to get the crisp output value. This step is a repeated process, after all adjustments are made, which allows the fuzzy expert system to be able to discriminate and classify the data set patterns of the different gases.

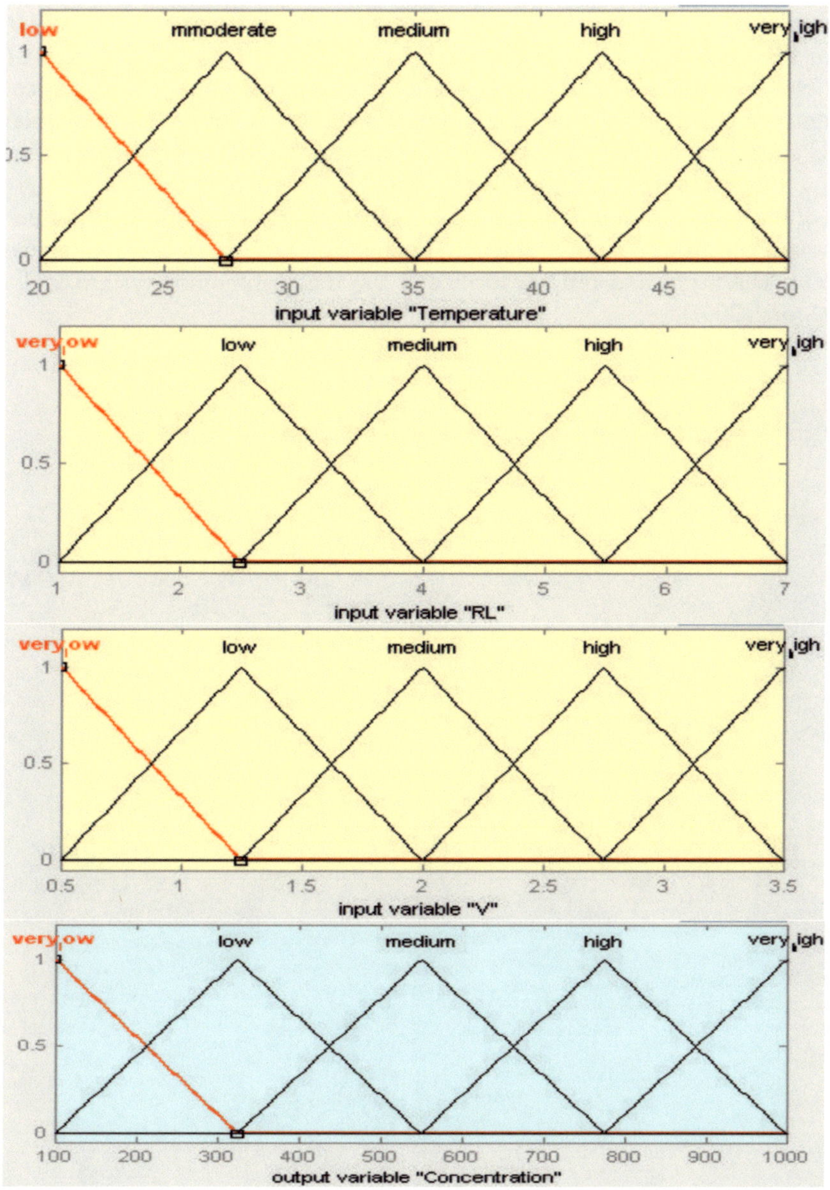


Fig. 40. Fuzzy membership functions with three input variables (Temperature, variable resistance, voltage of each sensor) and output variable (concentration).

Mamdani type fuzzy controller is used to construct the rules, which are extracted from the data driven from the microcontroller. It can be used to discriminate and classify the data set patterns for different gases according to the variation in different parameters, such as gas concentrations, variation in sensor's resistance and output voltage of microcontroller at different temperatures and to improve the sensor's selectivity for gas identification.

Due to the abundant number of membership function figures, the results are limited to representing the fuzzy logic output surface for each sensor. Fuzzy logic gives on line prediction of the concentration depending on the behavior of each gas with different sensors which are extracted from the experiments. The feature of each gas is detected, based on the fuzzy system. The input and output surface of the fuzzy inference system is illustrated in figs 41-60 (Morsi, 2007).

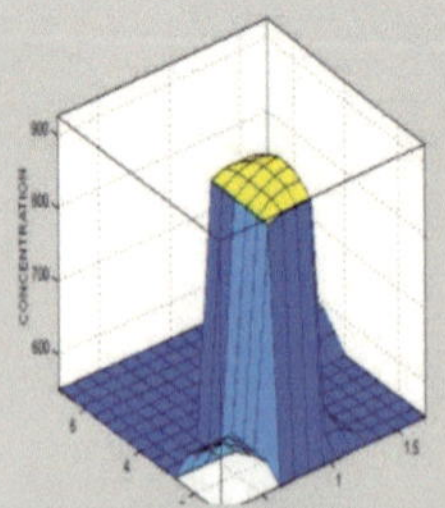

Fig (41) The behavior of TGS 822 output volt with Butane gas

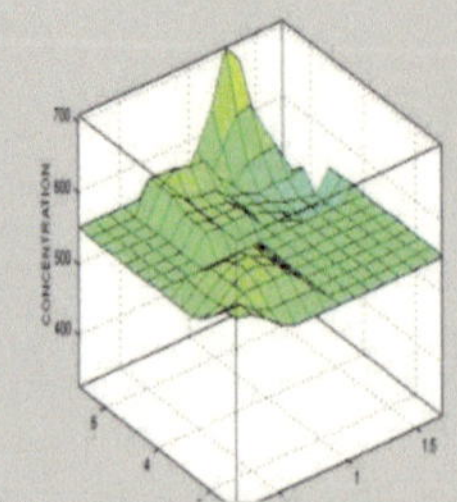

Fig (42) The behavior of TGS 822 output volt with Carbon

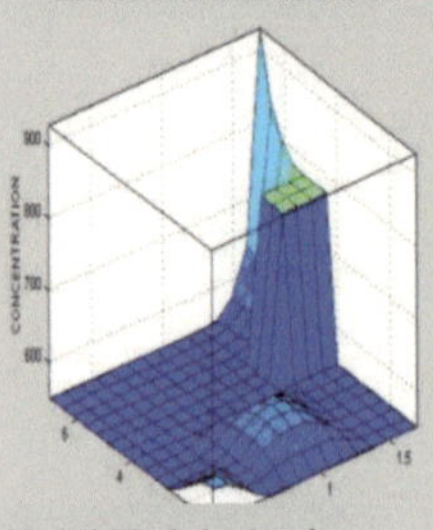

Fig (43) The behavior of TGS 822 output volt with Hydrogen gas with different concentration

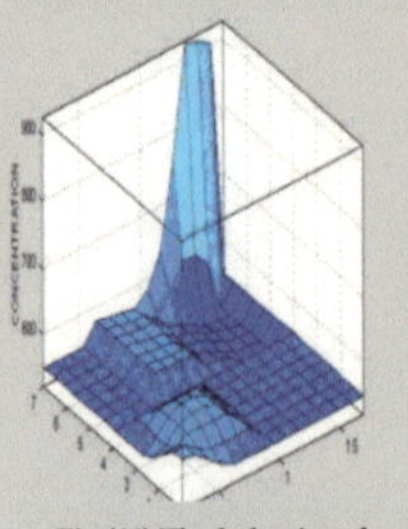

Fig (44) The behavior of TGS 822 output volt with Methane gas with different concentration

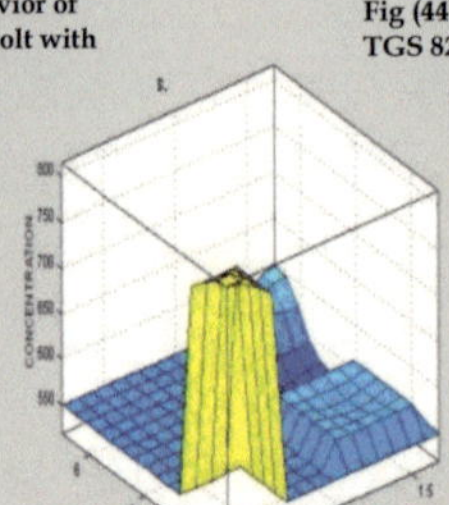

Fig (45) The behavior of TGS 822 output volt with Propane gas with different concentration

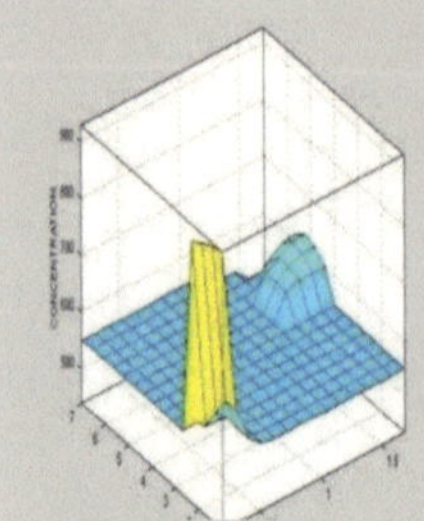

Fig (46) The behavior of TGS 2600 output volt with Butane gas

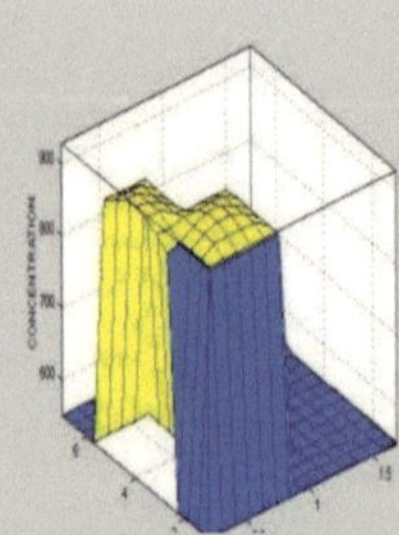

Fig (47) The behavior of TGS 2600 output volt with Carbon dioxide

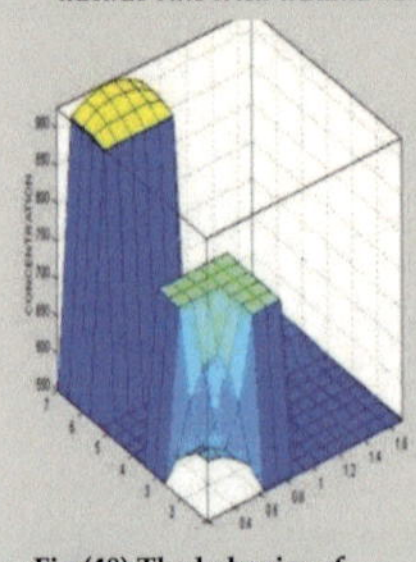

Fig (48) The behavior of TGS 2600 output volt with Hydrogen gas with different concentration

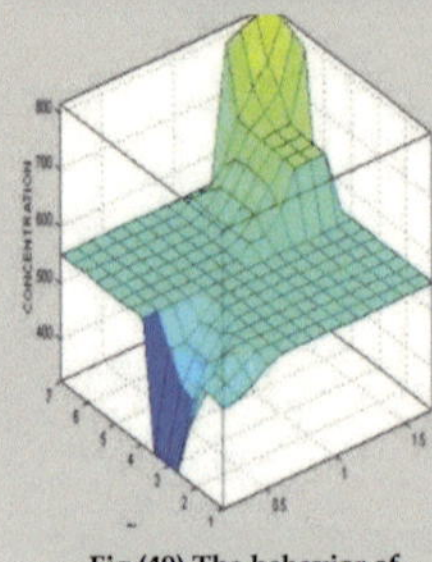

Fig (49) The behavior of TGS 2600 output volt with Methane gas with different concentration

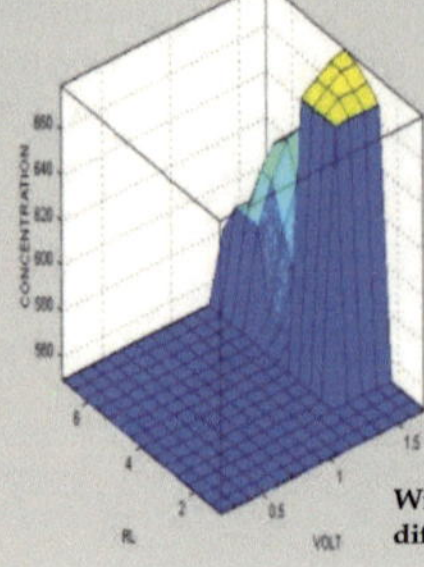

Fig (50) The behavior of TGS 2600 With Propane gas with different concentration

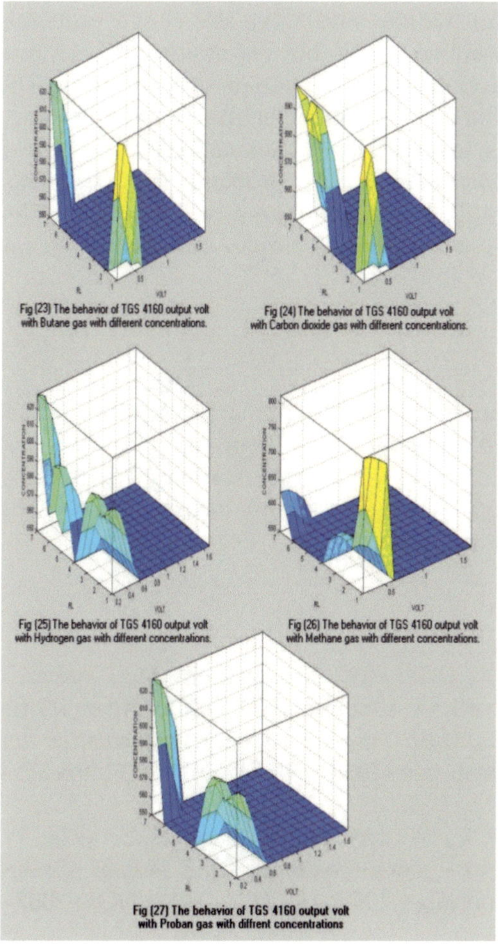


Fig (23) The behavior of TGS 4160 output volt with Butane gas with different concentrations.

Fig (24) The behavior of TGS 4160 output volt with Carbon dioxide gas with different concentrations.

Fig (25) The behavior of TGS 4160 output volt with Hydrogen gas with different concentrations.

Fig (26) The behavior of TGS 4160 output volt with Methane gas with different concentrations.

Fig (27) The behavior of TGS 4160 output volt with Proban gas with diffrent concentrations

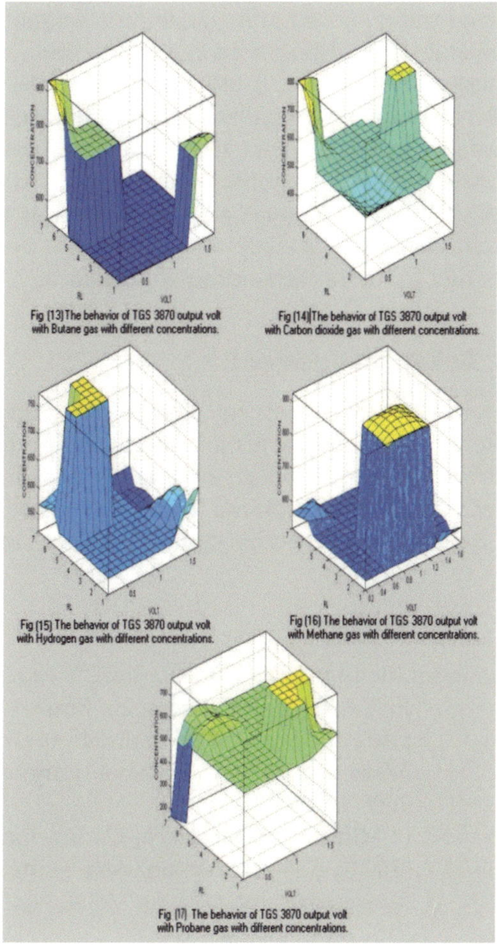


Fig (13) The behavior of TGS 3870 output volt with Butane gas with different concentrations.

Fig (14) The behavior of TGS 3870 output volt with Carbon dioxide gas with different concentrations.

Fig (15) The behavior of TGS 3870 output volt with Hydrogen gas with different concentrations.

Fig (16) The behavior of TGS 3870 output volt with Methane gas with different concentrations.

Fig (17) The behavior of TGS 3870 output volt with Probane gas with different concentrations.

## 7. Conclusion

The large scale of data is able to provide high-level information to make decisions about each gas achieved by using efficient and affordable sensor systems that show autonomous and intelligent capabilities. Measurements have been done using an electronic nose design, depending on commercially available gas sensors. An enormous data collected allows analyzing and characterizing of different gases. Several tests have been carried out by eliminating from the complete time series, a subset of data in a random way to evaluate the reliability of the developed model. The data set is characterized by several problems which can generate errors during processing and prediction phases inducing:

- Missing data, caused by the periodic setting or the stop function of instruments.
- Incorrect recording data occurred by errors in transmission, recording and non-setting of equipment.

Some interpolation and validation techniques to address and solve the above problems depend on building a mathematical model based on a suitable regression analysis and interpolation, which is able to describe the behaviour of daily average concentration. The aim of modeling for gases studies is to describe the peculiar characteristics of gases as alarm situations or risk events. Electronic nose provides, low cost, low maintenance small size, and in some cases low power consumption. The system can handle problems such as sensor drift, noise and non-linearity. It is used as a simple alarm level based on index data. This could be used as a stepping stone for the development of more complex systems, which are needed for more demanding applications.

## 8. Acknowledgement:

I would like to express my sincere gratefulness and gratitude to Prof. Dr. Moustafa Hussein Professor of Optical Communications and OSA member. Vice Dean for education and research affairs, College of Engineering and Technology in Arab Academy for Science, Technology and Maritime Transport, e-mail mosaly@aast.edu, for his tolerance in revising the chapter as well as his endless guidance and support.

## 9. References:

Amigoni, F.; Brandolini, A.; Caglioti, V.; Lecce, V.; Guerriero, A.; Lazzaroni, M.; Lombardi, F.; Ottoboni, R.; Pasero, E.; Piuri, V.; Scotti, O. & Somenzi, D. (2006). Agencies for perception in environmental monitoring. *IEEE Transactions on Instrumentation and Measurement*, Vol. 55. No.4. (august 2006), pp. (1038 - 1050), DOI 10.1109/ TIM, 2006. 877747.

Becker, I.; Mihlberger, S.; Bosch, C.; Braunmuhl, V., Muller, G.; Meckes, A. & Benecke, W. (2000). Gas mixture analysis using Micro - reactor systems. *IEEE Journal of micro electromechanical systems*, Vol.9, No.4, (december 2000), pp. (478 - 484), DOI S1057 - 7157 (00) 10867-4.

Bourgeois, W.; Romain, A.; Nicolas, J. & Stuetz, R. (2003). The use of sensors arrays for environmental monitoring: interests and limitations. J. *Environmental, Monitoring*, Vol.5, (october 2003), pp (852 - 860), ISSN: 10. 1039 / b 307905h.

Belhovari, S.; Bermak, A.; Wei, G. & Chan, P. (2004), Gas identification algorithms for microelectronic gas sensor, *Proceeding of instrumentation and Measurement Technology*, pp. 584 - 587, ISBN 0-7803 - 8248 Como, (may 2004), IMTC 2004, Italy.

Belhovari, S.; Shi, M.; Bermark, A. & Chan, P. (2005). Fast and robust gas identification system using an integrated gas sensor technology and gaussian mixture models. *IEEE Sensors Journal*, Vol.5, No.6, (december - 2005), pp. (1433 - 1444), DOI 510.1109/ JSEN, 2005. 858926.

Belhovari. S.; Shi, M.; Bermark, A. & Chan, P. (2006). Gas identification based on committee machine for micro electronic gas sensor. *IEEE Transactions on Instrumentation and measurement*, Vol. 55, No.5, (october 2006), pp (1786 - 1793), DOI S10.1109/TIM. 2006. 880956.

Clifford, K.H.; Robinson, A.; David, R. & Mary, J. (2005) Overview of sensors and needs for environmental monitoring. *Sensors*, Vol. 5, No. 28, (february 2005), pp. (4-37), ISSN 1424 - 8220.

Carullo, A. (2006). Metrological management of large - scale measuring systems. *IEEE Transactions on Instrumentation and Measurement*, Vol. 55, No.2, (april 2006), pp. (471-476), DOI 10.1109/ TIM. 2006. 870125.

Dong Lee, D. & Sik Lee, D. (2001). Environmental gas sensor. *IEEE Sensors Journal*, Vol.1, No.3, (october 2001), pp. (214 - 217), ISSN 1530 - 437 x (01) 09470-2.

Eberhart, R.; Simpson, P. & Dobbings, R. (1996). *Computational Intelligence PC Tools*, APRROFESSIONAL, ISBN 0-12-228630-8, USA>

Fleming, W. (2001). Overview of automotive sensors. *IEEE Sensors Journal*, Vol. 1, No.4, (december 2001), pp. (296 - 308), ISSN S1530-437X (01) 11158-9.

Getino, J.; Gutierrez, J.; Ares, L.; Robla, J.; Sayago, C.; Horrillo & Gap, J. (1995). Integrated sensor array for gas analysis in combustion atmosphere, *Proceeding on solid- state sensors and Actuators*, pp. 803 - 806, Stockholm, (june 1995), Transducers 95 Euro sensors 1x, Sweden.

Guardado J.; Naredo, J.; Moreno, P. & Fuerte, C. (2001). A Comparative Study of neural network efficiency in power transformers diagnosis using dissolved gas analysis, *IEEE Transactions on Power Delivery*, Vol. 16, No.4, (october 2001), pp. 643-647, ISSN 0885 - 8977 (01) 08497-7.

Ishida, H.; Nakayama, G., Nakamoto, T. & Morizumi, T. (2005). Controlling a gas/odor plume tracking robot based on transient responses of gas sensors. *IEEE Sensors Journal*, Vol.5, No, 3. (june 2005), pp. (537 - 545), DOI 10.1109 / ISEN, 2051 - 839597.

Josphine, B. & Subramanian, V. (2008). Electrinic noses sniff success. *IEEE Spectrum*, Vol.45, No.3, (march 2008), pp. (47 - 53), ISSN 0018 - 9235.

Kolen, P. (1994). Self- calibration / compensation technique for microcontroller based sensors arrays. *IEEE Transactions on Instrumentation and measurement*, Vol. 43, No.4, (august 1994), pp. (620 - 623), ISSN 0018 - 9456 / 94.

Luo, R.; Chen, C. & Luo, Y. (2002). Multisensor fusion and integration: approaches, applications and future research directions. *IEEE Sensors Journal*. Vol. 2, No.2, (april 2002), pp. 107-119. ISSN S 1530 - 437x (02) 03941 - 6.

Marco, S.; Ortega, A.; Pardo, A. & Samitier, J. (1998). Gas identification with tin oxide sensor array and self organizing maps: adaptive correction of sensor drifts. *IEEE Transactions on Instrumentation and Measurement*, Vol. 47, No.1, (february 1998), pp. (316-321), ISSN 0018 - 9456..

Morsi, I. (2007). A microcontroller based on multisensors data fusion and artificial intelligent technique for gas identification. *Proceeding of IEEE Industrial Electronics Society*, pp 2203 - 2208, ISBN 1-4244 - 0783 - 4107, Taipei, (november 2007), industrial electronics society, Taiwan.

Morsi-a, I. (2008). Discrimination of some atmospheric gases using an integrated sensor array, surface response modeling algorithms and analysis of variance (ANOVA), *Proceeding of IEEE Sensors and Application Symposium (SAS)*, pp. 140 - 145, ISBN 978 - 1 - 4244 - 1963 - 0108, Atlanta, (february 2008), IEEE Sensors, USA.

Morsi-b, I. (2008). Discrimination between butane and propane in a gas mixture using Semiconductor gas sensors and neural networks, *Proceeding of IEEE Sensors Application Symposium*, pp. 134-139, ISBN 978 - 1- 4244 - 1963 - 0108, Atlanta, (february 2008), IEEE Sensors, USA.

Morsi - b, I. (2008). Electronic noses for monitoring environmental pollution and building regression model, *Proceeding of IEEE Industrial Electronics Society*, pp. 1730 - 1735.

ISBN 978 - 1 - 4244 - 1766 - 7108 Orlando, (november 2008), IEEE industrial electronics society, Florida.

http://www.figarosensor.com (on line).

Smulko, J. (2006). The measurement setup for gas detection by resistance fluctuations of gas sensors, *Proceeding on Instrumentation and Measurement Technology*, pp. 2028 - 2031, ISBN 0-7803, 9360, 0106, Sorrento, (april 2006), IEEE instrumentation and measurement society, Italy.

Timothy, J. (1995). *Fuzzy Logic with Engineering Applications*, McGraw- Hill INC, ISBN 0-07-053917-0, New York.

Tanaka, K. (1996). *An Introduction to Fuzzy Logic for Practical Applications*, Springer, ISBN 0-387-94804-4, New York.

Wesley, J. (1997). *Fuzzy and Neural Approaches in Engineering*, John Wiley & Sons INC, ISBN 0-471-19247-3, 1, USA.

Wilson, D.; Hoyt, S.; Janata, H.; Booksh, K. & Obando, L. (2001). Chemical sensors for portable handheld field instruments. *IEEE Sensors Journal*, Vol.1, No.4 (december 2001), pp. (256-274), ISSN 1530 - 437X (01) 11120 - 6.

Weigong, J.; Chen, Q., Reu, M.; Liu, N. & Daoust, C. (2006). Temperature feedback control for improving the stability of a semiconductor metal oxide (SMO) gas sensor, *IEEE Sensor Journal*, Vol. 6, No.1, (february 2006), pp. 139 - 145, ISSN 10.1109/ JSEN, 2005. 844353.

Zylka, P. & Mazurek, B. (2002). Rapid dissolved gas analysis by means of electrochemical gas sensor, *Proceeding of 14th International conference on Dielectric Liquids*, pp. 325 - 328, ISBN 0-7803 - 7350 - 2102, Graz, (july 2002), ICDL 2002, Austria.

# Medical Image Intelligent Access Integrated with Electronic Medical Records System for Brain Degenerative Disease

Mei-Ju Su[a], Po-Hsun Cheng[b], Sao-Jie Chen[a], Chung-Yi Yang[d], Ping-Kung Yip[f], Daniel Racoceanu[gh] and Heng-Shuen Chen[ce]*
[a]*Graduate Institute of Electronics Engineering, College of Electrical Engineering and Computer Science, National Taiwan University*
*Department of Software Engineering, National Kaohsiung Normal University*
[b]*Department of Medical Informatics, College of Medicine, National Taiwan University*
[c]*Department of Family Medicine, National Taiwan University Hospital*
[d]*Department of Medical imaging, National Taiwan University Hospital*
[e]*Information System Office, National Taiwan University Hospital*
[f]*Department of Neurology, National Taiwan University Hospital*
[g]*IPAL-UMI CNRS 2955, French National Research Center , I2R, A*STAR, NUS, Singapore*
[h]*Faculty of Sciences, University of Besancon, France*
**Email: chenhs@ntu.edu.tw*
*National Taiwan University, Taipei, Taiwan*

## Introduction

As the computer data storage capacity increases and technology of digital imaging progresses rapidly, today we can access and manipulate massive image database on the Internet. How to search and access intelligently on content based image database become a prominent focus in the field of multimedia research. In this chapter, to support the diagnostic decision making, a new idea of grid-distributed, contextual, representation, use of specific visual medical knowledge, intelligent information access framework for medical images database was integrated with radiology reports and clinical department information. It will assist reducing the human, legal and financing consequences of these medical errors. A report by the American Hospital Association suggests that US hospitals use only 1.5%~2.5% of their Hospital Medical budgets on data information systems, which is less than the 5-10% of similar funds dedicated to such systems found in the budgets of other industries. Moreover, as computer data storage capacity increases and the technology involving digital imaging progresses rapidly, the traditional image has been replaced by Computer Radiography (CR) or Digital Radiography (DR) derived imagery, Computed Tomography (CT), Magnetic Resonance Imaging (MRI), and Digital Subtraction

Angiography (DSA). This advance reduces the space and the cost associated with X-ray films, speeds up hospital management procedures improving also the quality of the medical imagery-based diagnosis quality. American hospitals, in particular, often consult image diagnostic professionals from India via Internet due to budget consideration. The clinical information gathered by this study will alleviate the budget issue because the tele-consultation regarding image diagnostics will then be feasible.

For the current medical image database system, image retrieval can be performed by using keywords for searching in pre-interpreted reports. However, the characteristics of free-text reports may compromise with the effort for clarification from low level features such as color, shape, texture, to medium level features describing by collection and spatial relationships, or highest abstract features which are semantic or contextual. In 1990s, the content-based image retrieval (CBIR) started [1]and grew steadily over the last ten years. [2] There is growing interest in CBIR because of the limitations inherent in metadata-based systems. Textual information about images can be easily searched using existing technology, but requires humans to personally describe every image in the database. However, CBIR query uses a lot of computer power to process, and it can economize a large manpower. Therefore, the content-based retrieval of the medical image also becomes a significant field for medical assistance, medical education and medical research. At clinics, when a physician diagnoses a patient through the patient's medical images, he has to entry the PACS and RIS. And he makes a diagnosis in another system, EMR (Electronic Medical Records). [3]

In Taiwan, the National Taiwan University Hospital (NTUH), which is traditionally the leading medical center, has recently adopted a complete health recording system, including an Electronic Medical Record (EMR) system linked to Hospital Information System (HIS), Research and Information System (RIS), Picture Archiving and Communication System (PACS), and other clinical information systems. National Taiwan University (NTU), one of the research partners of ONtology and COntext related MEdical image Distributed Intelligent Access (ONCO-MEDIA) project1 is leading a study of the integration between the Content-Based Medical Image Retrieval (CBIR) and EMR systems as well as on its implications in providing improved clinical diagnostic and therapeutic decision support.

Dementia is the loss of mental functions -- such as thinking, memory, and reasoning -- that is severe enough to interfere with a person's daily functioning. Dementia is not a disease itself, but rather a group of symptoms that are caused by various diseases or conditions. Symptoms can also include changes in personality, mood, and behavior. In some cases, the dementia can be treated and cured because the cause is treatable. Dementia develops when the parts of the brain that are involved with learning, memory, decision-making, and language are affected by one or more of a variety of infections or diseases. The most common cause of dementia is Alzheimer's disease, but there are as many as 50 other known causes. Most of these causes are very rare. [5] Dementia is a word for a group of symptoms caused by disorders that affect the brain. People with dementia may not be able to think well enough to do normal activities, such as getting dressed or eating. They may lose their ability to solve problems or control their emotions. Their personalities may change. They may become agitated or see things that are not there. [6] Dementia has become more and more prevalent in recent years. In the United States, there are approximately 5 million people suffering from dementia and that number is projected to rise above 16 million by the year of 2050. Presently, Americans pay US$5000 per patient per year for dementia medication and associated nursing care costs [9] [10].

In Taiwan, there were approximately 140 thousand people suffering from dementia in 2005 and there will be 650 thousand dementia cases by the year of 2050. MMSE (mini-mental state examination) is commonly used in medicine to screen for dementia.The MMSE test is a brief 30-point questionnaire test that is used to screen for cognitive impairment. It is also used to estimate the severity of cognitive impairment at a given point in time and to follow the course of cognitive changes in an individual over time, thus making it an effective way to document an individual's response to treatment.

Since Dementia, as a disease, is an important and long term problem that causes significant burdens for families and societies, this study has endeavored to find a viable procedure to ameliorate the treatment of dementia patients and to enhance the early diagnosis and monitoring of its progression. [11]

In this chapter, we chose Dementia to establish a system for CBIR with EMR. Dementia is a neurological disease, usually the clinical course is long, and it represents a variety of characteristics in brain image such as CT (computed tomography), MRI (magnetic resonance imaging) or PET (Positron Emission Tomography). If the doctor wants to diagnosis a symptom, he needs a series of images to diagnose or decide for therapeutic strategies. Therefore, the image database correlated with clinical information would be crucial in care of a dementia patient. In addition, usually it is an intensive collaboration among neurologists, radiologists and other clinical specialties. This study focused on Dementia as a pathology model, in order to elaborate a prototyping system for CBIR with EMR. Dementia is a neurological disease, usually characterized by a slow histopathology, and presents itself with a variety of characteristic abnormalities in brain imagery such as CT, MRI, or PET. In the course of the treatment, a doctor may need a series of images to make the proper diagnosis or to make critical decision for therapeutic strategies. Therefore, an image database infused with clinical information could become a major component for the improvement of the dementia patient care. The chapter will describe a novel concept of Medical Image Distributed Intelligent Access Integrated with Electronic Medical Records is expected to enhance the early diagnosis and monitoring of disease progress.

## 2. Methods

**Integration of RIS, EMR, PACS and Clinics to Support Diagnosis**

At present, most hospitals store the medical images from CT, MRI, DSA and X-ray film in PACS. The clinicians make differential diagnosis of a patient in EMR system with references to laboratory results and image reports. Therefore, we have to provide the essential information from EMR, PACS and RIS to clinicians, such as neurologists, to support their decision. On the other hand, in the department of medical imaging, the radiologists also need to refer to medical information recorded by other specialties to interpret medical image for their reports on the RIS [7]. The image report by the radiologists could assist the clinicians to make correct diagnoses; however, the correct image interpretation also depends on the crucial medical information that clinical doctors must input. This co-dependence demonstrates the need for two-way communications between imaging professionals such as radiologists and their clinical counterparts that are treating the patients. Therefore, in this study, the integration of EMR, RIS and PACS and clinics input was implemented to establish a prototype model for intelligent access of medical image database, and retrieve clinical information automatically. (Fig.1.) The integrated user interface used the ICD-9 (International Classification of Disease, Ninth Revision) 331.0 code to identify and query its relative medical information and medical images from HIS, PACS or RIS. Therefore, the important thing is to define what the essential clinical information is.

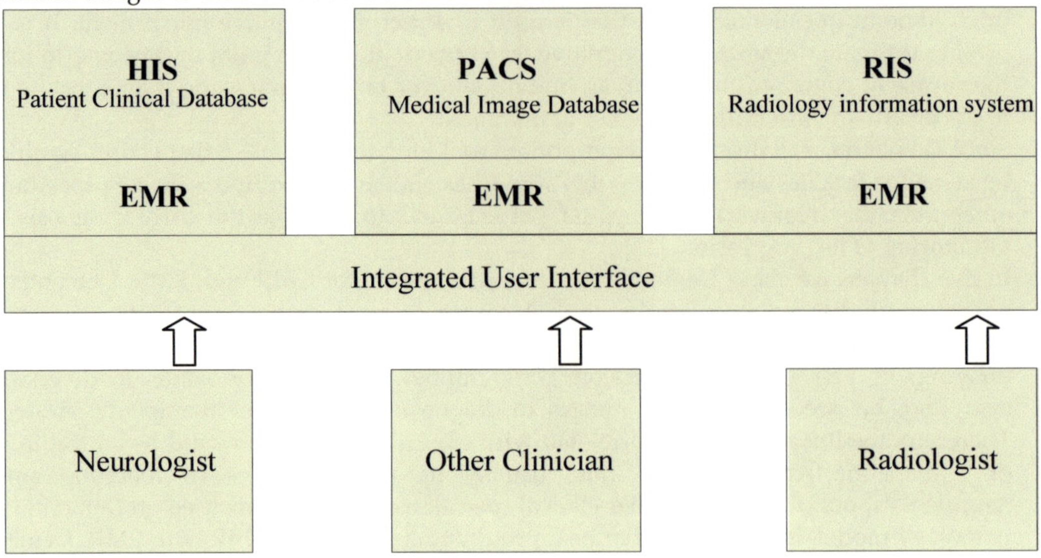


Fig. 1. System Structure of Prototype Model

### Inter-disciplinary collaboration

This important process was the collaboration of the interdisciplinary among neurology, medical informatics and radiology experts. In this study, a prototype model was designed to assist the procedure involving the physician-in-the-loop approach [4].In this prototype model, a group of neurologists and radiologists collaborated to establish a common language involving the image diagnosis. In the EMR integration with RIS and PACS, we based on the diagnostic criteria and practical guideline to satisfy the diagnosis procedure and requirement. Moreover, the establishment of the ontology of dementia was in accordance with the essential clinical information of dementia. The process flow chart was as follow:

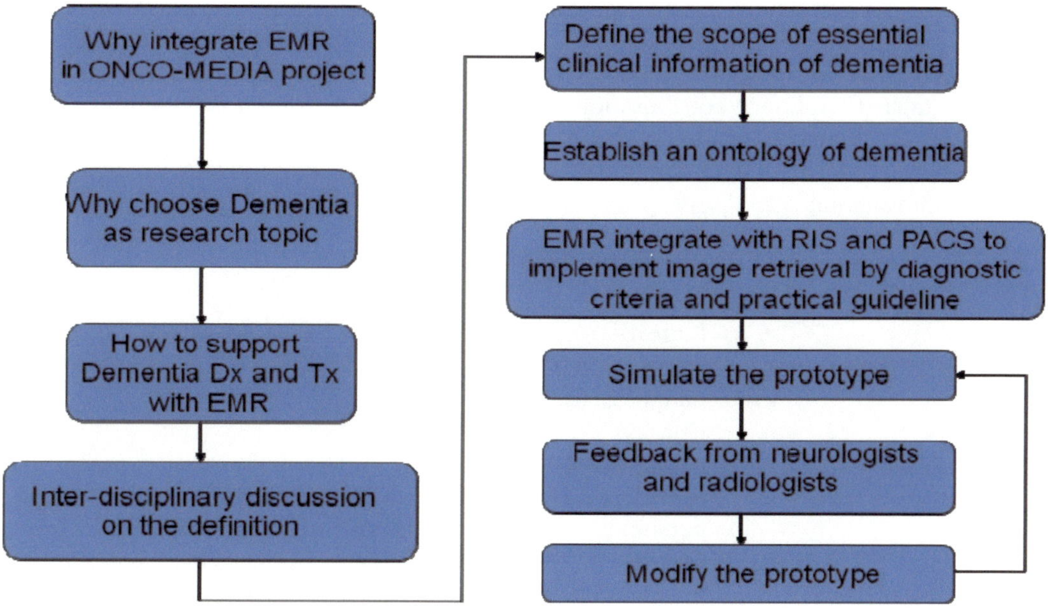


Fig. 2. Research flow chart

**Establishing a Definition of Essential Clinical Information in Dementia**

The Literature review is essential course before experts to define the essential clinical information. Therefore, journals, textbooks and clinical reports will be our guidelines. The UMLS [12] is a long-term project realized from 1986 by Library National of Medicine (LNM), the largest world's library in the biomedical domain of Maryland. This system is the result of the combination of 140 multilingual terminology databases, knowledge sources as well as tools in order to facilitate the tasks of accessing, researching, integrating and aggregating of biomedical and health information. The technical purpose of this system is to combine into a unified structure of different knowledge sources in the biomedical domain.[13] The purpose of NLM's Unified Medical Language System (UMLS) is to facilitate the development of computer systems that behave as if they "understand" the meaning of the language of biomedicine and health. Bio-medical information as a result of a large number of constantly increasing and are scattered in various database systems, so you want to search complete and no new information for easy, UMLS Thus came into being for the purpose of enhancing the capacity of the system, allowing the system to understand the readers biomedical aspects of meaning, and thus help readers information retrieval and integration. Therefore, we also have to depend on UMLS to support us to develop the dementia model. And the methods and steps, the experts discussed as follow:

Literature review from journals, textbooks and clinical reports

Selecting relevant medical image reports from department of medical imaging

Using representative cases to simulate medical image distributed intelligent access integrated with EMR to select crucial clinical information

Finalizing structure and items of essential clinical information regarding dementia

Dependence on the Unified Medical Language System (UMLS) to facilitate the development of a prototype model that follows the international language of biomedicine and health.

## 3. Results

**Essential Clinical information**

After the inter-disciplinary collaboration, we got the final definition of essential clinical information in dementia when the neurologist diagnoses in a clinic. In the model, the essential clinical information of dementia included is summarized as follows:

A. Base information
   a. Sex
   b. Age
   c. Country
   d. Residency
   e. Education (yr)
   f. Occupation (pre-retired work)
   g. Language (dialect)

B. Clinical history
   a. Handedness
   b. Age of onset
   c. Initial symptom sequence (multi-choice):i. memory, ii. personality, iii .language, iv. gait and v. bradykinesia
   d. Course: i. rapid progression (< 1 year), ii. chronic progression, iii. stepwise and iv. fluctuated
   e. Risk factors (multi-choice): i.CVA, ii.HTN, iii.DM, iv. cardiac disease, v. hyperlipidemia, vi. obesity, vii. physical inactivity, viii. vegetarian, ix. parkinsonism and x. family history

C. Clinical diagnosis
   a. Normal
   b. MCI (Mild Cognitive Impairment)
   c. AD (Alzeimer Disease)
   d. VaD (Vascular Dementia)
   e. Mixed type
   f. FTD (Frontotemporal Dementia)
   g. DLB (Dementia with Lewy Bodies)
   h. Dementia, other types

D. Lab
   a. CBC
   b. Electrolyte
   c. BUN/Cre
   d. GOT/GPT
   e. T4/TSH
   f. B12/folate
   g. Lipid profile
   h. VDRL
   i. Hachinski ischemic score
   j. MMSE
   k. CDR

The prototype system is designed to recognize a positive dementia diagnosis and reconfigure its patient information presentation accordingly. International Statistical Classification of Diseases and Related Health Problems (ICD) provides codes to classify diseases and a wide variety of signs, symptoms, abnormal findings, complaints, social circumstances and external causes of injury or disease.[14] The ICD-9(International

Classification of Disease, Ninth Revision) was published by the WHO in 1977.[15] In EMR of National Taiwan University, we use ICD-9. Each code of ICD-9 codes has a precise meaning, and as a whole it covers practically all known symptoms. ICD-9 codes 290-319 are mental disorders. And ICD-9 of dementia is 290. ICD-9 codes 320-359 are Diseases of the nervous system and code 331.0 is Alzheimer's disease. In diagnosis flow with the model of the research, an input of the ICD-9 331.0 code for Alzheimer's disease will alter and display the patient information, such as: base information, clinical history, lab results and medical images. (Fig. 3.)

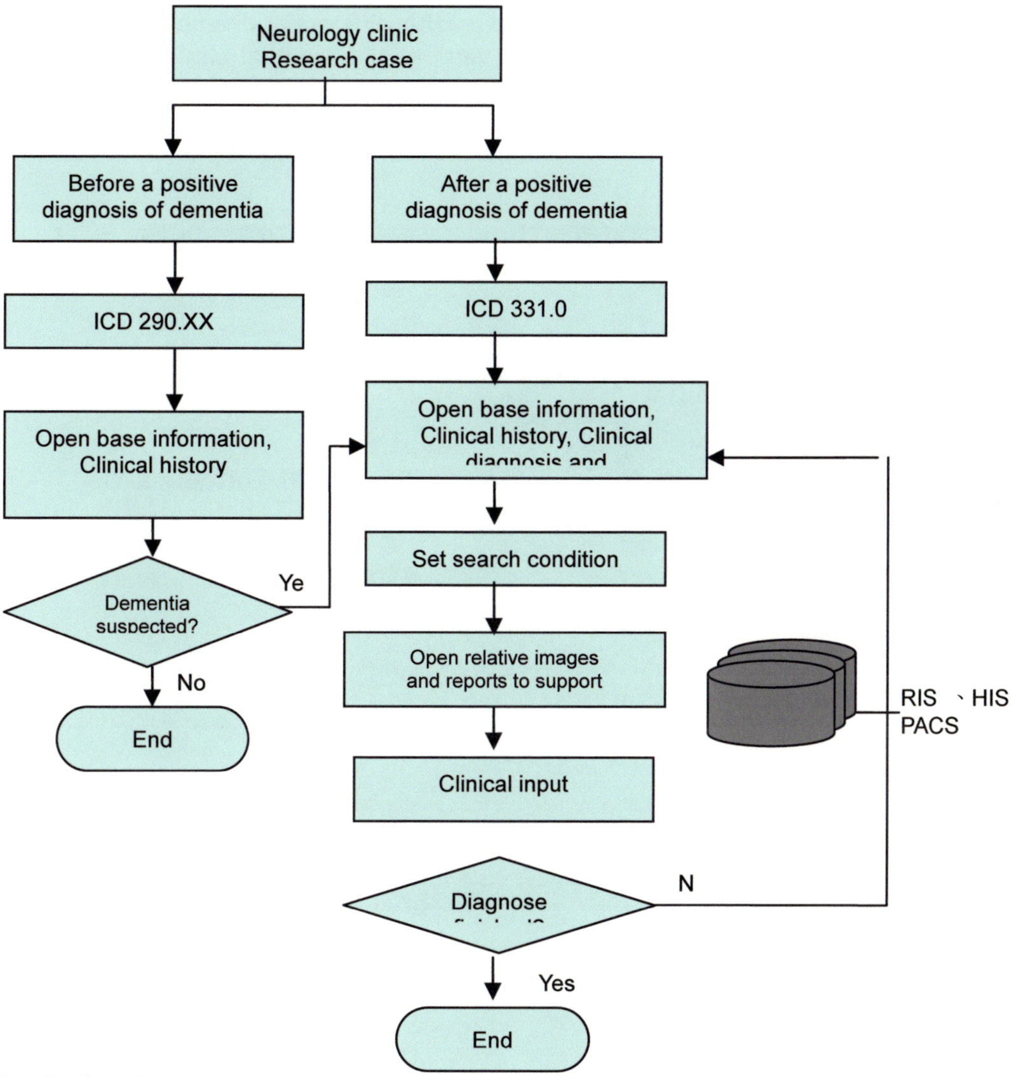


Fig. 3. Flow Diagram

On the other hand, if dementia has not been yet, the neurologists would still like to know the patient's base information, clinical history, and lab results. Using this clinical history, the

neurologists may make a choice reflecting the initial symptom sequence, course, and risk factors, which will also support him to make an early diagnosis in the future. (Fig. 3.)
With the established prototype model, the data schema of the essential clinical information of dementia will be integrated into the EMR user interface in the clinical department in the EMR system of NTUH. Clinical doctors can input the essential clinical information, such as base information, clinical history, clinical diagnosis, upon initiation of dementia diagnoses and the system will present a prompt with a pop-up menu for easy data entry. At the same time, the prototype model will automatically retrieve the relative medical images and image reports by the radiologists in order to support the diagnosis. (Fig.4)
Moreover, the radiologists get images from PACS with differential diagnosis of dementia and the RIS can simultaneously automatically retrieve the essential clinical information related to specific image characteristics defined by a consensus of the neurology and radiology experts (Fig.5.). In this way, both user interfaces are designed to open a pop-up window with the pull down bar when the clinician or radiologist is ready to input data into the system. (Figs 4-5) [8]

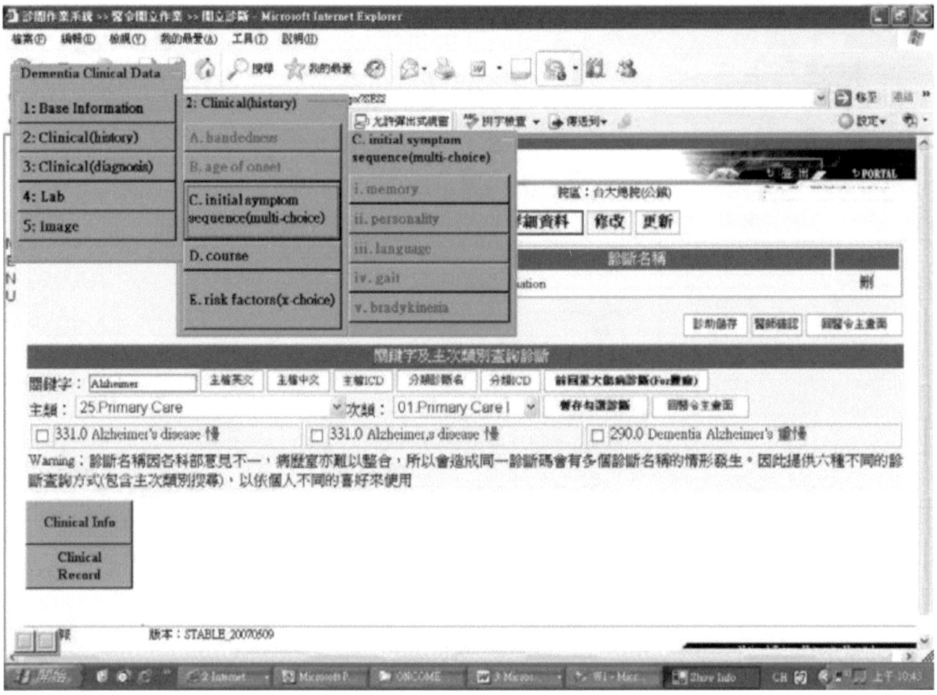


Fig. 4. Prototype Model: Clinical History

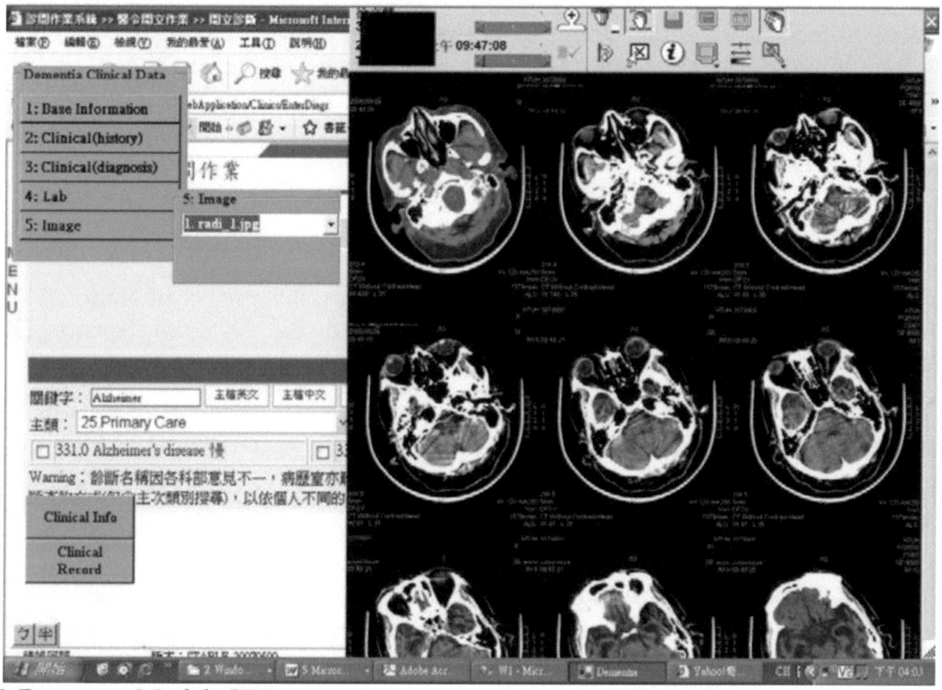

Fig. 5. Prototype Model: CT Image

## 4. Discussion

In this study, the intelligent information access framework for medical image databases was designed to integrate radiological reports and clinical information. The most important concern in this approach is the interdisciplinary collaboration among neurology, medical informatics and radiology experts. The second important concern would be the implementation with the critical and service-oriented hospital information system. Therefore, we will test the system by the physician-in-the-loop approach to enhance diagnosis practically and revise the system.

Moreover, we focused on decision support for dementia diagnosis, teaching and research. Therefore, we would retrieve images of similar patients via a medical grid by querying keywords of the base information, clinical History, clinical diagnose, Lab. we get the new retrieved image database for the patients. Therefore, we will analysis their medical image correlation by image processing and the relevance of the clinical data and images in order to assist diagnosis, research and teaching.

Security and privacy is also a very important issue in this field of research. First, we build trusted electronic relationships between healthcare customers, employees, businesses, trading partners and stakeholders. Therefore, when we use the patient's anamnesis, examination data, or medical images, whether we have the patient's permission or not, there must be a set of procedures to follow accordingly. We plan to consider the security and privacy function in the system, in the future.

The implementation of this prototyping system must be well organized and the initial testing done on an offline system. The clinical data could be backed-up and copied to a

separate system for the purposes of the trial. When the first prototype model becomes fully implemented, the system could be expanded by adding other neurodegenerative diseases one by one to enhance the power and comprehensiveness of the intelligent retrieval for clinical practice.
In the future, the system will be continuously developed to extend its spectrum of diseases and clinical specialties.

## 5. Acknowledgements

This research work was partially supported by the u-Hospital project in National Taiwan University funded by the Ministry of Education and the National Science Council (95R0062-AE00-05), Taiwan, and by the ICT-Asia ONCO-MEDIA project, France.

## 6. Reference

[1]H. Muller, N. Michoux, D. Bandon ,A. Geissbuhler; "A Review of Content Based Image Retrieval Systems in Medical", International journal of medical informatics, vol. 73, page(s): 1-23, 2004.
[2]W. Niblack, R. Barber, W. Equitz, M. D. Flickner, E. H. Glasman, D. Petkovic, P. Yanker, C. Faloutsos, and G. Taubin, QBIC project: querying images by content, using color, texture, and shape, in: W. Niblack (Ed.), Storage and Retrieval for Image and Video Databases, Vol. 1908 of SPIE Proceedings, pp. 173-187, 1993.
[3]Lei Zheng; Wetzel, A.W.; Gilbertson, J.; Becich, M.J.; "Design and analysis of a content-based pathology image retrieval system", IEEE Trans. Information Technology in Biomedicine,vol. 7, no. 4, Dec. 2003, page(s):240-255.
[4]Kak, A.; Pavlopoulou, C ;"Content-based image retrieval from large medical databases", Proceedings of the First International Symposium on 3D Data Processing Visualization and Transmission, 19-21 June 2002 Page(s):138 – 147.
[5]Joseph R Carcione, DO, MBA on January 01, 2007), "Alzheimer's Disease Guide", http://www.webmd.com/alzheimers/guide/alzheimers-dementia
[ 6]"Medline Plus: Dementia", http://www.nlm.nih.gov/medlineplus/dementia.html
[7]Bueno, J.M.; Chino, F.; Traina, A.J.M.; Traina, C., Jr.; Azevedo-Marques, P.M., "How to add content-based image retrieval capability in a PACS", Proceedings of the 15th IEEE Symposium on Computer-Based Medical Systems, 4-7 June 2002, page(s):321 – 326.
[8]Traina, A.; Rosa, N.A.; Traina, C., Jr, "Integrating images to patient electronic medical records through content-based retrieval techniques", Proceedings of the 16th IEEE Symposium on Computer-Based Medical Systems, 26-27 June 2003, page(s):163 – 168.
[9]"1.7m 'will have dementia by 2051", http://news.bbc.co.uk/1/hi/health/6389977.stm, 27 February 2007, BBC NEWS.
[10]"Report of Alzheimer's Disease Facts and Figures 2007", Alzheimer's Association,http://www.alz.org/
[11]"Taiwan dementia policy advocacy 2006", Taiwan Alzheimer's Disease Association, http://www.tada2002.org.tw/index.html
[12] http://www.nlm.nih.gov/research/umls/

[13]Le Thi Hoang Diem; Chevallet, J.-P.; Dong Thi Bich Thuy;" Thesaurus-based query and document expansion in conceptual indexing with UMLS: Application in medical information retrieval", Research, Innovation and Vision for the Future, 2007 IEEE International Conference on 5-9 March 2007 Page(s):242 - 246
[14 ] http://www.cdc.gov/nchs/about/major/dvs/icd9des.htm
[15] Yao-Yang, Shieh; Shaw, B.C., Jr.; Roberson, G.H.; "Internet Web-based teaching for cross-sectional anatomy and radiological imaging", Computer-Based Medical Systems, 1998. Proceedings. 11th IEEE Symposium, 12-14 June 1998 Page(s):192 - 197

# Use of RFID tags for data storage on quality control in cheese industries

Raquel Pérez-Aloe[(1)], José M. Valverde[(1)], Antonio Lara[(1)], Fernando Castaño[(1)], Juan M. Carrillo[(1)], José González[(2)] and Isidro Roa[(2)]
*Universidad de Extremadura[(1)]. Instituto Tecnológico Agroalimentario[(2)]*
*Spain*

## 1. Introduction

The current laws that regulate the food security in the European Union lay down the principles and general requirements of the food legislation. In the article 3 of the Regulation 178/2002 the traceability is defined as the "ability to trace and follow a food, feed, food-producing animal or substance intended to be, or expected to be incorporated into a food or feed, through all stages of production, processing and distribution". In addition, "the food traceability must be guaranteed in all the stages described above: production, transformation and distribution" which implies the obligation of being able of identifying every product in the company providing a complete information about it (Regulation 178, 2002).

Depending on the activity in the food chain three different types of traceability can be distinguished:

1) Back traceability, called *"suppliers traceability"* as well, refers to the possibility of having knowledge of what products are coming into the company, where are they coming from as well as which farmers are their suppliers.
2) Internal traceability or *"process traceability"* refers to the information about what is made, from what it is made, how and when it is made and the identification of the product.
3) Forward traceability or *"client traceability"* means the possibility of knowing what products the company delivers, when and to whom they have been supplied (Coscarón et al. 2007; Spanish Agency for Food Security, 2004).

Although the law imposes a generic obligation of traceability, it is not mentioned the way in which companies can achieve that goal (Decree 1808, 1991; Decree 217, 2004).

Nowadays, the sector of cheese production has no a procedure that exhaustively guarantees a proper traceability throughout all the fabrication stages. The main problem is the cheese ripening, done in special chambers as shown in Figure 1. The surrounding conditions in these rooms, such as humidity, temperature, product handling (turning), mould and flora growing avoid the individual labeling of the products. Is for this that the production and quality control are performed by batches and the data storage of the information is done manually by the company staff.

Moreover, if the cheese produced by a specific manufacturer has a Protected Denomination of Origin (P.D.O.) then the product must satisfy stringent requirements about the milk (origin, characteristics and preserving) and the elaboration, ripening and physical and physicochemical characteristics of the final result.

Fig. 1. A traditional ripening chamber

To have an idea, for example, the "Ibores" cheese (Spanish Southwest P.D.O.) has to be made with milk of mountain goats, with a preservation temperature less than 6° C, a minimum protein content of 6%, fat around 4%, pH higher than 6,5 and so on. One of the elaboration steps is the salting , which can be wet or dry, using only sodium chloride. In case of wet salting, the maximum stay time shall be 24 hours in a saline solution with a maximum concentration of 20%. Regarding the ripening time, it should be, at least, sixty days, being the finished product cylindrical with a height from 6 to 9 cm, diameter comprised between 12 and 15 cm and a weight from 750 to 1200 g. In the most traditional presentation, the cheese is coated with paprika or smeared with olive oil, appearing diverse colorations due to different moulds (Order 25/4, 1997). This is only a brief summary of the conditions that "Ibores" cheeses should meet in order to be qualified as product with P.D.O. The agency responsible for accrediting the P.D.O. is the Regulatory Board. Usually a technical expert visits the cheese industry requesting to the manufacturer a collection of data corresponding to the elaboration process to certify, if appropriate, the guarantee of origin and quality. Besides, the Regulatory Boards of P.D.O. are recognized as entities of product certification according to the European Standard EN 45011. This regulation shows in detail the criteria to be applied by these entities to perform a certification of products reliable and transparent. For instance, in the document that details the criteria to be evaluated by the technical staff of the Regulatory Board of P.D.O. "Torta del Casar", other Spanish Southwest P.D.O. (Order 11/1, 1999; Order 9/10, 2001; Order 6/5, 2002; Regulation 1491, 2003), appears that the Regulatory Board lays down a control based on sampling and analysis of milk and cheese. The results will be used in the development of a set of measurable data which will serve as basis for the accreditation process and to verify the adequacy of the dairy industry to the certification system. This system, in fact, is based on a procedure of self-control that includes several actions to be done by the person in charge of quality control in the company. These actions must be the periodic checking, as determined by the regulations, of the physical, physicochemical, microbiological and organoleptic parameters of the batches to be issued to the market, having a record of the results (CC/3, 2005; CC/4, 2007).

As it is clear from above, it is desirable that the cheese industry and the Regulatory Board of P.D.O. interact effectively and efficiently to achieve that the final product reaches the consumer with full guarantee of its origin, manufacturing process or quality. Therefore the main objective here will be to join efforts between the dairy companies, in terms of traceability, and the Regulatory Boards of P.D.O. with respect to their quality systems to certificate products. In this way, the binomial Company-Regulatory Board would have the necessary tools (hardware-software) that would enable compliance with current legislation regarding traceability, as well as a continuous quality improvement thanks to the optimization of the technological process according to the information obtained, respectively. The key points here would be the speed on getting the required information, the time saved and the simplification of tasks that would provide the implemented tool compared to the manual records of data usually done by both, the employees of the cheese industry and the technical staff of the Regulatory Board of P.D.O. in charge of the quality certification.

To achieve this goal, a system which deals with the use of Radio Frequency IDentification (RFID) has been developed. The RFID is a contactless method for data transfer in object identification. The transmission of data is carried-out through electromagnetic waves. The tag (transponder) consists of a microchip, as well as an antenna, which are usually put in some form of casing for protection against different environments. The RFID read/write device creates a weak electromagnetic field. If a RFID tag passes this field, the microchip of the transponder wakes up and can send or receive data without any contact to the reader. If the tag leaves the field, the communication gets interrupted and the chip on the tag stops working, but the data on the tag keeps stored (Finkenzeller, 2003). To provide the system with portability a PDA (Personal Digital Assistant) with reader and embedded antenna can be used. Figure 2 shows the usual components of a RFID system.

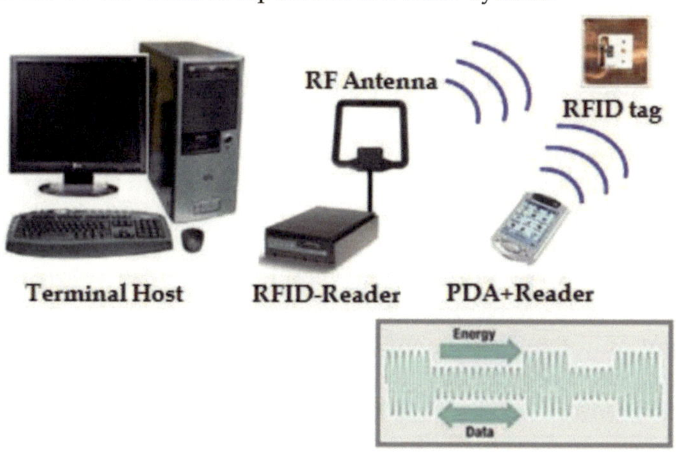


Fig. 2. Usual components of a RFID system

There are different RFID technologies available: passive tags have no own power source and take their energy directly from the magnetic field of the reader. Passive RFID tags do not need any maintenance, but the reading distance depends on the size and frequency of the transponder and antenna. Active tags are much more complex than passive tags and have an internal battery to increase the reading distances. The life time of active tags is limited through the battery. The semi-passive tags contain a power source, such as a battery, to power the microchip's circuitry. Unlike active tags, semi-passive tags do not use the battery to communicate with the reader. Communication is done in the same manner than passive tags do. Semi-passive tags might be dormant until activated by a signal from a reader. This conserves battery power and can lengthen the life of the tag. There are systems with 134 kHz, 125 kHz, 13.56 MHz, 868 MHz, 915 MHz, 2.45 GHz available, having different properties and reading distances depending on the environmental conditions.
Hence the main characteristics of a RFID system are:
- Communication done without physical contact between the reader and the tags.
- Soil resistant.
- No line of sight required.
- Read/Write memory.
- Possibility to store production and/or product data into the tag´s memory.
- Multi read /write capability.

Obviously, the use in dairy products of these "smart cards or tags" allows obtaining the benefits that come from the fact of providing the product with a "certain kind of intelligence", such as:
- To have only one identity.
- To be able to communicate with his environment in a efficient way.
- To be capable of obtaining and retaining the information about itself.

Also in this context, the RFID solution offers, versus the „traditional" bar code, the following advantages:
- Huge number of data in a reduced physical space.
- Automatic writing/reading in either individual or by batch mode. This is performed thanks to the use of anti-collision algorithms, which allow reading several RFID tags without interferences.
- Bar code needs visibility to work properly and the information stored can not be changed using the same tag.
- Bar code identifies a type of object. The RFID tag identifies an only object in an only way.
- Bar code is easily damaged in wet environments like are the ripening chambers where mould growing exists. In this case a RFID tag can be wrapped, for example, by *biofilm* without affecting the reading/writing process.

Barcodes are of course cheap to create, but they are limited in their storage capacity and are not flexible, when data needs to be changed.
Taking into account all the features mentioned above, a system based on the use of RFID transponders seems to be the most appropriate to carry-out the proposed tasks. The idea is to use RFID tags as physical support for storing the information required to perform a "complete traceability" in cheese industries, as well as facilitate the collection of data required by the technical experts of the Regulatory Boards in charge of quality certification (Pérez-Aloe et al., 2007). The application will perform the three types of traceability (vendor, process and customer) and an individual register of analysis and controls done in all the

production stages (milk reception, storage, fabrication, ripening, quality and yield control and pH measures) as well. In this way, the collected data corresponding to the process conditions (humidity, temperature, pressure, ventilation) including microorganism, biochemical and pH analysis and the connection of these data with the products provided by the different suppliers are increased. Then, the traceability will be granted, both on batches and on individual cheeses. This contributes to assure and certificate the quality, making easier the location, immobilization and in some cases the effective and selective recall when problems arise.
In this way, the device RFID would operate as an interface making easier and more efficient the exchange of data and information between the company and the technical staff of the Regulatory Board of the P.D.O. A sketch of this procedure can be seen in Figure 3.

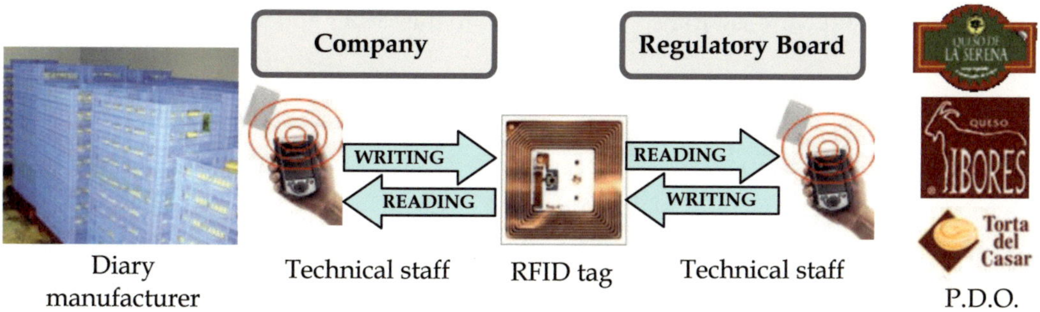


Fig. 3. Use of RFID tags in the integrated system of quality control Company-Regulatory Boards of P.D.O.

## 2. System implementation

The system developed is similar to that shown in Figure 2. It consists of two complementary systems; one is based on a personal computer (PC) and the other in a PocketPC (PPC). The PocketPC utility was implemented as a complement to the PC due to its portability. The Figure 4 presents a simplified block diagram of the two systems implemented.

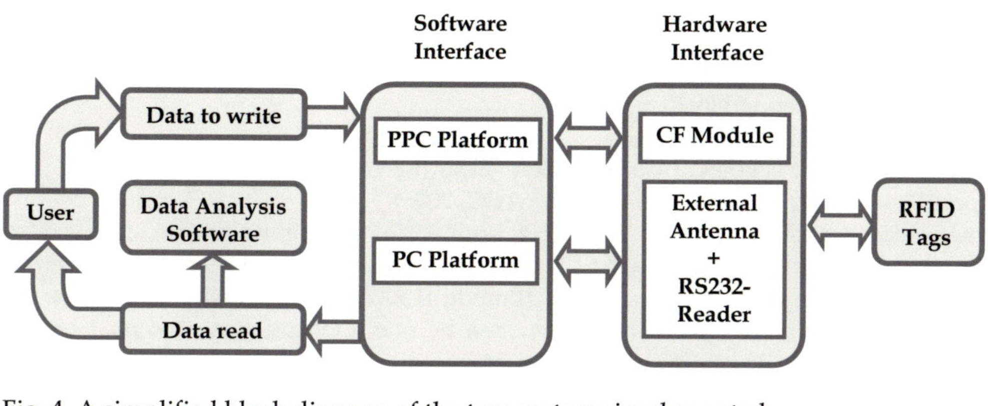


Fig. 4. A simplified block diagram of the two systems implemented

The PC system includes the S6350 midrange reader and the gate antenna series 6000 (Texas Instruments_RFID, 2002). The reader operates at 13.56 MHz and is able to communicate with tags that accomplish ISO 15693 protocol. The communication to the reader is done through a PC serial port, using a RS-232 data transmission protocol, with one start bit, 8 data bits, 1 stop bit and no parity. Several speeds can be selected within the range from 9600 bps to 57600 bps. The PC starts the communication with the reader, through a pair of request/response sequences accomplishing ISO 15693 standard, which establishes the request stream format as well as the fields size. Some of the commands supported by the reader can be used with addressing, i.e., read, write and lock. If addressing is used, the command will be sent to a single tag, and in the other case, the command will be broadcasted to all tags in the visible range of the reader. For example, Figure 5 shows the display of the reader utility after sending the command inventory. As it can be seen, as a response to this command, all transponders visible to the reader appear on the screen.

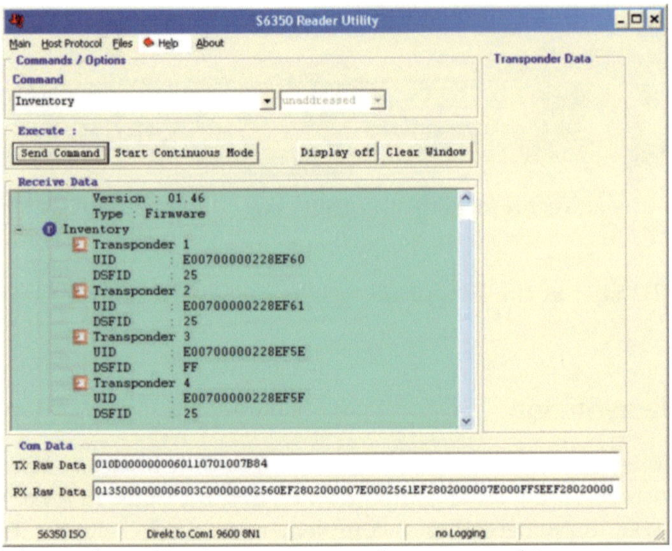

Fig. 5. Display of the reader utility in response to the command inventory

The system is also able to detect errors in such a way that if an error occurs during the communication, the reader will send an error code in the response stream to the PC. Some errors are tags not found in the vision range, a write attempt to a read-only block or an addressing to a non existing block.

Regarding the PPC system, it consists of:

- PDA with Windows PocketPC 2003® (Hewlett Packard iPAQ, 2003).
- Compact Flash reader with built-in antenna (ACG, 2006).

The hardware interface runs also at 13.56 MHz. Both ASCII and binary transmission modes are supported by the reader, but only ASCII mode has been developed because it simplifies the process. The transmission protocol is ASCII mode at 9600 bps. The PocketPC and the PC version are fully compatible, so that a tag written by one application can be read by the other without problems. The software was implemented with Microsoft® Embedded Visual C++ environment, and the source code includes the library supplied by the reader manufacturer. All the data stored in a tag are accessed and read in just 8 seconds.

Two different types of labels running at 13,56 MHz have been used in this application:

- Individual tags to be used to identify each cheese.
- Batch tags which store all data set and parameters related to its manufacturing process as well as information about the cheeses that belong to it.

Besides, two different rounded-shape tags with different sizes have been tested for individual labels, both on casein plate in order to improve the adherence to the cheese. The smaller one has a diameter of 9 mm and uses the chip I-Code SL2 ICS20 (Philips Semiconductors, 2003). The other one consists of a similar chip and has a size of 20 mm (Labelys, 2007). I-Code chip has a user memory of 128 bytes, divided into blocks of 32x32 bits. Of these 128 bytes, only 108 are addressable bytes (27x32 bits).

The tags HF-I ISO 15963 (Texas Instruments, 2005) have been selected to be utilized as batch labels due to their characteristics of thinness and flexibility. The tags have a 2 kBs user memory organized in 64 blocks x 32 bits as shown in Figure 6 (a).

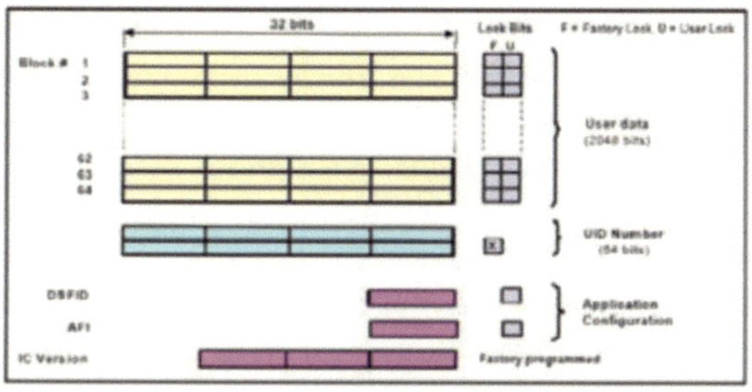


(a)

| Request | Request Code | Request Mode: Inventory | Addressed | Non-Addressed | Select | AFI |
|---|---|---|---|---|---|---|
| **ISO 15693 Mandatory and Optional Commands** | | | | | | |
| Inventory | 0x01 | ✓ | - | - | - | ✓ |
| Stay Quiet | 0x02 | - | ✓ | - | - | - |
| Read_Single_Block | 0x20 | ✓ | ✓ | ✓ | ✓ | ✓ |
| Write_Single_Block | 0x21 | - | ✓ | ✓ | ✓ | - |
| Lock_Block | 0x22 | - | ✓ | ✓ | ✓ | - |
| Read_Multi_Blocks | 0x23 | ✓ | ✓ | ✓ | ✓ | ✓ |
| Write_Multi_Blocks | 0x24 | - | - | - | - | - |
| Select Tag | 0x25 | - | ✓ | - | - | - |
| Reset to Ready | 0x26 | - | ✓ | ✓ | ✓ | - |
| Write_AFI | 0x27 | - | ✓ | ✓ | ✓ | - |
| Lock_AFI | 0x28 | - | ✓ | ✓ | ✓ | - |
| Write DSFID | 0x29 | - | ✓ | ✓ | ✓ | - |
| Lock DSFID | 0x2A | - | ✓ | ✓ | ✓ | - |
| Get_System_info | 0x2B | ✓ | ✓ | ✓ | ✓ | ✓ |
| Get_M_Blk_Sec_St | 0x2C | ✓ | ✓ | ✓ | ✓ | ✓ |
| **TI Custom Commands** | | | | | | |
| Write_2_Blocks | 0xA2 | - | ✓ | ✓ | ✓ | - |
| Lock_2_Blocks | 0xA3 | - | ✓ | ✓ | ✓ | - |

✓: implemented
-: Not applicable

(b)

Fig. 6. Characteristics of the tags used
(a) Memory organization. (b) List of commands.

Tags can contain read-only data (ROM) and read/write data (R/W). The stored data on blocks can be locked on factory or by user on an irreversible process, so data can not be modified any more. In other cases, tags can be reused for future utilizations.

All the tags have a locked field, the individual identification code UID (Unique IDentifier of the transponder) which is a 64 bits code, provided by the manufacturer and defined in ISO 15693 standard. AFI (Application Family Identifier, such as "transportation"," finance" ...)

code allows storing the type of application and DSFID (Data Storage Format IDentifier) the data format. Both of them are 1 byte blocks.

The HF-I tags commands list is seen in Figure 6 (b). Basically, two modes of reading/writing tags are available: single and multiple tag operation. In single tag operation, the first action is to detect a single tag, then the reader identifies the UID, and the subsequent reading/writing commands are referred exclusively to it. On the other hand, in the multiple tag operation the information is broadcasted to all the tags in the reader range.

The PPC utility includes routines for data interpretation and the communication protocol between the compact flash reader and the tags (AGC DLL, 2006). The procedure to establish communication between both devices and start sending commands is shown in Figure 7 (a). As it can be seen, the port where the reader is connected has to be detected and opened. If the port has been opened successfully then the reader is activated and ready to send a set of commands. Figure 7 (b) details the software code that performs the steps previously mentioned.

The "writing tag" command consists of 11 bytes in ASCII mode, so that the first two bytes indicate the address of the block to write, the following 8 bytes are the data to write and the last byte is the NULL or stop chain with all bits to zero. However, the "reading tag" command contains only 3 bytes, which refer to the block number to be read and the NULL byte. Moreover, the reader has a 512 bytes buffer, so once the command is sent and the reader receives the data, the utility can extract the required word from the buffer. The 512 bytes size allows the hardware to read all the tag blocks. Data are sent to the tags by means of a software application. This application is easy-to-use, so that any employee of the

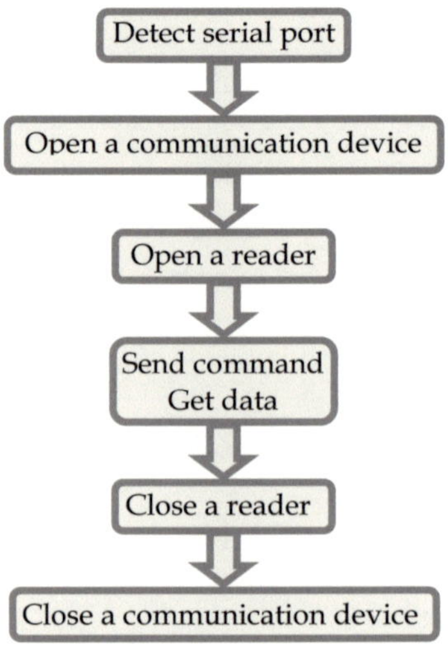


company of Regulatory Boards will be able to use it without difficulties. company or Regulatory Boards will be able to use it without difficulties.

```
// Initialise and open the communication port
        presetSettings* settings=new presetSettings();
        settings->baudRate =460800;
        settings->protocol=0;       // ASCII mode

           char puerto[30];          // Detects the PDA port where the // CF reader is connected

        RDR_DetectSerialPort(puerto);
```

```
if (RDR_OpenComm(puerto,0,settings)==0){  //and check if successful.  // Open the port
                                          If //command returns a 0 an error //has
                                          occurred
        MessageBox((CString)"Error.",(CString)"Información",MB_OK);
                                          //no need to specify the first //parameter in
                                          ASCII mode
}else{
                                          //If port has been opened //successfully then
                                          activate //the reader
        RDR_OpenReader(1,6);
        RDR_AbortContinuousRead(); //Stop the continuous
                                          //readout.Reading only on request
}
```

(a) (b)

Fig. 7. Procedure to establish the communication between the reader and tags
(a) Flow diagram. (b) Software code

The routine includes a "format tag option" which stores zeros in all blocks in order the tag to be reused for future activities. A scheme representing the mode in which data are stored in the tag memory and the data appearance on the PPC screen can be observed in Figure 8.
Regarding the data to be recorded in the tags, the writing process has to be optimized in order to store as much as possible cheese production parameters. The fields that will be saved on tags can contain numerical values (temperature, fat, etc.), alphanumerical values (type of milk, manufacturer, Batch, batch qualification, etc.) and data concerning key dates on production (elaboration, reception, ripening, etc.). Numerical data will be codified in binary, differentiating between integer and decimal part. The number of bits required for each part depends on the range of values and the precision used. In some cases, a data manipulation is performed. For example, if a variable varies from 3 to 5, for a value of 4.57, the integer and the decimal part are codified separately.

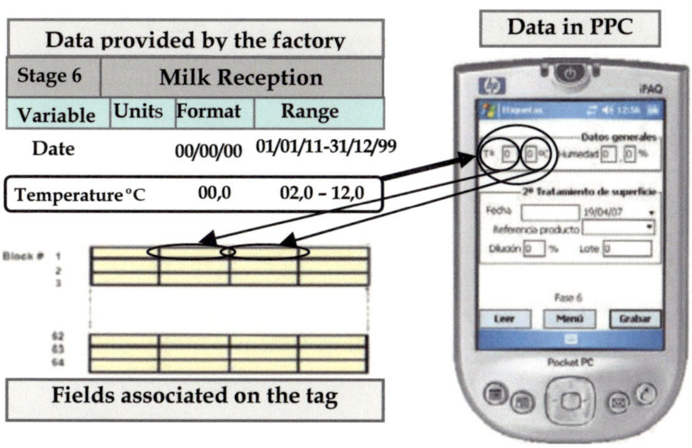


Fig. 8. Data recorded in tag and its representation on the PPC screen

Effective range of integer part has only 3 values (3, 4 and 5), and an offset of 3 is subtracted, so only 2 bits are needed (0 to 2) instead of the 4 bits needed if offset is not considered (0 to 5). On the other hand, alphanumerical values will be stored as a simple database, that is, assigning a numerical value to each data, i.e., type of milk can contain 4 values: "null",

"cow", "goat" and "sheep", that will be linked to numerical values 0, 1, 2 and 3, respectively.
Once all the fields and its associated number of bits are defined, the next step is to arrange the whole tag. The purpose is that each stage of the production process will be associated with a collection of blocks. Around two hundred variables related to the parameters involved in the different phases of the cheese fabrication can be recorded in a tag. Some of them appear in Table 1.

| Variable | Range |
|---|---|
| **General Data** | |
| *Product Code* | 1000-2000 |
| *Lot* | 010111-311299 |
| *Volume* | 500 lts-2500 lts |
| *Pieces* | 50 uds-300 uds |
| *Fit for consumption?* | yes/no |
| *Number of tags* | 000000-999999 |
| **Specific data for the different stages** | |
| *Reception date* | 01/01/11-31/12/99 |
| *Raw milk supplier* | Alphabetical |
| *Tank* | Alphanumerical |
| *pH* | 4,00 upH-7,00 upH |
| *Acidity* | 13,00 ºD-18,00 ºD |
| *Temperature* | 02,0 ºC-12,0 ºC |
| **Chemical analysis** | |
| *Fat* | 3,00 %- 8,00 % |
| *Protein matter* | 2.50 %-7,00 % |
| *Lactose* | 3,00 %- 6,00 % |
| *sodium chloride* | 0,80 %-2,20 % |
| **Microbiological analysis** | |
| *Listeria monocytogenes* | yes/no |
| *Salmonella spp.* | yes/no |
| *Staphylococcus aureus* | 0-20.000 ufc/gr |
| **Yield control** | |
| *Lot weight* | 50,0 kgr-400.0 kgr |
| *Lot yield (Volume/Weight)* | 4,00-12,00 |
| *Average unit weight* | 750 gr-1400gr |
| **Control of Clients** | |
| *Client Reference* | Alphanumerical |
| *Order number (units/kgr)* | 1-300/0,80-400 |

Table 1. Some parameters stored in the tags

## 3. Experimental results

The systems have been tested in the industries that collaborate in this work. Previous to place the prototypes in the companies, exhaustive tests were done on tags in laboratory in order to prove proper working under identical operation conditions than in factory. The simulated conditions were temperature, humidity, biological contamination, acid corrosion, ammoniacal gases and immersion on saline solutions, inhibiting substances, sugars, colorant pigments, preservative substances, oils action (Figure 9 (a)) and mould growing (Figure 9 (b)).

(a)

(b)

Fig. 9. Test on tags in laboratory
(a) Immersion on saline solution, olive oil and paprika. (b) Mould growing.

Besides, physical tests have been also made which include friction and flexibility because in ripening chambers, cheeses with its corresponding tags are subject to turns, shelving changes, frictions and personnel manipulations. In all these cases, no significant negative effects have been reported in communication with tags, with the exception of data reading with metallic materials in the range of the reader, which reported erroneous reading.
Finally, in order to confirm that tags were suitable to be attached to the products from the start of the fabrication to the end, the tags were placed on the surface of the cheese at the

beginning of the production. As can be seen in Figure 10, which corresponds to photographs taken at different stages of production, both types of tags used as individual labels remained

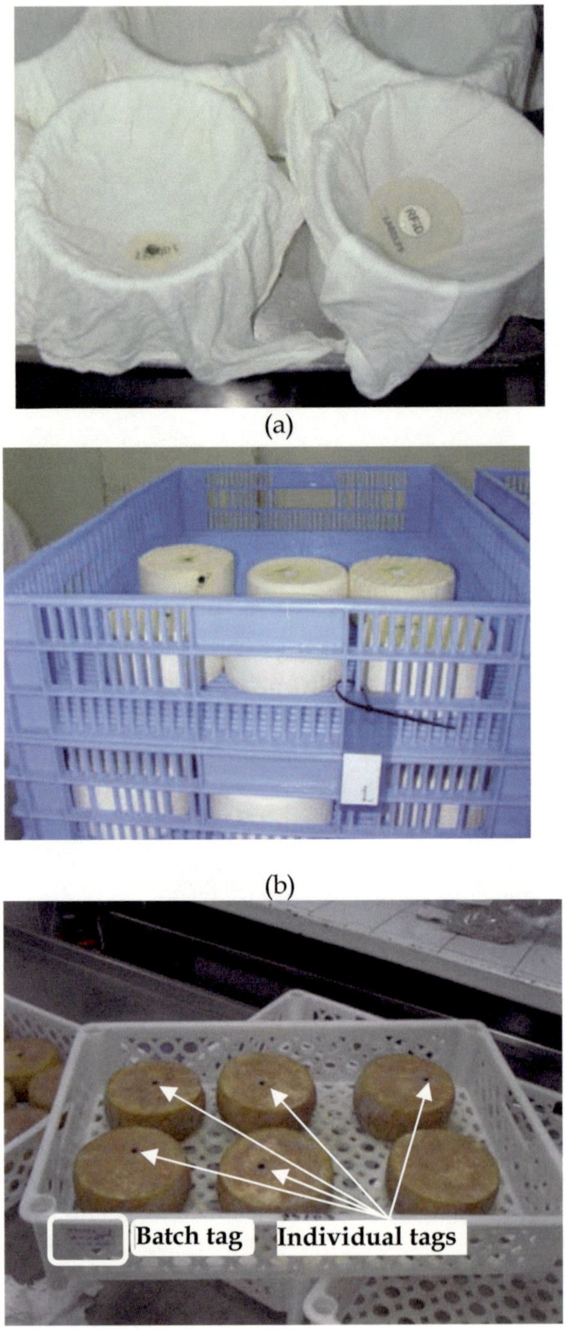


(a)

(b)

(c)

Fig. 10. Tags in different stages of production

(a) Before molding. (b) After pressing. (c) At the end of production attached to the rind of the cheese until the end of the process without reporting errors in the reading/writing process. Figure 10 also shows the containers with their batch labels.

Regarding the signal range, for the PC application the system is able to read/write tags inside a radius of around 20 cm, whereas the PPC reader has a limited range of around 25 mm, in both cases, enough for our purposes.
Finally, Figure 11 displays the way in which data are updated using the PPC system. The application is user-friendly so that employees of factories in charge of quality control and technical staff of Regulatory Board of P.D.O. responsible for quality certification could use the system easily.

Fig. 11. Data update in cheeses with attached RFID tags

## 4. Conclusion

Two different systems that perform the reading/writing task with RFID tags in a cheese industry have been implemented. One of them is based on a Personal Computer whereas the other solution uses a PocketPC providing the application with the required portability. The main objective has been to make available to the factory the complete traceability of the products, in individual and by batches mode, as well as to provide the technical staff of Regulatory Boards of P. D. O. with a tool that facilitates the process of quality certification.
The tags have been tested under different conditions of temperature, humidity, acid corrosion, ammoniacal gases and immerse in saline solutions with inhibiting substances, sugars, colorant pigments, preservative substances and oils. Besides, physical tests have been also made which include friction and flexibility. In all the situations, no significant negative effects have been reported in communication with tags, excepting for metallic materials in the range of the reader. Around two hundred variables related to the parameters involved in the different stages of the cheese production can be stored in the tag, which improve considerably the quality and yield control of the production plant.

## 5. Acknowledgements

This work has been financially supported by the Ministry of Infrastructures and Technological Development of the Government of Extremadura, under Grant PDT05A042 and PDT08A041 with the economic assistance of the European Union (FEDER).

## 6. References

ACG Multi ISO Plug-In Reader, (2006). ACG Identification Technologies, RDHP-0206P0-02

ACG RFID Reader DLL, (2006). User Manual, Rev 1.0, January 2006

Certification Criteria CC/3, (2005), Requirements to be met by the dairy industry, *Manual of quality of the Regulatory Board of P.D.O.*, Torta del Casar, (4), 1-8, Casar de Cáceres

Certification Criteria CC/4, (2007), Characteristics of the "Torta del Casar" Produced. *Manual of quality of the Regulatory Board of P.D.O.*, Torta del Casar, (5), 1-6, Casar de Cáceres

Coscarón, C.; Gil, M. & Legaz, E. (2007). *Revista Alimentaria*, No. 383, May 2007, 48-55, ISSN 03005755

Decree 1808, (1991) Which governs the indications or marks identifying the batch to which a foodstuff belongs

Decree 217, (2004), Which regulate the identification and registration of staff, facilities and containers involved in the dairy sector, and record the movements of the milk

Finkenzeller, K. (2003). *RFID Handbook: Fundamentals and Applications in contactless smart cards and identification*, John Wiley and Sons, ISBN 0-470-84402-7

Hewlett Packard iPAQ h5550 with Windows Pocket PC, (2003)

Labelys traçabilité, (2007). RFID casein plate

Order 25/4, (1997). Laying down the regulations of the Denomination of Origin "Ibores cheese" and its Regulatory Board

Order 11/1, (1999). Official recognition of the Designation of Origin "Torta del Casar"

Order 9/10, (2001). Adoption of the Rules of the Designation of Origin "Torta del Casar"

Order 6/5, (2002). Ratification of the Rules of the Designation of Origin "Torta del Casar"

Pérez-Aloe, R.; Valverde, J. M.; Lara, A; Carrillo, J. M.; Roa, I. & González, J. (2007). Application of RFID tags for the overall traceability of products in cheese industries, *Proceedings of 1st Annual RFID Eurasia Conference*, pp. 268-272, ISBN 978-975-01566-0-1, Turkey, September 2007, Istanbul

Philips Semiconductors, (2003). I-Code SL2 ICS20, Smart Label IC, Rev. 3.0, January 2003

Regulation 178, (2002). Laying down the principles and requirements of food law, establishing the European Food Safety Authority and laying down procedures relating to food safety

Regulation 1491, (2003). Registration of Protected Designation of Origin "Torta del Casar" in the Register of Protected Designations of Origin and Protected Geographical Indications

Spanish Agency for Food Security (2004). *Guide for the application of traceability in food companies.* Coimán S. L., NIPO 355-04-001-9, Madrid

Texas Instruments_RFID, (2002). HF Reader System Series 6000, S6350 Midrange Reader Module, September 2002

Texas Instruments_RFID, (2002). HF Reader System Series 6000, Gate Antenna, September 2002

Texas Instruments, (2005). Tag-it™ HF-I Plus Transponder Inlays, December 2005